Cognitive Perspectives
on Peer Learning

Cognitive Perspectives on Peer Learning

Edited by

Angela M. O'Donnell
Rutgers, The State University of New Jersey

Alison King
California State University San Marcos

1999

LAWRENCE ERLBAUM ASSOCIATES, PUBLISHERS

Mahwah, New Jersey London

45.00

Lawrence Erlbaum Associates, Inc., Publishers
10 Industrial Avenue
Mahwah, NJ 07430

Cover design by Kathryn Houghtaling Lacey

Library of Congress Cataloging-in-Publication Data

Cognitive perspectives on peer learning / edited by Angela M.
O'Donnell, Alison King.

p. cm. — (The Rutgers invitational symposium on education series)

"Based on original papers presented by the authors at the symposium on
Cognitive Skills and Learning with Peers, November 1, 1996, in New Brunswick, New Jersey, at the Rutgers Graduate School of Education"—Series
fwd.
Includes bibliographical references and index.
ISBN 0-8058-2447-2 (cloth : alk. paper) — ISBN 0-8058-2448-0
(pbk. : alk. paper).
1. Peer-group tutoring of students—Congresses. 2. Cognitive learning—Congresses. 3. Learning, Psychology of—Congresses. I. O'Donnell,
Angela M. II. King, Alison. III. Series.
LB1031.5.C65   1999
370.15'23—dc21   98-46511
                                                         CIP

Books published by Lawrence Erlbaum Associates are printed on acid-
free paper, and their bindings are chosen for strength and durability.

Printed in the United States of America
10 9 8 7 6 5 4 3 2

Contents

Series Foreword:
Rutgers Invitational Symposia on Education (RISE), Rutgers Graduate School of Education

The profession of education was shaken to its roots more than a decade ago, when national attention focused critically on education and on educators. Critics and friends raised basic questions about the profession, including whether educational professionals have successfully met the challenges that the students and the schools present and, even more fundamentally, whether they are *able* to meet those challenges. Beginning with the highly publicized *A Nation at Risk* (1983), seemingly endless and often contradictory criticisms, analyses, and recommendations appeared from virtually every segment of contemporary U. S. society.

In this explosion of concern and ideas for educational reform, we see a need for a general and national forum in which the problems of education can be examined in light of research from a range of relevant disciplines. Too often, analyses of very complex issues and problems occur within a single discipline. Aspects of a problem that are unfamiliar to members of the discipline are ignored, and the resulting analysis is limited in scope and thus unsatisfactory. Furthermore, when educational issues are investigated by members of one discipline only, there is seldom an attempt to examine related issues from other fields or to apply methods developed in other fields that might prove illumination.

The national debate on educational reform has suffered from this myopia, as problems and issues are identified and analyses and solutions often are proposed within the limited confines of a single disciplinary boundary. In the past, national discussions have been ill informed or uninformed by current research partly because there are far too few mechanisms for interdisciplinary analyses of significant issues.

The faculty of the Rutgers Graduate School of Education developed the Rutgers Invitational Symposia on Education to address this gap. Taking an interdisciplinary perspective, the series focuses on timely issues and problems in education. There is an accumulating corpus of high-quality educational research on topics of interest to practitioners and policymakers. Each symposium focuses on a particular problem, such as the potential teacher shortage, how to assess literacy skills, the structure of schools, and the effects of cognitive psychology on teaching mathematics. Each accompanying volume in the symposia series provides an interdisciplinary forum through which scholars can disseminate their original research and extend their work to potential applications for practice, including guides for teaching, learning, assessment, intervention, and policy formulation. These contributions increase the potential for significant analysis and positive impact on the problems that challenge educators.

The present volume, the 10th symposium, is dedicated to peer learning. Recently, much attention has centered on how children educate each other and how to maximize the cognitive benefits of peers learning form each other. The volume is divided into three sections plus an introduction. The first provides the theoretical rationale for the work that follows. Particular techniques originating from cognitive theories are given, and a section on the implications of peering learning for the classroom follows. The conclusion discusses key issues such as the following: Who benefits in peer learning? How do they benefit? What are the next steps for both research and practice in this important area?

This volume is based on original papers presented by the authors at the symposium on Cognitive Skills and Learning with Peers, November 1, 1996, in New Brunswick, New Jersey, at the Rutgers Graduate School of Education. It is with great pleasure that we contribute this volume to the series, The Rutgers Invitational Symposia on Education.

—Louise Cherry Wilkinson
Dean, and Professor of Educational Psychology
Rutgers Graduate School of Education

Introduction

ANGELA M. O'DONNELL
Rutgers, The State University of New Jersey

ALISON KING
California State University San Marcos

The goal of this book is to contribute to the literature on peer learning by focusing on approaches that are concerned with the cognitive processes underlying peer learning. The contents reflect a common concern with cognitive processes from developmental, information processing, or more generally, constructivist perspectives on peer learning. Because any text must address only a portion of the potential work available, we have not focused on the social aspects of peer learning. Although the social context of peer learning is clearly important, the focus of the book was less on the social aspects of the learning environment and more on the cognitive growth that occurs. We did not focus on the sociocultural influences on learning, although we also acknowledge the importance of relevance of such concerns. Both the social–motivational and sociocultural approaches to peer learning are well represented in the published literature (e.g., Johnson & Johnson, 1994; Resnick, Levine, & Teasely, 1991). The three parts of the book focus on (a) cognitive developmental theories underpinning many approaches to peer learning; (b) particular instantiations of cognitive approaches to peer learning; and (c) implications of cognitive perspectives on peer learning for teachers, teaching, and teacher education.

Any discussion of peer learning involves consideration of who is learning, how the role of peers with whom one works can be conceptualized, what it is that peers learn together, what changes as a result of the interaction, and how we can know what occurs in groups or what has been learned. The chapters in this book speak to these questions. The key question underlying many of these others is this: Why should we worry about the intricacies of interaction? There are both practical and theoretical reasons for doing so that are delineated in this book.

Peer learning or peer interaction is the subject of study in a wide variety of disciplines and for different purposes and may be considered from the perspectives of developmental psychology (social justice, play), social psychology (e.g., person perception, motivation, group processes), sociology (e.g., status characteristics, social categories, power and authority), humanistic psychology (e.g., helping and caring for one another), and cognitive psychology (e.g., how learning occurs, what is learned). In addition, interaction among peers is studied and interpreted from sociocultural perspectives (e.g., cultural influences on knowledge or interaction), sociocognitive perspectives (e.g., peer-induced conflict), and cognitive-developmental perspectives (e.g., gender-role development). Although there is a broad literature on peer interaction in developmental psychology, the educational implications of this work receive relatively little attention. The existing literature is also constrained by studies that rely on outcome measures that are largely concerned with the acquisition of factual knowledge and by the failure to address potential negative outcomes from peer learning. Futhermore, relatively little analysis of who learns and what they learn has been conducted within the context of peer learning research.

This book includes chapters that specifically examine cognitive-developmental theory and that may suggest mechanisms by which peers learn from one another. Cognitive elaboration perspectives on peer learning as expressed in specific techniques are also examined. It is important to note that we do not believe that cognitive-developmental and cognitive-elaboration theories provide independent explanations of cognitive processes, but we present them separately for purposes of clarity. The developmental theory described in the initial part of the book lays the foundation for the later descriptions of specific techniques, although many techniques reflect multiple influences. A number of the chapters in this volume address the contextual influences on peer learning, but this is not the primary focus of the book.

OVERVIEW OF CONTENTS

The remainder of the book is divided into three parts. The first part of the book (chaps. 1 and 2) includes two chapters that present the implications of the work of two major theorists in cognitive development. In Chapter 1, De Lisi and Golbeck discuss the implications of Piaget's theory of cognitive development for peer learning. They provide a framework within which the possibilities and limitations of peer interactions for children's cognitive development and school-based learning can be considered. Hogan and Tudge (chap.2) describe the implications of Vygotsky's theory for understanding the potential of peer learning. They provide an overview of Vygotsky's theory and discuss three aspects of development, noting that developmentalists often focus on a narrow interpretation of Vygotsky's work. They discuss several principles of the theory that are particularly salient for peer learning, including the concept of intersubjectivity and how it is achieved.

The second part of the book contains six chapters that describe a variety of peer learning techniques or models of collaboration, many of which are influenced by the work of Vygotsky and Piaget. Three of the chapters in this section specifically address the quality of discourse within a peer learning group (Person & Graesser,

Webb & Farivar, and King) and issues related to providing support for effective peer interaction. Two additional chapters by O'Donnell and by Palincsar and Herrenkohl extend this discussion. The final chapter in this section (Derry) provides a critique of these chapters.

Person and Graesser (chap. 3) analyze ongoing tutorial interaction and paint an interesting picture of the kinds of strategies adopted by unsophisticated tutors who employed politeness strategies that may have interfered with effective tutoring. King (chap. 4) describes the documented relation between the level of discourse within a collaborative peer-learning group and the level of achievement or productivity of group members. Webb and Farivar (chap. 5) are also concerned with the quality of discourse and examine the changes in the interactions of group members that occur over time during a semester-long program of peer learning in middle school mathematics classrooms.

Palincsar and Herrenkohl (chap. 6) describe three programs of research that focus on constituting learning communities in elementary and middle school classrooms. The programs are used to illustrate the complexities inherent in designing, implementing, and evaluating models of collaborative learning. In Chapter 7, O'Donnell examines potential difficulties in promoting effective group interaction. The potential benefits of structuring student interactions are discussed. A key assumption related to the use of scripted cooperation (described in detail) is that students may not naturally engage in the kinds of productive processes necessary for effective peer learning.

Derry (chap. 8) provides an overview of the contents of the five preceding chapters and points to common themes and concerns. She draws attention to problems inherent in the peer-learning literature in terms of an absence of an overarching theory within which specific practices can be couched. Derry notes the need for a theory of tasks and a need to focus on the quality of argument in collaborative groups. This chapter points to areas of future study.

The third part of the book contains four chapters that consider the role of the teacher and the skills needed by the teacher when using peer learning as an instructional strategy. Cooper (chap. 9) describes the general conditions that are necessary for effective peer learning and discusses the choices that classroom teachers must make in support of such learning. In Chapter 10, Meloth and Deering describe the difficulties experienced by teachers in implementing peer learning. They argue for the importance of the instruction provided to students before they work in groups, the teacher's monitoring of group activities, and the teacher's beliefs about learning and collaboration.

The complexity of preparing new teachers for the task of teaching and the additional complexity involved in preparing for work with other groups of students is addressed by Woolfolk Hoy and Tschannen-Moran in Chapter 11. The overall goal of their chapter is to examine how teacher education programs can prepare beginning teachers so that they develop expertise in peer-directed methods. In Chapter 12, Almog and Hertz-Lararowitz describe a model of professional development intended to assist teachers in developing the skills needed to work in classrooms of the future. The program described consists of three important elements: peer learning, group investigation, and the use of advanced technologies. The Conclusion to the book points to areas where research is still needed.

We acknowledge the support of the Graduate School of Education at Rutgers under the leadership of Dean Louise C. Wilkinson for the sponsorship of the 10th Rutgers Invitational Symposium in Education that brought the authors together. We thank Naomi Silverman of Lawrence Erlbaum Associates (LEA) for her support and assistance with this project. In addition, we thank Lori Hawver and Kathryn Scornavacca of LEA for assistance with the technical aspects of the production of this volume.

PART I

Cognitive Developmental Bases of Peer Learning: Overview

The two chapters in this part of the book (De Lisi & Golbeck, Hogan & Tudge) describe the basic principles of Piagetian and Vygotskian developmental theory and the implications of these theories for understanding peer learning. The inclusion of these chapters is an important aspect of this book, providing a thorough description of the theories that underlie many of the other materials in this book, and an in-depth analysis of the implications of these theories for peer learning strategies. Much of the work on peer learning relies on or references processes described in the theories of either Piaget or Vygotsky (e.g, sociocognitive conflict, scaffolding). Aspects of these theories are frequently misunderstood and misused. Piaget's theory of cognitive development is often given rather cursory treatment in general textbooks, a treatment that largely consists of an outline of his stages of cognitive development. Such textbooks rarely include a deep analysis of the processes by which cognitive growth occurs. Likewise, certain Vygotskian concepts are often used as markers rather than as explanations (e.g, the zone of proximal development).

De Lisi and Golbeck provide a detailed analysis of Piaget's theory and note that the search for logical coherence in understanding is only one of the options available to the learner. The possibility of bidirectional influences of peers in terms of growing understanding is developed by Hogan and Tudge. Both chapters alert us to the competence of the learner as being at the heart of the possible effects of peer learning. Both chapters also alert us to the possibility of mistaking immediate improvement for enduring change. Although much of the empirical work in these chapters was not conducted in a school setting, there are clear implications from this work for the analysis of peer learning processes in school and other settings.

CHAPTER ONE

Implications of Piagetian Theory for Peer Learning

RICHARD DE LISI
SUSAN L. GOLBECK
Rutgers, The State University of New Jersey

The underlying premise of this chapter is that Piaget's account of cognitive development provides important ideas and principles for educators who are interested in peer learning. Our task of communicating these ideas and principles is complex because Piaget's theory evolved over time (Piaget, 1970b) and is subject to alternative interpretations. In addition, some of Piaget's work has only recently been translated into English. There is disagreement as to whether or not Piaget understated the importance of social experiences and presented a view of cognitive development that is too biological and individualistic (Bovet, Parrat-Dayan, & Voneche, 1989; DeVries, 1997; Furth, 1987, 1996; Gopnik, 1996; Lourenço & Machado, 1996; Tudge & Rogoff, 1989; Tudge & Winterhoff, 1993b; Youniss, 1981; Youniss & Damon, 1992).

We find it helpful to segment the evolution of Piaget's theory into separate phases (Beilin, 1992; Chapman, 1988) and note that particularly in his early work (1920s–1930s), Piaget emphasized peer experiences as an important factor in child development. Although subsequent phases of Piaget's work no longer highlighted peer experiences, in our opinion, this was not reflective of a shift away from a social toward an individualistic psychology. Indeed, our major objective is to show how Piaget's (1985) "final" model of cognitive functioning, based on a self-regulatory process called *equilibration,* can serve as a useful framework to consider peer learning in educational settings.

We begin with a brief characterization of peer learning and its role in modern education. Peer learning is an educational practice in which students interact with other students to attain educational goals. One reason for the growing popularity of peer learning in schools is a shift away from traditional views of the teaching–learning process that stress knowledge transmission from teacher to pupil, in favor of *constructivist* approaches that emphasize discovery learning and view knowledge acquisition as a social activity (see Phillips, 1995, 1997, for an extended discussion of varied types of constructivism). Collaborative work between students has become an important means of implementing constructivist educational approaches. Professional associations such as the International Reading Association, the National Association for the Education of Young Children, and the National Council of Teachers of Mathematics have each endorsed peer learning as a means to enhance the teaching–learning process. Examples of peer learning techniques can be found in Part II of this book.

A second reason for the current popularity of peer learning derives from the fundamental task that schools face in preparing students for life after school in the workplace and in communities. Classroom-based peer learning activities are considered an important aspect of preparation for life after formal schooling ends. Learning how to work together cooperatively is a valued educational activity derived from the larger cultural context in which schools exist. Although this goal has been a part of school life for some time, it has traditionally been reserved for nonacademic activities. A third reason for the growing interest in peer learning is the pervasive introduction of technology in schools, especially computer networks, with its attendant opportunities and problems. Peer learning activities make it possible for students to work on projects that necessitate the sharing of technological resources. Finally, as schools and neighborhoods become increasingly connected to the Internet over the next 10 years, students will have virtually unlimited access to the products of efforts of others and will have the opportunity to interact and share ideas with students in both asynchronous and synchronous modes.

In summary, peer learning is viewed as a way to enhance learning outcomes and as providing formative experiences necessary for transition to, and full participation in, an American society that is increasingly technological and multicultural.

PIAGET'S CONSTRUCTIVISM

Piaget evolved a constructivist theory of cognitive functioning and development from around 1920 to 1980. Initially, Piaget wanted to explain the acquisition of logical and scientific thinking (Furth, 1981). He saw weaknesses in the two traditional philosophical answers of nativism (the categories of human knowledge are innate) and empiricism (the categories of human knowledge are directly shaped by experience). Although acknowledging that innate factors and experience played necessary roles in the formation of logical and scientific knowledge, he argued that neither of them (taken alone or together) was sufficient to explain the nature of knowledge acquisition. Piaget's alternative was constructivism, a process in which the individual reflects on and organizes experiences to create order in and adapt to the environment. According to Piaget (1971, 1978a, 1980), human beings are capable of extending biological programming to construct cognitive systems that interpret experiences with objects and other persons. Because the construction of cognitive systems takes time, it is often the case that the same "objective experience" will be interpreted and understood differently by two children who are at different points in the process of constructing cognitive systems. Constructivism has two related meanings in Piaget's theory. First, it refers to the refinement of existing cognitive systems over time. Piaget labeled this aspect of constructivism *development,* a process of change different from maturation and from learning. Second, it refers to the application of already formed cognitive systems that confer meaning in present circumstances. Toward the end of his career, Piaget (1985) articulated a model of constructivism that connects both senses of the term. Figure 1.1 presents an overview of this model and the relation between constructivism as meaning making in a given context based on assimilation–accommodation, and constructivism as change in cognitive systems over time.

The components of Fig. 1.1 are discussed next in order to show how Piaget's model of constructivism provides a strong foundation for the use of peer learning in classrooms. With respect to meaning making, teachers' use of peer learning may stem from a belief that "two heads are better than one." A student's meaning making in a given classroom context might be fundamentally different if the student works with other students rather than alone. This does not necessarily imply that collective meaning making is "better" than individual meaning making (see Hogan & Tudge, chap. 2, this volume). Piaget maintained that peer interactions provide rich and necessary contexts for students to revise their current cognitive systems. Reflecting on peer reactions and perspectives serves as a basis for a student to revise his or her cognitive system. Such revisions would, in turn, lead students to make new meanings. Permanent revisions to existing cognitive systems are only one of several possible outcomes to meaning making in a given context.

Application of Existing Cognitive Systems

In any given context, a person's level of success or understanding is partially determined by his or her cognitive system. Piaget is perhaps best known for his description of two major cognitive systems—a *sensory-motor system* that is developed soon after birth and an *operational system* that develops from the sensory-motor system in the second year of life. The components of the sensory-motor system are internal coordinations of external, goal-directed means–ends behaviors. The sensory-motor system is designed to attain success in an immediate context (Piaget, 1954). The components of the operational system are internal coordinations of internal thinking actions that seek to attain under-

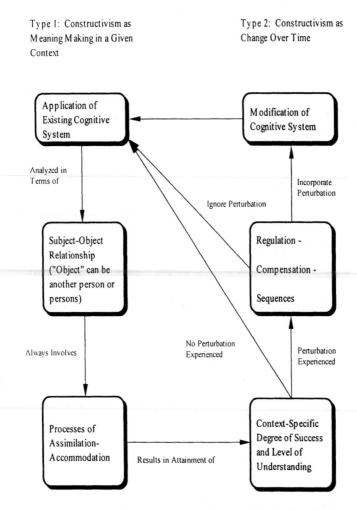

Type 1: Constructivism as Meaning Making in a Given Context

Type 2: Constructivism as Change Over Time

Application of Existing Cognitive System

Modification of Cognitive System

Analyzed in Terms of

Incorporate Perturbation

Ignore Perturbation

Subject-Object Relationship ("Object" can be another person or persons)

Regulation - Compensation - Sequences

Always Involves

No Perturbation Experienced

Perturbation Experienced

Processes of Assimilation- Accommodation

Results in Attainment of

Context-Specific Degree of Success and Level of Understanding

FIG. 1.1.   The relation between two types of constructivism in Piaget's theory.

standing in both immediate and anticipated contexts. The components of both systems consist of internal coordinations, but what distinguishes them is what is being coordinated—overt actions in the case of sensory-motor functioning and thinking actions in the case of operational functioning. Furth (1981) explained this point in detail.

Piaget subdivided both the sensory-motor and operational systems into *stages*. Each substage marks the degree to which the internal coordinations are coordinated. Successive substages reveal a greater degree of internal consistency and applicability across contexts. For example, pre-operational components differ from concrete operational components in that concrete operational components are capable of mental reversibility. A limitation to the components of the concrete operational system consists of not being able to reason logically from premises that are hypothetical or not subscribed to. This limitation is overcome with attainment of formal operational components.

Subject–Object Relations

Piaget described the functioning of cognition in terms of subject–object relations. According to Piaget, children develop an understanding of other people and objects in the environment from the actions that they perform with and on them. These actions are (in part) a function of the existing cognitive system. Piaget symbolized this aspect of the relation as going from "subject to object," or S → O. The actions that the child performs with others or on objects are also a function of the specific context of occurrence. Piaget symbolized this aspect of the relation as going from "object to subject," or S ← O. Taken together, Piaget's description of cognitive functioning as a subject–object relation can be depicted as S →← O. This forward and back, relational view of cognitive functioning differs from views placing greater emphasis on direct shaping by experience and reinforcement (S ← O), and also differs from views appealing to maturational sequencing of human cognition in which experience plays a minimal role (S → O). In these two perspectives, children are viewed as somewhat more passive (either subject to reinforcement control or the beneficiaries of evolutionary struggles worked out centuries before) than is the case in Piaget's relational view.

Piaget's extensive program of research provided the database from which he derived his descriptions of different cognitive systems and different subject–object relations. Because of his relational perspective, Piaget believed that in order to accurately describe cognitive systems, he needed to observe them in various contexts of occurrence. Piaget's books are full of examples in which the same child is successful in one situation, but unsuccessful in a slightly different situation. One general trend that emerged from Piaget's research was that cognitive systems in formation were found to be more heavily context dependent, whereas cognitive systems near completion were more internally consistent and reliable across contexts of occurrence.

Equilibrium Between Assimilation and Accommodation

Piaget's description of sensory-motor and operational functioning as relational highlights the importance of determining the relative contributions of the child and the environment in any specific situation. Children's actions and concepts are sometimes overly subjective, failing to account for aspects of the environment, including the perspectives of other persons. Conversely, children's actions and concepts are sometimes overly determined by environmental forces, including the perspectives of other persons, and do not reflect their true beliefs or capacities. Finally, it is possible for children's actions and concepts to reflect a balance or *equilibrium* between subjective and environmental components. Piaget discussed these three possibilities in terms of processes labeled *assimilation* and *accommodation*.

Assimilation is an incorporative process in which an object or event is "brought into" one or more cognitive system components in order to confer meaning. Children's actions and judgments are often misguided or incorrect from an adult perspective. Even in these circumstances, however, Piaget maintained that assimilation was responsible for the overt actions and judgments. Assimilation does not imply being correct or successful. The outer-directed process of accommodation occurs simultaneously with assimilation. In accommodation, one or more components take account of the particular features of the object or event being assimilated. Accommodation typically results in a momentary modification of a cognitive system component in order to adjust to present circumstances. Even if no modification is required, however, accommodation still occurs. Accommodation does not imply a permanent change or modification in a cognitive system or any of its components.

Piaget (1962) showed how children's use of symbols varies in the preponderance of assimilation or accommodation. For example, symbolic play entails a greater degree of assimilation than accommodation because the child alters the world through pretend play to serve her or his needs. In contrast, an attempt to imitate another person's behavior or commit something to rote memory requires more accommodation than assimilation. Piaget (1966) characterized intelligence as representing an equilibrium between assimilation and accommodation. His program of research on children's reasoning and problem solving indicated time and again that when cognitive systems are not in equilibrium, children's performance may vacillate between more accommodation than assimilation or more assimilation than accommodation. For example, Piaget and Inhelder's (1973) research on children's memory found that children could, in the short run, remember and reproduce configurations requiring logical understanding that was beyond their cognitive capacity due to successful accommodation of their perceptual and imaginal systems that carried over into short-term memory. Reproductions requiring longer term processes were unsuccessful, however, because understanding was insufficient to retain the "correct" image over time. In a different research project, Inhelder and Piaget (1958) found that young children tended to view themselves as causal agents for physical phenomena such as the period of a pendulum, despite explicit presentations of evidence to the contrary. In these studies, young children's initial and subsequent performance was incorrect due to a logical system not capable of controlling or isolating variables.

Piagetian theory does not specify which process—assimilation or accommodation—will dominate any given situation in which an equal balance is not possible. The pressure to perform in certain school situations, however, might well place a premium on students' accommodations to teachers' descriptions of correct procedures or answers. In many cases, these accommodations attain short-lived success and do not ensure a sufficient level of understanding to guarantee that the successful performance or correct answers will be replicated at subsequent points in time. Later in this chapter, we present a selective review of peer interaction studies conducted within a Piagetian framework. A key feature of these studies is the inclusion of delayed, individual posttests to check whether acquisitions during peer experiences reflect an intellectually healthy balance between accommodation (to peer ideas) and assimilation (to child's original ideas).

In Table 1.1, we list several forms of meaning-making behaviors to highlight their potential function and to note the relative contribution of assimilation and accommodation. For these and other behavioral forms in which there is an imbalance between assimilation and accommodation, it is an open question as to whether such an occurrence triggers change in the cognitive system that generated the imbalance in the first place. This important issue is discussed in the next sections of the chapter, as we move from the left- to the right-hand side of Fig. 1.1 in summarizing Piaget's constructivism.

Controlling the Sensory-Motor System to Attain Context-Specific Success

The adjustment and control of overt actions in the service of goal attainment was described by Piaget as occurring in a "quasi-automatic" fashion governed by a biologically given organizing function presumed to be part of the make-up of all living things. Infants and young children may be aware of their intentions and whether or not they were realized, but the means used to realize these intentions, that is, the actions themselves, are not analyzed and considered ahead of time. Instead, actions are modified in a trial-and-error fashion. Piaget characterized the sensory-motor system that governs overt actions as a powerful form of knowledge, capable of attaining success in certain situations (Piaget, 1954, 1976, 1978b). This powerful form of knowledge—sensory-motor organization—is available to human agents soon after birth and for the rest of the life course. Much of daily life is based on sensory-motor organizations that are simply taken for granted once they have been perfected and are often difficult to describe (e.g., crawling on all fours).

The sensory-motor system must, of necessity, account for the behaviors of other persons, because so many daily experiences involve other persons. Indeed many habits and behavioral expectations have their bases in social experiences from a very early age and predate mutual communication based on speech and language alone. Piaget (1981) and Piaget and Inhelder (1969) noted the mutual

TABLE 1.1
Forms of Individual and Self–Other Meaning Making

Behavioral Forms	Social Component	Function–Balance
Fantasy play including daydreaming	Child is alone but typically represents self-other experiences.	"Exercise" of previously developed understandings. Work on emotional conflicts.–*Assimilation*.
Parallel play	Child is in the company of another child who plays no role in child's play behavior. Play can reenact social experiences.	Same as above. Because other child is physically proximate, the potential to switch to an interactive form exists.–*Assimilation*.
"Look at what I can do!"	Child acknowledges other's presence and "uses" other person for self enactments.	Self verification via other demonstration.–*Assimilation*.
Cooperative exchanges with another child	Child–other child are equal partners and therefore are free to agree and disagree with one another.	Coconstruction of new understandings such as "genuine" reciprocity. Child and other are mutually engaged.–*Equilibrium*.
Peer regulation of child	Peer directs child's behavior but has to account for self's perspective and maintain attention.	Child is explicitly taught by another child based on mutual agreement or adult arrangement.–*Accommodation*.
Adult regulation of child	Adult directs child's behavior but has to account for child's perspective or get attention. Child is expected to obey directives.	Explicit teaching or behavior management by adult. Child learns about reciprocity by complement.[a]–*Accommodation*.
Modeling	Other person determines child's behavior if child is motivated to attend, retain, perform, etc.	Child attempts to perform behaviors enacted by another in order to acquire new behavior, flatter other, pretend to be the other, etc.–*Accommodation*.
Delayed imitation	Child is alone but reenacts other's behavior including self–other relations.	Attempt to consolidate previous experiences. Work on emotional conflicts. Incorporate in fantasy routines.–*Accommodation*.

[a]See Youniss (1981) for a discussion of various forms of reciprocity.

dependencies between the affective, cognitive, and social aspects of the sensory-motor system in the first 2 years of life.

Controlling the Operational System to Attain Understanding

Once the ability to conceptualize apart from overt action is developed during the second year of life, the organizing function now has another means to refine behavior. The possibility for "active" or deliberate cognitive adjustments exists once concept formation begins. These acts of mental conceptualization of action eventually lead to the ability to adjust actions or compare different actions prior to behaving with a deliberate plan in mind (De Lisi, 1987). At an even later point in development during early adolescence, thought becomes increasingly independent of overt actions such that actions themselves are no longer needed at all, or are only needed for purposes of verifying what has already been worked out in the mind. The long process of *functional interiorization* that began in infancy has been brought to completion once this level of cognitive performance has been achieved (Furth, 1981). Piaget (1976, 1978b) found that the ability to conceptualize actions develops slowly over time in early to late childhood, as children's spontaneous concepts often lag behind their successful actions. Such spontaneous concepts often serve as a filter for the process of conceptualization, such that descriptions by children of their own actions may be distorted by the children themselves to conform with the spontaneous concept.

In his earliest books on child development, Piaget often noted that young children's cognitive systems were insufficiently developed to attain "truly socialized" or adult levels of understanding of social phenomena. Lacking a fully developed cognitive foundation to understand and interpret social phenomena, Piaget (1954) maintained that young children tended to either "over assimilate" or "over accommodate" in social situations:

> In all the social behavior patterns of thought it is easy to see how much more easily the child is led to satisfy his desires and to judge from his own personal point of view than to enter into that of others to arrive at an objective view. But in contrast to this powerful assimilation of reality to the self we witness during the earliest stages of individual thought the child's astonishing docility with respect to the suggestions and statements of another person; the little child constantly repeats what he hears, imitates the attitudes he observes, and thus yields as readily to training by the group as he resists rational intercourse. In short, assimilation to the self and accommodation to others begins with a compromise without profound synthesis, and at first the subject wavers between these two tendencies without being able to control or organize them. (p. 409)

One of Piaget's earliest themes was that conceptual understanding results from organizations of social experiences. However, Piaget (1932b) felt that *cooperative* rather than *unilateral* social exchanges were needed to counter the child's tendencies toward overly subjective assimilation and overly docile imitative accommodation. Moreover, Piaget maintained that such cooperative relations were more likely to occur when children interacted with other children rather than with adults. (See DeVries, 1997, for an extended discussion of cooperation within child–adult and child–child relationships.) In Table 1.1, forms of social exchange in which children cooperate are distinguished from forms in which children or adults regulate other children's behavior. We revisit this issue in our later discussion of research on social justice and fairness.

EQUILIBRATION: FROM SUCCESS AND UNDERSTANDING
TO MODIFICATION OF THE COGNITIVE SYSTEM

Piaget's concept of equilibrium between assimilation and accommodation describes a desired state for intellectual functioning. In building on this idea in his later work, Piaget shifted his attention to an analysis of how change occurs in cognitive systems (right-hand side of Fig. 1.1). Piaget proposed that a process called *equilibration* leads to revisions in cognitive systems over time. Equilibration is a self-regulatory process leading from one equilibrium point to another equilibrium point. Piaget's analysis of the process of equilibration is based on the assumption that cognitive systems function via assimilation–accommodation. In fact, as we describe next, functioning of individual schemes and operations via assimilation–accommodation represents one of three main forms of equilibration.

Equilibration is a dynamic process in which the tendency to be *closed* or retain previously developed ways of interacting and understanding is counteracted by the opposite tendency toward *openness*, such that the present cognitive system is modified to capitalize on newly discovered means and insights. This dynamic tension between openness and closure is the motivational force for cognitive development (Piaget, 1971, 1978a, 1980).

Piaget (1985) based his model of equilibration on the following two postulates pertaining to assimilation–accommodation. In the following quote, *scheme* refers to a component of a cognitive system. The first postulate is this: "Every assimilatory scheme tends to incorporate external elements that are compatible with it. This postulate provides nothing more than an impetus for seeking; it makes activity on the part of the child necessary" (p. 6). The second postulate is as follows: "Every assimilatory scheme has to be accommodated to the elements it assimilates, but the changes made to adapt it to an object's peculiarities must be effected with loss of continuity. This postulate indicates that modifying a scheme must destroy neither its closure as a cycle of interdependent processes nor its previous powers of assimilation" (p. 6). From these two postulates we see that Piaget assumed that the motivation for assimilation is a built-in part of the cognitive system itself, and that the functioning of cognitive systems via assimilation–accommodation has the built-in possibility of creating a dynamic tension that can impel the system toward revision and change.

Piaget's research with children indicated that such revisions in cognitive systems may occur following either failure or success in goal attainment and understanding. Failure to attain a desired objective might cause a person to attempt new means of attainment and to reflect on those means. This process of reflection might then lead to a change in understanding. In the case of success, additional methods of attainment can be attempted "just to see if they will work too." Again, having attempted different means, the individual might then reflect on their relative strengths and weaknesses, and this process could result in a change in understanding. Thus, in Piaget's equilibration model, cognitive systems generate present, "online" cognitive behavior (such as means–ends goal attainment behaviors, logical reasoning, and causal reasoning), and also generate *perturbation–regulation–compensation* sequences that lead, sooner or later, to a restructuring of the cognitive system that was responsible for the original failure or success. Our discussion of research findings illustrates some of these points.

Three Forms of Equilibration

In order to have a model that covers both present, online cognitive behavior and changes in cognitive systems over time, Piaget recognized three main forms of equilibration. These pertain to the functioning of individual components of cognitive systems (cycle of individual cognitive components or basic subject ↔ object relation that functions via assimilation–accommodation), to interactions between or among two or more individual components (subsystem cycle), and to interactions between subsystems and the overall system (totality cycle). The first two types of equilibration describe current, online cognitive functioning. The last two types describe change in the cognitive system over time.

The first form of equilibration is the functioning via assimilation–accommodation of individual schemes and operations and pertains to present, ongoing cognitive construction. The second type of equilibration pertains to restructuring the relation within a scheme or restructuring the relationship between two or more schemes at the same level of complexity—a horizontal reorganization. The third form of equilibration pertains to a vertical restructuring of an entire set of schemes and operations with respect to the totality of which they are a part.

Perturbation–Regulation–Compensation Sequences

Piaget (1985) introduced several terms and concepts in presenting a revised model of equilibration. A core explanatory concept is the notion of a perturbation–regulation–compensation sequence that addresses the full range of human behavior from everyday habits to scientific reasoning. Several contingencies are dealt with in the model. First are situations in which no perturbations are experienced. In such cases, the need and possibility for behavioral and cognitive changes is not present and the cognitive system remains unchanged (see Fig. 1.1). The second general contingency is one in which perturbations are experienced. Having experienced a perturbation, the child may or may not seek to *regulate* his or her behavior. Piaget defined regulation of behavior as the modification of the repetition of an action based on the initial result of the action. Piaget stated that instead of seeking to regulate behaviors following perturbations, children often repeat the behavior without making any changes. Alternatively, children leave cognitive systems intact following perturbations because the perturbations lead the children to stop or go in a different direction. In short, Piaget acknowledged that in the everyday lives of real children, perturbations are no guarantee that regulations and compensations leading to cognitive changes will occur (see Fig. 1.1).

Equilibration as a process of self-regulation leading to changes in a cognitive system is only one of several options available to children when they experience perturbations. Such changes in the cognitive system can be considered to be a search for logical coherence or a deeper level of understanding (Furth, 1978, 1980). In situations in which one experiences perturbations such as a failure to understand or has a feeling that a deeper level of understanding is possible, a search for logical coherence or cognitive restructuring is only one of several possible options. Oftentimes, children ignore or repress cognitive failures or feelings of cognitive gaps. In such instances, there is no cognitive restructuring at the horizontal or vertical levels. Repression of cognitive failures can include self-deceptions in which the errors or failures are not acknowledged by the child. In other cases, adjustments that are made are momentary and do not result in change. Thus, being corrected by a teacher, parent, or fellow student may cause a child to change his answer but not result in a change in the cognitive system that generated the original wrong answer in the first place. Changing the answer is a response to public social pressure to correct one's mistake.

A second strategy for dealing with cognitive failures or feelings that one does not understand something also serves to protect the present system and leave it more or less unchanged. Here, the person deals with the difficult content in a playful fashion, knowing that it is too hard to deal with seriously. In this circumstance, the cognitive failures are acknowledged, but the person does not engage in cognitive effort to revise the cognitive system. Instead, the cognitive system is preserved by dealing with the failures or unexplained content in a playful fashion (see Furth, 1980).

Piaget's equilibration model was designed to account for situations in which either horizontal or vertical restructuring of cognition does occur. Here, cognitive failures and gaps in understanding are acknowledged and dealt with seriously. The child attempts to establish a new relation between his cognitive system and what he observes. As mentioned earlier, gaps in understanding may be "felt" following success as well as failure and can occur in situations in which the individual is working alone or with others. Because these changes are not the only or usual outcomes of cognitive functioning, Piaget referred to these as *reequilibrations* or *optimizing equilibrations*. Table 1.2 summarizes all of the *equilibration options* just described. Note that although most of the equilibration options are described in terms of individual behavior, all are applicable to situations in which two or more persons are interacting. It is unlikely that all mem-

TABLE 1.2
Equilibration Options in Piagetian Theory

Equilibration Option	Description	Result
Momentary assimilation–accommodation	Child is aware of intentions and progress toward goal attainment. Behaviors are modified accordingly.	Starting point for each of the remaining equilibration options.
Repress gaps or failures	Child ignores cognitive inadequacies that are felt momentarily.	Maintenance of cognitive system —no horizontal or vertical reorganization.
Playful response	Child deals with felt cognitive inadequacies by making light of them.	Maintenance of cognitive system likely, horizontal reorganization possible.
Imitation of other	Child deals with felt inadequacies by copying other person.	Maintenance of cognitive system likely, horizontal reorganization possible.
Search for logical coherence	Deliberate attempt to improve understanding following perturbations.	Conscious reorganization of conceptual understanding at horizontal or vertical levels.

bers of a group will repress gaps or failures. On the other hand, imitative and playful responses may be more likely in social than individual situations. It is an open question as to whether teams rather than individuals working alone are more likely to deliberately attempt to search for logical coherence following the experience of perturbations (see Moshman & Geil, 1998, for some promising findings in this regard). A related question is whether teams are more successful than individuals in reaching higher levels of understanding, once quests for logical coherence have been undertaken. Figure 1.2 depicts the three types of equilibration with behavioral examples. These issues are discussed in greater detail in the section of this chapter that discusses empirical research findings.

Perturbations Impel Change in Cognitive Systems

Piaget believed that persons at initial stages of development were likely to experience perturbations due to the tendency to focus on positive aspects of objects and experiences to the neglect of negative aspects. Piaget's considerable body of research on children's thinking provides evidence in support of this point. As an example, the reader may call to mind any one of Piaget's several conservation problems in which preoperational errors consist of focusing on the gain in one dimension to the neglect of the loss in a second, relevant dimension, leading to nonconservation judgments and explanations. Piaget maintained that better coordination of (understanding relations between) positive and negative aspects of situations are characteristic of higher levels of de-

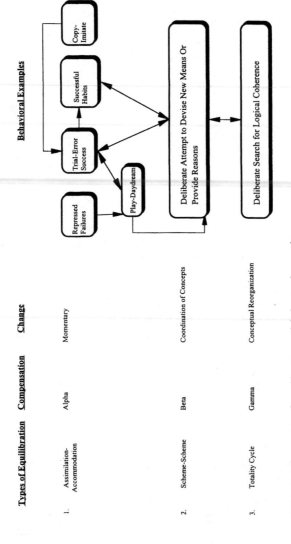

FIG. 1.2. Three types of equilibration with behavioral examples.

velopment. In short, the initial imbalance between positive and negative aspects typical of recently developed cognitive systems makes them prime candidates for experiencing perturbations.

As for perturbations, themselves, Piaget listed two main types—obstacles and lacunae (gaps). Obstacles are experienced as errors or failures to attain desired objectives and are regulated by negative feedback. Lacunae leave needs unsatisfied and are regulated by positive feedback that prolongs assimilative activities. Even in situations in which the child has successfully attained a desired objective, a lacuna may be experienced. Questions such as "Why did that work?" and "Could I do this some other way?" arise and are perturbatory. They lead the child to continue acting, testing the limits of present ways of succeeding, leading to the possibility of deeper understanding.

Regulations and Compensations

Having experienced a perturbation, a child may or may not engage in *regulatory activities*. Piaget identified several kinds of regulations of cognitive systems. We already discussed and distinguished between two main types of regulations, quasi-automatic and active, and means to achieve ends may be based on them. For example, the functioning of components of the sensory-motor system in terms of assimilation–accommodation occurs in a quasi-automatic fashion, below the threshold of awareness. The person is minimally aware of the accommodations made in the service of goal attainment, and focuses instead on the goal itself. Active regulation occurs when the person has to change means or chose between two or more means in order to attain a goal. A conscious choice or analysis of the situation is conducted. Quasi-automatic regulations are below the threshold of awareness. Thus, the original subject of action (sensory-motor components) becomes an object for a higher level concept or operation.

Regulations lead to one of three types of *compensations* (see Figs. 1.1 and 1.2). An *alpha* compensation is one in which the regulation of perturbations leaves the cognitive system unchanged. The subject cancels out the perturbation by ignoring it or by removing what bothers him. Alpha reactions are only partially compensatory, because no adjustments have been made to the cognitive system that just experienced a perturbation. The system is in danger of having the same perturbating elements arise. In *beta* compensations, the perturbation that sprang up externally is incorporated into the cognitive system, leading to enrichment of cognitive systems by integrating perturbations as internal variations and eliminating the perturbation as a perturbation. *Gamma* compensations consist of anticipating possible variations rendering perturbations to be potential transformations of an intact, highly developed cognitive system. Piaget's models of logicomathematical operations associated with each of the major stages of development are prime examples of *gamma* compensations.

Piaget (1985) listed four characteristics of regulatory compensations. First, every compensation acts against obstacles or gaps and at the same time draws useful information from these perturbations. Second, all compensations involve an evaluation of success and failure. Third, compensations tend to conserve states, sequences, schemes, or subsystems. Fourth, compensations are constructive in addition to being conservative. By acting against perturbations but drawing information from them, regulatory compensations gain in powers of anticipation, thus enriching the cognitive system.

Piaget noted the potential for peer interactions to cause perturbations for a child in several of his works, especially when discussing factors leading to development beyond egocentrism in childhood and adolescence. Thus, the idea of perturbation–regulation–compensation sequences has relevance for peer learning. Peers can present obstacles to a child's intended goals and methods of attainment. In addition, by indicating that a child's explanation is unclear or unsatisfactory, peers can stimulate lacunae in a child. Moreover, even without explicit queries by another, the process of attempting to formulate an explanation to another person can give rise to lacunae. With younger children, in particular, adults are more likely than peers to make sense of a child's egocentric communication, thereby reducing the chance of the experience of a lacuna. These examples illustrate how peer experiences may give rise to perturbations that serve to stimulate the process of equilibration. (See our later summary of a study by Dimant & Bearison, 1991, which illustrates the perturbation–regulation–compensation sequence with pairs of college students working on a combinatorial reasoning task.)

Piaget viewed individual cognitive operations and social cooperation as two sides of the same coin. Each is a component of a larger cognitive system and results from coordinations of, and abstractions from, the general properties of actions. As such, operations result from prior regulation–compensation sequences, and once constructed and stabilized, serve as regulators of behavior and thought as well. For example, on the individual side, young children anticipate and expect a series of five objects to continue to exist despite being hidden or covered, but also expect their number to increase in quantity after they are spread out. On the social side, young children understand that there are parental rules that must be obeyed, but understand the letter and not the spirit of these laws (Piaget, 1932b). In each case, the preoperational system is an advance over previous sensory-motor regulations but contains fundamental contradictions that will be corrected in turn by concrete operational systems.

The Functioning of Equilibration

Piaget's model of the functioning of equilibration includes two technical terms, observables and inferential coordinations, each of which must always be considered from the perspective of the subject under consideration. We shall not review all the various types of interactions described by Piaget (1985), but instead describe a general model:

> An observable is anything that can be established by immediate experience of the facts themselves. In contrast to this, coordinations involve inferences and go beyond what is observable. Such a distinction is clear, however, only when the subject is capable of objective observation and logically valid inferences. It is much harder when observations are inexact and when inferences include false implications. For that reason it will not do to define observables only in terms of perceptible characteristics. The subject often believes he perceives things that he does not perceive. Nor will it do to characterize coordinations by the verbal formulations subjects give of them. Implicit inferences play as great a role as those made partially explicit, if not a greater one. (p. 37)

Each term—observable and coordination—has a subject and an object component. Consider a causal interaction sequence. The subject first notes object observables (OBS O), and relates them to subject observables (OBS S). For example, the ball rolled (OBS O) when I pushed it (OBS S). All forms of sensory-motor equilibration stay on the observable level and do not entail inferential coordinations. If inferences linked to these observables are generated, they entail a reflection on the subject's actions and their effects on objects, which lead, in turn, to a conceptualization of object properties. The child may infer, for example, that some kind of power or force was transmitted from his hand to the ball, causing it to move (COORD S). The ball, in turn, may be classified as a type of object that can be moved with one's hands (COORD O). The general flow of this process is as follows:

$$OBS\ O \rightarrow OBS\ S \rightarrow COORD\ S \rightarrow COORD\ O \rightarrow OBS\ O \rightarrow etc.$$

(Piaget, 1985, p. 49).

The process of constructing inferential coordinations can lead the child to discover new observables. This leads to the following type of progression:

$$OBS\ O\ (n) \rightarrow OBS\ S\ (n) \rightarrow COORD\ S\ (n) \rightarrow COORD\ O\ (n) \rightarrow$$
$$OBS\ O\ (n+1) \rightarrow OBS\ S\ (n+1) \rightarrow COORD\ S\ (n+1) \rightarrow COORD\ O\ (n+1) \rightarrow$$
$$OBS\ O\ (n+2) \rightarrow OBS\ S\ (n+2) \rightarrow COORD\ S\ (n+2) \rightarrow COORD\ O\ (n+2)\ etc.$$

This diagram presents a summary of Piaget's final model of cognitive construction. The succession of levels (from n to n + 1 to n + 2, etc.) represents modification of the cognitive system as depicted in Fig. 1.1 and represents instances of either horizontal or vertical restructuring via beta and gamma compensations, as described in Fig. 1.2. Each individual row (level n alone, level n + 1 alone, or level n + 2 alone) represents meaning making in a given context as depicted in Figure 1 and represents instances of either momentary or horizontal restructuring via alpha and beta compensations, as described in Fig. 1.2.

LABORATORY AND CLASSROOM RESEARCH
ON PEER INTERACTIONS AND PIAGETIAN BEHAVIORS

In this section we illustrate how peer learning relates to Piaget's model of constructivism by reviewing empirical work on the role of peer interactions in children's understanding of social justice and fairness, and children's logical thinking and spatial reasoning. We have been highly selective in the research we describe here. First, we wish to illustrate the breadth of Piaget's framework. Piaget's views about learning and cognitive change are not specific to particular types of problems. For this reason, we chose to describe research on both social and logical reasoning. Second, because Piaget's model is developmental and addresses both ontogenetic and microgenetic change, we included research with participants from a wide age range. Third, we chose to include studies making use of well-researched and well-charted developmental tasks. By this, we mean that we chose tasks for which a clear developmental sequence has been identified.

Our review is necessarily constrained by our selection criteria, but our goal is to illustrate some of the points we made earlier. We focus on two issues. First, is there evidence that peer interactions have unique characteristics that foster children to construct new forms of meaning making? Second, what are the characteristics of peers' experiences that have been shown to foster growth and the modification of cognitive systems?

Peer Influences on Reasoning About Social Justice and Fairness

Piaget made some of his strongest statements about the role of peers in development during the early phases of his work, while he was studying children's moral reasoning (Piaget, 1932b). Research on peer interaction and moral reasoning has been generated from two main sources: the study of moral development and educational applications of Piaget's theory (e.g., DeVries & Zan, 1994; Kohlberg & Lickona, 1987).

Youniss and Damon (1992) summarized Piaget's views on socialization broadly, and on moral development in particular. They highlighted the fact that interpersonal relationships play an important role in the socialization process and described two types of relationships: those based on unilateral authority and those based on cooperation. Relationships of unilateral authority, such as a child–parent relationship, may generate respect for the views of the authority figure without a complete understanding of those ideas. Young children accept what they are told in a one-sided manner. By contrast, relationships of cooperation are symmetrical. Individuals contribute to interactions with more or less equal capabilities for communication and understanding. Unlike unilateral authority, cooperation implies that neither person holds a view without attending to the view offered by the other. Hence, there is a " tendency for each person to build on the other's ideas while explaining his own ideas to the other" (pp. 272–273).

Damon (1977) noted that Piaget depicted children's relationships with peers as the ideal context for cooperation, because children must cooperate to get along. In the process of discovering and practicing procedures that mediate peer cooperation, children form a common sense of social solidarity. Morality follows from these notions regarding relationships. As Youniss and Damon (1992) elaborated, Piaget proposed that morality is based on respect for persons rather than respect for tradition or rules: "Respect based on cooperation, however, allows views to be submitted to procedures that must follow the norms of reciprocity and discussion" (p. 274).

Several lines of inquiry followed from Piaget's work on socialization. Damon and Killen (1982) studied peer interaction and young children's reasoning about justice and fairness. If social interaction between equals fosters development, then opportunities to engage in peer debate and discussion should lead to more sophisticated patterns of thought. Damon and Killen explored this question by pretesting children from kindergarten through third grade for their reasoning about fairness in a social dilemma. Following the pretest, children were assigned to one of three conditions. In the experimental group, three children worked together to reach consensus on a new problem about fairness. The experimental group was further divided into triads of mixed ability and triads of comparable ability. In one control group, children worked individually with an adult experimenter on the same social reasoning dilemma. In the second control group, children received only the pretest and no additional experience. All children were then posttested individually. Peer interaction sessions were videotaped and discussions were transcribed. The transcripts were analyzed to capture both the discourse features of the peer debate and also to identify the interaction qualities linked to change. This design enabled a comparison of posttest results across the three groups as well as permitting an analysis of the peer debates.

Results showed that the experimental group improved from pretest to posttest, providing support for the hypothesis that peer interaction plays a role in cognitive growth. Although this change was small, the experimental interaction period was brief and occurred just once. Interestingly, these findings showed no differences in the amount of change in the triads of mixed ability and those of comparable ability. Also, within the mixed triads, there was no difference in the tendencies of the higher and lower level children to change. However, a close analysis of actual dialogue failed to reveal a consistent pattern of interaction related to improvement. Analyses of the interactions during the debates revealed that children who engaged in rejecting, conflict-filled modes of interaction tended not to advance. Lower level children who advanced tended to focus on solutions pertaining to them, and tended to accept or transform (through compromise or collaboration) the solutions of their peers. Higher level children who changed did so through social interaction processes that were more varied and diverse than those of lower level children.

Researchers in moral development have long acknowledged the significance of peer interactions for developmental change. Some investigations of social interaction and cognitive change make use of social dilemmas in which the needs of an individual are pitted against those of the group. Originally devised by Kohlberg (1963), these problems provide a well-researched set of tasks with clearly described developmental sequences. Social interaction provides opportunities to engage in role taking and social perspective taking. These activities lead to adjustments in interindividual cooperation and critical intraindividual coordinations. Social interaction, discussion, and dialogue about the dilemmas specifically, and social problems more broadly, are viewed as essential for cognitive advancement (see Blatt & Kohlberg, 1975; Colby, Kohlberg, Fenton, Speicher-Dubin, & Liberman, 1977, for additional work).

Interactions occurring during the discussion of moral dilemmas were examined directly by Berkowitz and Gibbs (1983) in a study of undergraduate dyads. Of primary interest were "those process features that relate to individual disequilibrium and the development of higher stages of moral reasoning" (p. 400). Berkowitz and Gibbs posited that moral development results from moral discussion in which discussants focus on the justification for their moral positions. The interpenetration of two or more moral reasoning systems was expected to produce conflict and optimize change.

Interpenetration of moral reasoning systems was assessed through discourse analyses. A mode of moral discussion labeled *transactive discussion* was identified and a coding system was devised. Transactive discussion is reasoning that operates on the reasoning of another. Development is believed to occur when each member engages his or her partner with his or her own reasoning. Rather than merely providing consecutive assertions, discussants *operate* on each other's reasoning in an ongoing dialogic dynamic.

Eighteen types of transactive behaviors (*transacts*) are included in this coding scheme. Transacts are coded as either lower level and representational, or as higher level and operational. Representational transacts represent another's reasoning, whereas operational transacts operate on or transform it. Operational transacts are the most advanced form of transactive behavior. Berkowitz and Gibbs (1983) tested the hypotheses that (a) dyads producing pre- to posttest change in moral reasoning would use more transactive behavior than dyads not producing change, and (b) operational transaction is more related than lower order forms of transaction to moral stage change. Berkowitz and Gibbs found support for both hypotheses. More transactive communication was shown in the dialogues of dyads demonstrating significant change in moral reasoning from pretest to posttest. Also, operational transaction appeared to be the crucial form of transactive communication associated with advancement in moral reasoning.

Taken together, these studies demonstrate that the joint resolution of socio-moral problems produces developmental change and that a crucial aspect of this process is the use of logic and reasoning. Figure 1.2 and Table 1.2 depict a search for logical coherence as one equilibration option in Piaget's theory and cooperative exchanges as one form of self–other meaning making.

Piaget believed that the asymmetrical nature of the adult–child relationship and the symmetrical quality of the child–child relationship were critical mediators in social interaction. If peer debate offers unique opportunities for transactive reasoning, then this should be evident in a comparison of child–child and child–adult discussion. Kruger and Tomasello (1986) explored this question in a study that compared children's use of transacts in their discussion of moral dilemmas with peers and with adults. It was predicted that children in peer dyads would use transacts more often because of the roughly egalitarian structure of the dyad. Children with adults were expected to use transacts less often, instead deferring to adult authority. Girls aged 7 to 11 participated in this study. Dyads were created by pairing half the girls at each age level with a familiar peer and pairing the remaining girls with their mothers. Dyads met and were read two story-dilemmas taken from a positive justice interview scale. The dyads were instructed to consider all possible solutions to the dilemma and to discuss them until they reached a consensus. Participants were encouraged to talk for as long as they liked and advised to consider all solutions to avoid a superficial discussion. The experimenter left the room and the discussion was tape-recorded. Discussions were subsequently transcribed and coded for the occurrence of transactive statements. As expected, a greater proportion of the target participants' conversational turns were identified as transacts when paired with peers than when paired with adults. These findings support Piaget's contention that children's moral discussions with peers are qualitatively different from moral discussions with adults. Adult–child asymmetry was observed in dyads with 11-year-olds as well as 7-year-olds.

In a subsequent study, Kruger (1992) explored the role of dyadic interaction on change in children's level of reasoning about moral dilemmas. If transactive discussions are related to change in moral reasoning, then discussion between peers, as opposed to discussion between parent and child, should be related to greater change. Furthermore, across both types of situations, the increased use of transactive discussion should predict change. Kruger explored these questions in a study of transactive discussions between peer and adult–child dyads among 8-year-old girls. Each target child was randomly assigned to either a peer or adult condition in which she discussed two moral dilemmas with either a friend or with her mother. Prior to the discussion episode, children were pretested for moral reasoning and afterward they were posttested. Results showed that the two groups did not differ on the pretest. However, at posttest, children who had discussed moral dilemmas with their peers produced higher levels of reasoning than those who discussed the dilemmas with their mothers. This is consistent with the hypothesis that peer discussions or cooperative exchanges produce greater changes in moral reasoning than do adult child discussions or adult-regulated exchanges.

How did the interactions occurring during the discussion of the moral dilemmas actually differ across peer and child–adult pairs? First, target girls in peer dyads as compared to those in adult–child dyads were expected to use more transacts, to use them more spontaneously, and to focus their transacts on their partners ideas, rather than their own. Second, the use of spontaneous transacts in discussion, no matter the partner, was expected to be positively related to moral reasoning level at posttest. Discussions of the moral dilemmas were analyzed by coding each conversational turn and were coded as nontransactive or transactive. Three specific types of transacts were coded, each with two orientations: transactive statements (self-oriented or other oriented), transactive questions (self-oriented or other oriented), and transactive responses (self-oriented or other oriented). The results showed that all participants generated the same proportional numbers of transacts in their conversations. However, consistent with predictions, group differences appeared in the types and orientations of the transacts. Target girls paired with peers produced more other-oriented statements than did those paired with adults, and peer partners produced more other-oriented statements than did adult partners. Hence, peer dyads were characterized by their mutual use of other-oriented transactive statements. In contrast, target girls paired with adults produced more self-oriented responses that did those paired with peers. Adult partners produced more other-oriented questions than did peer partners. Adult–child dyads were characterized by a pattern of adult questions and child responses.

Four dimensions of dyadic discussion style were defined. An egocentric style combined self-oriented statements by targets with self-oriented statements by partners and represents an absence of engagement with the partner and a focus on the self. A Socratic style was defined as involving other-oriented questions by the partner and self-oriented statements by the target child and represents a target's passive engagement in the transactive dialogue as compliance with the partner's request for transacts. An egalitarian style was defined as other oriented statements by both partners. It features spontaneous collaboration between partners in transactive dialogues. Finally, in leadership style, the target child exhibited spontaneous control over the interaction. Each dyad received a score for each of the four discussion styles and the two groups were compared. There were no differences between the groups in use of the egocentric style. However, adult–child dyads made more use of Socratic style interaction whereas peer dyads made more use of egalitarian style interaction and leadership style interaction.

An examination of the relation of the differential use of transacts by participants in the two conditions and posttest reasoning showed that the individual transact measures alone were not significant predictors. Regression equations that included the measures of discussion style, which incorporated transacts, were significant. For the sample as a whole, leadership style and egalitarian style were the best positive predictors of posttest reasoning. These two styles included greater spontaneity and activity by the target participant. For adult–child dyads considered alone, egalitarian style was predictive and for peers alone, leadership style predicted reasoning.

Three important conclusions can be drawn from this study. First, peer interaction during middle childhood supports moral reasoning, as children paired with peers, rather than adults, showed more change in reasoning. Second, there is an important difference in the quality of the discussion between peer dyads and adult–child dyads. Children assume a more active role in the transactions with peers. In contrast to peer dialogues, children discussing dilemmas with adults were more likely to assume a passive role. This supports the idea that active engagement is critical for the development of moral reasoning. Third, the use of reasoning in discussions with peers was predictive of change in moral reasoning. Across both the peer dyads and the adult–child dyads, the use of active reasoning by the child led to more sophisticated reasoning at posttest. This type of reasoning was more likely to occur in peer dyads than child–adult dyads.

A different approach to peer interaction and social reasoning is evident in the work of DeVries and colleagues. DeVries and Goncu (1987) studied peer relations and the construction of social knowledge in classroom contexts. They hypothesized that classrooms in which cooperative relationships were explicitly emphasized would lead children to exhibit higher levels of interpersonal negotiation strategies. Four-year-old children from a constructivist classroom and Montessori preschool classroom were observed. These two preschool programs provide distinctly different sorts of experiences to children in their ongoing daily interactions at school. The constructivist approach emphasized cooperation and collaboration both among children and between teacher and child. The constructivist teacher attempted to promote children's autonomy and self-regulation through reducing the exercise of adult power and through upholding the value of cooperation and mutual agreement among children. In contrast, a Montessori preschool, although encouraging children's active involvement with materials and the environment, downplayed peer interaction in collaborative, consciously shared experiences. Furthermore, the role of the teacher in the Montessori classroom was quite different than in the constructivist classroom. The teacher stood back and allowed children to work independently in the classroom. The teacher did not become an active participant in children's activities. Instead, the teacher was a guide or director helping children to understand the proper use of the materials. The teacher was emotionally restrained and more often the observer of activity rather than an active participant. Given this difference in educational programs, DeVries and Goncu explored the effects of experience in these two types of child-centered programs on children's sociomoral development. Specifically, they expected that the children in the two different settings would differ in the quality of their interpersonal negotiation strategies during play. Children in the constructivist classroom were expected to be more advanced and were expected to resolve conflicts more cooperatively.

Children from both classrooms were observed as they played a board game with a peer. Children's interactions during the game-playing situation were videotaped and transcribed. Interactions were then coded for their level of interpersonal understanding using a measure developed by Selman (1980). Strategies employed by children during the ongoing interaction were coded by evaluating each *turn* in the conversation. Four levels were identified. Level 0 referred to "raw will" without any reflection of the other's point of view. Level 1 referred to a one-way understanding of negotiated interaction that focused primarily on the self. At Level 2, the actor demonstrates an awareness of other individuals as planful and having opinions, feelings, and behaviors that impact on those of the self. Level 3 strategies include negotiations that express an awareness of the complexity of the actual interaction process and of the individual's awareness of the multiple meanings in group processes. Results showed that the children in the constructivist program were more advanced in their stage of social-cognitive competence than children from the Montessori program. This was evidenced by an analysis of the interpersonal negotiation strategies used and in children's management of conflict. The Montessori children showed themselves less able than constructivist children to regulate their social behavior in effective ways in the absence of adult regulation. Children from the constructivist program manifested greater valuing and coordination of thoughts, feelings, and wishes of self and other (even during conflict) than did children from the Montessori classes.

Further evidence for the influence of the classroom environment on children's interpersonal understanding was provided by a larger follow-up study conducted by DeVries, Reese-Learned, and Morgan (1991) and DeVries, Haney, and Zan (1991). DeVries, Reese-Learned, et al. (1991) compared kindergartners from three different types of classroom: one based on a constructivist approach, as described earlier; one based on a direct-instruction approach; and a third making use of an eclectic orientation. As in the earlier study, children's enacted interpersonal understanding was studied through an analysis of children's interactions while they played a board game and divided stickers. Children in all three classes showed a predominant use of Level 1 strategies but the children in the constructivist group consistently had the highest percentage of Level 2 strategies. The direct-instruction group consistently had the lowest. The constructivist group was more interpersonally active, having a greater number and variety of negotiation strategies and shared experiences. When group differences in the use of Level 0 strategies appeared, the constructivist classroom had the lowest number of strategies and the direct-instruction classroom the highest. No gender differences, no differences in cognitive understanding of the game, and no differences in mothers' reported child-rearing techniques were found. Importantly, although the direct-instruction group had significantly higher scores on preschool-screening tests and first-grade achievement tests, the differences between direct-instruction and constructivist groups disappeared by third grade. The work by DeVries and her colleagues demonstrates that classroom organization and curriculum impact children's ability to engage effectively with peers. Greater interpersonal competence and understanding may provide a basis for transactive dialogue and increased social understanding.

In sum, findings from several independent research programs support the following ideas: (a) peer collaboration and interaction serve to enhance children's socio-moral reasoning, (b) change toward higher levels of reasoning is most likely to occur when discussion and dialogue are transactive in nature, (c) peer–peer interactions are more likely to support such interactions than adult–peer relations, and (d) classroom experiences supporting cooperation influence children's interactions within small groups so that children are more likely to demonstrate greater interpersonal competence and understanding.

Peer Influences on Logical and Spatial Reasoning

Piaget's work in the development of logical and spatial thinking has had a profound impact on mathematics and science education in the United States. This is evidenced by the current standards of the National Council for Teachers of Mathematics (1989) and a perusal of journals for math and science educators. However, the relation between Piaget's theoretical work and educational practice is complex and indirect. The theory provides a clear set of assumptions and testable assertions about processes of knowledge acquisition and development. Our summary and discussion of research on peer influences on children's logical and spatial thinking is intended to illustrate some of the points made in earlier portions of the chapter.

Many of the studies included in this section were published many years ago. We thought it useful to revisit some of these "old" studies in light of more recent work on equilibration. Points made in the earlier portion of the chapter regarding assimilation, accommodation, and various forms of self–other meaning making are well illustrated by this earlier work.

The logical and spatial tasks Piaget and his colleagues presented to children attracted tremendous attention from researchers in cognitive development. One line of work particularly relevant to this chapter centers on the hypothesis that peer interaction provides a powerful context for supporting change in logical and scientific reasoning (Glachan & Light, 1982; Murray, 1983a; Perret-Clermont, 1980; Perret-Clermont, Perret, & Bell, 1993). In a thoughtful discussion of the literature on peer interaction and cognitive change, Glachan and Light (1982) identified three categories of experimental studies of child–child interaction for performance on Piagetian tasks. These include (a) the child observing the performance of a more advanced child, (b) the child actively interacting with a more advanced child, and (c) the child interacting with a child of his own level. Glachan and Light referred to the first category as modeling studies. They note that most of this work is grounded in social learning theory. The second two types of studies have arisen from a Piagetian framework.

The social learning hypothesis predicts that peer interaction enhances development because the child is provided with a more capable individual serving as a model. Progress in reasoning is attributed to the observation of the other successfully completing the task. Interaction with the model as well as interaction with the physical materials employed in the task is not required for change to occur. A number of studies exploring the role of models as change agents in concrete operational tasks show that modeling can enhance subsequent performance on the observed task (Kuhn, 1972; Murray, 1972; Rosenthal & Zimmerman, 1972; Zimmerman, 1974). Changes are maintained at a posttest several weeks later.

Modeling is one of the forms of individual and self-other meaning making we identified in Table 1.1. It is best understood in terms of the application of existing cognitive systems and functioning via assimilation and accommodation of individual schemes and operations as they pertain to present ongoing cognitive construction. This is the first form of equilibration we discussed. Modeling as a source of change is problematic from a Piagetian standpoint because the participant appears to be passive. As noted in Table 1.1, the imitative nature of modeling is largely accommodative and lacks the balance or equilibrium necessary for the second and third forms of equilibration characterized by the reorganization of schemes at the same or different levels.

However, Kuhn (1972) demonstrated that under certain circumstances, modeling may induce reorganization of schemes. She showed that exposure to a model functioning just slightly beyond the participant's current level (or level at pretest) can induce enduring change. She also found that modeling was ineffective when models functioned far in advance of the participant. Glachan and Light (1982) suggested that a child may be mentally active without necessarily being physically active: "Thus the success of the modeling procedures need not be interpreted in terms of passive imitation, and can even be seen as a kind of 'tacit interaction' between subject and model" (p. 245). This early work illustrates the dynamic aspects of Piaget's model of learning. Type 1 and Type 2 constructivism (see Fig. 1.1) are closely related, and through the application of existing cognitive systems children might then modify this system.

A different approach to modeling studies was provided by the work of Murray and colleagues. Botvin and Murray (1975) compared children who engaged in active interaction with other children and materials to children who merely watched this interaction. In the active interaction condition, groups of children (both conservers and nonconservers) were asked to reach consensus on six conservation problems. (This condition is similar to the "cooperative exchanges" form of meaning making shown in Table 1.1.) Children in the modeling condition were all nonconservers who watched the experimenter elicit a judgment and an explanation from each member of an interaction group before and after consensus was achieved. A no-treatment control group was also employed. Children in the modeling group and the active interaction group improved from pre- to posttest relative to those in the control group. The Botvin and Murray study differs from earlier work in that the children in the modeling condition were exposed to several different models who expressed and defended differing viewpoints. Conflicting judgments and explanations may have played an important role in change. In later work, more emphasis was placed on cognitive dissonance than modeling. By exploring role playing, (i.e., by asking children to pretend), Murray, Ames, and Botvin (1977) demonstrated that nonconserving and transitional participants who gave conserving judgments and reasons in role playing (similar to delayed imitation in Table 1.1) made large and significant gains on conservation posttests.

In the work addressing features of *cooperative exchanges* (Table 1.1) between children, experimental conditions were designed in which participants actively interacted with other children on solutions to conservation tasks and other concrete operational problems. Findings from a number of studies have shown that in active encounters between conservers and nonconservers, nonconservers yield to conservers more often than the reverse (Miller & Brownell, 1975; Silverman & Geiringer, 1973; Silverman & Stone, 1972). This understanding appears to be retained and is demonstrated on later posttesting up to a month after interaction. Many children who acquired conservation during the interaction session also introduced novel arguments.

Miller and Brownell (1975) considered why nonconservers were more likely to yield to conservers than vice versa. To establish whether or not conservers were generally more socially dominant, they asked pairs of children a variety of control questions unrelated to conservation. Conservers "won" 41 arguments and nonconservers won 38. In contrast, on conservation questions, conservers won 59 debates and nonconservers won only 8. Miller and Brownell noted that on the conservation questions, conservers were likely to assert their answers, produce counterarguments, and manipulate the stimulus materials. Nonconservers appeared to be limited to a restatement of their original response. Conservers, they suggested, exert a stronger social influence during conservation arguments because a belief in conservation is typically held more firmly than a belief in nonconservation.

The interaction studies described all incorporated a nonconserving child paired with a partner who both disagreed and offered a concrete operational solution. It is important to clarify the extent to which disagreement, independent of the provision of an operational solution, promotes cognitive change. The issue of contradiction and the resolution of contradiction through peer interaction is at the heart of Piaget's early work as well as the research on change in moral reasoning discussed in the previous section. Several lines of research have addressed the issue of contradiction and its resolution through interaction on concrete and formal operational tasks.

Doise and his colleagues investigated the effects of contradiction on the responses of nonconservers. Using a conservation-of-length task, Doise and his colleagues found that children progressed as a result of being presented with a solution that contradicted their own, even if the contradiction was not a correct solution (Doise, Mugny, & Perret-Clermont, 1975). Interaction with another child offering a conflicting solution led to improved performance because the contradiction fosters the consideration of other perspectives on task solutions. Similarly, pairs of nonconserving children manifesting different incorrect answers progressed, whereas pairs of nonconservers who used the same inferior solution did not (Doise et al., 1975).

Contradiction and its social resolution were also studied by Ames and Murray (1982). They presented nonconservers with one of four situations in which conflicting, but still incorrect, information about the conservation problem was provided. First, in a social interaction condition, children were paired with another nonconserving child who had offered a different nonconserving response. Children were presented with a new conservation problem and told to figure out together what the correct answer was. Second, in a model condition, children were asked to listen to a peer respond to a conservation question. The model's response was wrong, but different from the target child's response. Third, children in the pretense condition were asked to pretend the opposite of what they had asserted during the pretest. Fourth, in the nonpeer conflict condition, children were presented with two conservation items from among those they had failed. However, the items were modified so as to emphasize a contrasting nonconserving response. Finally, there was a no-treatment control condition. The treatment was presented within 1 week of the pretest and was followed by an immediate posttest. A delayed posttest was also presented 4 weeks later. Results showed that the social interaction group (the only condition permitting cooperative exchanges) outperformed the other four groups on both the immediate and the delayed posttest. Apparently, the social interaction situation stimulated the spontaneous generation of conservation responses (i.e., the vertical restructuring of cognitive systems). Importantly, this understanding was sustained through both immediate and delayed posttests. Such effects were not seen in any of the other experimental conditions, indicating that social interaction provides a unique and important context for stimulating change.

More recent work has drawn on Piaget's later work on equilibration in an effort to clarify the specific aspects of the social situation impelling modification of the cognitive system. This work helps to illustrate the second and third forms of equilibration depicted in Fig. 1.2—specifically the horizontal and vertical reorganization of schemes. This work also illustrates the search for logical coherence described in Table 1.2. Several researchers have drawn on the notion of sociocognitive conflict to understand the role of social interaction in cognitive change. Through social interaction, some form of cognitive disconfirmation occurs. Such disconfirmation triggers a search for logical coherence and deliberate attempts to improve understanding following the cognitive perturbation. Initial work focused on the notion of sociocognitive conflict and the rather simplistic idea that discussion characterized by a comparison of conflicting viewpoints would lead to the discovery of more adequate, logically coherent, and "better" understanding. Some researchers have used a spatial perspective-taking problem to explore this issue. For example, Bearison, Magzamen, and Filardo (1986) hypothesized that task-relevant disagreements and contradictions would be more effective at promoting cognitive gains than dyadic interactions lacking these kinds of cognitive disconfirmations. A spatial perspective-taking task was chosen because it required the active manipulation of task materials, thus allowing for the expression of verbal as well as enactive disagreements between partners in the experimental (dyadic) condition.

Pairs of children worked together on a spatial perspective-taking task and were compared with controls who completed the task alone. Among the experimental group, particular interaction strategies that reflected aspects of sociocognitive conflict (expressed verbally or enactively) were derived from videotapes of the interaction sequences. Distinctions were made between conflicts that consisted of simple statements or gestures of conflicting views and those that included reasons or logical justifications. Children aged 5 to 7 were included.

Although overall, children working in dyads did not perform significantly better than children working alone, several critical features in the frequency and quality of social interactions were found to promote cognitive growth. A curvilinear relation between the expression of sociocognitive conflict and cognitive change was found. Children, particularly boys, who expressed a moderate amount of conflict with their partner during the problem-solving situation did show a higher level of pretest to posttest change than either the low-conflict or high-conflict groups. Furthermore, there was a significant difference between this subgroup of experimental participants and the control group. Bearison et al. (1986) reported that among the males, there was an optimal range of frequencies for the expression of verbal disagreements. Too few or too many were not associated with significant, positive change. Enactive agreements, even if accompanied by verbal explanations, failed to predict change. These findings provide mixed support for the broad hypothesis that sociocognitive conflict supports cognitive change. Among the young children working on a spatial perspective-taking task, some boys appeared to benefit from the opportunity to work with peers, and these benefits were accompanied by discussions characterized by disagreements and explanations. Patterns were more complex for girls and did not fit neatly with theoretical expectations.

Peterson and Peterson (1990) examined the sociocognitive conflict among deaf children when engaged in a spatial perspective-taking problem. Children made use of a peer debate procedure. Past work has shown that deaf children lag behind hearing children in their mastery of Piagetian concrete operational tasks. It has also been suggested that deaf children have a weaker drive toward cognitive equilibration because they are often exposed to overprotective, conflict-avoidant child rearing methods. Such parenting strategies may lead to a high tolerance for ambiguity. It was hypothesized that deaf children would be relatively ineffective when given the opportunity to debate with peers in spatial perspective-taking tasks, showing little or no subsequent gain in reasoning. Deaf children aged 5 to 13 worked on spatial perspective-taking problems with peers who had likewise failed a pretest or alone. Contrary to the hypothesis, children who had worked with a peer showed significant improvement from pretest to posttest. These children disagreed actively and productively with one another. No such improvement was shown by the control participants who worked alone. Peterson and Peterson emphasized that the task they used was especially well suited to the needs of these children. Both enactive and verbal disagreements were measured, and enactive disagreements were easily expressed (i.e., one child relocating an object placed by the other child). Interestingly, children who made extensive use of verbal explanation showed less progress on the posttest than children who used more enactive strategies. However, verbal explanations accompanying disagreements were rare and occurred in only 3 of the 12 dyads. Peterson and Peterson concluded that deaf children are able to benefit from peer debate and the sociocognitive conflict such debate engenders on spatial perspective-taking problems. These studies are consistent with the notion that peer collaboration facilitates a search for logical coherence and a reorganization of existing cognitive schemes. Particularly striking here is the notion that children initially and individually lacking an understanding coconstruct an understanding of the perspective-taking problem.

We characterized sociocognitive conflict as an indicator of a "search for logical coherence." Yet, nowhere in the first portion of the chapter did we mention the notion of sociocognitive conflict. Whereas sociocognitive conflict might mark a perturbation in reasoning, cognitive change will occur only if the perturbation leads to an attempt to improve understanding followed by a conscious reorganization of conceptual understanding (see Fig. 1.1). As we noted in Table 1.2, such a search for logical coherence is only one of several responses that might occur following a perturbation.

Dimant and Bearison (1991) focused on the consequences of a perturbation among peer dyads working on a formal reasoning task. Specifically, they targeted the generation of theoretically relevant interactions that reflected the potential to evoke perturbations and resolutions (i.e., peer-induced disequilibrium) in a combinatorial reasoning task. Results showed that only experimental participants who had above the mean number of theoretically relevant interactions had individual pretest to posttest scores that significantly exceeded those of controls. As Dimant and Bearison noted, "it is not peer interaction per se that facilitates cognitive growth but [rather] particular and theoretically relevant features of peer interaction that account for gains" (p. 283).

The focus on theoretically relevant interactions including both conflict and its resolution marked a departure from past research strategies. Golbeck (in press) attempted to apply this framework to an analysis of elementary age children's reasoning about invariant horizontality in the physical world. Golbeck was interested in the role of peer collaboration in children's acquisition of spatial knowledge. Children aged 10 and 12 were pretested for their knowledge of horizontality. They were assigned to one of three conditions for subsequent problem solving experience: (a) working alone on subsequent water-level problems, (b) working with a peer of comparable understanding, and (c) working with a peer of a differing level of understanding. All children were given containers partially filled with liquid and were asked to represent the water surface in two-dimensional drawings. Hence, all children were able to receive feedback from the materials. Interactions sessions were videotaped and transcribed; all children were then posttested individually. Whereas all three groups showed an improvement from pretest to posttest, change was greatest for those children working with a peer. The analyses of the interactions employing Dimant and Bearison's (1991) coding scheme failed to show a relation between theoretically relevant interactions and change. However, for children in the matched-peer condition, there was a relation between procedural, task-oriented talk and improvement on the posttest. Among the unmatched peers, there was a relation between explanations about how to draw the water surface and improvement from pretest to posttest. Overall, discussions were marked by very little conflict. Perhaps these dialogues are better understood as efforts to make meaning in context (Type 1 constructivism in Fig. 1.1). From this perspective, joint meaning making rather than the generation and resolution of perturbations is the focus of activity.

Levin and Druyan (1993) explored social interaction and cognitive change on a *development-prone* problem and *development-resistant* task. The development-prone task was similar to a Piagetian assessment and required a judgment about the speeds at which two objects traveled around a circular track. Because the objects moved side by side, one moved faster. The development-resistant task was one shown to evoke scientific misconceptions. It was similar to the first problem, except both objects were attached to a common carrier. Specifically, two animals were riding side by side on a carousel. An individual displaying the misconception asserted that both dogs on the carousel were moving at the same speed. This judgment was often backed up with the statement that two parts of a single object cannot move at different speeds. Levin and Druyan put forth the interesting hypothesis that success on the first type of problem will improve as a result of opportunities for peer collaboration, whereas performance on the second problem will deteriorate. They tested these hypotheses with 6th-, 8th-, and 10th-grade students. Participants were pretested and assigned to groups of four to complete the test problems. Each group was in turn assigned to one of three conditions for the intervention; videotaped group transaction, individual multiple-choice testing (in which alternative answers to the problems were presented), or a no-intervention condition. Following the intervention, all participants were posttested individually on the same problems and two transfer problems. Several months later, all participants were interviewed again on the same problems.

As expected, participants showed higher success rates on the first problem with increasing age. Among the 10th graders, 64% passed after intervention. However, a different pattern was shown on the "common carrier" misconception problem. The percentage of students passing this problem increased slightly between 6th (13%) and 8th grade, but there was no difference between 8th (22%) and 10th graders (24%). As predicted, the intervention had different effects on the two types of tasks. Transactions seemed to promote performance on the autonomous motion problem (two separate objects moving) by encouraging progress and discouraging regression more than the other treatments. In contrast, transaction seems to have a bidirectional effect on the common carrier problem (the single object problem evoking misconceptions), by encouraging both progress and regression more than the other treatments.

For our purposes, it is useful to view the development-prone and development-resistant tasks as problems of very differing levels of difficulty. The common carrier misconception problem is significantly more difficult than the alternative problem. Presenting a group of students with a problem far beyond their grasp will not necessarily result in productive discussion and cognitive change. Indeed, as Levin and Druyan (1993) showed, a decline in correct responding and more deeply entrenched misunderstanding may result. These findings illustrate our point that there are many equilibration options, some of which do not lead to "positive" change (Table 1.2).

Recently, Moshman and Geil (1998) examined collaborative reasoning among college students. They presented students with a problem requiring the use of the falsification strategy in hypothesis testing. Specifically, a hypothesis concerning a set of four cards is presented and students are asked to decide which card must be turned to examine whether or not the hypothesis is true or false. Past research has shown that very few college students select for examination those cards that could falsify the hypothesis, although it has been shown that performance on the problem can be enhanced through variations in instructions, content, and context. Moshman and Geil considered this problem from a Piagetian perspective, arguing that an abstract understanding of the role of falsification in hypothesis testing develops over the course of adolescence, but that strategic application of this emergent competence is dependent on the situation. They expected that groups of people working on the four-card problem would fare better than individuals working alone. College students were randomly assigned to one of three groups: an individual control condition, an interactive group (students worked in groups of five or six), or an individual–interactive group (students first worked alone and then in groups of five or six). After groups reached what appeared to be a unanimous judgment, students recorded and explained the solution individually.

Correct solution patterns were far more common among groups than among students working alone. In the individual condition only 10% of the students selected the correct answer, whereas more than 70% of the groups selected the correct pattern. Analyses of the individual change patterns within the individual–interactive group showed that 37 of 57 students changed their responses after collaboration; all but 2 of these were in a positive direction. Although this finding would be stronger if Moshman and Geil had included a delayed posttest, as most of the other researchers we described ded, the trend toward improved understanding is striking. Furthermore, improvement was demonstrated even among groups in which no member initially provided a correct solution. Examples of the group dialogue illustrate participants' discovery of the centrality of the falsification strategy and the irrelevance of additional information to support the hypothesis.

In discussing their findings, Moshman and Geil (1998) addressed the issue of cognitive change in peer interaction as a process of conflict or a process of cooperation. They noted that this is a false dichotomy: "There were indeed conflicting views, and choices among these views, within every group in our study. These conflicts, however, took place within a cooperative context in which group members focused not on proving their own views correct but on co-constructing a consensus solution that could be justified to everyone's satisfaction" (p. 245).

SUMMARY

The literature on peer interactions and children's logical and spatial reasoning that we reviewed provides evidence that peer interactions can promote advancement in performance on Piagetian assessments and other tasks interpreted within a developmental framework and can support cognitive change. Dialogue and discussion serve to support change more effectively than independent, individual work. This does not mean that all instruction is best presented in such a format. Tasks need to be carefully chosen and matched to capabilities of the individual learners. One cannot infer from these findings that children will learn specific curriculum skills and knowledge objectives simply by putting children in groups. However, it is likely that small-group discussions on topics of interest to children requiring the use of logic and reasoning at an appropriate level of difficulty will be beneficial. It is also likely, given the right setting, that children working in small groups or dyads will generate more sophisticated and creative answers to challenging questions than children working alone.

There are, however, limitations to the work described. None of the research on logical and spatial thinking described here has been conducted in classrooms. Such work is badly needed and should focus not only on outcomes, or change from pretest to posttest, but also on the processes characterizing individual learning within social contexts. The studies we reviewed show that sociocognitive conflict in the absence of cooperation is unlikely to provoke change. Researchers and practitioners need a more detailed understanding of the way interactions between individuals support vertical and horizontal reorganization of cognitive schemes.

A second limitation of this research focuses on the generalizability and endurability of cognitive change. Most of the studies we described included a delayed posttest. Some included an assessment on a related task. It is difficult to make statements about cognitive change without such assessments and in the future, researchers should try to include such measures. It is not easy to operationalize Piaget's theory in a manner that fully respects the integrity of individual learners' cognitive systems, captures the complexity of the social situation, and enables a test of theoretically relevant transactions with the environment. Efforts to maintain the internal validity of experimental designs undermine the external validity of the research. In the future, such studies must be complemented by parallel work within classroom settings on school tasks.

GENERAL GUIDING PRINCIPLES FOR PEER LEARNING FROM PIAGET'S THEORY

We conclude our chapter with a few guiding principles for school-based peer learning gleaned from our summary of Piagetian theory and research.

1. Peer learning groups are composed of individual learners. These individuals each make meaning, discover problems, and resolve problems within their individual minds. These constructivist processes are depicted in Figs. 1.1 and 1.2. Although social contexts support and enhance these processes, ultimately they occur within the minds of individuals. This implies that as educators employ peer learning techniques, they must not loose sight of the interactions occurring between individuals within groups.

2. Peer interactions have the potential to foster intellectual growth in ways not easily replicated by children working alone or children working with adults.

3. Attainment of educational objectives using peer learning is a joint function of students' cognitive systems and the particular content area being worked on by the peer team. From a Piagetian perspective, the important question is not "will children learn from peer team experiences?" Instead, the issue is the *quality of learning* or level of understanding vis-à-vis the educational objective. Piagetian theory suggests that students' cognitive systems are important to consider because they influence the ability both to work cooperatively in teams and to understand the curriculum content. Teachers need to have an understanding of what their students are capable of in terms of cooperating toward attainment of stated project goals. Teachers also need to have an understanding of their students' knowledge (observables and inferential coordinations) of the curriculum

content and reasonable expectations as to how they might change in the course of the project.

4. Success at the level of action precedes understanding at the level of conceptualization. Learning a series of actions from a peer via modeling or demonstration (copying observables) does not guarantee that the two peers share the same level of understanding (inferential coordinations). It is best to check on the level of understanding reached by each member of the team (see #1 in this list).

5. Piagetian theory predicts that change in concepts is most likely to occur when assimilation and accommodation are in balance. Such a balance is more likely to occur in cooperative situations characterized by mutual respect, rather than unilateral authority. It is important that school learning experiences, whether individual, teacher–student, or student–student, are conducted in a classroom in which participants respect each other. Adults may need to underscore the importance of respecting others as students interact with each other in formats that are more impersonal (e.g., communicating asynchronously via e-mail).

6. Even in the most optimal environments, change in meaning making is not the "default" option for cognitive systems. Instead, systems tend to conserve their present ways of functioning and need to experience perturbations in order for change to be possible. Having students work together versus alone is not enough to ensure that change in cognitive systems and performance occurs. Instead, the nature or quality of the peer interactions is crucial. Task-relevant peer engagement characterized by questioning, explanations, and predictions leads to perturbations that in turn lead to modifications of cognitive systems. A challenge for constructivist educators is to document other ways in which peer experiences facilitate positive changes in individual cognitive systems, enabling new forms of meaning making to occur in classrooms. The constructivist theory and research findings we described do not offer cookbook methods for how to organize classrooms and instruction to attain educational goals. Instead, the ideas provide a perspective on peer learning that educators must adapt for the particular circumstances and contexts in which they work (Piaget, 1932b).

CHAPTER TWO

Implications of Vygotsky's Theory for Peer Learning

DIANE M. HOGAN
The Children's Research Centre, Trinity College, Dublin

JONATHAN R. H. TUDGE
University of North Carolina at Greensboro

The terms *peer learning* and *cooperative learning* have been used to describe quite different forms of interactions, with different goals, peer arrangements, and types of activities. In this chapter, we focus specifically on peer learning that is related to collaborative problem solving, typically involving two children. The roots of research on this type of peer learning are not in the field of education, but in developmental psychology, with much of the research occurring in university laboratories or in school, rather than involving the study of group processes in the classroom.

In what ways is Vygotsky's theory relevant to a discussion of collaborative peer learning? Vygotsky's theory views human development as a sociogenetic process by which children gain mastery over cultural tools and signs in the course of interacting with others in their environments. These others are often more competent and help children to understand and use in appropriate ways the tools and signs that are important in the cultural group into which they have been born. This process of interaction between the child and a more competent other is said to effect development if the interaction occurs within the child's zone of proximal development.

Although this summary is true to Vygotsky's position, we must not conflate Vygotsky's theory with one small part of the theory; we need to go further if we are to make progress in our understanding of collaboration from a Vygotskian perspective. When scholars study collaboration using a Vygotskian framework, the most commonly cited concept is that of the zone of proximal development, although this concept is hardly the theory's cornerstone. Our argument is that the application of Vygotsky's theory to collaborative problem solving (as to anything else) requires more than pairing a child with a more competent other and focusing simply on the interactions between them (or, for that matter, on the results of those interactions). Rather, it requires an interweaving of different aspects of development, involving the individual and the cultural-historical as well as the interpersonal, and focusing on the processes of development themselves. Research that dwells solely on interpersonal aspects, relying on the concept of the zone of proximal development, reduces the theory in a way that seriously detracts from its value.

As DeLisi and Golbeck (chap. 1, this volume) and others (Azmitia & Perlmutter, 1989; Chapman & McBride, 1992; Perret-Clermont, 1980; Tudge & Winterhoff, 1993b) make clear, the issue of peer collaboration is also addressed from a Piagetian perspective. Vygotsky-inspired research into peer collaborative problem solving has been less plentiful because Vygotsky, unlike Piaget (especially in his work on moral reasoning), did not emphasize the particular benefits of peer collaboration and focused more on adult–child interaction. Vygotsky's theory, however, has tremendous implications for our understanding of peer collaboration.

We divided the chapter into two major sections. In the first section, we discuss the major aspects of development (cultural-historical, interpersonal, and individual) that characterize Vygotsky's theory. In the second section, we review recent research on peer collaboration that purports to be set within a Vygotskian framework, and examine recent empirical evidence about the conditions under which learning in the course of peer collaboration is most likely to occur.

For the purposes of this discussion, each of these aspects of development (cultural-historical, individual, and interpersonal) will be treated as separate things. This is purely a heuristic device, as they do not operate separately, and Vygotsky's theory requires understanding of their interrelatedness. We cannot understand the interpersonal processes that go on between people (whether child–child or adult–child dyads) without knowing something about the individual characteristics (such as age, gender, motivation, competence) that each participant brings to the relationship. At the same time, we cannot understand the interactions between these individuals without knowing something about the broader context that provides much of the meaning. This context is both microsystemic (is this collaboration taking place in school or home?) and macrosystemic (the culturally and historically derived meanings and status of collaborations between children, of what is considered appropriate behavior in the home or in the school, and so on). The systemic nature of Vygotsky's theory, as is true of Bronfenbrenner's ecological systems theory (Bronfenbrenner, 1989, 1993; Bronfenbrenner & Ceci, 1994; Tudge, Gray, & Hogan, 1997), should force researchers to analyze the interweaving of these aspects of development.

ASPECTS OF DEVELOPMENT

Culture, History, and Phylogeny

Much of Vygotsky's writing was concerned with evolution, in particular focusing on how humans can be distinguished from other animals, and especially from those closest to humans. Drawing on Darwin, Kohler, Koffka, and others, Vygotsky and Luria (1993, 1994) argued that tool use in apes and chimps constituted the evolutionary link between the animal world and humankind. However, "in spite of the fact that the ape displays an ability to invent and use tools — the prerequisite for all human cultural development — the activity of labor, founded on this ability, has still not even minimally developed in the ape" (Vygotsky & Luria, 1993, p. 74). The use of tools in labor and, yet more important, the use of psychological tools, was critical in the development of human culture, because tools stand as mediating devices between humans and their environments. Just as environments influence people's development, people actively change their environments. This is true whether one designs a stick to be used later for digging and planting (a physical tool), or uses a knot tied in a rope or gives another person a lynx's claw as an aid to memory (examples of psychological tools cited by Vygotsky & Luria, 1993, pp. 102–108). The most powerful psychological tools are signs and symbols, including language, without which neither collaboration nor culture can occur. Culture, Vygotsky (1997) argued,

> creates special forms of behavior, it modifies the activity of mental functions, it constructs new superstructures in the developing system of human behavior. . . .
> In the process of historical development, social man changes the methods and devices of his behavior, transforms natural instincts and functions, and develops and creates new forms of behavior — specifically cultural. (p. 18)

The nature and form of historical developments, in any culture, necessarily have an impact on the thinking, literacy, numeracy, art, and so on, that develops in that culture. These developments, in turn, have a profound effect on the ways in which children's development proceeds in different cultural groups. As Vygotsky (1994a) argued in the first sentence of his 1929 paper titled "The Problem of the Cultural Development of the Child": "In the process of development the child not only masters the items of cultural experience but the habits and forms of cultural behavior, the cultural methods of reasoning" (p. 57).

These developments, of course, have a profound effect on the ways in which children's development proceeds in different cultural groups. The presence or absence of certain types of institutions (e.g., schools), technologies, and semiotic tools (e.g., pens or computers) as well as variations in the values, beliefs, and practices of different cultural groups are interdependent with differences in the ways in which children's development proceeds (Bornstein, 1991; Harkness &

Super, 1996; Hogan, 1996; Rogoff, 1990; Tudge, Shanahan, & Valsiner, 1997; Whiting & Edwards, 1988). The same point is of course true when considering the same cultural group over historical time (Elder, Modell, & Parke, 1993). The study of any aspect of children's development, peer learning included, cannot ignore the cultural and historical context within which that development occurs.

Individual Aspects

It is also critical to bear in mind the dialectical relation between the child and the cultural environment, for although the environment supplies the "habits and forms of cultural behavior" the individual is actively involved in "mastering" those habits and forms (Vygotsky, 1994a, p. 57), and acquiring "as [his or her] personal property, that which originally represented only a form of [his or her] external interaction with the environment" (Vygotsky, 1994b, p. 352). The ways in which this process took place was one of Vygotsky's main areas of interest, including the study of children who were deaf or blind. In his discussion of early development, Vygotsky argued that biological and maturational aspects of development (the "natural line") as well as aspects of the physical, social, and cultural environment (the "cultural line") had to be considered to make sense of development. "Both plans [sic; 'planes'] of development—the natural and the cultural—coincide and merge. Both orders of changes mutually penetrate each other and form in essence a single order of social–biological formation of the child [sic; 'child's'] personality" (Vygotsky, 1997, pp. 19–20).

This set of mutually interpenetrating influences cannot, of course, be separated into specific cultural and natural lines. Nonetheless, individuals bring their own uniqueness to any interaction. Characteristics that contribute to that uniqueness include gender, developmental status (prematurity or full-term birth), pubertal timing, physical or mental attributes, temperament, age, as well as what each individual brings in terms of personal history up to the point at which his or her development is being considered (Valsiner & Litvinovic, 1996). These characteristics are socially rooted, of course, but at the same time are unique to each individual—their own "personal property" (Vygotsky, 1994b). They will be expressed in different ways according to the specifics of the task and of the interacting partner, but any discussion of peer collaboration cannot ignore what each individual brings to the collaborative process.

By way of illustration of what Vygotsky meant by individual differences over time, he described four stages that children pass through in the course of memory development and the understanding of arithmetic (Vygotsky, 1994a). In both cases, what was critical was the development in the child of the use of mediational means, in particular pictures and speech. Vygotsky argued that initially, in the early preschool years, children rely on their natural or "primitive" behavior to try to remember some items. In the second stage, they can use the mediational means (e.g., some type of representation of the items), but only if there is a clear connection between the item and the representation. If the link is not obvious, the children are as likely to remember something that was in the representation but had nothing to do with the item to be remembered. The third stage is one in which children start to use the mediating devices more actively, inventing linkages between the item and the representation even when there is no obvious connection. The final stage in the process is one in which the entire process becomes internal, and external mediational means are no longer required.

Vygotsky (1987) clearly stressed the individual's active role in development. Moreover, although he believed that collaboration with others was important, he made clear that its effectiveness has limits, limits that are set by the current developmental state of the individual: "We said that in collaboration the child can always do more than he can do independently. We must add the stipulation that he cannot do infinitely more. What collaboration contributes to the child's performance is restricted to limits which are determined by the state of his development and his intellectual potential" (p. 209).

Interpersonal Aspects

The third interrelated aspect of development deals with interactions with others, something that occurs from the moment of birth. As Vygotsky and Luria (1994) argued, the "entire history of the child's psychological development shows us that, from the very first days of development, its adaptation to the environment is achieved by social means, through the people surrounding him. The road from object to child and from child to object lies through another person" (p. 116). Vygotsky's best-known concept, the zone of proximal development, is most relevant in relation to this aspect of development. Contrasting traditional (and, indeed, contemporary) measures of intellectual development (the "actual" level, as determined by tests of what the child can currently do independently) with the proximal level (what the child can do with assistance of someone more competent, whether adult or child), Vygotsky (1987) argued that "the zone of proximal development has more significance for the dynamics of intellectual development and for the success of instruction than does the actual level of development" (p. 209). Instruction, therefore, "*is only useful when it moves ahead of development. When it does, it impels or wakens a whole series of functions that are in a stage of maturation lying in the zone of proximal development*" (p. 212). The zone is not, therefore, some clear-cut space that exists independently of the process of joint activity itself. Rather, it is *created* in the course of collaboration: "We propose that an essential feature of learning is that it creates the zone of proximal development; that is, learning awakens a variety of developmental processes that are able to operate only when the child is interacting with people in his environment and in collaboration with his peers" (Vygotsky, 1978, p. 90).

The specific mechanisms that allow the child to construct higher psychological structures, according to Vygotsky, are internalization and externalization.

Children internalize or interiorize the processes occurring in the course of the interaction with the more competent member of the culture—they "grow into the intellectual life of those around them" (Vygotsky, 1978, p. 88). Internalization is not a matter of mere copying and is "far from being a purely mechanical operation" (Vygotsky & Luria, 1994, p. 153), because this would preclude the emergence of novelty. Rather, children transform the internalized interaction on the basis of their own characteristics, experiences, and existing knowledge. Development is thus a process of reorganization of mental structures in relation to one another (Vygotsky, 1994a). In subsequent interactions with the social world, the transformed knowledge–structures contribute to its reconstruction. Those who have already aided the child may assist in this process by encouraging externalization: "The teacher, working with the school child on a given question, explains, informs, inquires, corrects, and *forces the child himself to explain*" (Vygotsky, 1987a pp. 215–216, italics added).

Vygotsky did not distinguish between social and cognitive development as contemporary Western psychologists do. In Western societies, cognitive processes are seen as internal and individual, and social processes as external and mutual (Forman, 1992). Vygotsky, by contrast, distinguished between interpsychological (or intermental) and intrapsychological (or intramental) processes. Interpsychological process are socially regulated and mediated. Intrapsychological processes (e.g., voluntary memory, selective attention, logical reasoning) begin as interpsychological, so they are always in some sense social, as they are based on social interaction. But both intra- and interpsychological processes are cognitive when they are engaged in problem-solving activities. Therefore social and cognitive processes are not separate entities but rather are interdependent. Although Vygotsky focused a great deal of attention on cognitive development, and it is primarily in this sphere that research based on his ideas has been conducted, he cautioned against ignoring socioemotional dimensions of development:

> Among the most basic defects of traditional approaches to the study of psychology has been the isolation of the intellectual from the volitional and affective aspects of consciousness. The inevitable consequence of the isolation of these functions has been the transformation of thinking into an autonomous stream. Thinking itself became the thinker of thoughts. Thinking was divorced from the full vitality of life, from the motives, interests, and inclinations of the thinking individual. (Vygotsky, 1987, p. 50)

Vygotsky did not explain the nature of specific psychological mechanisms. An example of such a mechanism is the kind of mental representation of social interactions that form in the internalization process. Vygotsky, however, saw this as essentially a mediated process. The social process passes through a link, a psychological tool. One such tool is a sign, and for Vygotsky the most important type of sign in the transformation of thinking from other- to self-regulation was language.

This focus on these processes of development was clearly important to Vygotsky, but he did not restrict them to discussions of instruction (Nicolopoulou, 1993). In a 1933 lecture, Vygotsky (1978) argued that play is highly important in young children's development, not least because it helps them in the use of symbolic forms: "In play thought is separated from objects and action arises from ideas rather than from things: a piece of wood begins to be a doll and a stick becomes a horse" (p. 97). Meanings of things are thus detached from their typical appearance and serve as mediating devices between objects and ideas, in just the same way that the written word will come to have that function for literate children. Vygotsky (1987) concluded that "play creates a zone of proximal development of the child. In play a child always behaves beyond his average age, above his daily behavior" (p. 102).

It is at this level of analysis that attention can be focused on the actual processes of interaction between the developing individual and his or her environment. That environment is of course a social environment, for although it can be thought of as purely physical (in the case of solitary play), the social is nonetheless present in the provision of play materials, space or time for play, prior knowledge of what are considered appropriate and inappropriate ways in which to play with the materials, and so on. Interpersonal interactions are necessarily key to understanding peer learning, for although we need to know about individual characteristics of the two or more individuals involved, the interactions between them are crucial.

We now turn from a purely theoretical discussion to an examination of empirical research on peer collaborative problem solving, focusing largely (although not exclusively) on research that has been placed within a Vygotskian framework. We then discuss the implications of this work for both peer learning and the theory itself.

RESEARCH ON CHILDREN'S COLLABORATIVE PROBLEM SOLVING

Vygotsky concentrated more on the cultural-historical aspects of development and had relatively little to say about microgenetic problem-solving scenarios that characterize much of the research on social interaction and problem solving (van der Veer & Valsiner, 1994). Nonetheless, the concept of the zone of proximal development and the notion that a potential level of development could be achieved by the child under guidance of adults or peers has inspired research on social interaction and problem solving with important implications for his theory. Although there has been relatively little research on peer collaboration from a Vygotskian perspective, substantial evidence has accumulated that social interaction can be beneficial to children's learning, as Vygotsky hypothesized. Research inspired by both Vygotskian and Piagetian theory has shown that peer collaboration can facilitate better performance when one child is more advanced (Ames & Murray, 1982; Bearison, Magzamen, & Filardo, 1986; Chapman & McBride, 1992; Doise & Mugny, 1984; Light, 1983, 1986; Mackie, 1983; Murray, 1972, 1983b; Perret-Clermont, 1980; Perret-Clermont & Schubauer-Leoni, 1981; Tudge, 1989, 1992; Tudge & Winterhoff, 1993b; Tudge, Winterhoff, & Hogan, 1996).

It thus appears that children's problem-solving ability can improve when they work together. There are, however, some discrepancies in the literature as to the conditions under which such benefits are likely to be seen (Chapman & McBride, 1992; Tudge et al., 1996). Social interaction does not have uniform effects and the assumption that all social interaction has beneficial effects and none that are detrimental may be untenable. Several studies have found that children have not improved during collaborative problem solving (Doise & Mugny, 1984; Mugny & Doise, 1978; Perret-Clermont, 1980; Russell, 1982). In addition, evidence has accumulated indicating that under some conditions collaboration may in fact have detrimental effects (Levin & Druyan, 1993; Rosenthal & Zimmerman, 1972, 1978; Tudge, 1989, 1992; Tudge & Winterhoff, 1993a; Zimmerman & Lanaro, 1974). The findings suggest that benefits may depend on a complex set of factors. Such factors may include the particular age and ability level of the children and of their partner, the children's motivation to collaborate, and the extent to which they are exposed to more sophisticated reasoning by a partner and are willing to accept and use that reasoning independently. The nature of the task will also have an influence, as the situations and activities will pose challenges to the ways in which children had previously used certain cognitive operations. The institutional and cultural supports for collaboration will also interact with the other factors. Under what conditions is cognitive growth most likely to be fostered when children collaborate? In the discussion that follows, we focus on individual, interpersonal, and cultural-historical factors separately, although we wish to be quite clear that this organization is for heuristic purposes only.

INDIVIDUAL FACTORS

Individual factors differentiate individuals from one another and include age, gender, and personality and socioemotional factors. It is critical, from the point of view of Vygotsky's dialectical approach, to consider what the individual brings to the learning situation. Although the emphasis is clearly on sociocultural context in Vygotsky's theory, dialectical models stress the interrelatedness of person and environment. Thus, it is not the case that the social or cultural context determines the process or outcome of collaborative learning. Rather, individual and contextual factors interact and mutually affect each other. Age and gender are two factors that are typically viewed as individual characteristics by scholars who have focused on peer collaboration. Perceptions of what can be achieved, either individually or collaboratively, by children of different ages or gender, however, are more than "individual" characteristics, but clearly of interpersonal and sociocultural relevance. Nonetheless, they are usually treated as individual factors.

Age

Research on peer collaboration is typically conducted using school-aged children, but the extent to which younger children can benefit from peer collaboration has been debated in the literature (Azmitia & Perlmutter, 1989). The issue arises out of apparent differences between Piagetian and Vygotskian theory. Piaget argued that the greatest benefits of peer collaboration would be achieved when children had reached the concrete operational stage, whereas Vygotsky, by contrast, believed that social interaction was important for children's development from birth, when adults first begin to encourage children to communicate, plan, and remember. However, he did not state that this would necessarily be the case for interaction with peers (Tudge & Winterhoff, 1993b).

Research has been inconclusive on this issue. Cooper (1980) found that 5-year-olds were more likely to get involved in discussion and collaboration than 3-year-olds on a balance scale task, and Azmitia (1988) found little evidence that discussion helped 5-year-olds learn a model copying task. Tudge and Winterhoff (1993a), on the other hand, using a mathematical balance beam task, found that 5- to 6-year-old children performed better when they worked with a more competent partner than when working alone or with a less competent partner. In related research, 5-year-olds were as likely to benefit from collaboration as 8- to 9-year-olds (Tudge, 1992). Most commentators concur that further research is needed to ascertain age-related constraints on the benefits of social interaction (Azmitia & Perlmutter, 1989; Forman, 1992; Tudge & Rogoff, 1989). The discrepant results outlined here point to the need for studies that vary age levels and that incorporate preschool children. Vygotsky believed that biological factors would place limitations on children's development of higher psychological functions. He was very unclear, however, about how these factors operate and did not specify how the organically based elementary processes relate to the development of the higher functions (Wertsch & Tulviste, 1992). This is an area that warrants further research and theory development.

Gender

Gender is generally underexplored as a potential factor influencing children's collaborative efforts apart from work reported by Bearison and his colleagues, conducted from a Piagetian perspective (Bearison et al., 1986). Gender differences have been found in the way in which children use language in interaction in other areas of research (Ellis & Gauvain, 1992). In two studies of peer collaboration set within a Vygotskian framework, gender differences were reported. Ellis and Gauvain found sex differences in the way boys and girls exchange information in same-sex pairs. Tudge (1992) reported that although, on average, girls and boys did not differ in their overall initial level of reasoning (rule use) in a balance beam task, there were differences in performance following collaboration. Specifically, girls were more likely to regress, following collaboration with other girls, than were boys who had worked with boys, in part because the girls seemed more interested in preserving good relations with their partners than in arguing with one another. The findings of these studies indicate that gender is an area deserving greater attention.

Further work is also necessary to identify other individual factors that may influence the success or failure of collaborative learning among peers, the most obvious of which is individual motivation to collaborate and learn. This issue is discussed further here, as well as in other chapters in this volume (e.g., Palincsar & Herrenkohl, chap. 6, and Webb & Farivar, chap. 5).

INTERPERSONAL FACTORS

Interpersonal factors are processes taking place between individuals. Vygotsky argued that social interaction is the forum in which change in individuals and contexts occurs. Much of the research on peer collaboration set within a Vygotskian framework targets interpersonal factors and has led both to advancement of Vygotsky's theory and to greater understanding of the conditions under which social interaction is most likely to lead to developmental advance in children's thinking. The interpersonal factors discussed here include the nature of the pairing, including a contrast of adult–child with child–child pairing (because this has important implications for collaborative learning and for Vygotsky's theory), and the implications of pairing children of different competency levels, both when independent feedback is provided and not provided. The role of interpersonal socioemotional factors, including motivation and relative confidence of the partners, is also discussed. Finally, we discuss the findings regarding achievement of joint understanding of the problem.

Adult–Child and Child–Child Pairing

Vygotsky's theory that higher mental functions originate in shared problem solving, during which children learn more skilled approaches in interaction with a more competent partner, has received most attention as it relates to adult–child rather than peer interaction. This may be because it is frequently viewed as the opposite to Piagetian approaches to cognitive development. Piaget believed that social interaction was likely to be most beneficial when the relationship between partners was socially symmetrical. Children would be more likely to enter into a true negotiation of reasoning with partners who are not seen as holding positions of authority, or as experts (see, e.g., DeLisi & Golbeck, chap. 1, this volume; DeVries, 1997; Tudge & Rogoff, 1989; Tudge & Winterhoff, 1993b). Vygotsky did not address the issue of social hierarchy, but stressed the importance for development of collaborating with a more competent partner (asymmetry in knowledge rather than in social relations), and in his own work referred more to adults in his discussions of the zone of proximal development. Is social interaction only valuable when children are paired with adults, or can interaction with peers also be valuable? Research set within both Piagetian and Vygotskian frameworks indicates that collaboration both with adults and peers can have positive effects on children's cognitive development in the course of collaboration, yet research comparing adult–child and child–child pairing has had somewhat mixed results.

In a study conducted by Radziszewska and Rogoff (1988), target children were 9 to 10 years old. In the peer dyads children were class friends and adult–child dyads were mother–daughter and father–son pairs. The dyads were given maps of an imaginary town, with a school and 23 stores, and two lists of errands. The task was to devise the optimal route for one car from school and back to retrieve the items on the two lists. To produce this route, the pair had to consider relative distances for locations they had to visit, as well as for alternatives (on every list there were two items that could be bought at either one of two stores). Pairs were told that they would later be asked to plan a trip alone, and collaboration rather than instruction was stressed. At individual posttests, target children who had collaborated with adults performed significantly better than those who had worked with peers. Results indicated that adult–child pairs were more likely to use sophisticated planning strategies—they planned sequences, whereas peer dyads used more one-step moves (similar to those used by younger children working alone), and this proved more effective.

A study by Gauvain and Rogoff (1989) looked at the effects of sharing responsibility during joint planning with a peer or with an adult partner on later individual performance. The participants were 5-year-olds, and the study was of a similar design to the study just described, except that participants were not aware that they would receive a posttest. During planning, adult–child dyads produced slightly more efficient routes than did peers or solitary children and showed more concern with definition of task and efficiency. However, when they later planned routes alone, there was no difference in efficiency, indicating that the children had not made their parents' more efficient strategies their own.

Studies conducted by Ellis and Rogoff (1982, 1986) focus on peer versus adult tutoring (the authors argued that these can be viewed as instances of collaborative problem solving). Differences were found in the way in which adults and children teach: Children's teaching depended more on demonstration and modeling and their verbal instruction was less complex. Children were less effective as teachers on complex laboratory classification tasks, seeming to have difficulty coordinating the multiple demands involved in managing the instructional task. The strategies used by the two kinds of dyads were compared in a task involving classification of either grocery items or photos of common objects on kitchen shelves in colored boxes (Ellis & Rogoff, 1986). The task of the more advanced partner was to prepare child learners to perform the task independently for a later test. Child teachers tended to focus more on the immediate task of putting the items in the right locations and seldom explained the categorization rationale, whereas adult teachers placed more emphasis on the long-term goal of having the child learn the categorization scheme for a later memory test. It was concluded that the benefits of having an adult partner were greater than those associated with having a peer partner.

As a whole, this research provides support for the theory that a zone of proximal development can be constructed with either an adult or peer, but indicates that pairing with an adult has different consequences (often more beneficial) for children's learning. This has important implications for Vygotsky's theory, because in his discussion of the zone of proximal development, he did not differentiate between the potential effects of either type of partnership. Although the focus of this chapter is on peer interaction, we return to the issue of the relative benefits of adult–child and child–child pairing in our discussion of the processes occurring in social interaction that are most likely to foster cognitive growth.

Competency Levels Between Peers

Vygotsky's (1978) theory suggests that cognitive growth may occur not only when children are assisted by an adult but also when children collaborate with a more competent peer. There has been considerable support for this idea in research inspired by both Vygotsky's and Piaget's theories. Some research shows that interaction between children of the same cognitive level can be beneficial, as long as interpersonal conflict is engendered (Ames & Murray, 1982), but that collaboration is more effective when a child is paired with a more advanced partner.

The findings are somewhat mixed, however. Although the majority of research indicates that children who work with a more competent partner improve more than those who have an equally or less competent partner, recent work by Tudge and his colleagues (Tudge et al., 1996) demonstrates an exception. Children were pretested individually and classified according to the level of "rule" they used to predict the movements of a mathematical balance beam when different combinations of weights were placed at varying distances from the fulcrum. The rules (of which there are six levels) correspond to children's increasing ability to take into account weight and distance to solve the problems. Children either worked alone or were paired with same-sex partners who used the same rule, a higher rule, or a lower rule at pretest. Some children received feedback from the materials and some did not. In the collaborative sessions, they were asked to predict the workings of the beam (whether it would fall to either side or stay balanced when blocks holding it in place were removed) and provide justification for their predictions. When children disagreed, the experimenter asked them to discuss the problem until they reached agreement. After agreement had been reached, they were again asked to provide justification. Tudge and his colleagues reported that although working with a partner was somewhat more effective than working alone, this was only true under conditions of no feedback. Working with a more competent partner was not more effective than working with an equally competent partner or working alone—especially when the child did not receive feedback from the materials.

The concept of the *zone of proximal development* has generally been taken to imply that neither the task difficulty nor the guidance given to children should be too far in advance of their current level of ability. Tudge et al. (1996) tailored the problems given to target children in each dyad so that the most difficult problem could be solved by using the rule one higher than they had used at pretest. Their partners had used a rule no more than two higher than that of the target children. This kind of pairing was more effective in bringing about cognitive growth than was the case in previous studies (Tudge, 1989, 1992), when the problems were not tailored in this way. In the earlier studies, children's improvements were not as pronounced. Results obtained to date are generally supportive of Vygotsky's belief that learning is most likely to occur when help is "proximal" to the curent level of the child. In research currently underway by Tudge and his colleagues, both competency level and difficulty task are varied to investigate the limits of proximity to current level for cognitive growth to occur.

Vygotsky's theory of development (particularly his concept of the zone of proximal development) is typically taken to mean that the effects of social interaction will always be positive and never detrimental to cognitive functioning (van der Veer & Valsiner, 1994), although Vygotsky (1934, cited in Wertsch, 1985) stated that instruction should be in *advance* of the child's current level for learning to occur. The work of Tudge (1989, 1992), and of Levin and Druyan (1993) indicates that when children are exposed to reasoning that is *below* their own current level, the effects of collaboration can be detrimental. When children were paired with a less competent partner in Tudge's balance beam experiment (but when feedback was not a condition), some children regressed in their reasoning. Specifically, if a child could be persuaded by a less competent partner to accept reasoning that was less advanced, regression was likely to occur. Tudge suggests that functions that are not fully formed (those that Vygotsky referred to as *embryonic*) may be more malleable, so that development can be either in the direction of progression or regression. In Tudge's rule system, some rules allow children to consistently predict the workings of the beam (i.e., how it will behave when weights are added in certain configurations and at certain distances from the fulcrum). Other rules do not allow for such consistent prediction. Tudge (1989, 1992) found that children who used rules on the pretest that were least open to consistent predictability of the working of the balance beam were most likely to develop—but development could be either in the direction of advance or decline, depending on whether they were paired with a more or less competent partner.

Levin and Druyan (1993) found that children regressed on a task involving a misconception about movement and speed. The experiment was based on the belief in *single object–single motion*. The misconception is that two parts of a single object cannot move at different speeds. Children were shown video simulations of dogs moving on a screen. In one simulation, two dogs run on a track and are unattached (*autonomous carrier*); on the other, the two dogs are carried by a rotating carousel (*common carrier*). The problem is to work out whether the dogs are moving at the same speed in each scenario and, if not, which is moving faster. Children who gave discrepant responses to the second problem at pretest were paired (one child offering the misconception as a solution, the other giving the scientific solution). On the autonomous carrier problem, children who were paired with a more competent partner were likely to improve. On the second problem (common carrier), involving the misconception, the more competent children (those who had originally given the scientific [correct] solution) were likely to regress as a result of collaboration.

These studies suggest that regression is not only possible but also likely, depending on the level of competency of a partner as well as on the nature of the task. The findings have important implications for Vygotsky's concept of the zone of proximal development and its functioning, broadening it in a manner that is compatible with Vygotsky's thinking to include the possibility of developmental decline as a consequence of interaction in the zone of proximal development. Tudge (1992) suggested that it may be possible to construct a zone of proximal development either in front of or behind the child's current level of reasoning. The question remaining unexplored is whether there are limits on the degree to which children will decline. For example, when children decline to a level that is not malleable, or to a fully matured (lower) level of reasoning, will developmental decline stop? This can be tested by varying the degree to which the partner is less competent than the target child.

Interpersonal Socioemotional Factors

Vygotsky assumed that children would be motivated to learn from their more competent partners, and there is some empirical evidence to support this. Ellis & Rogoff (1982) found that children will initiate their own involvement in problem-solving activities when their partners are ignoring their presence or doing little to encourage joint participation. But what compels children to accept the reasoning of another once collaboration has begun? Why do children internalize knowledge at higher (and lower) levels? Although his primary concern was with the processes of development and particularly the transformation from intermental to intramental functioning, Vygotsky's theory did not deal adequately with this question beyond specifying a process of internalization and externalization. The lack of attention paid to this question by researchers interested in peer collaboration may be due to the difficulty associated with its investigation (Ellis & Gauvain, 1992). One way in which the issue has been explored is in terms of the relative confidence of collaborating partners, that is, as an interpersonal issue. Another important factor may be children's prior relationships, but this question has received little empirical attention to date.

Tudge (1989, 1992) raised the issue of whether researchers have confounded competence and confidence in children, particularly in Piagetian studies that involved pairing conservers with nonconservers. Results of these studies invariably report improvement of nonconservers. This can be explained, Tudge argued, by the fact that conservers (according to Piaget) are necessarily more confident, because they see the logical necessity of their position. As a result, their less confident partners accept their reasoning. The nature of the rules children used to predict the working of the balance beam in Tudge's own studies (1989, 1992; Tudge et al., 1996) may be associated with differences in the confidence of children's reasoning. As discussed earlier, three of the rules necessarily involve some inconsistency in prediction, whereas three others allow consistent prediction. Children using rules involving some inconsistency at pretest were more likely to improve when paired with a child using a higher, consistent rule and to regress when paired with a partner using a lower, consistent rule. About twice the number of children who had used a rule allowing consistent prediction at pretest continued to use that same rule than did children who used a rule that involved uncertainty. In short, less confident children were likely to accept the reasoning of their partner, even when it was at a lower level than they began with, and these developmental regressions were stable.

Levin and Druyan (1993) came to a similar conclusion regarding their finding that children who held the scientifically correct solution to a problem about movement and speed were likely to regress when paired with a child who held a misconception about movement and speed. Misconceptions are intuitive concepts that are resistant to change even in the face of scientific evidence to the contrary, perhaps because the solutions are (apparently) self-evident. Children who held the scientific misconception at pretest were likely to have been more confident of their position and children who offered the scientific solution, having little evidence from everyday life to reinforce their thinking, were less confident.

These studies clearly point to the relevance of affective factors in children's learning. Work by Forman and her colleagues (Forman, 1992, Forman & McPhail, 1993) may point the way to more fine-grained analysis of such emotional factors as children's task goals and the processes by which they come to reach intersubjectivity. This group of researchers analyzed children's verbal communication to try to understand the process by which intersubjectivity is achieved. Forman (1992) analyzed discourse between peers, basing her definition of discourse on Ochs' (1990) view that whereas language (explicit verbal arguments) may reduce our understanding of context, discourse, by contrast, relates language to the norms, preferences, expectations, and so forth, that are implicit in communication. Discourse is the more appropriate form of analysis, Forman argued, from a Vygotskian perspective, because it implies a social process that takes context-based factors into account, and because its focus is on speech as a mediational tool. Forman (1992) argued that intersubjectivity is built on the interpsychological activity of discourse:

> What children learn from discourse is a set of implicit principles of cooperative interaction and procedures for making inferences about what people mean by what they say. These conversational influences are different from the inferences employed in formal deductive arguments. Conversational inferences are the means by which children take an active role in the co-construction of knowledge. (p. 148)

Thus, analysis of discourse can lead us to a better understanding of how intersubjectivity is achieved. We can learn, for example, how children gain the ability to combine the conversational discourse used outside the context of school with the kind of logical argument necessary to successfully solve an academic problem as a team. Forman's work indicates that successful achievement of intersubjectivity requires that children coordinate their interpersonal wishes to dominate or to please their partner with the need of the dyad to work together to solve the problem. Forman and McPhail's (1993) analysis of speech registers enabled them to see how children reflect on and modify their initial task goals so that they can come to a shared understanding of the task and collaborate. This is clearly a promising avenue for further research that may help to tease out the process by which knowledge comes to be jointly constructed.

Joint Understanding

Several studies, including those conducted with peer dyads only and those in which peer pairing has been compared with child–adult pairing, indicate that having a more competent partner is not a sufficient condition for cognitive growth to occur. It is also important that children be exposed to a higher level of reasoning than that which they exhibited at pretest, and that they accept that reasoning. In Tudge's (1989) study, children were asked to provide justification for their predictions during the experiment (no feedback was given). Reasoning could be provided at the same level as the partner's, or at a higher or lower level. The effects of the quality of this reasoning were substantial. When children were exposed to reasoning at a higher level, they were likely to start to use a higher rule themselves, although not in all cases. In some instances, children accepted their partner's more sophisticated reasoning during the collaborative session, but did not proceed to use (adopt) it at subsequent individual posttests. Similar results were reported in a later study (Tudge, 1992). For advances to occur, the more competent partner had to verbalize his or her reasoning and the less advanced child had to accept it.

Ellis and Rogoff (1986) found that peers communicated their reasoning poorly to their partners in comparison to adults in the course of a joint planning task. In subsequent individual posttests, children who had worked with a peer showed more of a tendency to use less effective, step-by-step approaches to the planning task than did those paired with an adult. Radziszewska and Rogoff (1988, 1991) reported a similar phenomenon. The greater success of the adult–child pairs than the child–child pairs could be explained by the fact that children in the former type of dyad were exposed to more sophisticated reasoning than was the case in the peer dyads, if only because adults were much more likely to verbalize their thinking about potential strategies (98% of adults did so). Indeed, these were virtually the only children who heard strategy statements. These findings suggest a strong role for verbalization of reasoning by partners as a condition under which cognitive growth is more likely to occur during peer collaboration. Although Vygotsky did not explicitly state that this should be a condition for social interaction to be beneficial, it is quite compatible with his thinking about the importance of language as a mediating mechanism inherent in the process of social interaction and internalization. The research just outlined supports and further clarifies this thinking, underscoring the importance for children of hearing verbalized reasoning at a higher level. It indicates that simply hearing another's more advanced thinking does not necessarily lead to learning; there must also be a process of negotiation, through which children reach a joint understanding of both the task at hand and the solution, for children's thinking to advance.

Scholars in the Vygotskian tradition have stressed the need for children to come to joint understanding of a problem on the basis of having taken each other's perspective into account. The concept has been related to the linguistic concept of intersubjectivity as used by Rommetveit (1975) in work by scholars such as Gauvain and Rogoff (1989) and Wertsch (1985). The less advanced child is assumed to be interested in learning from the more competent partner, and the expert is viewed as having responsibility for adjusting to the level of support or guidance to fit within the child's zone of proximal development (Tudge & Rogoff, 1989).

Research by Ellis and Rogoff (1982, 1986) indicated that it is important that the more competent partner understands what the less advanced partner needs and is able to adjust the degree of support they give to match that. Adults were found to be more skilled at doing this with children than were peers. Gauvain and Rogoff (1989) found that those children who shared responsibility for the task and made joint decisions with their partner were most likely to improve. In later solitary trials, having had a partner per se was not related to improved plan effectiveness or use of foresight; those who had shared responsibility during collaborative sessions were more likely to use advanced scanning and more efficient routes than children who had not, and these children were also more likely to be responsible for decision making. This was true for adult–child and peer dyads. These findings are consistent with Vygotsky's position that knowledge is first social and later individual, in the sense that knowledge is created in the course of interaction with another, rather than simply preexisting in the environment.

In research that has focused solely on peer collaboration, Forman and Cazden (1985) looked at the joint problem-solving activities of 9- to 14-year-olds, using Piaget's chemical task and a projection of shadows problem. The authors were interested in how peers came to a shared understanding of the task. They found that it was more important for partners to coordinate their perspectives and coconstruct a joint answer (*interpsychological regulation*) than it was for them to have a different perspective to start off with for peer collaboration to be beneficial.

Interaction Style

What influences the process of coming to a joint agreement on a problem? One factor may be the way in which children interact with one another. Styles of interaction will significantly affect the experience of *guided participation*—the idea that negotiation of a problem is most likely to be beneficial when the more competent partner has the skills and motivation to tailor the help given (the kind of reasoning provided) to a level appropriate for the less advanced partner (Rogoff, 1990; Wertsch, 1985). However, it is also important for the less advanced partner to be motivated and actively involved in the process, as exemplified by research reported elsewhere in this volume (Palincsar & Herrenkohl, chap. 6; Webb & Farivar, chap. 5).

In the literature on collaborative problem solving, the issue of the role of interaction style for cognitive growth has largely centered around whether cooperative styles are the most likely to produce growth (Azmitia & Perlmutter, 1989). Most studies of elementary school children seem to indicate that cooperation is more conducive to learning than domination by one child. Children can benefit from an activity if they are jointly involved in the problem solving, although it has also been shown that children can improve from simply copying a model (Azmitia & Perlmutter, 1989). Dominant styles may be preferable at the early stages of interaction if the child is a novice, but when the child's competence is increased, a more cooperative style may be better. Forman and Cazden (1985), in their work with peer dyads, found a correlation between the level of social interaction children used (the degree to which both children were involved with each other) and learning. Three styles of interaction were discerned as the children worked on problem-solving tasks. The first was a parallel form, in which there was no exchange. The second was an associative form, in which children tried to exchange information but did not attempt to coordinate their roles. Finally, there was a cooperative form, in which both children constantly monitored each other's work and played coordinated roles in carrying out the task. Cooperative interaction was associated with the most advanced cognitive operations in reaching solutions to the task.

Research also suggests that the capability of more advanced partners to provide support at an appropriate level is an important feature of interactional style. As discussed previously, Vygotsky's view was that development of cognitive abilities is facilitated by help from a partner that is targeted to somewhat in advance of the child's current level. This sensitive support facilitates the transition from shared to self-regulated cognitive processes as the child is supported in taking on an increasingly active role, or in what Rogoff (1990) termed *guided participation*. This shift in responsibility has been explored somewhat in comparison studies of adult–child versus peer pairings but very little in research on peer interaction. In one such study, Ellis and Rogoff (1986) found that peers were not as good as adults in scaffolding the performance of another. In Ellis and Rogoff's comparison of adult–child and child–child dyads, the child teachers tended to give learners too much responsibility and not enough guidance. Adult teachers played a dominant role early on, but then gradually withdrew their support on the basis of what the child appeared to need. Child teachers tended to allow insufficient participation by learners but did seem to be aware of the learner's need for more information and guidance and to become gradually more effective in imparting this over time. Gauvain and Rogoff (1989) concluded that child teachers (e.g., trained peers) may not be sensitive to the appropriate level for learning in the less advanced child. Child teachers "did not involve the learners at a comfortable level allowing the learner some degree of participation without requiring the learner to do much alone prematurely" (p. 303). These findings provide support for the Vygotskian emphasis on joint construction of solutions to problems as the means through which advances in children's psychological functioning comes about. At the same time, it calls into question the extent to which peers can be expected to be able to successfully coconstruct a zone of proximal development in interaction with less advanced peers, because even if a peer knows what the less advanced child needs, he or she may have difficulty adjusting to an appropriate level and adjusting as the child improves over time. The findings of Ellis and Rogoff (1982, 1986) and Gauvain and Rogoff (1989) are consistent with the emphasis of Vygotskian scholars on the importance of partners' achieving joint understanding and definition of goals (intersubjectivity; Tudge & Rogoff, 1989). They serve to illustrate the important role of sensitivity to the level and needs of the less advanced child and of ability to adjust guidance to the appropriate level.

What influences interaction styles? Ellis and Rogoff (1986), in their work involving classification tasks, found one factor to be the nature of the task. Partners who were acting as tutors in this study tended to be more dominant in their style of interaction on tasks that resembled activities in the home than on tasks that resembled school activities. However, research on peer collaboration has not yet found satisfactory answers to the question of how children come to collaborate and, as a result, to learn. Overall, knowledge about the process that brings children together to work out a joint solution is limited, although other chapters in this volume (e.g., those by King, chap. 4; Palincsar & Herrenkohl, chap. 6; and Webb & Farivar, chap. 5) are very helpful. We still know comparatively little, however, about children's initial task goals, about how they modify or redirect their individual and interpersonal goals and preferences to meet the task of negotiating as part of a dyad. We know that it is important for children to accept a higher level of reasoning but do not know what compels them to do so. We know that guided participation facilitates learning, but we do not understand what motivates a more advanced partner to provide continuous, progressive support as the less advanced child moves toward greater responsibility. These are questions about socioemotional factors, an area that has received little attention in the literature.

Feedback

Another area that has received limited attention is that of feedback that comes not simply from the collaborating partners, but from the materials themselves. For a child to receive confirmatory feedback that the proposed solution is correct presumably provides a boost to his or her confidence, and no doubt helps a dyad achieve joint understanding. In studies of social interaction, feedback has sometimes been available, sometimes not. What is striking about the majority of the research is that the potential effects of feedback separate from those of the interaction process have not been examined. In some studies in the tradition of Vygotskian theory, for example, when model copying is used (e.g., Wertsch, 1979; Wertsch & Hickmann, 1987) and feedback is inherent in the task, it is not possible to determine whether it is the effects of the social interaction process or of feedback that underlie the results observed. In one study involving social interaction between 3- to 5-year-old children and their mothers (Freund, 1990), the separate effects of feedback or social interaction were examined. One group of children interacted with their mothers in the course of the problem-solving task and received no feedback from the experimenter as to whether their solutions were correct; another group did not interact with their mothers but did receive feedback at the end of the task. Children who collaborated with mothers improved more than those who got feedback. However, because mothers typically regulated their children's problem solving, it can be seen as a kind of feedback in itself, and because Freund did not control simultaneously for feedback and social interaction, the separate effects of each on children's performance were unclear.

Two studies questioned the nature of the separate effects of feedback from the materials and social interaction among peers. Ellis and Siegler (1994) studied fifth graders' mathematical problem solving with decimal fractions, alone and in dyads, with some children receiving feedback as to the correctness of their responses and some not. None of the children who did not receive feedback gave correct responses at the posttest, irrespective of whether they worked alone or with a partner, whereas a significant number of those who received feedback answered correctly. The most successful problem solvers were children who received feedback and worked with a partner—they were more than twice as likely to answer correctly at posttest than singletons who received feedback. Tudge et al. (1996) studied children engaged in a problem-solving task using a mathematical balance beam. Children were in three groups: 6-year-olds, 7-year-olds, and 8- to 9-year-olds. Some of the children worked in pairs and some alone, some received feedback from the materials and some did not. Children who received feedback from the balance beam improved significantly more than those who did not. Those who worked with a partner performed better than those who worked as singletons, but only when they did not receive feedback; children working as singletons with feedback did better than children who worked with a partner, a finding that contrasted with most previous research on the effects of peer collaboration. Tudge and his colleagues speculated that having a partner may serve as a distraction, encouraging social interaction that is not related to the task, and that when singletons got feedback they used it. When no feedback was provided to singletons, most continued at the same level or declined. Just receiving feedback was not enough to help a child advance in the level of reasoning they used to solve the balance beam problems, however. The children most likely to improve were those who were exposed to, and accepted, a higher level of reasoning. These findings suggest that a partner may not be necessary, if the problems given are tailored to the level of the child and contingent feedback is given. But when no feedback is given, having a partner may be more conducive to learning. It appears that our understanding of the impact of competency levels and task difficulty on children's collaborative problem solving can be enhanced greatly by taking feedback into account.

Our final point relating to interpersonal factors in collaborative problem solving is that most studies involving contrasts between dyads (or small groups) and individuals assume that individuals are working alone, simply because they have no partner. In fact, of course, the social world is always present, sometimes in the person of the researcher, who is there ostensibly simply to observe but in fact provides a high degree of regulation. Even if the researcher is "present" only by virtue of a camera, the social world is clearly present. It is present in the materials provided, the way in which the child is asked to attempt the experimental problem, the unusual circumstances in which the setting is arranged (from a university laboratory to a relatively secluded area in the child's school), and in so many other ways.

CULTURAL-HISTORICAL CONTEXTUAL FACTORS

Discussion of cultural-historical or sociocultural factors is rare in the Vygotsky-based literature on peer collaboration (far less common than studies that examine adult–child collaboration), but even more rare are studies that incorporate analysis of cultural-historical or sociocultural factors into the design. We identified three such studies, one conducted by Tudge (1989) comparing children from the (now former) Soviet Union and the United States on a problem-solving task, a second conducted by Ellis (1987) comparing Navajo and Euro-American children on instructional strategies, and a third by Tudge and Winterhoff (1993b). In each case, the researchers attempted to explain differences in collaborative problem solving by invoking knowledge of historically formed features of the cultures involved.

Tudge (1989) used a mathematical balance beam with 5- to 7-year-old same-sex pairs. The findings were virtually identical across the two cultural groups: when children who used an "unconfident rule" were paired with a higher level partner, they were likely to improve with a confident partner but likely to regress if the more confident partner's rule was lower than their own. In the United States, however, boys made greater pretest to posttest improvements than girls, and the latter were more likely to regress. In the Soviet Union, there were no gender differences. Tudge argued that cultural norms about gender could explain these findings. In the United States, boys tend to be socialized to think of themselves as being good at mathematics and scientific thinking relative to girls. In the Soviet Union, by contrast, girls were not raised to see themselves as inferior in this area. Girls in the United States may also be more ready to agree in order to preserve friendship or to please, although this may mean declining in the sophistication of their reasoning.

In a second study that addressed sociohistorical factors, Ellis (1987) compared Navajo and Euro-American children's instructional strategies. Using a three-dimensional battery-operated maze game called "The Way to the Store," pairs of 9-year-olds were asked to teach individual 7-year-olds (i.e., these were groups of three children). Cultural differences were found in the manner in which instruction was carried out, with Euro-American children relying more on verbal instruction than Navajo children. However, the proportion of useful task information to overall information conveyed was greater for Navajo groups. There were also differences in degree of involvement in the task and division of instruction. Overall, Navajo children appeared to be more supportive partners and to collaborate more effectively. The authors related these findings to differences in cultural values for talking and for collective rather than individual achievement.

A third study did not incorporate analysis of cultural-historical factors into the initial design but discussed findings with reference to sociohistorical factors.

In his discussions of sociohistorical development, Vygotsky emphasized the importance that changes in the sociopolitical landscape and its associated institutions could have for children's development. One such institution is formal schooling, which Vygotsky expected to have implications for the development of higher mental processes. Tudge and Winterhoff (1993a) argued that school experience is sometimes confounded with age. They studied 5-year-olds collaborating on a problem-solving task. Their results suggested that children who were longer in school were more familiar with expectations and requirements of school and with interacting with peers and teachers. Specifically, children who were longer in school (not older children) used a significantly higher rule at individual pretest than peers with less school experience. In addition, there were differences in the degree to which children benefited from receipt of feedback, depending on amount of experience with formal schooling; those with more experience benefited more.

SUMMARY OF RESEARCH FINDINGS AND IMPLICATIONS FOR VYGOTSKY'S THEORY

As a whole, research on peer collaboration in the past decade has led to greater specification of the conditions under which collaboration is most likely to foster cognitive growth. It is now clear that social interaction cannot be assumed to have blanket effects and certainly cannot be assumed to be always beneficial. For example, competency has a complex relation with feedback, such that when children receive contingent feedback from the materials, it may even be preferable to work as a singleton. Other conditions that affect the degree to which social interaction among peers can be expected to lead to developmental advance are the age of partners (although the findings are mixed), and the relative competence of partners; being paired with a more competent partner is generally preferable, whereas pairing with a less competent partner may lead to regression. In addition, there is evidence that cognitive growth is most likely to occur when tailoring occurs at three levels; tailoring of the level of reasoning to which children are exposed (competency level of partner), of the difficulty of the task, and of the support given by the social partner. Further research is needed to investigate optimal adjustment of these three features of social interaction to the child's current level. It also appears critical that more competent partners verbalize their reasoning and that less advanced children accept reasoning at a higher level than they started out with. Furthermore, the greater the extent to which partners are involved in the task, treat it as a joint endeavor, and come to a shared understanding, the more likely it seems to be that children will learn. Finally, the children's perception of their partner's reasoning (perhaps because he or she is more confident) may be conducive to development, but whether this is developmental advance or decline depends on whether the more confident partner is also the more competent. These findings can only be taken as suggestive of conditions under which development may be fostered, and not to represent optimal conditions for learning. There are no optimal conditions that have universal application irrespective of context.

Strengths and Weaknesses of the Research and Implications for Vygotsky's Theory

The studies discussed here generally provide support for Vygotsky's theory that children's development can be fostered both by adults and by more competent peers. It also extends and clarifies that theory in important ways but fails to address it in others. One of the greatest strengths of this body of literature is that process has received at least as much attention as outcomes, in keeping with Vygotsky's own interests. Although many researchers look at pretest and posttest differences in attempting to specify the optimal conditions for development to occur, attention has been paid to the question of how shared knowledge is created and how more competent partners facilitate the internalization of this knowledge.

The studies reviewed here generally support Vygotsky's theory. Indeed they provide evidence that knowledge can be constructed socially—it can exist as a social interactional process prior to being internalized and used independently by children (a basic premise of Vygotsky's work). It provides support also for the concept of the zone of proximal development. A number of studies indicate that less advanced children can move to a higher level of thinking with the help of a more competent partner. Several important conditions are attached to this however. Whereas Vygotsky (1978) loosely grouped adults and more competent peers together in his discussion of the zone of proximal development, several of the studies outlined here indicate that there may be differences in the consequences of working with an adult and working with another child, arising perhaps from adults' greater skills at tailoring their support to a level that is conducive to learning. There may also be age constraints on the potential for social interaction to help foster cognitive growth, but this is an area that needs further research. Vygotsky believed that there were limits on the extent to which constructing the zone of proximal development could result in higher levels of thinking, and this has also found support. One notable extension to Vygotsky's formulation of the concept of the zone of proximal development is the finding that social interaction with a less competent peer can lead to regression. Although this is not incompatible with Vygotsky's views (he specified that help should be provided in advance of the child's current level), it makes explicit the possibility that development can proceed either in the direction of advance or decline, and therefore that a zone of proximal development can be constructed ahead of or behind the child's current level of cognitive ability. The limits to which this can occur have not yet been investigated. Research outlined here also suggests that development is likely to occur (as Vygotsky hypothesized) when children's thinking is at an immature stage. One reason why thinking that is not yet fully formed is more open to development (in either direction) appears to be that children at such stages behave less confidently than those who hold greater conviction about the correctness of their thinking. Children's social partners need not necessarily be more competent to be more self-assured. These findings both support and extend Vygotsky's conceptualization of the zone of proximal development. Research also indicates that when feedback is provided, the relation between relative competency of partners and the likelihood of cognitive growth is complicated. As mentioned earlier, when feedback is available, it may actually be preferable to work as a singleton than with a partner. This issue was not discussed by Vygotsky, but has implications for real-life settings. If children are paired at school to work collaboratively, then it is necessary to understand the potential benefits when feedback will also be provided.

The studies discussed here also help to clarify and extend our understanding of the processes of constructing joint understanding and of the transition from shared to self-regulated thinking. The findings are consistent with Vygotsky's beliefs. For example, Vygotsky believed that the joint construction of knowledge is mediated by psychological tools, and particularly by language. Research discussed previously indicates that verbalization of a more sophisticated level of reasoning by the more advanced partner is strongly related to cognitive advance. Vygotsky also believed that children were actively involved in this process—one study reviewed here found that children will initiate their own involvement in a task when the more competent partner does nothing to involve them. In addition, several studies found that improvement in performance was related to the degree to which children were actively involved in the task—it must be a joint, rather than a parallel, effort. Vygotsky did not explain the conditions under which internalization of shared knowledge is most likely to occur, other than saying that construction of a zone of proximal development facilitates this. Research reviewed here suggests that children are most likely to adopt the higher level of thinking and use it independently when the more competent partner helps to guide and support the less advanced partner to take progressively more responsibility, monitoring change and gradually withdrawing support as appropriate. Another important contribution, as mentioned earlier, is the finding that not every partner is equally able to adjust their help in an appropriate manner.

The weakness of this body of literature, to return to the argument we made at the outset of this chapter, lies in the insufficient attention paid to elements of Vygotsky's thinking that are critical tenets of cultural-historical theory. The most important of these is perhaps sociocultural factors which, for Vygotsky, gave meaning to microgenetic and ontogenetic development. Indeed, interpreting development in terms of historically formed contexts lies at the heart of cultural-historical theory. The majority of recent research cannot be generalized beyond the White middle-class Western populations on which it was conducted. The cognitive tools, approaches to problem solving, and interaction styles may differ greatly across cultural contexts both outside and within the United States (Ellis & Gauvain, 1992), leading to potentially quite different interpretations of results.

The second missing element is related to the first, which is that apart from Forman's work, studies of peer collaboration have not given very much attention to semiotic mediation. Whereas most research focused on identifying the optimal conditions for development to occur, Forman and her colleagues (Forman & Cazden, 1985; Forman & McPhail, 1993) directed their attention to analysis of children's use of language (speech registers and discourse) in social interaction. This work may help to further our understanding of the process by which intersubjectivity is constructed. Forman's research has perhaps come closest to taking the broader context into account, because her focus is on discourse (which implies looking not merely at verbal arguments but at the implicit message about the context-based norms, expectations, etc., in communication) rather than language.

Finally, although Vygotsky believed that it was critical to our understanding of developmental processes, the issue of mediation of effective peer learning by socioemotional factors has been explored very little. It appears that researchers are just beginning to recognize their potential influences (Ellis & Gauvain, 1992). One area that could be explored in further research is children's prior relationship with their partner. From an early age, peer interactions among children occur mainly between friends (Azmitia & Perlmutter, 1989). It may make a difference to the nature of the interaction whether partners have previously (and positively) spent time together. In a few studies, friends performed better than non-friends, perhaps because friends' conversations have more mutuality and involvement than those between non-friends (Berndt, 1987). This might mean that they understand each others' needs more, and so could give better guidance. Friends are more likely to resolve conflicts equitably than are non-friends (Hartup, 1992), and this might have implications for the degree to which children are able to achieve shared understanding of the task. In addition, friends are more likely to give explanations for their actions (Nelson & Aboud, 1985). This is a factor that may be of extreme importance, because a key process identified in whether children improve in the course of interaction is whether they are exposed to and accept the reasoning of their partner (Tudge, 1989, 1992; Tudge et al., 1996). Finally, friends are more likely to try to get their partner to change their mind—to challenge the position of the other and advance their own (Nelson & Aboud, 1985), a factor that may also be important for the processes involved in convincing the other to accept their reasoning.

Conclusions

The small number of research studies that investigated Vygotsky's theory that children's learning can be fostered by their interaction with more competent peers resulted in several important clarifications and extensions of Vygotsky's theory. Our understanding of the effects of social interaction among peers, and of the mechanisms leading to those effects, has progressed from a general acceptance that all social interaction necessarily leads to cognitive growth to a growing awareness of the complexity of factors that can serve to facilitate or hinder developmental advance, and even to lead to decline. Many questions remain unanswered regarding the processes by which children can influence each other's cognitive development. This research has not uncovered the specific mechanism that brings about the collaborative process or what motivates children to change their current way of thinking in favor of new (or perhaps old) knowledge. We are coming closer to understanding the conditions under which children in collaborative situations are likely to reach a joint situational definition that provides the foundation for self-regulation of cognitive processes, but we do not understand the nature of the transformation process as children internalize social relations. Neither do we understand the findings in terms of the sociohistorical contexts that give them meaning. Because research has typically focused on peer collaboration in middle-class Western cultures, we know little about the sociocultural factors that may influence cognitive interaction.

If socioemotional factors remain an understudied phenomenon, and individual and interpersonal participant characteristics remain an unknown, we will be left with the unappealing scenario envisioned by Vygotsky, where "thinking is inevitably transformed into an autonomous flow of thoughts thinking themselves" (1934, in Wertsch, 1985, p. 89). If research on peer collaboration continues to overlook sociohistorical contexts, we will be left with the untenable assumption, from a Vygotskian perspective, that context is irrelevant to children's development.

PART II

Cognitive–Elaborative Approaches to Peer Learning: Overview

The six chapters in this part describe a variety of techniques that depend to a greater or lesser extent on cognitive elaboration theory (Slavin, 1995). Such approaches are based on general information processing theory and suggest that in order to remember information and connect it to existing knowledge, a student must restructure the information or elaborate on the information (Wittrock, 1978, 1990). The chapters also draw on the cognitive-developmental theories of Piaget and Vygotsky described in Part I of this book. In addition, many of the chapters in this part are strongly influenced by sociocultural perspectives on learning and often reflect cognitive-constructivist perspectives.

The chapters in this Part II describe specific techniques or models of collaboration. Three of the chapters (chaps. 3, 4, & 5) specifically address the quality of discourse within a peer learning group and issues related to providing effective support for productive interaction. Two additional chapters (chaps. 6 & 7) extend this discussion. The last chapter in this part provides a commentary on these chapters. Because the various chapters included here describe specific techniques, we thought it important to end this part of the book with a chapter that provided some integration of the other chapters. The final chapter by Derry draws attention to the underlying themes or ideas that are common to these chapters.

CHAPTER THREE

Evolution of Discourse During Cross-Age Tutoring

NATALIE K. PERSON
Rhodes College

ARTHUR G. GRAESSER
University of Memphis

It has been well documented that one-to-one tutoring is an effective method of instruction. Reported effect sizes have ranged from 0.4 to 2.3 standard deviation units when tutored students are compared to classroom instruction or other control groups (Anderson, Corbett, Koedinger, & Pelletier, 1995; Bloom, 1984; Cohen, Kulik, & Kulik, 1982; Mohan, 1972). These effect sizes are quite surprising considering that a normal tutor typically has minimal tutoring experience, lacks expert domain knowledge, and has received no training in sophisticated tutoring techniques (Fitz-Gibbon, 1977; Graesser & Person, 1994). Although the majority of studies that report the benefits of tutoring primarily focused on outcomes, some of the more contemporary research is aimed at understanding the tutoring process (Fox, 1991, 1993; Graesser, Bowers, Hacker, & Person, in press; Graesser & Person, 1994; Graesser, Person, & Magliano, 1995; Lepper, Aspinwall, Mumme, & Chabay, 1990; Merrill, Reiser, Ranney, & Trafton, 1992; Person, Graesser, Magliano, & Kreuz, 1994; Putnam, 1987). Many of these researchers have attempted to understand the effectiveness of normal, unskilled tutors by systematically analyzing the collaborative dialogue that occurs between tutors and students.

The purpose of this chapter is to illustrate the pedagogical mechanisms that facilitate learning during normal one-to-one tutoring interactions. We believe that the advantages that one-to-one tutoring has over other learning methods are best understood by analyzing the contributions that tutors and students make while attempting to answer a question or solve a problem. In a number of previous publications and manuscripts, we documented the pedagogical tactics and strategies that tutors frequently implement during these interactions. We also provided substantial evidence that tutors rarely employ sophisticated tutoring techniques that are often incorporated into structured tutoring facilities in school systems and intelligent tutoring systems on computers (Graesser et al., in press; Graesser & Person, 1994; Graesser et al., 1995; Person, 1994; Person et al., 1994). In this chapter, we illustrate some of our previous claims about tutor strategies via actual tutoring dialogue excerpts. The chapter contains four sections. We first briefly describe the two tutoring samples that we used in our analyses. We then discuss the five-step dialogue frame that is prevalent in tutoring sessions but not in classrooms. A general understanding of the five-step frame is important because many of our subsequent arguments are housed within this framework. The third section provides a brief overview of sophisticated strategies that are rarely implemented by normal tutors. The last section illustrates the pedagogical strategies and dialogue moves that normal tutors did use in our tutoring samples.

TWO TUTORING SAMPLES

Tutoring protocols were collected from two naturalistic tutoring samples. The students in the first sample consisted of 27 undergraduates enrolled in a psychology research methods course who were required to participate in the tutoring sessions in order to fulfill a course requirement. The instructor of the research methods course identified six topics that are typically difficult for students to master. These topics included (a) operationally defining variables, (b) interpreting graphs, (c) statistics, (d) designing an experiment to test a hypothesis, (e) factorial designs, and (f) interpreting interactions. A counterbalancing scheme ensured that each student attended two different tutoring sessions with two different tutors.

The tutors for the research methods sample were three psychology graduate students who were recommended by a faculty member and were considered to be competent in the area of research methodology. Each of the tutors had some prior tutoring experience but not in the area of research methods.

The students in the second sample consisted of 13 seventh graders who were having difficulty in algebra and who were recommended for tutoring by their algebra instructors. They were tutored on topics such as fractions, exponents, positive and negative numbers, and algebra word problems. This sample included all of the algebra tutoring that took place at this particular middle school during a 1-month period. Therefore, it should be noted that this sample is representative of the tutoring that takes place in school settings.

The tutors for the algebra sample were 10 high school students who had performed well in previous mathematics courses. None of the tutors in these two samples had extensive tutoring experience (approximately 9 hours each), had ever received formal training in tutoring strategies, or could be considered experts in their respective domains. Therefore, these tutors were typical of the tutors who typically work with students in school settings. The algebra tutors all attended the same school as the seventh-grade algebra students and were roughly 3 years older than the tutees.

The tutors and students in the two samples, however, should not be considered peers in the sense that their level of expertise is fundamentally equal. Other researchers have investigated learning situations in which two peers with roughly equal knowledge collaborate to solve a complex task (O'Donnell, Dansereau, Hythecker, et al., 1988; O'Donnell et al., 1990; Rogoff, 1990). Our tutors are not peers in this sense.

All tutoring sessions were videotaped and transcribed. The research methods sample had 44 hours of tutoring, whereas the algebra sample had 22. Some of the sessions in the research methods sample could not be transcribed because of poor sound. A full account of our data collection, transcribing procedures, coding methods, and statistical analyses can be found in several previous articles (Graesser & Person, 1994; Graesser et al., 1995; Person et al., 1994; Person, Kreuz, Zwaan, & Graesser, 1995). Our previous analyses indicated virtually no differences between the two samples in terms of the dialogue patterns, pedagogical strategies, and tactics that were employed by the tutors. Therefore, we do not attempt to differentiate these two samples in our illustration of such patterns, tactics, and strategies.

THE FIVE-STEP DIALOGUE FRAME

Some researchers have characterized classroom interactions in terms of a three-step dialogue frame. The sequence of these three steps involves: (1) the teacher's request for information from a student, (2) the student's answer, and (3) the teacher's evaluation of the student's contribution. Mehan (1979) referred to these three steps as initiation, response, and evaluation, whereas Sinclair and Coulthart (1975) referred to them as question, answer, and evaluation. Regardless of the labels (IRE or QAE), neither of these three-step frames requires extensive input from the student.

The dialogue frame that is prevalent in tutoring consists of five steps rather than three. Our previous publications provide detailed descriptions of the five steps (Graesser & Person, 1994; Graesser et al., in press; Graesser et al., 1995). A brief description of the five steps follows:

1. Tutor asks a question (or alternatively provides a problem for the student to solve).
2. Student answers the question.

   3. Tutor gives feedback on the answer.

   4. Tutor and student collaboratively improve the quality of answer.

   5. Tutor assesses student's understanding of the answer.

The five-step dialogue frame is illustrated in the following exchange from a tutoring session on the topic of factorial designs (research method).

Example 1

Step 1	1:1	TUTOR:	So, how many F scores would be computed?
Step 2	1:2	STUDENT:	Three.
Step 3	1:3	TUTOR:	Three [agreeing with the student].
Step 4	1:4	TUTOR:	And what numbers [referring to a matrix of cell means] would you use?
	1:5	STUDENT:	You would do one for humor [one of the independent variables].
	1:6	TUTOR:	And what does that tell you?
	1:7	STUDENT:	I'm not sure [laughs].
	1:8	TUTOR:	OK, why do you do an F score? What is an F score?
	1:9	STUDENT:	To see the size, uh, significance?
	1:10	TUTOR:	The size of significance.
	1:11	STUDENT:	The size of significance.
	1:12	TUTOR:	Right, how statistically significant a variable is.
	1:13	STUDENT:	Right.
	1:14	TUTOR:	So, you are right, you would have three [F scores]: one for caffeine, one for humor, and one for . . . ?
	1:15	STUDENT:	The scores . . . from caffeine and humor.
	1:16	TUTOR:	Interaction, the interaction of the two, right?
	1:17	STUDENT:	Um hmm.
	1:18	TUTOR:	[Explains independence of main effects].
Step 5	1:19	TUTOR:	Do you see what I'm saying?
	1:20	STUDENT:	Um hmm.

The nature of this dialogue is quite different from what typically occurs in classroom interactions. Notice that Step 4 consists of multiple turns that allows the tutor and student to elaborate on ideas raised in the earlier steps. It would be quite difficult for a teacher in a classroom to craft such an elaborative dialogue that would meet the needs of a particular student (see King, chap. 4, this volume, for a classroom strategy in which students can provide elaborated help to one another). Although many of our subsequent claims involve each of the five steps, we believe that the heart of the tutoring process lies in the collaborative exchanges that occur in Step 4. More specifically, the pedagogical strategies that tutors implement during Step 4 facilitate student learning and ultimately account for the advantages that one-to-one tutoring has over other learning methods. Before these strategies are discussed in detail, we would first like to familiarize the reader with some of the strategies that normal tutors do not employ during tutoring sessions.

PEDAGOGICAL STRATEGIES THAT NORMAL TUTORS DO *NOT* EMPLOY

In previous analyses, we examined the extent to which normal, unskilled tutors utilized learning components that have been advocated in contemporary pedagogical theories and intelligent tutoring systems (Graesser et al., in press; Graesser et al., 1995; Person, 1994). Some of these components include active student learning, error diagnosis, anchored learning, student modeling, and sophisticated tutoring strategies. The results of several in-depth analyses of the tutoring protocols indicated that tutors typically do not include these components; thus, they cannot account for the effectiveness of normal one-to-one tutoring. A brief overview of some of our findings regarding these components is provided in this section.

One-to-one tutoring seems to be the optimal environment for a student to become an active, self-regulated learner. Educational researchers have routinely advocated learning situations that would encourage students to be inquisitive, self-motivated, and in charge of rectifying their own knowledge deficits (Brown, 1988, 1992; Bruner, 1961; Papert, 1980; Piaget, 1952; Scardamalia & Bereiter, 1991; Wittrock, 1990; Zimmerman, Bandura, & Martinez-Pons, 1992). We found that 80% of the questions that occur in a tutoring session are asked by the tutor, with tutees taking little responsibility for their own learning by asking questions (Graesser et al., in press; Graesser & Person, 1994; Graesser et al., 1995; Person et al., 1994). Of the questions asked by tutees (20%), less than one third were posed to address a true knowledge deficit (e.g., "What is an antagonistic interaction?"). The majority of student questions (54%) were about procedures (e.g., "Are you on page 109?") or attempts to confirm their preexisting beliefs (e.g., "Don't you have to have at least three groups to do an F test?"). Although these student questioning rates do not appear to be very encouraging, they are somewhat higher (but not substantially higher) than what typically occurs in a classroom. Students in classroom settings collectively ask 3.0 questions per hour (Dillon, 1988; Graesser & Person, 1994). It may be the case that students need to be trained to ask good questions and to become active, self-regulated learners (King, 1992a; Palincsar & Brown, 1984; Pressley, 1990; Pressley, El-Dinary, & Brown, 1992).

According to proponents of error diagnosis approaches, the tutor (human or computer) is responsible for identifying the student error, diagnosing the cause of the error, and shepherding the student through a correct solution path (Anderson, Corbett, et al., 1995; Lesgold, Lajoie, Buzno, & Eggan, 1992; Reiser, Connelly, Ranney, & Ritter, 1992). These approaches may require extensive negative feedback from the tutor, which may be disheartening for a student who is having difficulty in a subject. We found very little evidence that normal tutors opt for such approaches. When a student committed an error, the tutor pointed out the cause of the error 8% of the time and provided an entire solution path only 6% of the time. This does not mean that tutors do not address student errors. They do indeed address the errors; they simply do not handle them with sophisticated error diagnosis approaches.

Anchored learning occurs when students acquire important concepts and principles from authentic, highly situated problems or examples (Bransford, Goldman, & Vye, 1991; Goldman, Pellegrino, & Bransford, 1993; Schank & Jona, 1991). These problems or examples typically require students to actively solve problems that have real-world application and personal relevance. For example, the Cognition and Technology Group at Vanderbilt (1993) developed the Jasper series, a set of video-based adventures that are designed to teach children via intriguing, contextually rich problems. In one episode, Jasper and the other characters must save an eagle that has been injured in a meadow. At the end of this episode, the students in the classroom are challenged to save the eagle. Our tutors, however, did not present problems of this kind. Person (1994) examined the nature of the tutor-generated examples in the research methods sample. Only 2% of the 847 tutor-generated examples were classified as authentic, situated examples. It may not be feasible for normal tutors to use situated problems given the time constraints of a typical 1-hour tutoring session. That is, situated problems may take many hours to solve, and tutors may feel compelled to expose the student to as much material in the session as possible, rather than work just one problem in depth. If this is indeed the case, anchoring learning is not a component that can account for the positive outcomes of normal tutoring.

In an ideal world, a tutor (or teacher) would be able to deduce precisely what the student knows and accurately detect the student's knowledge deficits. Designers of intelligent tutoring systems refer to this inference capability as *student modeling*. These designers have attempted to build intelligent tutoring systems that can infer the knowledge states of the student on the basis of the student's questions, answers, and errors (Anderson, Conrad, & Corbett, 1989; Anderson, Corbett, et al., 1995; Larkin & Chabay, 1992; Ohlsson, 1986; Sleeman & Brown, 1982; VanLehn, 1990). Learning occurs as the knowledge base of the tutor converges with the knowledge base of the student. Roschelle (1992) argued that this convergence of shared knowledge is the basis of collaborative learning. Our analyses indicated that the convergence of shared knowledge during the course of tutoring is infinitesimal at best. One line of evidence for this claim involves the feedback that tutors provide to students (Graesser et al., 1995). Our analyses indicated that tutors are more likely to give positive feedback (32% of the time) after student errors than negative feedback (14% of the time). For vague or incoherent student answers, the tutors gave positive feedback 45% of the time and rarely provided any negative feedback (4% of the time). If tutors were truly tracking the knowledge of the students, the tutors' feedback patterns should have been more compatible with the students' contributions. Example 2 illustrates the indiscriminate feedback that tutors often provide students. The example was extracted from a research methods tutoring session on variables. The tutor is attempting to explain why subject variables are not susceptible to random assignment.

Example 2

2.1 TUTOR: Subject variables can't be manipulated, because they are people variables. You can't manipulate social economic status. You can't manipulate sex. You can't manipulate age, because they're all part of the person. Um, you can't [randomly] assign someone to be married, single, or divorced. Another example, you can't assign somebody who abuses the child or not abuses the child. These are called subject variables.

2.2 STUDENT: Yeah, but, I don't understand what you mean.

2.3 TUTOR: Well, you have this whole group of people, uh, say your subject pool, and you're doing a study on child abuse and how that affects you at a later age. You can't take the subjects, divide them in half randomly, and make half of them abused.

2.4 STUDENT: Yeah, because they might lie.

2.5 TUTOR: Well, yeah, that's just something you can't do, you can't make them abused children when they are adults.

In Turn 2.5, the tutor provides positive feedback even though the student's previous contribution is blatantly error ridden. According to Person et al. (1995), tutors may attempt to minimize criticism or negative feedback because such acts would violate politeness rules of normal conversation (see Brown & Levinson, 1987, for additional information on politeness). That is, negative feedback is a face-threatening act that could cause to the student to shut down (Lepper et al., 1990). It is possible for tutors to give explicit, unambiguous negative feedback and still be polite. This is illustrated in Example 3. This example was taken from an algebra tutoring session on fractions.

Example 3

3.1 TUTOR: Let's try this one, 5/18ths minus 3/6ths.

3.2 STUDENT: Uh, this one would just go like that [pointing to a previously worked problem]?

3.3 TUTOR: Well, um, actually, no, no, you couldn't do that. Sorry.

The tutor's feedback in Turn 3.3 is explicit and negative yet he manages to incorporate two politeness strategies. In the beginning of the turn, the tutors pauses ("um") and at the end of the turn, he apologizes ("Sorry"). These two politeness strategies allow the tutor to provide straightforward feedback in a kinder, gentler way. The tutor in Example 2 could have provided similar feedback; perhaps this would have prevented the student from maintaining the belief that dishonest participants are a problem in random assignment.

Additional evidence also suggests that very little convergence of meaning occurs between tutors and students. This line of evidence involves student questions. As stated earlier, intelligent tutoring systems that adhere to student modeling approaches are often designed to infer a student's knowledge state from the questions that the student asks. Person et al. (1994) reported that student achievement was significantly correlated neither with the frequency of student questions nor the proportion of student questions that reflect knowledge deficits. That is, good students and poor students asked roughly the same number of questions. Therefore, tutors cannot rely on student questions to gauge their understanding. Good students did ask a higher proportion of deep-reasoning questions; however, the overall frequency of these questions was very low (only 8 per hour). Hence, tutors should be cautious in using these student questions as a measure of student understanding.

Sophisticated tutoring techniques have been endorsed by researchers in psychology, education, and cognitive science. Some of these techniques include the Socratic method (Collins, 1985; Stevens, Collins, & Goldin, 1982), modeling-scaffolding-fading (Collins, Brown, & Newman, 1989; Rogoff, 1990), building on prerequisites (Gagné, 1977), and cascade learning (VanLehn, Jones, & Chi, 1992). We searched the tutoring protocols for vestiges of these sophisticated techniques and came up virtually empty handed (Graesser et al., 1995; Person, 1994). In a qualitative analysis of the protocols, Person et al. (1995) conducted an extensive search to find collaborative exchanges that capture the essence of Socratic tutoring. Example 4 was the only instance of a such an exchange. This research methods student is attempting to design a study that would determine the relation between divorce and depression in children; he does not understand that this can only be accomplished by using a correlational approach.

Example 4

4.1	TUTOR:	Tell me first, ah, what kind of experiment would it be? I mean, what method? Would it be . . . are you going to have an experimental design?
4.2	STUDENT:	Yes.
4.3	TUTOR:	You are?
4.4	STUDENT:	Probably so, um, because not all children, if they're depressed are going to be . . . you're not going to be able to look at any data on depressed children. Well, I mean, let me start over. You can look at data on depressed children and whether or not their parents are divorced, but if you wanted to really test your hypothesis, it would be better if you conducted an experimental research design.
4.5	TUTOR:	OK, I'm curious, OK, now how would we go about doing that? OK, this is all up to you.

During the next five turns (4.6–4.10), the student struggles to come up with a design. The tutor offers minimal input during these turns (e.g., "OK," "um hmm"). Socratic tutoring often requires the tutor to maintain the erroneous beliefs of the student until the student recognizes the errors. After letting the student flounder for several minutes, the tutor asks a question that forces the student to rethink his answer.

> 4.11 TUTOR: . . . I could be wrong, but are you manipulating anything?
> 4.12 STUDENT: No, you're absolutely right. No, I'm not.

There are several reasons why Socratic tutoring may be absent in most normal tutoring interactions. It requires extensive practice on the part of the tutor, is very time-consuming, and also requires high levels of domain knowledge (Collins, Warnock, Aeillo, & Miller, 1975). As Example 4 illustrates, students may wander down many unproductive paths before realizing the defects in their thinking. Hence, Socratic tutoring along with other sophisticated techniques may conflict with the time constraints of a typical tutoring session and require extensive training on the part of the tutor. It is not surprising that normal tutors virtually never use them.

PEDAGOGICAL STRATEGIES THAT *DO* OCCUR IN NORMAL TUTORING

This section describes the strategies and dialogue moves that normal, unskilled tutors employ during tutoring sessions. In the first portion of this section, we focus on Step 1 of the five-step dialogue frame and demonstrate how tutors control the tutoring agenda by following curriculum scripts. The subsequent discussion concentrates on Step 4 of the frame. We show how tutors use strategies such as hinting, prompting, splicing, pumping, and summarizing to facilitate student learning, strategies we believe to be major contributors to the overall effectiveness of normal one-to-one tutoring. Actual dialogue excerpts are provided to illustrate these strategies.

Curriculum Scripts

Other researchers have reported that skilled tutors adhere to curriculum scripts (McArthur, Stasz, & Zmuidzinas, 1990; Putnam, 1987). A curriculum script consists of a set of subtopics, examples, and questions that is constructed prior to the tutoring session. We are quite convinced that unskilled tutors also adhere to these scripts. In a previous analysis, we examined the tutors' questions and subtopics that occurred in the tutoring protocols (Graesser et al., 1995). We found that 73% of tutor questions and subtopics were inspired by curriculum scripts, a result confirmed by Person's (1994) separate analysis of the source and the rate of occurrence of tutor-generated examples, in which she found that 78% of the tutors' examples were motivated by curriculum scripts. Hence, we are quite certain that normal, unskilled tutors follow these scripted game plans.

We are not convinced, however, that the prevalence of curriculum scripts in normal tutoring contributes to its overall effectiveness. First, teachers in classrooms follow prepared lesson plans and therefore, curriculum scripts are not unique to normal tutoring. Second, the tutors did not alter their scripts to satisfy the intellectual needs of particular students. Presumably, a good tutor should be sensitive to the needs of the student and should adjust the level of instruction accordingly. We found that the tutors asked the same questions and provided the same examples regardless of the achievement level of the student. This is illustrated in Examples 5 and 6. In both of these examples, the tutor is attempting to explain the many components of a 2×2 factorial design. She used this hypothetical example in every tutoring session on factorial designs. The student in Example 5 is a good student (he received an A in the course), and his contributions indicate that he understands this example. The student in Example 6, however, is not a very good student (she received a C– in the course). Her contributions indicate that she does not fully understand this example.

Example 5

5.1	TUTOR:	OK, let's see, I use the example of . . . Let's suppose we are trying to protect America from a new street drug called Moodflakes. So we are trying to evaluate the threat posed by Moodflakes to the youth of America. OK. So, we are looking at the reaction time task which involves pressing a button at the sound of the buzzer. OK, to evaluate the effect of the drug, OK, we are going to compare Moodflakes to say a placebo, Cornflakes, to see if Moodflakes differentially affects the performance on the reaction time task. Also, we want to see if Moodflakes might have a differential effect depending on the environment it's used under. So we are going to look at a noisy environment versus a quiet environment. *OK, so, so* we're looking at the difference between Moodflakes and Cornflakes, and we're looking at noisy environments and quiet environments, OK?
5.2	STUDENT:	OK.
5.3	TUTOR:	All right, so what sort of variables do we have here?
5.4	STUDENT:	OK, we have the dependent variable.
5.5	TUTOR:	Which is what?
5.6	STUDENT:	The reaction time.
5.7	TUTOR:	OK.
5.8	STUDENT:	One independent variable would be–
5.9	TUTOR:	[interrupts] call it A.
5.10	STUDENT:	OK, we have ah . . . type of drug. The second one would be, ah, type of environment.
5.11	TUTOR:	OK, environment. OK, so how many IVs do we have here, obviously?

5.12 STUDENT: Ah, two.
5.13 TUTOR: OK, so how many levels do we have for IV one?
5.14 STUDENT: Two.
5.15 TUTOR: OK, and what are they?
5.16 STUDENT: Moodflakes, placebo.

Example 6

6.1 TUTOR: Why don't we say we are looking at trying to protect America from a new street drug called Moodflakes? OK?
6.2 STUDENT: Moonflakes.
6.3 TUTOR: MOODflakes, that's right.
6.4 STUDENT: Kind of like Kellogg's Cornflakes [laughs].
6.5 TUTOR: That's right. Let's say we wish to evaluate the threat posed by this drug called Moodflakes, and we're, we're using a reaction time task which involves pressing a button after a buzzer has sounded, to ah, to measure the effects of Moodflakes, OK? And we're gonna compare the effects of the Moodflakes to a standard dose of, a standard dose of the Moodflakes to the standard dose of a placebo treatment, Cornflakes, OK?
6.6 STUDENT: [laughs].
6.7 TUTOR: All right, um, why don't we say we're looking at subjects tested under 2 different conditions: a noisy environment, where they have a real noisy room with lots going on, or a quiet room, OK? All right, let's think, what are your variables involved in this experiment?
6.8 STUDENT: You have your (pause), one of your independent variables would be (pause).
6.9 TUTOR: You can call it IV one.
6.10 STUDENT: OK, that would be . . . the real thing which is the placebo.
6.11 TUTOR: OK, in other words, the IV is what?
6.12 STUDENT: The drug?
6.13 TUTOR: In other words, type of drug.

It takes the next 23 turns (6.14–6.36) for the tutor and student to articulate the other independent variable (i.e., type of environment, noisy versus quiet).

6.37 TUTOR: OK, what other variable have we got running around?
6.38 STUDENT: Well, you have to put things I guess (laughs), um (pause)
6.39 TUTOR: OK, in other words?
6.40 STUDENT: Dependent.
6.41 TUTOR: Right!
6.42 STUDENT: I thought we were looking for the third independent.
6.43 TUTOR: Nope, just a third type of variable.
6.44 STUDENT: OK, that's [the student pauses and doesn't know the answer].
6.45 TUTOR: Reaction time.

These two dialogue examples are typical of how the tutors adhered to their curriculum scripts across several tutoring sessions on the same topic. The tutor's contributions remain curiously similar, whereas the two students' contributions are drastically different. One would expect a tutor to provide (or restructure) problems that are manageable for students with different abilities. We did not find this to be the case. One explanation for this finding may be that normal, unskilled tutors are not capable of accurately gauging student ability. For tutors to augment their tutoring plans to accommodate a particular student, they must be able to accurately assess what the student knows. The accurate assessment of student knowledge is a critical component of several sophisticated tutoring techniques. For example, modeling-scaffolding-fading techniques require that tutors structure problems so that students with different knowledge levels can make relevant contributions (Rogoff, 1990; Rogoff & Gardner, 1984; Vygotsky, 1978). For these techniques to be successful, the tutor must know the boundaries of the student's knowledge. Evidence suggests that skilled (or expert) tutors are capable of restructuring the tutoring agenda to accommodate the needs of particular students (McArthur et al., 1990). However, this does not seem to be the practice of normal, unskilled tutors. It apparently is the case that unskilled tutors lack the training and experience to accomplish such a feat.

Conversational Moves That Occur in Step 4

Earlier in the chapter, we indicated that tutors do not give discriminating feedback to student answers in Step 3 of the dialogue frame. We also noted that tutors do not ignore student errors. In the remainder of the chapter, we illustrate the strategies and discourse moves that tutors use to handle students' errors and facilitate student contributions. In Step 4, the tutor and student collaboratively work to improve the quality of the student's contribution. It would be impossible for a teacher in a classroom to have a conversation with each student in the class in order to obliterate each of their misconceptions about a particular topic. We believe that the conversational moves that occur in Step 4 account for the differences between tutors and teachers, and ultimately, are responsible for the learning advantages that tutoring has over typical classroom learning. This section discusses and illustrates five conversational moves that are used by tutors in Step 4: hinting, prompting, splicing, pumping, and summarizing.

Hinting. Hinting is one tactic that tutors occasionally use to correct students' errors and misconceptions (Fox, 1991, 1993; Graesser, 1992; McArthur et al., 1990, Merrill et al., 1992). When providing a hint, the cognitive burden is assumed by both the tutor and the student. The tutor knows the answer but is reluctant to simply give it to the student. Therefore, the tutor must produce a hint that will provide enough information to steer the student in the right direction. Several of our analyses revealed that tutors frequently provided hints after students' error-ridden contributions. In one analysis of deep-reasoning questions, tutors provided hints after students provided error-ridden answers 27% of the time (Graesser et al., in press). Person (1994) found that tutors provided hints 11% of the time after student errors and 16% of the time when the students were unable to provide any answer at all. Example 7 illustrates a tutor providing hints after the student is unable to construct a correct answer. This example was extracted from one of the research methods tutoring sessions on interactions. During the course of the example, the tutor provided the student with a number of hints that enabled the student to make correct contributions. The tutor constructed some hypothetical cell means for a 2 × 2 factorial design. The tutor also depicted the results in a graph.

Example 7

7.1 TUTOR: Okay, here are our results [referring to the four cell means and the graph]. Okay, what's going on here? Do our variables have a main effect?

7.2 STUDENT: Uh, ENVIRONMENT [one of the independent variables] is related to DRUG [the other independent variable], uh, (pause). I'm not sure.

7.3 TUTOR: Okay, forget about ENVIRONMENT for now, and let's just concentrate on DRUG.

7.4 STUDENT: Uh (pause).

7.5 TUTOR: Okay, if you can't determine a main effect from the graph, why don't you look at the cell means. Remember how we computed the marginal means for each variable earlier?

7.6 STUDENT: Kinda.

7.7 TUTOR: Okay, forget about the graph and compute the marginal means for DRUG.

7.8 STUDENT: Five and nine, so there is a main effect for DRUG.

7.9 TUTOR: Yep.

The student appears to be on the wrong track during Turn 7.2. In Turn 7.3, the tutor provided a hint in order to refocus the student. The tutor also provided additional hints in at Turns 7.5 and 7.7. Rather than explicitly telling the student whether there was a main effect for each of the independent variables, the tutor provided hints about the computation that is involved in main effects. It is interesting to note how the tutor's hints became progressively more specific until the student could supply a correct answer.

Prompting. In many ways, prompting is a fill-in-the-blank technique. Tutors will often begin a phrase that includes information that is relevant to the topic and then pause. The pause and intonation of the tutor's contribution will signal the student to supply the missing information. Prompting is very similar to providing a hint, although prompting typically requires less cognitive effort on the part of the student. With a hint, the student is still required to do much of the problem solving (as in Example 7). Prompting, however, typically requires a minimal contribution from the student. Example 8 illustrates prompting and is taken from the algebra sample.

Example 8

8.1 TUTOR: And you would multiply that by . . . ?
8.2 STUDENT: 6, 42.
8.3 TUTOR: Yeah.

There are two possible reasons why tutors use the prompting strategy. The first involves the time constraints of the tutoring session. Tutors may attempt to expedite the tutoring process by providing much of the context and perfunctory information that is needed to solve problems. If the tutor required the student to assume all of the cognitive burden involved in solving a problem, many topics would not get covered.

The second reason addresses collaborative mechanisms in normal discourse (Clark & Schaefer, 1989). In normal conversation, listeners are expected to help speakers repair speech errors by filling in missing words. Tutors may exploit this aspect of normal conversation in order to get students to actively participate in the session. Tutors must be careful, however, to provide students with adequate cues; otherwise the student may become confused. The following example illustrates how the prompting strategy went terribly awry in a research methods tutoring session. The tutor wanted the student to explain the difference between graphs that depict frequency distributions and those that depict descriptive statistics.

Example 9

9.1 TUTOR: But if you've calculated the scores, and you're using statistics, and you've calculated the means. Down here [points to the X axis] you would put (pause)? And up here [points to Y axis] you would put (pause)?
9.2 STUDENT: [looks at tutor with a blank stare]
9.3 TUTOR: This is important because there's a difference between the frequency distribution and this.
9.4 STUDENT: If you give me some FACTS [she is shouting], I can do it, I just can't do it abstract!
9.5 TUTOR: OK, all right.
9.6 STUDENT: I mean, you're saying blank and blank, and I don't know what blank and blank ARE, so how could I tell?!

Splicing.   Splicing is a phenomenon that occurs in practically all forms of discourse in which there are two or more speech participants (Falk, 1980; Ferrara, 1992; Graesser, 1992; Lerner, 1991). According to Ferrara (1992), splicing occurs when the words of two speech participants interlock to make a meaning-ful utterance. Splicing requires a high degree of cooperation between speakers. Tutors frequently interrupt students to insert correct information. The splicing phenomenon is illustrated in Example 10, an excerpt extracted from an algebra tutoring session.

Example 10

10.1 TUTOR: The angles of a triangle add up to?
10.2 STUDENT: 360.
10.3 TUTOR: 180.
10.4 STUDENT: Hmm.
10.5 TUTOR: 180, a circle is all the way around and that's 360 degrees.
10.6 STUDENT: OK, uh, I don't get this stuff.
10.7 TUTOR: Circles?
10.8 STUDENT: Right.
10.9 TUTOR: Before we look at circles, you know what "d" is, right?
10.10 STUDENT: Ah [doesn't know the answer].
10.11 TUTOR: Diameter, you see the center of the circle?
10.12 STUDENT: Sure.
10.13 TUTOR: You drop one [point] on one side, and you drop one on the other and when you connect them, it [the line] has to go through the center. . . . The diameter is the longest segment between two points in a circle.
10.14 STUDENT: OK.

At Turn 10.3, the tutor splices in the correct information after the student's error-ridden response. At Turn 10.11, he splices in the correct answer when the student fails to provide any answer. We found splicing to be the most prevalent strategy employed by tutors to handle student errors. In an analysis of deep-reasoning questions, tutors spliced in the correct answer 38% of the time after student errors (Graesser et al., in press; Graesser et al., 1995). Person (1994) re-ported that tutors used the splice strategy after 31% of students' error-ridden answers and 21% of students' partial answers (answers in which the student is only able to supply a portion of the answer) while they collaboratively worked through example problems. It may be the case that splicing is so entrenched in normal conversation that tutors do it unknowingly. On the other hand, perhaps tutors can sense when students are unable to supply correct answers. If this is the case, tutors may jump in with the answer to avoid embarrassing the student.

Pumping. A pump refers to a tutor pumping a student for additional infor-mation. Tutors employed this tactic approximately 14% of the time when stu-dents failed to provide answers or provided error-ridden contributions (Person, 1994). Example 11 illustrates the pumping tactic in the context of a tutoring ses-sion on factorial designs.

Example 11

11.1 TUTOR: Look at this graph. Is there a main effect for B [one of the independent variables]?

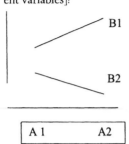

11.2 STUDENT: Well, the two lines share a midpoint [This is an error, the lines do not share a midpoint].
11.3 TUTOR: Uh huh?
11.4 STUDENT: So, there's no main effect for B.
11.5 TUTOR: Uh huh, for B?
11.6 STUDENT: Yeah.
11.7 TUTOR: Well, not exactly. The lines for 6 don't share a midpoint; there is an effect for B.

The tutor is pumping for more information in Turns 11.3 and 11.5. There are two possible reasons for tutors using pumps. First, when the tutors pump for more information, most of the cognitive burden rests with the student. Therefore, tutors may employ this tactic so students will reason aloud and possibly even realize their own errors. Second, a tutor may employ this tactic to gain a better understanding of the student's error. That is, the pump buys the tutor more time to better interpret the student's misconception.

Pumping appeared to be a popular tactic in Step 4 even when no student errors were committed. In Example 12, the tutor pumps the student for additional information after each student contribution. In this example, the onus is on the student to solve the problem rather than on the tutor. This excerpt was extracted from a research methods session on graphing.

Example 12

12.1 TUTOR: Why don't you draw for me a negative linear relationship.
12.2 STUDENT: Negative?
12.3 TUTOR: Sure.
12.4 STUDENT: OK [student draws the X and Y axes]. OK, negative is like for instance, ah, here's an example that was in the book [Draws a line that depicts a negative linear relationship and labels both axes of the graph]. A negative correlation would be let's say, um, people wanting to help, um, someone in trouble.

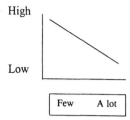

12.5 TUTOR: Uh huh? What is this [pointing to Y axis]?

12.6 STUDENT: [pointing to Y axis] This is the probability that they would help and this [pointing to the X axis] is, ah, the circumstances, ah, whether there's few people around or whether there's several.

12.7 TUTOR: OK? So?

12.8 STUDENT: OK, so that's negative. The probability that someone will help is negatively correlated with the number of bystanders.

12.9 TUTOR: Right.

Summarizing. The multiple turns that occur in Step 4 allow the tutor and student to collaboratively construct a correct answer or solution to a problem. Once a complete answer is constructed, a good tutor should require the student to do the summarizing or recapping. This would allow the student to receive additional practice, as well as demonstrate his or her mastery of the problem. However, we found that tutors are significantly more likely to summarize the correct answers or example solutions than the students, 1.6 versus .04, respectively (Graesser et al., 1995). A tutor summary is provided in Example 13. This exchange occurred near the end of a tutoring session in research methods; the tutor is summarizing an earlier discussion on scales of measurement.

Example 13

13.1 TUTOR: Do you have any questions over any of the material? Is there anything that was, that I went over that wasn't really clear or anything that the book did?

13.2 STUDENT: Not really.

13.3 TUTOR: OK, I'm just going to ask you some questions to review.

13.4 STUDENT: OK.

13.5 TUTOR: OK, nominal, scales, uh, just scales, you got your nominal, uh, ordinal, interval, uh, ratio. OK, nominal scales?

13.6 STUDENT: A categorical type thing.

13.7 TUTOR: An example would be, uh, male, female, married, single, divorced, whatever—all those things, things you can't attach a number to, you can't quantify it. We call that nominal.

13.8 STUDENT: [nods head].

13.9 TUTOR: An ordinal scale, uh, it's very, it's like being able to quantify it. An example the book uses is the movie rating system.

13.10 STUDENT: [nods head].

13.11 TUTOR: One star, two star, three star, four star? You know a four-star movie
                is better that a three-star movie, and three's better than two, and
                two's better than one. But you don't know that a four-star movie is
                twice as good as a two star, and you don't know that the difference
                between a one star and a two star is the same as the difference
                between a three star and a four star.

13.12 STUDENT: [nods head].

During the next 17 turns (13.13–13.29), the tutor provided lengthy examples
for interval and ratio scales. The student never contributed more than a head
nod or an "OK." This exchange would have been the perfect opportunity for the
student to demonstrate her knowledge of these scales. For example, the tutor
could have asked the student to provide the labels for the scales as well as the examples. Normal, unskilled tutors may be unaware that student summaries are
effective pedagogical tools (Palincsar & Brown, 1984). Tutors may need training
to learn how to routinely implement effective pedagogical strategies. On the
other hand, tutor summaries may contribute to the overall effectiveness of one-
to-one tutoring in that they are typically concise and error free, whereas student
summaries may be lengthy and unintelligible. We are not arguing that student
summaries are adverse pedagogical tools. Rather, the constraints of a typical
tutoring session may not be suitable for student summaries.

CLOSING COMMENTS

In this chapter, we attempted to illustrate the strategies that normal tutors employ with dialogue excepts from actual tutoring sessions. We believe that the
learning advantages that one-to-one tutoring has over other learning environments is largely due to the conversational moves or strategies that tutors use in
Step 4 of the five-step dialogue frame. These moves and strategies include hinting, prompting, splicing, pumping, and summarizing. We also described some
well-known learning components (i.e., active student learning, error diagnosis,
anchored learning, student modeling, and sophisticated tutoring strategies) and
discussed how they are conspicuously absent in normal tutoring sessions. Thus,
we hope that we have provided a clearer distinction between what occurs in normal tutoring versus that which allegedly occurs in expert or intelligent tutoring
settings.

ACKNOWLEDGMENTS

This research was funded by the Office of Naval Research (N00014-90-J-1492,
and N00014-92-J-1826) and the Center for Applied Psychological Research at the
University of Memphis in grants that were awarded to Arthur C. Graesser.

CHAPTER FOUR

Discourse Patterns
for Mediating Peer Learning

ALISON KING

California State University San Marcos

This chapter presents three discourse patterns that have been developed by King for use by peer learning groups to mediate their own learning. These three discourse patterns are designed to facilitate different types of learning: complex knowledge construction, problem solving, and peer tutoring. The theoretical basis of these mediational models is presented as are research findings showing empirical support for their effectiveness. Discussion focuses on ways in which these discourse patterns promote interactive cognitive activity as well as the metacognitive processes needed to regulate that activity.

INTERACTION AND LEARNING

Any peer learning context provides opportunities for learners to interact with each other in verbal and nonverbal, paralinguistic ways. Interaction can take a variety of forms such as providing physical assistance with a task, physically or verbally guiding another's performance of a skill, providing verbal or gestural cues or hints for solving a problem, and mutual discussion about the topic or activity being pursued. From a Vygotskian perspective on learning (Leont'ev, 1932; Luria, 1928; Vygotsky, 1929, 1978), these social contexts provide a learning arena for the development of individuals' cognitive abilities. In this view, learning is socially constructed during interaction and activity with others. During such interaction, individuals engage in the exchange of ideas, information, perspectives, attitudes, and opinions. The interaction also provides opportunities for individuals to model their patterns of reasoning, thinking strategies, and problem-solving skills on those of their peers. As a result of this type of interaction, individuals internalize knowledge, meanings, and skills from each other; they also collaboratively build new knowledge and meaning. Thus, from this social constructivist theoretical perspective, during such interactive learning activities, peers are said to *mediate* each other's learning.

Examination of the interaction between individuals reveals specific ways in which learning is mediated by the discourse itself. In general, different types of interaction facilitate different kinds of learning. For example, learning factual material may simply require rehearsal of material and can be accomplished through group discourse that consists of merely requesting and providing information. In contrast, more complex learning—often referred to as higher level learning, such as analyzing and integrating ideas and solving ill-structured problems—calls for the construction of new knowledge. For individuals to be successful in such higher level complex learning, they must go beyond memorizing information to thinking with that information and thinking about how that information relates to what they already know. According to many theoreticians (e.g., Noddings, 1989; Tudge, 1990b; Vygotsky, 1978), to promote such high-level learning in a group context, the discourse within the group must be of a comparably high cognitive level. Such discourse would consist of, for example, thought-provoking questions, explanations, speculations, justifications, inferences, hypotheses, and conclusions.

This relation between the level of discourse within a collaborating pair or group of learners and the level of learning or achievement of the individuals has been documented by several researchers. For example, in a series of studies of peer interaction and learning, Webb (1989) consistently found that giving detailed elaborate explanations to others in the group is a strong predictor of achievement; that is, the student who does the explaining is the one who benefits. Other researchers have found similar positive learning effects for explanation giving (Chi & VanLehn, 1991; King, 1990a; Swing & Peterson, 1982). In an analysis of naturally occurring group interaction during problem solving, a positive relation emerged between children's level of verbal interaction and their problem-solving success (King, 1989b). In that study, the pairs of students that were successful in the task were the ones that asked more task-related questions of each other and reached higher levels of strategy elaboration than did unsuccessful pairs. Subsequent studies (e.g., King, 1990a, 1991, 1992b, 1994b; King & Rosenshine, 1993) showed that students can successfully be taught various strategies for asking such task-related thought-provoking questions of others in the group. These questions then elicit explanations, inferences, speculations, and other such elaborated responses, which in turn have a direct positive effect on individual achievement. Chan, Burtis, Scardemalia, and Bereiter (1992) also analyzed the constructive cognitive activity of students in learning groups and the contribution that activity made to learning. The children in that study were instructed in how to give "deep thinking" responses to text statements; then the researchers read a series of text statements to each child individually and asked them to respond. Chan et al. (1992) defined deep thinking as generating *thinking ideas* (describing a new realization, attempting to solve a problem, or trying to understand a difficult point) as opposed to *easy ideas*. Results of that study showed clear evidence that the level of cognitive constructive activity a child engaged in, from simple retelling of details and knowledge from the text (low) to problem solving and extrapolation beyond the text (high), had a direct effect on learning.

The interaction among individuals in a group can promote learning in several ways. In a group learning context, members of a group must talk to each other about the task, presenting their ideas and perspectives, asking questions, providing information, suggesting plans of action, and so on. Even without any responses from others, thinking aloud to the group in this way is a meaning-making process in itself. Thinking aloud can alter the individual's knowledge structures. It can provide the opportunity for individual members to clarify their own ideas, elaborate on them, evaluate their existing knowledge for accuracy and gaps, integrate and reorganize knowledge, or in some other manner reconceptualize the material (Bargh & Schul, 1980; Brown & Campione, 1986). This sort of cognitive change affects subsequent learning and performance.

Proponents of theories of the social construction of knowledge (e.g., Bearison, 1982; Damon, 1983; Mugny & Doise, 1978, Perret-Clermont, 1980; Vygotsky, 1978) suggest that when individuals make their thinking explicit and available to the group in this way, it sets the stage for dealing with conceptual discrepancies that emerge within the group and for the negotiation of meanings in general. When interacting in cooperative discussion contexts, individuals often discover that their own perceptions, facts, assumptions, values, and general understandings of the material differ to a greater or lesser extent from those of others with whom they are interacting. When these conceptual discrepancies emerge, individuals often feel the need to reconcile them. To do so, they must negotiate understanding and meaning with each other. This meaning negotiation, this coconstruction of knowledge, occurs through individuals' explaining concepts to each other, defending their own views, asking thought-provoking questions, hypothesizing, speculating about alternative interpretations, evaluating suggestions for feasibility, revising plans, and in general arriving at agreed-on meanings and plans. As Cobb (1988) pointed out, individuals engaged in such meaning negotiation with others are continually reorganizing and restructuring their own knowledge and thinking processes. Working alone would not result in the same extent of cognitive change. Thus, through interaction that is characterized by such a high level of discourse, group members mediate each other's learning.

However, students do not often engage in this level of discourse spontaneously. Learners generally do not elaborate on material unless they are prompted to do so (Britton, Van Dusen, Glynn, & Hemphill, 1990; Spires, Donley, & Penrose, 1990). Neither do they spontaneously activate and use their relevant prior knowledge (Pressley, McDaniel, Turnure, Wood, & Ahmad, 1987), or ask many thought-provoking questions during discussion without specific training in question asking (King, 1990a, 1992b). In fact, students working in groups appear to be more focused on finding the right answer than in mediating each other's problem solving (e.g., Vedder, 1985) and problem-solving groups tend to operate at a concrete specific level in a step-by-step manner (rather than at an abstract, planful level) unless the teacher intercedes with explicit guidance in how to interact (Webb, Ender, & Lewis, 1986). In general then, it appears that students will interact with each other at a very basic level unless they are taught specific skills of higher level discourse.

PROMOTING EFFECTIVE DISCOURSE
FOR MEDIATING PEER LEARNING

How can high-level discourse be promoted within collaborating groups? Some attempts to do so have focused on structuring the interaction so that students are forced to follow a particular pattern of talk in the group, thus controlling student mediation of learning. Methods of structuring the interaction can include scripting the interaction, giving specific task instructions, assigning particular roles, modeling, and instruction in specific discourse skills. For example, in Dansereau's (1988) *Scripted Cooperation* procedure, the script specifies and directs the processing activities students engage in during learning, thus directing students into a specific sequence of discourse: summarizing, error feedback, elaboration (see also O'Donnell, chap. 7, this volume). In Scripted Cooperation, the focus of the structure (and the resulting discourse) is on learning factual material, primarily through rehearsal and the procedure is very effective for that purpose. *Reciprocal Teaching* (Palincsar & Brown, 1984) also relies on structuring the interaction to promote specific discourse: questioning, summarizing, clarifying, predicting. Reciprocal Teaching has been found to be highly effective for understanding and remembering prose.

In both Scripted Cooperation and Reciprocal Teaching, group members mediate each other's learning. In both of these approaches, however, the highly structured interaction dictated by the procedures is thought by some to be too constrained to be conducive to the higher order thinking required for generative learning (Cohen, 1994b; Rosenshine & Meister, 1994; Salomon & Globerson, 1989). This is in spite of the fact that the Scripted Cooperation procedure does include an elaboration phase. Although the structure of the Scripted Cooperation and Reciprocal Teaching approaches facilitates fact learning, Salomon and Globerson speculated that the same structure may thwart the independent thinking necessary for analytical and generative learning and impede the kind of free exploratory activity needed for solving ill-structured problems (see Salomon & Globerson for a fuller discussion of this point). According to Cohen

(1994b), group interaction must be structured in order to promote the kind of high-level discourse necessary for peer mediation of problem solving and generative learning. That structure, however, needs to be flexible enough to provide students freedom to adapt those discourse skills and patterns to their particular task demands and group needs. Such freedom within structure is a delicate balance in group learning contexts.

Although high-level discourse can be promoted by structuring the interaction among group members in peer learning contexts, modeling also plays an important role in this process—in particular, modeling of questioning, reasoning patterns, and problem-solving strategies. For example, even when students are not explicitly taught the skills of summarizing or elaboration, their abilities in these areas could be enhanced through observing and imitating their peers' use of these skills. Similarly, sharing questions and responses with one another helps the group develop models of expert questioning and responding.

The three discourse patterns presented in the following sections of this chapter were developed to assist peer learning groups in mediating their own learning. Each discourse pattern is unique and was designed to facilitate a particular type of learning: complex knowledge construction (King, 1989a, 1994b), problem solving (King, 1991), and peer tutoring (King, 1994a, 1997; King, Staffieri, & Adelgais, 1998). These discourse patterns have been found to promote not only interactive cognitive activity, but also the metacognitive processes necessary for monitoring and regulating that activity.

DISCOURSE PATTERNS FOR PEER MEDIATION OF COMPLEX KNOWLEDGE CONSTRUCTION[1]

Guided Peer Questioning (developed and refined by King, 1989a, 1992b, 1994b) is a question-asking and -answering procedure designed to promote interaction and learning in small groups of peers. Group interaction is guided by the questions group members pose to the group. Group members are trained in how to ask thought-provoking questions and how to provide elaborated responses. Thus, the thought-provoking questions promote high-level discussion, which has been found to result in high-level learning (King, 1990a; King, 1994b; King & Rosenshine, 1993).

This procedure is guided by structured question "starters" such as, "Why is . . . important?" "How is . . . similar to . . . ?" "How does . . . relate to . . . ?" "What is an example of . . . ?" "What does . . . remind you of? And why?" These open-ended question starters are provided to members of the learning group, who

---

[1] Part of this section of the chapter is adapted from material appearing in King, A., "Teaching effective discourse patterns for small group learning," in R. Stevens (Ed.), *Teaching in American schools* (1998, pp. 121–139). Adapted by permission of Prentice Hall.

then use the question starters to guide them in generating their own specific questions related to the material being studied. When using Guided Peer Questioning, students first (individually) select a few of the open-ended, content-free questions from a larger list and generate several content-specific questions by "filling in the blanks." Then, after writing their questions, students get into groups where they take turns posing their specific questions to their group to stimulate discussion. Because students have been trained in how to provide elaborated responses (e.g., explanations, justifications, and rationales) to questions they are asked (King, 1994b), the quality of the ensuing discussion is enhanced.

The question starters were designed to prompt students to monitor their comprehension, actively process information, and construct new knowledge. Different kinds of question starters promote different levels of learning, from comprehension to knowledge construction. On a comprehension-monitoring level, asking and answering these questions is a form of self and peer testing, allowing students opportunities to check how well they (and their peers) understand the material as well as to clarify misunderstandings, correct errors, and fill in gaps in knowledge. At a more complex level of learning, asking and answering thought-provoking questions forces students to actually think about the material (rather than just memorize it), organizing the information, integrating it with prior knowledge, and reconceptualizing it in various ways. Answering such questions requires students to examine alternative perspectives, make connections among ideas, and generate explanations, elaboration, speculations, inferences and other forms of new knowledge.

A series of studies (King, 1989a, 1990a, 1992b, 1994b; King & Rosenshine, 1993) revealed that when students were taught to ask each other these thought-provoking questions during learning, their questions prompted high-level interaction and learning. In two studies (King, 1994b; King & Rosenshine, 1993), students learned to use these open-ended *comprehension questions* (ones that check for how well the material is understood) and thought-provoking *connection questions* (integration question—ones that ask for integration of concepts in some manner). Figure 4.1 shows the set of question starters selected for use in a research study with fourth graders (King, 1994b).

During peer interaction, clear patterns of discourse emerged that were dictated by the particular type of the open-ended question posed (comprehension or connection). As the complexity of questions increased from comprehension to connection, there was a corresponding increase in the complexity of discourse, from comprehension to knowledge construction to extended knowledge construction. Thus, use of the Guided Peer Questioning procedure promoted three types of discourse patterns, each of which is discussed in turn. The results of both studies (King, 1994b; King & Rosenshine, 1993) showed that these discourse patterns mediated learning as measured by tests of inference and factual recall as well as knowledge mapping.

---

comprehension questions

> Describe . . . in your own words.
>
> What does . . . mean?
>
> Why is . . . important?

connection questions (integration questions)

> Explain why . . . .
>
> Explain how . . . .
>
> How are . . . and . . . similar?
>
> What is the difference between . . . and . . .?
>
> How could . . . be used to . . . ?
>
> What would happen if . . . ?
>
> How does...tie in with ...that we learned before?
>
> What is a new example of ...?
>
> What are the strengths and weakness of ...?

FIG. 4.1. Thought-provoking question starters for fourth graders. King, 1994b, adapted by permission.

Comprehension Discourse Pattern

Some of the content-free open-ended questions (e.g., "Describe . . . in your own words" and "What does . . . mean?") were designed to prompt children to generate comprehension questions (King, 1994b; King & Rosenshine, 1993). These types of questions were intended to be used by learners to monitor their comprehension of terms, processes, and the like covered in the material being studied. Such comprehension questions (e.g., "In your own words describe an echinoderm" and "What does zonation mean?"), are not very thought-provoking in the sense that they are memory based—they simply ask for recall of material previously presented. But they do require students to restate definitions, descriptions, and procedures by paraphrasing in their own words. These comprehension questions were intended to induce some reconceptualization on the part of the responder and at the same time elicit evidence of real understanding (i.e., indications that knowledge had been assimilated into the responder's cognitive structures) because of the need to paraphrase instead of stating definitions verbatim.

The typical discourse pattern that emerged with comprehension questions consisted of the following sequence: comprehension question → paraphrase of definition or description → corrections and addition of detail (if necessary) →

new question (often an integration question building on the preceding definition or description and asked by either the same questioner or another group member). Figure 4.2 shows this typical comprehension discourse pattern.

Following is an excerpt of a typical comprehension discourse pattern. This dialogue was excerpted from the recorded interaction of a pair of fifth graders discussing a lesson on zonation in tide pools (King & Rosenshine, 1993). Those students had received prior training in how to use the content-free question starters to prompt and guide their discussion.

JANELLE: In your own words describe what the word camouflage means.
KATIE: Camouflage means that an animal makes its skin or fur the same color as its surroundings.
JANELLE: So predators can't see it so easy.
KATIE: Yeah! Why is an animal that has camouflage better off than an animal without camouflage?

COMPREHENSION DISCOURSE PATTERN
prompted and guided by the content-free comprehension questions student pairs are trained in

comprehension question --> comprehension statement (paraphrased definition or description showing comprehension) --> corrections and addition of detail (when necessary) --> new question

asks for a process or term from the text or teacher presentation to be described or defined in students own words-- to check comprehension

provides a paraphrased definition, description, and other material paraphrased in students' own words

TYPICAL KNOWLEDGE CONSTRUCTION DISCOURSE PATTERN
prompted and guided by the content-free integration questions student pairs are trained in

integration question --> statement showing construction of new knowledge --> new (usually related) integration question

goes beyond what was explicitly stated in text or teacher lesson, connects two ideas together, or asks for an explanation, inference, justification, etc.

makes new connections or goes beyond what was provided in the text or teacher presentation ; explanations, inferences, relationships between ideas, justifications, statements linking lesson content to material from outside the text or teacher presentation (prior knowledge and personal experience)

EXTENDED KNOWLEDGE CONSTRUCTION DISCOURSE PATTERN
prompted and guided by the content-free integration questions student pairs were trained in

integration question --> statement showing construction of new knowledge --> supplemental knowledge construction statement --> supplemental knowledge construction statement --> supplemental knowledge construction statement --> new (usually related) integration question

goes beyond what was explicitly stated in text or teacher lesson, connects two ideas together, or asks for an explanation, inference, justification, etc.

makes new connections or goes beyond what was provided in the text or teacher presentation -- explanations, inferences, relationships between ideas, justifications,-- statements linking lesson content to material from outside the text or teacher presentation (prior knowledge and personal experience)

FIG. 4.2. Comprehension and knowledge construction discourse patterns: increasing complexity of questions results in increased complexity of discourse.

Analysis of this discourse sequence suggests that Janelle's question prompted Katie to remember the definition of camouflage presented in class and then paraphrase it to demonstrate her understanding of the term. Katie's response appears to be accurate and stated in her own words. However, Janelle apparently feels that it is incomplete or needs some clarification or elaboration, so she adds a rationale for camouflage. Thus, the two girls together are collaboratively reconstructing (coreconstructing?) the definition of the term as presented in class. Mediating each other's understanding of camouflage in this fashion results in a more complete definition than either girl would likely have arrived at on her own.

Knowledge Construction Discourse

The open-ended integration (connection) questions require high-level cognitive activity of both questioner and responder. To generate these questions, the questioner must think about how ideas relate to each other and the responder must go beyond what is explicitly stated by connecting two or more ideas together, or providing explanation, inference, speculation, or justification. Analysis of peer interaction in two studies (King, 1994b; King & Rosenshine, 1993) revealed that these integration questions elicited highly elaborated responses that corresponded to the type of question posed. For example, when a content-free integration question of the comparison–contrast form such as "Compare and contrast . . . to . . ." was used by upper elementary grade students to generate their own content-specific integration question such as "Compare and contrast tide pools to inland pools," and that specific question was posed by a student to a learning partner, the integration question elicited a highly elaborated comparison based on the material being studied. Typically, such a response was followed by another question. Thus, the discourse consisted of the following sequence: thought-provoking integration question → statement connecting two or more ideas or an elaborated explanation → new question. Such typical discourse was designated as a knowledge construction discourse pattern because it showed evidence of new knowledge being constructed in the course of the partners' interaction.

The following example, taken from the same transcript of Katie and Janelle, illustrates such a knowledge construction discourse pattern.

JANELLE: What do you think would happen if there weren't certain zones for certain animals in the tide pools?

KATIE: They would all be, like, mixed up—and all the predators would kill all the animals that shouldn't be there and then they just wouldn't survive. 'Cause the food chain wouldn't work—'cause the top of the chain would eat all the others and there would be no place for the bottom ones to hide and be protected. And nothing left for them to eat.

JANELLE: O.K. But what about the ones that had camouflage to hide them?

Examination of this Janelle–Katie dialogue segment reveals that Janelle began by asking Katie to speculate about what it would be like if there were no zonal distinctions in a tide pool. This was a high-level integrative question that asked Katie to go beyond what they learned in class about the different zones. In posing her question, Janelle was asking Katie to analyze what they already knew about the features of the several tide pool zones and the characteristics of the different animals that inhabit specific zones. She was also seeking help to construct new knowledge about the relations between the characteristics of zones and the characteristics of their inhabitants. Clearly, Janelle had already begun on her own to think about those relations. In fact, she could not have generated the question without having begun to consider how a particular zone in a tide pool affects the animal life living in it. However, in verbalizing her question, she drew Katie too into thinking about possible connections. According to Katie's analysis, the animals' characteristics would remain the same, but with the zone distinctions removed, inhabitants would be more vulnerable to predators; they would all eat each other and the food chain would collapse. In her analysis, not only was Katie apparently building new understandings about the importance of the distinctions among the zones in a tide pool, she was also gaining experience in the skills of reasoning through a new situation and communicating to others the product of her reasoning. Katie's response was clearly a thoughtful, elaborated one. Thus, in asking her initial question, Janelle was mediating Katie's learning (as well as her own). It is unlikely that either girl alone would have speculated about such a situation; and if they had, it is doubtful that they would have actually analyzed the hypothetical situation to arrive at such a plausible scenario.

When Janelle asked her follow-up question "But what about the ones that had camouflage to hide them?" the question appears to have raised a conceptual discrepancy between the two girls' perspectives on what would happen. Janelle's question implied that camouflaged animals may pose an exception to Katie's claim that "there would be no place for the bottom ones to hide." During social construction of knowledge, challenging each other's perspectives on an issue or offering another point of view induces sociocognitive conflict (Mugny & Doise, 1978), which often leads to subsequent resolution through discussion. Thus, Janelle's question furthered the mediational process by challenging Katie (and herself) to think about a possible exception within their scenario. This conceptual discrepancy begs to be resolved through further peer discussion. In negotiating understanding and coconstructing meaning through this sort of high-level discourse, Janelle and Katie were mediating each others' learning (Cobb, 1988; Noddings, 1989; Tudge, 1990b).

Extended Knowledge Construction Discourse Pattern

In a significant number of instances of knowledge construction interaction in the two studies (King, 1994b; King & Rosenshine, 1993), after the initial question had elicited a response, that response in turn prompted further elaboration from others in the pair or triad, including the questioner. Those multiple responses built onto each other to propel the discussion forward. These extended discourse sequences typically consisted of the following patterns: thought-provoking integration question → statement connecting two or more ideas or an elaborated explanation → addition of other newly constructed knowledge (often multiple contributions) to extend the discussion (occasionally including a statement such as an inference or generalization that served to "conclude" the issue or point raised by the question) → new question (usually prompted by discussion just generated and extending that discussion). This discourse pattern was called *extended knowledge construction discourse pattern*. Figure 4.2 compares this extended knowledge construction discourse pattern with the typical knowledge construction discourse pattern discussed previously.

Following is a representative discussion from an earlier part of the same transcript showing an example of the extended knowledge construction discourse pattern:

KATIE: How are the upper tide zone and the lower tide zone different?
JANELLE: They have different animals in them. Animals in the upper tide zone and
          splash zone can handle being exposed—have to be able to use the rain
          and sand and wind and sun—and they don't need that much water and
          the lower tide zone animals do.
KATIE: And they can be softer 'cause they don't have to get hit on the rocks.
JANELLE: Also predators. In the spray zone it's because there's predators like us peo-
          ple and all different kinds of stuff that can kill the animals and they won't
          survive, but the lower tide zone has not as many predators.
KATIE: But wait! Why do the animals in the splash zone have to survive?

In this dialogue segment, Katie's initial question asked Janelle to compare two specific tide zones. Katie's question is considered an integration question in this case (rather than a simple recall question) because, whereas the features of the different zones were covered during the lesson, the differences between them were not explicitly pointed out. Therefore, Katie's question asked for her and Jannelle to integrate what they already knew (the characteristics of two specific zones) and compare those characteristics to identify differences, that is, to develop new knowledge on their own by extension from their existing knowledge. Again, as with Janelle in the previous discussion, Katie must have already begun to think about this issue of how the zones differ just to have been able to pose the question. In asking Janelle to think about this issue, Katie was guiding Janelle's thinking, and this is an indication of Katie mediating Janelle's learning about tide pools. In her response, Janelle thought her way through a comparison of the animals in the two zones, thus extending her own (and probably Katie's) understanding of tide pools. Janelle's initial response focused on how the animals inhabiting the zones differ from each other and she only implied that the water levels differ too. The girls' responses played off of each other as they each contributed material to elaborate the comparison. They continued to mediate each others' learning with Katie's follow-up question on the issue of survival (brought up by Janelle in her last contribution). Katie's question "But wait! Why do the animals in the splash zone have to survive?" challenged Janelle's (apparent) assumption that survival is desirable. According to theories of the social construction of knowledge (e.g., Cobb, 1988; Mugny & Doise, 1978; Perret-Clermont, 1980; Vygotsky, 1978), such challenges to one's perspective on an issue serve to mediate learning by inducing sociocognitive conflict and its possible resolution through subsequent discussion. As before, it is unlikely that either girl alone would have considered these matters and developed on her own the extended understandings that resulted from such peer mediation.

The typical discourse patterns initiated by integration questions and comprehension questions were knowledge construction discourse patterns and comprehension discourse patterns, respectively. Results of two studies (King, 1994b; King & Rosenshine, 1993) showed that these discourse patterns mediated science learning for fourth and fifth graders.

Although these discourse patterns may appear similar to the initiation–response–evaluation discourse pattern commonly seen in classroom discussion (Mehan, 1979), there are important differences in both content and process. For example, the typical initiation–response–evaluation discourse pattern is teacher led. The teacher initiates by asking a question, the student responds by answering the question, then the teacher evaluates that response, and the sequence is repeated (Mehan, 1979). Also, those teacher questions are often low-level ones (Dillon, 1988; Graesser, 1992); and responses usually consist of retelling (reproducing) information already learned and can be readily evaluated as right or wrong. In contrast, the discourse patterns illustrated here (as shown in the Janelle–Katie dialogues) are initiated by student-generated questions. In the case of the knowledge construction discourse patterns, those student-generated questions are high-level, integrative, thought-provoking ones. Further, those questions generally elicit thoughtful, elaborated student responses that are characterized by integration of ideas into newly constructed knowledge. These responses are often followed by a related follow-up question. Thus, during such peer dialogue, new knowledge is socially constructed (Bearison, 1982; Damon, 1983; Perret-Clermont, 1980; Vygotsky, 1978).

Students occasionally posed factual recall questions although they had not been trained in asking such questions. When a factual question was asked (e.g., "What are the three colors of marine algae?") it was followed by a response consisting of simple restatement of factual information recalled from memory (e.g., "Green, brown, and red"), generally with no further elaboration from the group (King, 1994b; King & Rosenshine, 1993). This response was in sharp contrast to the kind of discourse elicited by an integration or comprehension question. Most of the questions asked by the untrained control group students in those two studies were factual questions; those students were not taught any questioning skills but were told to ask and answer each other's questions (King, 1994b; King & Rosenshine, 1993).

Effectiveness of Knowledge Construction Discourse Patterns

In both of these Guided Peer Questioning studies (King 1994b; King & Rosenshine, 1993), when a factual question was asked, it was generally followed by a simple restatement of factual material. When a comprehension question was asked, it was followed by paraphrase of recalled material. Integration questions elicited a thoughtful, elaborated response (often several) showing that new knowledge had been constructed, either by integrating several previously encoded ideas or in some other way extending the knowledge beyond what had been originally presented. Our observations revealed that these discourse patterns were dictated by the format of the actual questions posed, and those questions elicited responses that corresponded in form to the questions asked (King 1994b; King & Rosenshine, 1993). In the case of the comprehension and integration discourse patterns, those student self-generated questions were themselves controlled by the format of the provided content-free questions. Those questions were used to prompt generation of content-specific questions, which in turn elicited responses that corresponded to the questions asked in terms of the type of thinking required and indications of either comprehension of knowledge or construction of new knowledge.

It should be noted that significant differences exist between Guided Peer Questioning on the one hand and Scripted Cooperation and Reciprocal Teaching on the other in terms of controlling peer interaction. First, Guided Peer Questioning promotes learning that goes far beyond fact learning and encoding of material explicitly presented. It provides a context and skills for mediating the social construction of new knowledge. Second, the guided questioning–responding process itself has a great deal of flexibility built into it, and the procedure almost guarantees flexible use. Although the group interaction is structured at a fundamental level, through the forms of the question starters, guided questioning was designed to provide freedom within structure. For example, students are not required to ask any particular question; rather, they choose which question starter to use. Research shows that freedom to choose which questions to use in generating questions is a significant factor in the effectiveness of Guided Peer Questioning (see King, 1994c, for a comparison of Guided Peer Questioning with and without choice of question starters). Furthermore, although students learn and practice the questioning skills and responding skills in a structured way at first, they soon become very flexible in generating questions on an as-needed basis—rather than in a routinized way.

Students' freedom to choose which questions to use in guiding their generation of specific questions is only one aspect of the flexibility inherent in Guided Peer Questioning. Once students, even as young as fourth graders, understand how thought-provoking integration and comprehension questions differ from fact questions, and once they have learned the structure for generating their own questions, they need very little encouragement to adapt the process for flexible use. We found that they frequently adapt the given form of a question to fit the context without losing the question's thought-provoking quality (King 1994b; King & Rosenshine, 1993).

A DISCOURSE PATTERN FOR PEER MEDIATION OF PROBLEM SOLVING[2]

An inquiry-based procedure for peer mediation of problem solving has also been developed (King, 1991). This procedure is based on a sequence of *strategic questions* that learners use to guide their cognitive and metacognitive activity and interaction during problem solving. These strategic questions were designed specifically to be compatible with a problem-solving process in order to help problem solvers be strategic (intentional and planful—rather than resorting to methods of trial and error and chance) during their problem solving.

The strategic questions are of three types: planning questions, monitoring questions, and evaluation questions. Figure 4.3 shows the full set of strategic questions used in one research study (King, 1991). During problem solving, learners in small groups or pairs engage in asking and answering these questions with each other to prompt their partners and themselves to plan, monitor, and assess their problem-solving process and problem solution in an ongoing strategic manner. The questions are made available to learners on handheld prompt cards. The format of the particular questions and the sequence of questions is deliberately structured to guide students through the stages of problem solving and help them to monitor their progress toward a solution. To this end, the strategic questions are constructed and arranged to follow the stages of the problem-solving process (e.g., problem identification and representation, search for a solution path, implementation of a solution, and evaluation [Gick, 1986]), and they include such questions as "What is our plan?" "What do we know about the problem so far?" "What strategy are we using?" and "Do we need a different strategy?"

These general strategic questions were also designed to prompt meaningful cognitive and metacognitive activity at the various stages of problem solving. For example, asking and answering these questions was expected to help students clarify the problem, think about the problem in new ways, access their existing knowledge and strategies, and formulate and provide explanations to their partners.

---

[2]Some material in this section has been adapted from King, A. (1991), "Effects of training on strategic questioning on children's problem solving success. *Journal of Educational Psychology, 83,* 307–317. Adapted with permission from the American Psychological Association.

PLANNING

1.   What is the problem?
     What are we trying to do here?
2.   What do we know about the problem so far?
     What information is given to us?
     How can this help us?
3.   What is our plan?
4.   Is there another way to do this?
     What would happen if...?
5.   What should we do next?

MONITORING

1.   Are we using our plan or strategy?
     Do we need a new plan?
     Do we need a different strategy?
2.   Has our goal changed?
     What is our goal now?
3.   Are we on the right track?
     Are we getting closer to our goal?

EVALUATING

1.   What worked?
2.   What didn't work?
3.   What would we do differently next time?

FIG. 4.3.   Strategic questions for guiding problem solving.
King, 1991, reprinted by permission.

To identify or define the problem, one member of a group or pair might select the question "What are we trying to do here?" It was expected that in answering this question together, the students would determine the nature of the problem more precisely. A question such as "What information is given to us?" would help students access their prior knowledge, whereas the question "Is there another way to do this?" would foster greater access to known strategies. To generate new ideas and unique perspectives, they might ask "What would happen if . . . ?" or "What should we do next?" To monitor their progress at any point they might ask "Are we getting closer to our goal?" In addition to asking and answering these specific questions, students are encouraged to ask other sorts of thought-provoking questions to elicit further elaboration. Engaging in this questioning–answering discourse pattern during problem solving allows students to share information and perspectives, negotiate understanding, and truly coconstruct their problem-solving plans, strategies, solution paths, and the like. Such questioning also promotes students' self-monitoring and regulation of their problem solving.

Student Problem-Solving Discourse Patterns

The sequence of strategic questions provided to the students in one study (King, 1991) structured their interaction in predictable ways during problem solving. Clearly discernible discourse patterns emerged from analysis of that interaction. In general, when students asked strategic questions, the responses elicited were of three different kinds: thoughtful elaborated responses (explanations, justifications, information, and methods needed for solving the problem), related elaboration questions, and nonelaborated statements. In that study (King, 1991), the strategic questions were often posed as more specific versions of the provided questions (e.g., "Can we get the diagonal stripe in another way?" in place of "Is there another way to do this?") or as a more personalized variation of the provided question (e.g., "What are we gonna do now?" for "Do we need a different strategy?"). A typical problem-solving discourse pattern was initiated by a strategic question that elicited one or more thoughtful, elaborated strategy-oriented or solution-oriented responses and one or more elaboration questions, which in turn elicited more elaborated responses as well as nonelaborated responses. This typical discourse sequence is portrayed in Fig. 4.4.

Responses were considered thoughtful, elaborated ones if they were solution- or strategy-oriented. Such responses include explanations of a concept or process, clarification of an idea, analysis of a situation (e.g., "No, that's not what they have. They have a stripe, probably thin, then they have a punch, some squares—two—then they have a rotate—135, probably 135, then it has a rotate again ..."), elaborated descriptions of how to do something (e.g., "Let's turn the square and punch, we're sorta right on the rotate because 135 did it, so let's try 135"), a rationale for using a particular strategy or plan (e.g., "See how we wanted this at 45—45 is going this way, so if we can go this way, these two will end here"), a justification for trying a particular approach, or a reason why an attempt was successful or unsuccessful (e.g., "If it would have turned and rotated like this it would have worked"). Nonelaborated statements included giving directions, the correct answer, or other information without any explanation or elaboration (e.g., "Punch two squares" or "This will make it").

Elaboration questions are thought-provoking questions that ask for further specific elaboration, clarification, or specific elaborated help in the form of an explanation or reason (e.g., "What happened to the three circles?"), or for detailed directions for how to execute a specific previously planned move (e.g., How can we turn it?"). Students' elaboration questions frequently consisted

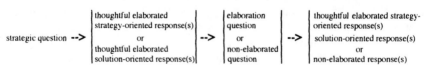

| strategic question --> | thoughtful elaborated strategy-oriented response(s)
or
thoughtful elaborated solution-oriented response(s) | --> | elaboration question
or
non-elaborated question | --> | thoughtful elaborated strategy-oriented response(s)
solution-oriented response(s)
or
non-elaborated response(s) |

FIG. 4.4.   Problem-solving discourse patterns.

simply of "Why?" or "How come?" The comprehension questions and some of the integration questions used in the knowledge construction discourse patterns (discussed in the previous section) are also considered elaboration questions. In contrast, nonelaboration questions were those that asked for "the right answer," simple information, or some other nonelaborated response (e.g., "How many stripes do we make?").

Examples of Problem-Solving Discourse Patterns

Several segments of strategic problem-solving dialogue from the interaction between pairs of fifth graders are shown below (King, 1991). These segments are representative of the discourse of the students trained to use strategic questioning, and they illustrate the role that those questions play in the problem-solving process. All dialogue is taken from transcripts of the final problem-solving session. During that session, students worked in pairs at computers to solve a problem of replicating a given complex design on the computer screen using "The Factory," a program designed to promote problem solving. During this session, students were neither prompted to use their questioning strategies nor were their prompt cards listing the questions in Fig. 4.3 provided to them.

In "The Factory," students create "products" on a simulated assembly line that they design from as many as eight machines that either rotate, stripe, or hole-punch a square of "raw material." Students were told they were to design a sequence of machines that would, when used in sequence, turn the raw material into a product that replicates the given pictured design (selected from the manual accompanying "The Factory" and representative of the highest difficulty level of that program). One machine rotates the square 45°, 90°, 135°, or 180°; a second machine punches one, two, or three holes (square or round) through it; and a third machine places thin, medium, or thick stripes on it.

> MARK: Okay. What are we trying to do?
> CRAIG: First of all, we're gonna try and solve this problem. No more than 8 machines.
> MARK: We have to make it look like this (pointing at the picture of the design). First—what we need to do is rotate.
> CRAIG: Why? No—no—not rotate—'cause it's like this (pointing at the pictured design)—so this is how it starts out—we'll just make a stripe—Okay?
> MARK: Yeah—stripe—medium.

In this beginning part of their interaction, Mark's strategic question "What are we trying to do?" prompts Mark and Craig to check that they understand and agree on what the problem is and what its parameters are. Asking and answering a problem-identification question in this manner is an important first step in the planning phase (or problem-representation phase) of problem solving. In answering this question, they identify that the problem is to make their product look like the pictured design using "no more than 8 machines." Mark goes on to say what action needs to be taken first, that is, he begins a plan. However, Craig disagrees and a sociocognitive conflict arises in the form of a discrepancy between their suggestions of how to begin. This discrepancy is precipitated by Craig's elaboration question "Why?" (which he himself goes on to answer). This conflict is apparently resolved when Craig provides an explanation for why he wants to make a stripe first—to make it look like the pictured design. Thus, together their response to Mark's initial strategic question is a solution-oriented first step.

Shortly thereafter, Craig asks another strategic question, "What are we gonna do now?" to generate new ideas—directions, plans, strategies. This particular strategic question prompts them to consider what direction (plan) they should pursue now or what new approach (strategy) they should use.

CRAIG: **What are we gonna do now?**
MARK: Yeah. You got to put three. No, wait—see—look—look—three—
CRAIG: **Why?**
MARK: 'Cuz look—I'll show ya why. I'll show ya—because we already put that there and it is going (inaudible) in there—and nothing is going to happen because we have to get over there—so it's 3. Just do 3—I bet you it will.
CRAIG: No. 'cuz there's 2 square holes already—then we'll have 4—too many
MARK: Good going. Rotate 45.
CRAIG: It's already 45. **What are we trying to do?**
MARK: We're trying to figure out if our hypothesis was correct.
CRAIG: But it's not right.
MARK: I forgot the other 45° angle—I know I forgot it—see look—I know I forgot the 45. **What now?** I need a pencil (picks up pencil to sketch sequence of moves).
CRAIG: Well I don't think you should write it—I'm gonna push return to see if it (their factory) works.
MARK: No! Wait—I know I forgot the 45. Watch. Watch. One punch—rotate 45— goes to the next—circle punches—goes to—. **What did you do that for?** Two circle punches. **Why did you do 2 circle punches in a row?**
CRAIG: I think I put too many things. It's just the opposite of what we wanted. I should have put this here and that there. Hold on—hold on—.
MARK: **Are we going to have to start all over?** Darn it! We have to start all over.

Mark's response to Craig's initial strategic question was apparently insufficient for Craig because he asked an elaboration question ("Why?"). Mark gives an elaborated response—an attempted explanation, which is matched by an elaborated explanation from Craig. After more turns of talk consisting of nonelaborated responses, Craig asks another strategic question "What are we trying to do?" to get them back on track in terms of a plan. Although Mark's answer about their hypothesis in not specific (and therefore probably not very helpful), he goes on to ask a strategic question, "What now?" In answering this question himself by saying "I need a pencil," Mark shows that he is selecting a different problem-solving strategy, namely, using a pencil to sketch out the sequence of machine moves (a graphic representation of the solution). A conflict arises when Craig says he does not think Mark should use a pencil—perhaps implying that doing so may not conform to the problem parameters—and goes on to suggest his own alternative strategy of checking to see the sequence of machines as represented on the computer screen to determine if their factory will work. In doing so, Craig is trying to get the same information as Mark would get by sketching with a pencil, but Craig's strategy would be clearly "allowed" within the problem boundaries as they had defined them at the beginning. As they analyze the diagram on the screen, Mark asks two elaboration questions ("What did you do that for?" and "Why did you do 2 circle punches in a row?") that help them identify their errors and lead them to evaluate their problem solving by figuring out what they could have done differently. Evaluating their progress in this way is another important part of the problem-solving process. Finally, by asking the strategic question, "Are we going to have to start all over?" Mark is monitoring their plan and strategy—their problem-solving process.

Effectiveness of the Problem-Solving Discourse Pattern

The effectiveness of training in this discourse pattern was assessed in a study with fifth graders in a school problem-solving context (King, 1991). Students who were trained in asking and answering the strategic questions were more successful at problem solving than unguided questioners and control students. Problem-solving success was measured by both a written test of problem-solving ability and solving a novel problem. In addition to outperforming their untrained peers in problem solving on that test and the novel problem, the trained students also asked more strategic questions and gave more explanations to each other during actual problem solving than did their peers. Analysis of transcripts of peer interaction revealed that those explanations were actually prompted by the strategic questions and by related thought-provoking questions asked by the trained questioners. Thus, results of that study indicated that using strategic questioning to guide problem solving prompts patterns of discourse that, in turn, promote problem-solving success.

Why are Discourse Patterns Prompted by Strategic Questions Effective?

Training in the guided questioning discourse pattern teaches students how to ask for and get explanations, justifications, information, methods, and other elaboration useful for solving a problem. That is, strategic questioning promotes problem-solving success by controlling the content of the interaction between partners; in particular, by inducing task-appropriate, effective questioning and responding discourse.

Asking strategic questions is intended to prompt students to activate their existing knowledge regarding problem solving, analyze components of a problem, reconceptualize the problem, evaluate alternatives, and access strategies already in their knowledge base. To answer the strategic questions, students generate elaborations (explanations, applications, details, relations, and consequences) about the problem, which in turn lead to success in solving the problem.

Furthermore, asking and answering strategic questions with their partners during problem solving is expected to promote the emergence and resolution of sociocognitive conflict (Mugny & Doise, 1978). The strategic questions are intended to uncover any differences between students' prior knowledge structures and current mental representations of the problem; then, through explaining and defending their views to their partners, those conflicts can be resolved. Those strategic questions were designed specifically for the purpose of inducing individuals to explain their ideas, reasoning, goals, solution strategies, and the like to their partners. As pointed out previously, during that explaining process, the explainers elaborate and reorganize their own conceptual structures to some extent (see Bargh & Schul, 1980). Also, in order to coordinate their problem-solving plans and activity with their partners (i.e., to decide on a single course of action), individuals must further modify their own mental representations of the problem and its various solution paths and bring them into accord with those of their partners (Cobb, 1988). By requiring students to explain and justify their thinking to their partners, guided strategic question asking and answering encourages this sort of reconceptualizing on the part of students. In the King (1991) study, guided questioners gave substantially more explanations to each other than did the unguided questioners and controls, suggesting that answering the problem-solving questions posed by their partners may have induced some degree of change in students' thinking about the problem; particularly the kinds of reconceptualizations indicated previously.

In that study, the social context of guided strategic questioning also provided opportunity for modeling of effective cognitive and metacognitive behavior. First, the question asking and answering was modeled by the teacher during initial instruction; furthermore, ongoing modeling of these problem-solving processes occurred as partners interacted with each other during problem solving. For example, when partners described their reasoning and generally engaged in thinking out loud during problem solving, their externalized thinking provided effective models of the basic mental processes involved in being strategic during problem solving, and their partners were provided the opportunity to model their own strategic thinking on that of their peers.

Thus, in general, this strategic questioning discourse pattern appears to promote problem-solving success by teaching students how to be strategic problem solvers, that is, how to engage in appropriate and effective discourse during problem solving; specifically, how to ask for and get useful information, plans, and strategies for solving the problem.

A DISCOURSE PATTERN FOR PEER TUTORING

Recently, a procedure for mediating peer learning in a reciprocal tutoring context was also developed (King, 1994a, 1997). This peer tutoring model is called ASK to THINK—TEL WHY®©.[3] This guided peer tutoring model addresses both cognitive and metacognitive aspects of learning. The procedure utilizes five different types of questions that tutoring partners sequence to scaffold learning from comprehension checking and consolidation of prior knowledge to building of new knowledge and monitoring thinking.

Coaching Learning in a Guided Peer Tutoring Model

The ASK to THINK—TEL WHY®© tutoring model includes a question-asking component based on the knowledge construction pattern of discourse (discussed earlier), but extends and modifies that pattern to more closely emulate a Vygotskian process of mediating learning (Vygotsky, 1978). The model emphasizes intentional mediation of peer learning through the use of reciprocal tutoring roles, supportive communication skills, question-asking skills and skills of sequencing those questions, as well as elaboration skills and specific skills in explanation giving.

In ASK to THINK—TEL WHY®©, the roles of tutor and tutee embody clearly differentiated discourse modes. When in the tutor role, tutors only ask questions and do not explain or give answers in any other way. They ASK to THINK®©. When they are in the tutee role, students explain but do not ask questions. They tell why. This clear differentiation between the roles is intended to make it easier for tutors to focus on asking questions rather than lecturing or talking at the tutee. Staying in the questioning mode is more likely to elicit explanations and other elaboration from the tutee (the kinds of verbalization known to promote learning for the tutee). To emphasize this role-based distinction in voice, the partner in the tutor role is called the *questioner* and the tutee is the *explainer*.

The focus of the tutor role in this peer tutoring model is on the use of guided inquiry with five types of questions: review questions, thinking questions, probing questions, hint questions, and metacognitive questions. Students in the tutor role use these questions to prompt their partners to make corresponding responses. An emphasis of this model is on the tutor's sequencing of the questions asked, beginning with review questions, proceeding to more sophisticated thoughtful questions, and asking hint questions and probing questions as needed. When appropriate, tutors also ask metacognitive questions to monitor the thinking and learning process. The sequence is designed to generally follow

---

[3]"ASK to THINK—TEL WHY" and "ASK to THINK" are registered trademarks and the tutoring procedure itself is copyrighted by Alison King, 1991 and 1994. Neither the names "ASK to THINK—TEL WHY" or "ASK to THINK" nor the particular tutorial procedure known by that name and described herein may be used for any commercial, research, or training purpose whatsoever without prior written permission from Alison King.

three phases: assessment and consolidation of prior knowledge, construction of new knowledge, and monitoring of thinking processes. Thus, in this model, the tutor serves as a coach to scaffold the joint knowledge construction activity to progressively higher levels.

Assessment and Consolidation of Prior Knowledge. Tutors ask review questions (e.g., "What does . . . mean?" and "Describe . . . in your own words.") to prompt the partner to restate what can be recalled about the material. Those review questions elicit definitions, descriptions, explanations, and the like from the tutee. Review questioning and answering helps partners review and consolidate the material that was presented to them in a teacher's lesson or the text. These questions also serve as a way of checking to see how well partners understand the material. By asking and answering review questions at the beginning of the discussion, partners engage in assessment and consolidation of prior knowledge and establish a common knowledge base on which to build. Then, through asking and answering thinking questions (and hint and probing questions as needed), they can proceed to construct new knowledge onto that base. If an answer to a review question is incomplete, the tutor asks probing questions or hint questions to help the tutee fill in gaps in knowledge, correct misunderstandings, and clarify material. Probing questions (e.g., "I don't understand. What do you mean by that?" and "Tell me more about . . . ") ask the tutee to expand on an idea, clarify a point, be more explicit, or in some other way elaborate. Hint questions provide clues or partially framed answers in the form of a question (e.g., "Have you thought about . . . ?" and "How can . . . help you?"). Tutors ask hint questions when tutee responses are incorrect or partial.

Construction of New Knowledge and Monitoring of Thinking. Thinking questions ask tutees to go beyond the material as explicitly presented to make connections among ideas, note relationships within that material (e.g., comparison–contrast, cause–effect), or make links between the new material and their own prior knowledge and experience—that is, to construct new knowledge. Such questions include "What is the difference between . . . and . . . ?" "What are the strengths and weakness of . . . ?" and "What do you think would happen to . . . if . . . ?" (These are the connection questions from the Guided Peer Questioning strategy discussed in a previous section). Thinking questions are more effective at this stage of the tutorial process because partners have established a solid knowledge foundation on which to build due to the effects of the previous review questioning. Asking and answering thinking questions and hint and probing questions induces the learners to build new knowledge through their explanations and elaboration and connect that new knowledge to existing (now activated) knowledge.

Monitoring (metacognitive) questions are called *thinking-about-thinking* questions; examples include "What led you to that belief?" and "Describe how you arrived at that answer." These questions are used throughout the knowledge-construction process and are asked to help the tutee "unpack" the thinking involved in a previous answer. Thinking-about-thinking questions function as a way for the tutor to monitor the thinking process of the tutee; and, as importantly, they serve as a form of self-monitoring of thinking for the tutee.

To help them remember the five kinds of questions and the sequence in which to use them, students are provided with handheld prompt cards showing several question starters in each of the five categories of question types along with a reminder of the sequence. Students as young as fourth grade have successfully used this questioning process and the question labels embodied in the acronym (King, Burton, Galloway & Verdusco, 1996).

Pattern of Questioning–Answering Interchange. The typical sequence of a question–answer interchange between tutor and tutee who are using the ASK to THINK—TEL WHY®© peer tutoring model is shown (adapted from King, 1998a). This particular interchange shows 10 *moves*—a move is defined as a tutor question or a tutee answer. However, depending on the quality of responses, a typical question–answer interchange may have as few as six such moves because when answers are well developed on the initial try, hint and probing questions may not be required.

Questioner asks **review question**
Explainer gives **response** that shows comprehension of the point questioned
Questioner asks **thinking question** building on explainer's response to review question
Explainer gives **response** that is not complete
Questioner asks **probing question**
Explainer gives **explanation** or other response that is still **not adequately elaborated**
Questioner asks **hint question**
Explainer gives **adequately elaborated plausible explanation** or other response
Questioner asks **thinking-about-thinking question**
Explainer gives **response** indicating thinking about the thinking involved in previous response

The tutor's role also includes use of supportive communication skills: listening attentively (using eye contact, nodding, saying *Uh-huh*), providing "thinking time" (waiting at least 5 seconds in silence after asking a question, cf. Rowe's, 1986, "wait time"), giving feedback on accuracy and completeness of an answer (e.g., by saying "Well done" if partner's answer is plausible or "No, that's not quite right" if not), and giving encouragement (e.g., by smiling, saying "You're doing great!" or "I know you can do this").

The tutee's role is to TEL WHY®© (the acronym used to remind students of this role). When in this role, students tell—rather than ask. They explain rather than simply describe. They link the ideas within the material to each other and to the world outside the text or lesson. Tutees are trained to do so by telling *why* and *how* as opposed to telling *what* (describing); and by using their own words rather than repeating verbatim what they have heard or read. Being able to paraphrase material into their own words generally demonstrates real understanding as opposed to memorization.

The ASK to THINK—TEL WHY®© model of peer tutoring is highly transactive in nature—characterized by reciprocity, mutuality, and interdependence in the joint construction of knowledge. The use of reciprocal tutor–tutee roles (partners exchange roles) promotes interdependence and mutuality between the tutoring pair. Furthermore, the question-asking and -answering process itself has transactivity built into it: a question asked by one person is dependent on the previous response made by the other; and the other's answer to the question is generally framed by that question and at the same time often dictates, to a great extent, the next question posed. Partners depend on each other for what and how they learn. Thus, scaffolding and guidance are mutual. What they learn and how they learn it is a back-and-forth process—mutually determined. This reciprocity and interdependence of interaction, the mutuality of scaffolding and guidance, creates a *transactive* process where both people participate equally in mutual assistance and mutual learning (King, 1998a). The ASK to THINK—TEL WHY®© model of peer tutoring is described in more detail elsewhere (King, 1997; King et al., 1998).

Peer Tutoring Discourse Pattern of ASK to THINK—TEL WHY®©

The typical discourse pattern used in ASK to THINK—TEL WHY®© peer tutoring (King, 1997) shows the ways in which tutoring partners jointly scaffold their learning to progressively higher levels.

The ASK to THINK—TEL WHY®© discourse pattern is quite different from the naturalistic untrained tutorial dialogue pattern observed by Graesser, Person, and Magliano (1995), although there are some similarities. In their observations of naturally occurring tutorial dialogue, Greasser et al. (1995) identified a five-step dialogue frame that is frequently followed in tutorial interaction. That frame goes beyond the three-part initiation–response–evaluation frame commonly used by classroom teachers (Mehan, 1979). Although the dialogue pattern observed by Graesser et al. (1995) begins with initiation–response–evaluation—tutor asks question, student answers question, tutor gives short feedback—this sequence is followed by tutor improves quality of answer, tutor assesses students' understanding. The ASK to THINK—TEL WHY®© discourse pattern also begins with question asking, question answering, and evaluative feedback; however, rather than the tutors themselves improving the quality of the tutees' answers as observed by Graesser et al., tutors ask questions to prompt the tutees to do this cognitive activity on their own. In ASK to THINK—

TEL WHY®© tutors scaffold tutees' elaboration and extension of answers and their development of relationships, explanations, justifications, inferences—that is, their construction of new knowledge—after which they prompt tutees to assess their own understanding as well as their thinking process. Thus, this tutoring process involves the tutee and tutor jointly in the knowledge-construction process. In contrast, Graesser's observations indicate that in untrained tutoring, the tutor does most of the cognitive work. Generally, ASK to THINK—TEL WHY®© is more transactive than untrained tutoring, has more moves, and is more complex; ASK to THINK—TEL WHY®© uses sophisticated teaching–learning strategies. In contrast, Graesser et al. (1995) found untrained tutors rarely used Vygotskian or Socratic approaches.

Example of Peer Tutoring Discourse Pattern

A segment of interaction of a pair of students using the ASK to THINK—TEL WHY®© questioning–answering tutorial model is shown here to illustrate the typical discourse pattern of this model. It is followed by an analysis of that interaction in terms of the tutor and tutee roles and other aspects of the tutoring model.

JAMIE: Okay. Summarize involuntary muscles in your own words. (*review question*)

KEISHA: Involuntary is where they are automatic. They just work automatically. You don't have to even think about it. Like the blinking of your eyes. And your heart pumping and relaxing. You don't have to tell your stomach to digest your food. It just does it on its own. It's just like you don't have to think about it. (*comprehension statement*)

JAMIE: Is there anything else? Like is there anything else I need to know about an involuntary muscle? (*probing question*)

KEISHA: Um, no.

JAMIE: Okay. Just that they work automatically. (*feedback on accuracy of response*) Well then, describe voluntary muscles in your own words. (*review question*)

KEISHA: Voluntary muscles, um, you need to think about it consciously—messages get sent to the brain and the nerves make it move—like it's not automatic to walk—your brain is sending the messages to do it. (*statement showing comprehension*)

JAMIE: Good. (*feedback*) Can you give an example of what you mean, like what do you mean they give your brain messages and your brain gives a signal down to your nerves or . . . ? (*probing question*)

KEISHA: Like, let's say you're playing a game of baseball when the ball's coming just to the bat—well, your brain sends a message to your hands and your arms for you to swing the bat. (*statement showing integration of concepts by use of example*)

JAMIE: Okay. (*feedback*) Well—What is the difference between voluntary muscles and involuntary muscles? (*thinking question*)

KEISHA: Voluntary muscles you have to think consciously about it to get it to work and involuntary muscles, they're automatic. They function without you thinking about it. Like the blinking of your eyes randomly. You just do it you know. (*statement showing integration of concepts by linking differing aspects*)

JAMIE: And is there anything else I need to know about the two? (*probing question*)

KEISHA: They're both very different jobs. Without them both I guess you got to (unintelligible) both at the same times.

JAMIE: How are they similar—how are the two kinds of muscles similar? (*thinking question*)

KEISHA: Well, they're both muscles. They both make your body function. There's not really a better one between the both of them. They're both needed. (*statement showing integration of concepts by linking differing aspects—evaluation statement*)

JAMIE: How did you figure that out? (*thinking-about-thinking question*)

KEISHA: Well I pictured them—and then looked at the picture to compare. (*statement showing unpacking of the thinking process*)

JAMIE: Okay, that's good. (*feedback and praise*) Your turn.

Jamie begins the discussion by asking a review question. In asking Keisha to "Summarize involuntary muscles in your own words," Jamie is prompting Keisha to review the lesson. She is also assessing how well Keisha understands the term *involuntary muscles*. Keisha's response shows that she understands the term well. Nevertheless, Jamie probes to see if there is more to tell by asking a probing question. "Is there anything else? Like is there anything else I need to know about an involuntary muscle?" After no further elaboration from Keisha, Jamie gives feedback on the accuracy of Keisha's answer and asks a second review question. Although Keisha's answer is accurate (and Jamie gives her feedback to that effect), Jamie follows up with a probing question that asks Keisha to be explicit by giving an example. The response that Keisha makes is a well-elaborated example having to do with hitting a ball with a bat. Her example shows that she can apply her definition of voluntary muscles to an everyday activity.

At this point it appears that Jamie has decided that they have established an agreed-on understanding of what voluntary and involuntary muscles are. With that knowledge base established, Jamie (after providing feedback on the accuracy of Keisha's answer) goes on to ask Keisha to compare the two kinds of muscles so as to identify their differences and later on, their similarities—both are high-level thinking questions. Keisha's initial response shows integration of concepts by linking differing aspects of the two kinds of muscle; and after Jamie probes for more (by asking "And is there anything else I need to know about the two?"), Keisha goes on to develop a more elaborated comparison–contrast between the two kinds of muscle.

When she says "There's not really a better one between the both of them. They're both needed," Keisha shows that she has evaluated the role of the two kinds of muscles and arrived at a judgment about their relative value based on the criteria of function. Evaluation is considered a very high level of cognitive activity (Bloom, 1956). When Jamie asks Keisha to monitor her own thinking process (by asking a metacognitive question, "How did you figure that out?"), Keisha's response shows that she is aware of using a visualization strategy and she is able to articulate about it.

It should be noted that, throughout the students' interaction, Jamie supports Keisha's responding activity by giving feedback (e.g., "Good," "Okay," and "Okay, that's good") and by waiting after she asks a question to allow Keisha some time to think about her response before making it. Although, in the research study that this dialogue is taken from (King et al., 1998), tutoring pairs generally gave feedback and thinking time, they did not use another of their trained supportive communication skills: providing encouragement. Regarding questioning, tutors stayed in the questioning mode almost exclusively; and they asked all of the five kinds of questions with the exception of hint questions. Apparently, asking hint questions in a situation as spontaneous as transactive tutoring is very difficult.

Effectiveness of the Peer Tutoring Discourse Pattern

A guided sequenced-questioning model of peer tutoring, called ASK Your Partner to Think®© (developed previously by King, 1993), is identical to ASK to THINK—TEL WHY®© except that it lacks the thinking-about-thinking type of questions. An experimental study was conducted comparing that guided sequenced-questioning model of tutoring to use of two other models of peer tutoring, a questioning-explanation model and an explanation-only model (King et al., 1998). That study was designed to assess the effectiveness of that guided sequenced-questioning tutoring model and to determine the role of the sequenced-questioning component of the model (King et al., 1998). Performance data from fact and inference tests revealed that seventh-grade students using the sequenced-questioning model outperformed their classmates who used the other two models of tutoring. The sequenced-questioning model of tutoring was found to promote knowledge construction, knowledge retention, and ability to transfer. Analysis of peer interaction data of pair tutoring sessions showed clear differences in patterns of discourse among the three experimental conditions. In all three conditions, the discourse patterns corresponded to the patterns of interaction in which students were trained; and across treatments, the tutoring pairs that demonstrated the highest level of learning also engaged in the highest level of elaborated discussion. We concluded that the sequenced-questioning component of that tutoring model played an important role in its effectiveness.

More recently, a study was conducted to determine what role the metacognitive questions in ASK to THINK—TEL WHY®© might play in a sequenced-questioning tutoring process (King et al., 1996). The ASK to THINK—TEL WHY®© model of tutoring was compared to the ASK Your Partner to THINK®©

model. Fourth graders using the ASK to THINK—TEL WHY®© model performed better than their classmates using ASK Your Partner to THINK®© in ability to construct new knowledge and on level of awareness of their thinking processes involved in doing so. And, 12 weeks later, those same students continued to perform better on knowledge construction related to the material studied and were significantly more aware of the thinking processes they used in constructing that knowledge. Analyses of process data confirmed that those thinking-about-thinking questions made an important contribution to the effectiveness of the tutoring model. We concluded that the ASK to THINK—TEL WHY®© model of peer tutoring was more effective than the same model without metacognitive questions because training in metacognitive questioning improved students' awareness of their thinking processes, which in turn may have enhanced their ability to construct knowledge both during peer tutoring per se and subsequently on written tests.

IMPLICATIONS FOR PRACTICE

The three discourse patterns presented in this chapter can be used by peer learning groups to mediate their own learning within a variety of higher level learning contexts: complex knowledge construction (King, 1989a, 1994b), problem solving (King, 1991), and peer tutoring (King, 1994a, 1997; King et al., 1996; King et al., 1998). Although mediated learning is usually accomplished in a context where a more expert child or adult scaffolds learning for a less able child, this kind of pairing is not often available in today's classrooms (see King, 1997, for a discussion of this point). Rather, most classroom peer learning activity is between peers who are of comparable ability, where neither partner is more knowledgeable in the material being learned. Consequently, such learning tends to be limited to review and remediation of material not yet mastered. Although this kind of learning is useful, it is not higher order complex learning. Higher order complex learning takes place when learners actively construct meaning for themselves from what is presented to them; such complex learning includes analyzing and integrating ideas and solving ill-structured problems. During higher order learning, learners go beyond the factual information presented to generate relationships among those facts, make inferences, generalizations, speculations, comparisons, and the like; that is, to construct new knowledge. In today's schools, there is a real need for this kind of learning. There is also a real need for peer-directed learning approaches that are effective for higher order complex learning and at the same time can be used by those who are truly peers—same ability age mates.

The three peer learning discourse patterns presented in this chapter have been found effective for promoting higher order complex learning. All three approaches are easy to implement in classroom settings and children as young as fourth grade have used them successfully. Each discourse pattern was designed to structure interaction in peer learning contexts so that learning is mediated by the discourse itself. Each pattern promotes interactive cognitive activity as well as those metacognitive processes necessary for monitoring and regulating such activity. These approaches to peer-mediated learning can be implemented in any classroom to facilitate same-ability peers in successfully scaffolding each other's learning.

CHAPTER FIVE

Developing Productive Group Interaction in Middle School Mathematics

NOREEN M. WEBB
University of California, Los Angeles

SYDNEY FARIVAR
California State University, Northridge

The past 20 years have seen a tremendous increase in the use of peer-directed small-group work in schools. Some of the reasons for this upsurge are noted in the introduction to this book and also in Chapter 1 by De Lisi and Golbeck. For our purposes, a main reason for putting students into groups is to give students an opportunity to learn from each other. Students can learn from each other in many ways, for example, by giving and receiving help, by recognizing and resolving contradictions between their own and other students' perspectives, and by internalizing problem-solving processes and strategies that emerge during group work (Bearison, Magzamen, & Filardo, 1986; Brown & Palincsar, 1989; Webb & Palincsar, 1996). This chapter focuses on the mechanism of helping behavior, specifically the exchanging of explanations about the content being learned.

Many researchers have explored the power of giving and receiving explanations in peer-directed small groups (Brown & Palincsar, 1989; King, 1992b; Peterson, Janicki, & Swing, 1981; Saxe, Gearhart, Note, & Paduano, 1993; Slavin, 1987; Webb, 1991; Yackel, Cobb, Wood, Wheatley, & Merkel, 1990). However, when and how exchanging explanations promotes learning is not fully understood, and it is not clear how to promote explanation giving in the classroom. In this chapter, we examine both issues in the context of a semester-long program of peer learning in middle school mathematics classrooms. We explore the link between the behavior of students in small groups and their learning—concentrating on the kinds of explanations that students receive and what students do with those explanations—and the effects of the instructional program on students' behavior.

The following sections (a) briefly review theoretical and empirical literature on the kinds of helping behavior that have been shown to predict achievement in peer-directed small groups, (b) describe the instructional program designed to increase students' ability to help each other, (c) describe the kinds of helping behavior found to predict achievement during the instructional program, (d) present a detailed case study of the evolution of verbal interaction in four groups over the course of the instructional program, and (e) discuss the implications of the findings for classroom practice, research, and theory.

THEORETICAL PERSPECTIVES AND REVIEW OF RESEARCH

As described in Chapters 1 and 2, the theories of Vygotsky and Piaget suggest several mechanisms by which students learn by working with other students in collaborative settings. In Vygotsky's (1981a) view, the mental functioning of the learner develops through a process in which the learner internalizes and transforms the content of social interaction. A key element of Vygotsky's theory is the "zone of proximal development," the difference between what a child can achieve independently and what he or she can accomplish with help from a more experienced and capable person (see Hogan & Tudge, chap. 2, this volume, for a detailed analysis). By participating in social interaction within the zone of proximal development, students learn to internalize the skills they practice (Tudge & Rogoff, 1989). To be able to adjust the interaction so that it is at an appropriate level for the child's zone of proximal development, the more capable person must be able to understanding the child's thinking and communicate in ways that the child understands. The process of enabling a child to carry out a task or solve a problem that the child would not be able perform without assistance is called *scaffolding* (Wood, Bruner, & Ross, 1976). Peers may be advantaged in providing scaffolding because of their understanding of and familiarity with other children's misunderstandings, and their ability to explain concepts in familiar terms (Brown & Palincsar, 1989; Noddings, 1985; Vedder, 1985; Vygotsky, 1981a).

The Piagetian perspective (see De Lisi & Golbeck, chap. 1, this volume) is commonly identified as sociocognitive conflict theory in which cognitive conflict arises when there is a perceived contradiction between the learner's existing understandings and what the learner experiences in the course of interacting with others (Piaget, 1932a). One possible response to this contradiction is that the learner may reexamine and question his or her own ideas and beliefs, seek additional information to reconcile the conflicting viewpoints, and try out new ideas (Forman & Cazden, 1985; Gilly, 1990). De Lisi and Golbeck (chap. 1, this volume) provide a detailed analysis of how equilibration processes may operate to restore cognitive balance or resolve conflict.

The mechanisms by which sociocognitive conflict (Piaget) and internalization of social processes (Vygotsky) produce cognitive development are not completely understood. The giving and receiving of explanations by group members may provide a window on the operation of these underlying mechanisms. In the Vygotskian approach, explaining is probably a fundamental component of the interaction between more-capable and less-capable peers. The less-capable person learns from the explanations given by the more-capable person. By receiving explanations from the more-capable person, the less-capable person can correct misconceptions, fill in gaps in his or her understanding, strengthen connections between new information and previous learning, and develop new problem-solving skills and knowledge (Mayer, 1984; Sweller, 1989; Wittrock, 1990).

In the Piagetian perspective, although the processes learners use to resolve cognitive conflict are not described explicitly in the theory and are rarely observed in empirical research, it is also likely that explaining is important. When students work together, resolving cognitive conflict may entail a series of negotiations in which students explain their viewpoints to each other. Students may learn by giving explanations to each other and may learn from the explanations given by others. In the process of giving explanations and justifying their perspectives to others, students may clarify or reorganize material in new ways in their own minds, recognize and fill in gaps in their understanding, recognize and resolve inconsistencies, develop new perspectives, and construct more elaborate conceptualizations than they would when learning material by themselves (Bargh & Schul, 1980; Benware & Deci, 1984; King, 1992b; Yackel, Cobb, & Wood, 1991). In the process of receiving explanations, they may compare their own perspectives to those of others, and make adjustments in their own understanding as a result. Except in situations where a student is already an expert, it seems likely that peers working together can potentially benefit from both giving and receiving explanations. They can benefit from receiving explanations from students who have more knowledge or a better understanding or a different perspective, and they can benefit from giving explanations that help them clarify their own understanding.

Previous research found that giving explanations is more predictive of achievement than is receiving explanations and that giving explanations is usually positively correlated with achievement (King, 1992b; Webb, 1991). Empirical results on the relation between receiving explanations and learning are inconsistent and weak (Webb, 1991; Webb & Farivar, 1994). Receiving a response that has no elaboration or receiving no response, in contrast, is usually negatively related to achievement (Webb, 1989).

The missing link in the research on receiving explanations may be that additional conditions must be satisfied for help received to be effective (see Webb,

1989, 1991; Webb, Troper, & Fall, 1995). Explanations must satisfy four conditions. They must be (a) relevant to the target student's need for help, (b) timely, (c) correct, and (d) sufficiently elaborated to enable the target student to correct his or her misconception or lack of understanding. Although the giver of the explanation has some responsibility for meeting these conditions, such as being willing to help and willing to expend effort to provide relevant and elaborated explanations, the target student also has some responsibility. To receive maximum benefit from receiving help, the target student must express a need for help that clearly conveys his or her area of difficulty or misunderstanding, or lack of understanding. In order to do this, the target student must carry out the steps in Nelson-Le Gall's (1981, 1985; Nelson-Le Gall, Gumerman, & Scott-Jones, 1983) comprehensive, five-step model of children's help seeking. The target student must be aware that he or she needs help, be willing to seek help, identify someone who can provide help, use effective strategies to elicit help (e.g., ask explicit, precise, and direct questions; Peterson, Wilkinson, Spinelli, & Swing, 1984; Wilkinson, 1985; Wilkinson & Calculator, 1982a, 1982b; Wilkinson & Spinelli, 1983; see also Webb & Kenderski, 1984; Webb et al., 1995), and be willing to reassess his or her strategies for obtaining help.

Vedder (1985) proposed three other conditions for learning that concern how the student receiving an explanation responds after receiving help. First, the target student must understand the explanation. Second, the student receiving help must have the opportunity to use the explanation to solve the problem or carry out the task for herself or himself. Anecdotal observations suggest that groups do not always provide such opportunities for practice, preferring instead to do the work for the student who needs help (Shavelson, Webb, Stasz, & McArthur, 1988; Vedder, 1985). Third, the student must use the opportunity for practice by attempting to apply the explanation received to the problem at hand. The failure to meet these conditions of effective help may be one reason why receiving help is usually not correlated with achievement. The learner must, in other words, be an active participant in the learning process and engaged in constructive activity.

The notion of the learner as an active participant in the learning process finds support in both theoretical and empirical work. Active participation of the learner is a critical feature in both Piaget's and Vygotsky's perspectives on learning. In Piaget's perspective, the learner is actively involved in resolving cognitive conflict. In Vygotsky's perspective, the learner actively interprets functions occurring in social interaction. Tudge (1990a, p. 7) quoted Vygotsky (1987) to show the importance of the active participation of the less-competent partner, as well as the more-competent partner, during social interaction: "The teacher, working with the school child on a given question, explains, informs, inquires, corrects, and *forces the child himself to explain*" (pp. 215–216; italics added). With help and support from the more-competent partner, the less-competent partner practices skills and gradually internalizes them so he or she can perform them without assistance, and they become part of his or her individual repertoire (Vygotsky, 1978, 1987). In a recent study of text comprehension in which students worked individually, for example, Chan, Burtis, Scardamalia, and Bereiter (1992) found that the level of constructive activity (e.g., from low level to high level: states the topic, repeats text, paraphrases text, refers to personal knowledge, constructs inferences) significantly predicted new learning.

It is important, given the theoretical and empirical support for the importance of the learner's participation, that the help seeker in a group have an opportunity to do something with the help they receive. Carrying out further activity after receiving explanations may benefit the learner in several ways. First, during the process of using the explanation to try to solve the problem, students may generate self-explanations that help them internalize principles and construct specific inference rules for solving the problem (Chi & Bassock, 1989; Chi, Bassock, Lewis, Reimann, & Glaser, 1989). Second, attempting to solve problems may help students monitor their own understanding and help them become aware of misunderstandings or lack of understanding (Chi & Bassock, 1989). Unless students attempt to solve problems for themselves without assistance, they may falsely assume that they know how to solve the problems. Furthermore, observing other students solve problems correctly may also give students a false sense of competence (see Nelson-Le Gall, 1992). Third, attempting to solve problems may help make the group aware of a student's misunderstandings or lack of understanding. Otherwise, the group may rely on students' own admissions of whether they understand (e.g., "I get it"), which may not always be accurate (Shavelson et al., 1988). It may be necessary for the group to watch students solve a problem incorrectly to understand the exact nature of their difficulty and to formulate additional explanations as necessary.

The study described in this chapter focuses on explanations that students working in cooperative groups give each other, the activity that students engage in after they receive help, and the relations between these kinds of peer interactions and learning. The context of this study was a cooperative learning program, conducted during three curriculum units, that was designed to promote active participation of students working in groups with particular emphasis on the giving of elaborated explanations. Previous analyses of data from this program were reported elsewhere (Webb & Farivar, 1994) but did not include the coding of multiple levels of explanations or the activity students engaged in after receiving help. A second article (Webb et al., 1995) did code multiple levels of explanations and activity after receiving help for two of the units presented here (Units 1 and 2). This chapter presents modified results from that article and extends the analyses to the third curriculum unit (Unit 3). The next section describes the cooperative learning program and the design of the study. Subsequent sections describe the results of the quantitative analyses of the entire sample and the results of in-depth analyses of four groups.

THE COOPERATIVE LEARNING PROGRAM
AND THE DESIGN OF THE STUDY

In this program, students worked in small peer-directed groups on a set of problems assigned daily. The goal of small-group work was for all students to help each other learn how to solve the problems. Although students were given instruction and practice in developing communications, helping, and explaining skills, their actual group work was fairly unstructured and with rare exceptions (such as the person assigned to ask the teacher for help if the group had a question), students were not given specific roles to play during group interaction

Cooperative Learning Program

The cooperative learning program had four sequential sets of activities designed to develop students' ability to work effectively in small groups. (For a complete list of activities used in the study, see Farivar & Webb, 1991.)

Preliminary Activities. Prior to engaging in any group work, students carried out a set of inclusion activities to familiarize them with their classmates and to help them feel more comfortable interacting with their classmates to lessen feelings of awkwardness once they were assigned to small working groups.

Developing Communication Skills. The second set of activities was designed to develop students' basic communication skills and to help students learn how to interact with others and to work effectively in small groups. The teacher introduced norms for group behavior, and the class discussed and made charts for posting in the classroom that summarized them (e.g., attentive listening, no put downs, 12-inch voices—no yelling, equal participation by everyone, zero noise level signal; Gibbs, 1987). Classes also discussed and made charts of social skills to use in small groups: checking for understanding, sharing ideas and information, encouraging, and checking for agreement (Johnson, Johnson, & Holubec, 1988). These activities were essential in promoting a classroom climate within which productive cooperative work could occur. Groups filled out "group processing" sheets to check whether they carried out these skills while working in their groups. These social skills set the stage for explanation giving by emphasizing understanding and sharing ideas, rather than focusing on the correct answers. Finally, to build team cohesion, each small group chose a group name and created a group sign. This activity reinforced the group's identity and enabled teachers to use the groups' names instead of students' names when calling on them.

Developing Help Giving and Help Receiving Skills. The third set of activities was designed to develop students' ability to help each other while working on problems in small groups. To help students realize the value of active participation compared to only observing others, to reinforce the importance of reciprocal communication, and to show the importance of question asking as well as question answering, students gave directions about drawing figures to another student who either was or was not allowed to ask questions, and then compared and discussed the two experiences. To introduce specific helping skills based on research on effective help seeking (Nelson-Le Gall, 1981, 1985; Nelson-Le Gall et al., 1983), the teacher displayed and discussed charts of behaviors for students to engage in when they did not understand how to solve a problem and when they gave help to another student. The chart of behaviors for students who needed help listed the following steps: recognize that you need help, decide to get help from another student, choose someone to help you, ask for help, ask clear and precise questions, and keep asking until you understand.

The chart of behaviors for students who gave help listed the following steps to foster explanation giving: notice when other students need help; tell other students to ask you if they need help; when someone asks for help, help him or her; be a good listener; give explanations instead of the answer; watch how your teammate solves the problem; give specific feedback on how your teammate solved the problem; check for understanding; praise your teammate for doing a good job. (For examples of each step in these charts, see Farivar & Webb, 1994.) As a practice activity, students carried out these skills in their small groups while solving novel math problems. Students also completed checklists of these help-giving and help-receiving behaviors after group work to increase their awareness of which skills their groups used and where they needed to improve.

Developing Explaining Skills. The final set of activities focused primarily on developing students' ability to give explanations and secondarily on active participation of the person needing help. In one activity adapted from the study of Swing and Peterson (1982), students performed skits in front of the class to demonstrate "good" helping and "unhelpful" helping. In the skit for good helping, one student explained to another student how to carry out the steps in solving a problem, gave the other student an opportunity to try to solve the problem, corrected the other student's errors with explanations of what should have been done and why, asked follow-up questions to make sure that the other student understood, and gave praise for work well done. In the skit for unhelpful helping, one student gave the other student only the answer and did not describe how to solve it, told the other student to hurry up, and told the other student to concentrate on getting the answer rather on understanding how to solve the problem (see also Farivar & Webb, 1994). The class discussed differences between the skits and how they applied to their own small-group work.

Students also carried out Pairs-Check (Kagan, 1989). In this activity, groups split into pairs and members of a pair took turns solving problems while their partner watched and acted as a coach and helper. If a student had difficulty or made an error, the "coach" was responsible for explaining how to solve the problem, for monitoring how the student reworked the problem, and for ensuring that the student understood how to solve the problem correctly. After each problem, the two pairs in the group compared answers to make sure that they were all solving the problem correctly. They worked as a group to resolve any discrepancies between the work of pairs. This activity was designed to give students practice with all aspects of "teaching," from giving help to monitoring other students' understanding and giving other students opportunities to solve problems for themselves.

Design and Procedures of the Study

Sample. The cooperative learning program was implemented in six seventh-grade general mathematics classes representing a range of achievement levels (184 students) at an urban middle school in the Los Angeles metropolitan area. The composition of the classes was similar in terms of student achievement, gender, and ethnicity. Students had little or no previous experience working collaboratively with other students. Two teachers each taught three classes. The ethnic breakdown of the sample was 55% Latino, 26% White, 14% African American, 3% Asian American, and 2% Middle Eastern or Other. Nearly all students were proficient in English and many were bilingual.

Instructional Conditions. The six classes were divided into two instructional conditions that varied in the amount of preparation that classes received. In Condition 1, four classes (two from each teacher) worked in cooperative groups throughout the semester and carried out all of the communications activities described in the previous section: preliminary activities (at the beginning of the semester, prior to small-group work), developing communication skills (in conjunction with a curriculum unit on decimals), developing help-giving and help-receiving skills (in conjunction with a curriculum unit on fractions), and developing explaining skills (in conjunction with a curriculum unit on percentages). In Condition 2, the remaining two classes (one from each teacher) carried out the cooperative learning activities one curriculum unit behind the classes in Condition 1. They worked individually for the curriculum unit on decimals and worked in groups for the curriculum units on fractions and percentages. The sequence of activities for the classes in Condition 2 was preliminary activities (at the beginning of the semester), developing communications skills (in conjunction with the unit on fractions), and developing help-giving and help-receiving skills (in conjunction with the curriculum unit on percentages). Classes in Condition 2 did not carry out the activities on developing explaining skills.

Procedures. On the basis of pretest scores on general mathematics achievement, ethnic background, and gender, students were assigned to small groups so that all were heterogeneous and reflected the mix of backgrounds in the class as closely as possible. Three achievement strata were defined in each class on the basis of the pretest scores: high (top 25% of the sample), medium (middle 50%), and low (bottom 25%). Groups were formed so that each had one high-achieving student, one low-achieving student, and two medium-achieving students.

Teachers participated in seven full-day workshops that covered issues of group work, the mathematics content to be taught, and how to integrate them. The teachers synchronized their lesson plans so that all classes followed the same schedule of classroom activities (except for the planned variation between conditions on preparation for group work). At the beginning of each curriculum unit, all classes carried out the communications activities corresponding to that phase of the program in conjunction with activities and instruction in the mathematics content.

At the beginning of each class period, the teacher introduced the whole class to the material to be covered that day and solved a few example problems with the class. For classroom instruction involving small-group work, groups worked on the class assignment, either problems assigned in the textbook (general mathematics for Grade 7; Eicholz, O'Daffer, & Fleenor, 1989) or teacher-prepared activities (e.g., calculating sales tax for meals selected from restaurant menus). The teacher reminded the class about the norms for behavior that had been most recently introduced, and reminded students to consult each other first before asking her for help. The teacher circulated among groups, watching groups work and answering questions where necessary. At the end of each class period, groups turned in their classwork and spent 5 minutes completing and discussing their checklist of expected behaviors for group work. Periodically, the teacher discussed the groups' experiences in the whole-class setting. The teacher administered a weekly quiz to all students. Students completed a posttest at the end of the unit. For traditional classroom instruction, students completed the same classwork at their seats and could ask questions of the teacher but not other students.

On one day during each curriculum unit, classes working in small groups were tape-recorded for the entire class period. During Unit 1 (decimals), students were tape-recorded while trying to determine the costs of long-distance telephone calls with varying costs for the first part and later parts of the call (e.g., "Find the cost of a 30-minute telephone call in which the first minute costs $0.22 and each additional minute costs $0.13"). During Unit 2 (fractions), students were tape-recorded while adding fractions with like or unlike denominators (e.g., $\frac{3}{4} + \frac{2}{3}$). During Unit 3 (percentages), students were tape-recorded while converting decimals to percentages and percentages to decimals (e.g., "Convert 0.36 to a percentage" and "In order to find the sale price of a $12 shirt that is on sale for 25% off, convert 25% to a decimal").

The reward structure used in during the study was mostly individual (about 80%). Students' grades on all tests and quizzes were based on their own individual scores. For classwork and homework, students received two scores: one individual score (points for submitting the work) and one group score (a score on the quality of the work based on one randomly selected paper from their group). Teachers instituted this small-group reward component to increase individual accountability and group pressure on individuals to complete homework and classwork (to increase the rate of return of homework and classwork).

RELATIONS AMONG RECEIVING EXPLANATIONS, CONSTRUCTIVE ACTIVITY, AND ACHIEVEMENT[1]

This section summarizes the results of analyses concerning the level of help given in small groups and the subsequent constructive behavior of students after receiving help. The specific issues investigated were the level of elaboration in the help given in groups; the kinds of behavior students engaged in after receiving help; the relations among level of help received, subsequent constructive activity, and achievement; changes over the course of the program in the level of helping behavior and constructive activity; and the relation between behavior and achievement.

Coding of Explanations, Constructive Activity, and Achievement

For all students who indicated a need for help, three general categories of behavior were coded: (1) the level of elaboration in the help that the student received, (2) the level of activity in the work that the student carried out after receiving help, and (3) the level of activity in the work that the student carried out on subsequent problems during group work. Two raters coded student interaction, and agreement between the raters was high (correlations between raters ranged from .86 to .99).

Elaboration of Help Received. The coding of the help that a student received distinguished among six levels of elaboration from highest elaboration to lowest elaboration: (6) a verbally labeled explanation of how to solve part or all of the problem, (5) a numerical rule with no verbal labels for the numbers, (4) a numerical expression, (3) a sequence of unconnected numbers or numbers to copy or operations to perform, (2) the answer only, and (1) no response or a noncontent response.

The main distinction between Level 6 and Level 5 was the verbal labeling of

---

[1]Parts of this section are based on "Constructive activity and learning in collaborative small groups" by Noreen M. Webb, Jonathan D. Troper, and Randy Fall (1995), *Journal of Educational Psychologist, 87,* 406–423. Copyright by the American Psychological Association, Inc. Adapted here with permission.

numbers. For the problem of finding the cost of a 30-minute telephone call in which the 1st minute costs $0.22 and each additional minute costs $0.13, an example of a Level 6 explanation is "Multiply 13¢ by 29. Because 29 minutes are left after the 1st minute" and example of a Level 5 explanation is "This is 30, so you minus 1. You use 29." The verbal labeling that differentiates a Level 6 explanation from a Level 5 explanation (in the foregoing examples, "29 minutes left after the 1st minute" instead of just the numbers "30, . . . minus 1 . . . 29") was thought to make it easier for the student receiving the explanation to construct a self-explanation about how to solve the problem (Chi & Bassock, 1989).

Level 4 help was a numerical expression specific to a particular problem, without any indication of the underlying rules for solving the problem idiosyncratic to a single problem, and did not apply to other problems that students worked on. Students giving Level 3 help did not provide a connected expression, but just gave numbers for another student to copy (e.g., "Put 13 on top; 29 on the bottom. Then you times it"). Level 2 help was just the answer (e.g., "I got $3.77"). Level 1 help consisted of no response at all or a noninformational response ("Just do it the way she [the teacher] said").

Activity on the Current Problem After Receiving Help. The coding of the activity that the student carried out on the current problem after receiving help also distinguished among six levels, from most constructive to least constructive: (6) reworks entire problem from the beginning or explains how to solve it to another student, (5) applies a numerical rule that another student had given and completes the problem, (4) finishes numerical calculations that another student had set up, (3) copies work from another student's paper or writes down the calculations as another student says them aloud, (2) acknowledges the help received without carrying out further work on the problem, and (1) says nothing and the observer notes that the student is not working on the problem individually. The order of the levels of constructive activity depended on how much work the student carried out and how independent a student's work was from the work of others in the group.

Activity on the Next Problem. The coding of the activity that the student carried out on the next problem distinguished among three levels from most constructive to least constructive: (3) solves the problem correctly without assistance from anyone else (works independently, explains how to solve the problem to another student, or takes the lead in setting up and solving problems while collaborating with others), (2) copies or finishes the calculations that another student set up (works collaboratively with others but does not set up the problem or the calculations), and (1) does no work on the next problem. Activity on the next problem was not coded if a student had trouble on the next problem or if the class ended before a student had an opportunity to try to solve the next problem.

Two achievement test scores were created for each instructional unit: a specific posttest score that was the total of the items on the posttest pertaining to the material that was covered on the day groups were tape-recorded, and a general posttest score that was the total of all items on the posttest. The specific posttests focused on the cost of long-distance telephone calls (Unit 1), addition of fractions with like or unlike denominators (Unit 2), and converting decimals to percentages and percentages to decimals (Unit 3). Internal consistency alpha reliability coefficients for the specific and general posttests ranged from .70 to .97.

Frequencies of Behavior and Changes Over Time

Frequencies of Behavior. Table 5.1 gives the frequencies of all verbal behavior variables for students who worked in groups during all three instructional units (Condition 1). Table 5.2 gives the frequencies of behavior for students who worked in groups during the second and third instructional units (Condition 2). The majority of the requests for help resulted in responses that included some elaboration of the problem that went beyond just the answer. The percentages of responses to requests for help that included some elaboration ranged from 62% to 75% across the two tables.

After receiving help, students engaged in different kinds of constructive activity on the current problem, as can be seen in Tables 5.1 and 5.2. The percentage of time that students carried out no further work on the problem after receiving help was substantial, and the percentages of activity that consisted of only acknowledging the help received or saying nothing at all ranged from 33% to 54% across Tables 5.1 and 5.2. Most of the activity that students did carry out was minimal, either copying another student's work or finishing calculations that another student had set up. Only a minority of the activity was at a level that indicated that students actively applied the help they received to try to solve the problem for themselves, either reworking or explaining the problem or applying to the current problem a numerical rule that another student had stated.

The third category of behavior in Tables 5.1 and 5.2 shows the activity that students engaged in on the problem subsequent to the one in which they indicated a need for help. Students showed a considerable range of constructive activity. Fairly often, students worked the problem without assistance from anyone else. In a substantial number of instances, however, students carried out only minimal work on the next problem, merely copying others' work or finishing calculations that other students had set up, or did no work at all on the next problem.

Comparison Between Cooperative Learning Conditions for Each Curriculum Unit. Across the three curriculum units of the cooperative learning program, there was an increased emphasis in classroom activities on giving explanations instead of only the answer and on actively seeking help when confused or unsure, as well as an increased emphasis on active participation by all group members.

Two sets of predictions were made on the basis of the sequential and cumulative nature of the program. First, it was expected that, within a curriculum unit, students who had received more communications training (Condition 1) would give more elaborated help and would exhibit more constructive activity than students who had received less communications training (Condition 2). Second, it was expected that, for classes within each instructional condition, the frequency of elaborated help and constructive activity would increase over time across the three instructional units.

TABLE 5.1
Means and Standard Deviations of Frequencies of Student Behavior and
Achievement (Condition 1: Classes in Small Groups During All Units)[a]

	Unit 1 (Decimals)[b]		Unit 2 (Fractions)[c]		Unit 3 (Percentage)[d]	
	M	%[e]	M	%[e]	M	%[e]
Indicates a need for help	2.35		1.97		1.41	
Receives help						
Level 6: Labeled explanation	.88	37	.74	38	.31	22
Level 5: Unlabeled numerical rule	.16	7	.64	32	.29	20
Level 4: Numerical expression	.28	12	.10	5	.14	10
Level 3: Numbers to write or copy	.25	11	.00	0	.29	20
Level 2: Answer only	.32	14	.41	21	.31	22
Level 1: Noncontent or no response	.47	20	.08	4	.10	7
Average level of help received	4.15		4.46		3.97	
Constructive activity: Current problem						
Level 6: Reworks or explains problem	.28	12	.10	5	.20	15
Level 5: Applies another's numerical rule	.11	5	.18	9	.27	20
Level 4: Finishes another's calculations	.60	26	.49	25	.20	15
Level 3: Copies work	.44	19	.31	16	.24	17
Level 2: Acknowledges help received	.25	11	.28	14	.24	17
Level 1: Says nothing	.63	27	.59	30	.22	16
Average level of constructive activity (current)	3.31		2.74		3.46	
Constructive activity: Next problem[f]						
Level 3: Solves problem without assistance	.74	57	.61	37	.62	49
Level 2: Copies or finishes another's work	.19	15	.29	18	.56	44
Level 1: Does no work	.37	28	.74	45	.09	7
Average level of constructive activity (next)	2.34		1.98		2.46	
Mathematics pretest[g]	.58		.56		.61	
Specific posttest[g]	.49		.52		.59	
General posttest[g]	.62		.40		.53	

[a] Adapted from "Constructive activity and learning in collaborative small groups" by Noreen M. Webb, Jonathan D. Troper, and Randy Fall (1995), *Journal of Educational Psychology, 87,* 406–423. Copyright 1995 by the American Psychological Association, Inc. Adapted here with permission. [b] $N = 57$. [c] $N = 39$. [d] $N = 49$. [e] Percentage of indications of a need for help that led to this response. [f] $N = 51$ for Unit 1, $N = 38$ for Unit 2, $N = 45$ for Unit 3. [g] Proportion of items correct.

TABLE 5.2
Means and Standard Deviations of Frequencies
of Student Behavior and Achievement
(Condition 2: Classes That Worked in Small Groups During Units 2 and 3)[a]

	Unit 2 (Fractions)[b]		Unit 3 (Percent)[c]	
	M	%[d]	M	%[d]
Indicates a need for help	1.54		1.38	
Receives help				
Level 6: Labeled explanation	.42	27	.14	10
Level 5: Unlabeled numerical rule	.54	35	.24	18
Level 4: Numerical expression	.17	11	.14	10
Level 3: Numbers to write or copy	.00	0	.33	24
Level 2: Answer only	.33	21	.38	28
Level 1: Noncontent or no response	.08	6	.14	10
Average level of help received	4.19		3.16	
Constructive activity: Current problem				
Level 6: Reworks or explains problem	.08	5	.00	0
Level 5: Applies another's numerical rule	.08	5	.24	17
Level 4: Finishes another's calculations	.67	44	.10	7
Level 3: Copies work	.12	8	.29	21
Level 2: Acknowledges help received	.17	11	.24	17
Level 1: Says nothing	.42	27	.52	37
Average level of constructive activity (current)	3.02		2.53	
Constructive activity: Next problem[e]				
Level 3: Solves problem without assistance	.55	39	.48	40
Level 2: Copies or finishes another's work	.35	25	.43	36
Level 1: Does no work	.50	36	.29	24
Average level of constructive activity (next)	1.97		2.28	
Mathematics pretest[f]	.58		.59	
Specific posttest[f]	.53		.56	
General posttest[f]	.38		.48	

[a]Adapted from "Constructive activity and learning in collaborative small groups" by Noreen M. Webb, Jonathan D. Troper, and Randy Fall (1995), *Journal of Educational Psychologist, 87*, 406–423. Copyright 1995 by the American Psychological Association, Inc. Adapted here with permission. [b]$N = 24$. [c]$N = 21$. [d]Percent of indications of a need for help that led to this response. [e]$N = 20$ for Unit 2, $N = 21$ for Unit 3. [f]Proportion of items correct.

Comparison of the frequencies of behavior for Unit 2 (Fractions) for students who had participated in two phases of the cooperative learning program (Condition 1: Table 5.1) and students who had participated in only one phase of the cooperative learning program (Condition 2: Table 5.2) show only slight and statistically nonsignificant differences between conditions. Students in Condition 1 in Unit 3 received more elaborated help and engaged in a higher level of constructive activity on the current problem than did students in Condition 2 (average level of help received: $t = 2.11$, $p < .05$; average level of constructive activity on the current problem: $t = 2.22$, $p < .04$). The difference between conditions for the level of constructive activity on the next problem was not statistically significant.

Changes in Behavior Over Time. The second set of predictions concerned changes in student behavior over time. Contrary to the prediction, the level of helping behavior and constructive activity did not increase consistently over time. First, in both instructional conditions (Condition 1: Table 5.1 and Condition 2: Table 5.2), the level of elaboration of help given remained fairly constant over time. The only effect that seemed to correspond to predictions was the decrease in giving no response (Level 1 help) from the first unit to later units in Table 5.1. Second, the levels of constructive activity did not increase over time. The only noteworthy trend was the lower incidence of saying nothing at all after receiving help (Level 1 constructive activity) during Unit 3 than during Units 1 and 2 (Table 5.1).

The data in Tables 5.1 and 5.2 suggest that the cumulative effect of the program was not greater than phases of the program considered separately. Differences in the mathematics content from unit to unit may have masked any effects of the cooperative learning program over time. That is, some mathematics topics and kinds of problems may be more conducive than others to giving explanations with a high level of elaboration or in promoting constructive activity. The third unit involved the conversion of decimals to percentages and percentages to decimals. The only step to explain in many of these problems was the placement of the decimal point. These problems probably gave students little opportunity to create elaborated explanations in comparison to the first two units involving the calculation of the costs of long-distance phone calls (Unit 1) or adding fractions with like and unlike denominators (Unit 2). In sequencing content in the classroom, therefore, placing content that is "explainable" early may help give students practice and familiarity with giving elaborated explanations and prevent the bad habit of giving nonelaborated responses.

Predicting Achievement and Behavior in Small Groups

One goal of this study was to link the various kinds of help giving during classroom practice to achievement. Table 5.3 gives the results of multiple regression analyses predicting achievement from instructional condition (working in small groups during all three units or only during Units 2 and 3), pretest scores, and the three kinds of behavior measured in this study: the level of help received, the level of constructive activity on the problem on which help was needed, and the level of constructive activity on the next problem. The best predictors of achievement were students' pretest scores and their constructive activity on the problem after the one on which they needed help. The level of help received and the level of constructive activity on the problem on which students needed help were generally not significant predictors of achievement.

TABLE 5.3

Multiple Regression Coefficients Predicting Posttest Achievement From Behavior and Pretest Scores[a]

| | Unit 1 (Decimals) | | | | Unit 2 (Fractions) | | | | Unit 3 (Percentage) | | | |
| | Specific Posttest | | General Posttest | | Specific Posttest | | General Posttest | | Specific Posttest | | General Posttest | |
Predictor	r	B	r	B	r	B	r	B	r	B	r	B
Instructional condition	—	—	—	—	-.02	.00	.04	.07	.06	.02	.13	.12
Pretest	.47***	.30**	.43**	.29*	.54***	.28**	.55***	.31**	.24	.18	.40**	.36**
Level of help received	.43**	-.08	.34*	-.06	.13	-.03	.12	-.10	.04	.06	-.03	.01
Level of constructive activity: Current problem	.59***	.31*	.43**	.10	.40**	.05	.45***	.18	.28*	.10	.21	.02
Level of constructive activity: Next problem	.64***	.43**	.59***	.49***	.73***	.59***	.72***	.51***	.49***	.44***	.32**	.27*

[a]Adapted from "Constructive activity and learning in collaborative small groups" by Noreen M. Webb, Jonathan D. Troper, and Randy Fall (1995). *Journal of Educational Psychologist, 87,* 406–423. Copyright 1995 by the American Psychological Association, Inc. Adapted here with permission.

Note: r = zero-order correlation. B = standardized multiple regression coefficient.

*p < .05. **p < .01. ***p < .001.

Further multiple regression analyses were carried out to determine the predictors of constructive activity (see Table 5.4). The most important predictor of constructive activity on the next problem was constructive activity on the current problem. Applying help received to the current problem made it more likely that students would be able to solve the next problem. Second, in all three units, the level of help received was a significant predictor of constructive activity on the current problem. Receiving high-level explanations enabled students to carry out constructive activity on the current problem. Taken together, the results of the multiple regression analyses reported in Tables 5.3 and 5.4 suggest the following sequence of effects:

Level of help received → Level of activity → Level of activity → Achievement
(current problem)   (next problem)

Although the level of help received did not directly predict achievement, it was an important first step in the sequence of behaviors that predicted achievement.

Interestingly, pretest scores were usually not significantly related to level of activity on the current and next problems. Constructive activity was not simply an indicator of mathematical ability: Students with higher mathematics pretest scores did not always exhibit higher levels of activity than students with lower mathematics pretest scores. Although level of help received was a strong predictor of level of activity on the current problem, much of the variance was left unexplained, showing that other factors accounted for carrying out constructive activity.

EVOLUTION OF GROUP INTERACTION IN FOUR GROUPS

The results in the previous section showed that the level of help received is an important component in peer interaction and predicts achievement outcomes through the mediating variable of constructive activity. The level of help received did not increase consistently over the course of the semester-long program. To better understand the dynamics of group interaction in this study, we examined the experiences of four groups in detail in this section. The groups were drawn from classes that received all three phases of the instructional program in communications and helping skills. The primary criterion for selecting groups was that the membership stayed as intact as possible from beginning to end of the study. Two groups were selected from each of the teacher's classrooms. The analyses of these four groups focused on the level of help received (corresponding to the variables presented in Tables 5.1 and 5.2), the kinds of questions that students asked, and verbal references that students made to the kinds of interaction being promoted in the instructional program.

Table 5.5 presents the data on these variables for each of the four groups. The data are presented for each group as a whole. Consistent with the results pre-

TABLE 5.4
Multiple Regression Coefficients Predicting Level of Constructive Activity From Behavior and Pretest Scores[a]

| | Unit 1 (Decimals) Constructive Activity | | | | Unit 2 (Fractions) Constructive Activity | | | | Unit 3 (Percent) Constructive Activity | | | |
| | Current Problem | | Next Problem | | Current Problem | | Next Problem | | Current Problem | | Next Problem | |
Predictor	r	B	r	B	r	B	r	B	r	B	r	B
Instructional condition	—	—	—	—	-.10	-.13	.01	.05	.25*	.17	.13	.04
Pretest	.25	.15	.25	.08	.19	.13	.44***	.35**	.29*	.33**	.08	-.07
Level of help received	.54***	.51***	.55***	.29	.47***	.46***	.18	-.11	.26*	.28*	.02	-.10
Level of constructive activity: Current problem	—	—	.58***	.36*	—	—	.53***	.52***	—	—	.41***	.45***

[a] Adapted from "Constructive activity and learning in collaborative small groups" by Noreen M. Webb, Jonathan D. Troper, and Randy Fall (1995), *Journal of Educational Psychology, 87*, 406–423. Copyright 1995 by the American Psychological Association, Inc. Adapted here with permission.

Note: r = zero-order correlation. B = standardized multiple regression coefficient.

*p < .05. **p < .01. ***p < .001

TABLE 5.5
Frequencies of Behavior in Four Groups

	Group 1 Unit			Group 2 Unit			Group 3 Unit			Group 4 Unit		
	1	2	3	1	2	3	1	2	3	1	2	3
Indicates a need for help[a]	9	1	6	12	2	1	9	0	2	2	2	5
Level of help received												
6: Labeled explanation	5	1	0	4	1	0	3	—	0	0	0	0
5: Unlabeled numerical rule	0	0	0	1	0	12	—	0	0	2	1	0
4: Numerical expression	2	0	1	2	0	0	1	—	0	0	0	0
3: Numbers to copy	1	0	2	0	0	0	0	—	0	0	0	3
2: Answer only	0	0	3	3	0	0	2	—	2	0	0	1
1: Noncontent or no response	0	0	0	2	1	0	1	—	0	2	0	0
Asks for help[b]	18	3	18	12	17	10	16	0	6	9	2	16
Specific question	5	1	7	9	13	4	8	—	0	2	1	1
General question or statement	13	2	11	3	4	6	8	—	6	7	1	15
References to desired behaviors	9	13	1	3	0	2	1	2	1	1	0	8
Work together	5	1	1	1	0	0	0	1	1	1	0	0
Understand or learn	2	3	0	0	0	1	0	1	0	0	0	3
Help (general)	1	8	0	2	0	1	1	0	0	0	0	0
Explain	1	1	0	0	0	0	0	0	0	0	0	5
References to undesirable behaviors	0	0	3	0	0	0	1	0	0	1	0	0
Work alone	0	0	2	0	0	0	0	0	0	0	0	0
Get answer only	0	0	1	0	0	0	0	0	0	1	0	0
Do not help	0	0	0	0	0	0	1	0	0	0	0	0

[a]Number of math problems on which a student made an error or asked a question. [b]Number of questions asked (may include multiple questions per problem; see text).

sented earlier, the level of elaboration in the help received did not consistently increase over time in these groups. Furthermore, there was no tendency for the frequency of help at a particular level (e.g., labeled explanations, or answers only) to change consistently over time.

Questions Asked: Specific Versus General

Previous research has shown that asking specific questions targeting a particular aspect of the problem is more likely to elicit high-level explanations than is asking general or vague questions about the problem (e.g., Webb & Kenderski, 1984; Webb et al., 1995) and students were directed to "ask clear and precise questions" in the third unit. The questions that students asked each other in these four groups, then, were coded as specific if they referred to a particular number or part of the problem (e.g., "Why did you have to subtract 1?") and were coded as general questions otherwise (e.g., "How do you do it?"). Questions about the final answer to the problem were also counted as general questions, such as "How did you get 6.4?"

In Table 5.5, the frequencies for "asks for help" are higher than "indicates a need for help" because all questions were counted as asking for help, no matter how many questions were asked about the same problem, whereas all questions that a student asked about a problem were coded as one indication of a need for help. Sometimes students asked the same or a similar question repeatedly for the same problem, persisting until they got a response:

STUDENT 1: "Is 7/9 the lowest terms for number 5?"
STUDENT 1: "Is number 5, 7/9 the lowest term?"

The previous example was coded as one indication of a need for help but was coded as two questions. In other cases, students asked questions of the person giving an explanation and the questions were counted as multiple questions but only as one indication of a need for help:

STUDENT 1:   Times 30. Damn, times it times 29. Sorry.
STUDENT 2:   Times 29?
STUDENT 1:   Yes, you still need your first additional minute.
STUDENT 2:   How do you get times 29?
STUDENTS 1, 3: You minus one. You just take away one from the . . . OK. 'Cause you still need your first additional minute.
STUDENT 2:   I didn't hear a word you all just said.

Students tended to ask more general questions than specific questions (Table 5.5) but there was not a consistent increase over time in either the number of specific questions or in the proportion of questions that were specific. Moreover, there was no apparent relation between the number or proportion of specific questions asked in the group and the level of explanations given in the group.

References to Group Norms and Behavior

To investigate students' awareness of the group norms and kinds of behavior that were being promoted in this program, we coded students' verbal references to norms and desired behaviors in these four groups, which resulted in two categories of references: (a) to desired behavior and (b) to undesirable behavior. Examples of each reference are given in Table 5.6.

Groups varied considerably in the nature and frequency of their references to group norms and desired (or undesirable) behavior and these references showed some correspondence with the level of help given in the group. Group 1 gave numerous references to desired behaviors in the first two phases of the study (Units 1 and 2), emphasizing the importance of working together, understanding and learning, helping each other, and explaining how to solve the problems; much of the help given was at a high level of elaboration. In the third phase of the study (Unit 3), this group made only one reference to desired behavior and this was a general one: the importance of working together. Moreover, this

TABLE 5.6
References to Group Norms and Behavior in Four Groups

Category	Examples
Desired Behaviors	
Working together	OK. We're on a roll, so let's wait for Miguel to catch up so we can all do number 3.
	We are all supposed to all do these together.
	Your're supposed to be working with the group.
	You're not done until we're all done.
Understanding or learning	You gotta understand.
	You have to learn.
	I can't tell you [just] the answer.
	Give it back. You had to understand the work.
Helping	Look, if you don't know how to do it, then I'll help you.
	You need help?
Explaining	Do you want us to explain it to you?
	They're all trying to explain it to him and they won't explain it to me.
	I'm just explaining to her how to do the work here. See? Now I can't reach over to just tell her how to do it.
	Explain your answer.
Undesirable Behaviors	
Working alone	You guys do your own. I'm gonna redo it.
	I like to do them on my own.
Getting only the answer	You have to tell me the answer.
	Let me copy it.
Not helping	Don't ask me how to do it.

group made several references to undesirable behavior, including the wish to work alone and the demand for the answer. Consistent with the references to desired and undesirable behavior in this phase, the level of help given was at a fairly low level. Students gave each other numbers and answers to copy. It is not clear whether the quality of the help given deteriorated because of the nature of the task or because a low-achieving member of the group who had been the recipient of much of the high-level explaining was absent on the day of recording.

Group 2 referred to desired behavior during Units 1 and 3 and also showed some high-level explaining during these units. During Unit 2, this group made no references to desired or undesirable behavior. They did, however, ask each other many questions about how to solve the fractions problems. Furthermore, most of their questions to each other targeted specific aspects of the problem (see Table 5.5), which may account for the high-level explanation given in this phase. Because this group was involved in asking each other questions from the very beginning of group work on the day they were tape-recorded, there may have been no reason for them to refer to the norms for group work and desired behavior. They were already engaged in desired behavior. It is possible, then, that students refer to norms or desired behavior mainly when they are not already engaged in desired behavior and as a way of getting the group back on track if they start to exhibit undesirable behavior. The nature of the references to desired behaviors (see Table 5.6) provides some support for this hypothesis. The clearest examples are the references for working together and for understanding or learning. Students often admonished the group to work together when they were not doing so. Students typically mentioned the importance of understanding or learning when another student asked to copy or receive the answer. Groups may make explicit references to group norms and desired behavior primarily to stop undesirable behavior from occurring or continuing. If a group does not refer to group norms and desired behavior, we cannot assume that the group is not aware of them.

Group 3 made only a few references to desired or undesirable behavior during each unit. During Unit 1, the fact that half of the questions they asked each other were specific questions may have accounted for the occurrence of some high-level explanations. During Unit 2, members of this group worked on the problems separately and did not ask each other any questions. During Unit 3, only one student mentioned the importance of working together and no other behaviors were mentioned. Furthermore, all of the questions asked were at a very general level ("How do you do it?" "I don't get it"). Again, it is unclear if the lack of high-level explaining results from the nature of the task content or the fact that no one expressed the importance of understanding or explaining and there was a lack of specific questions.

Group 4 was the only one of the four groups to show improvement over time in their behavior and awareness of the desired group norms and behaviors. During Unit 1, one student repeatedly asked for help and the group was very reluctant to help this student. At the beginning of group work, the group insulted this student when he asked for help:

STUDENT 1: I need help.
STUDENT 2: Now that just proves one thing now, doesn't it?
STUDENT 1: Yes, turd, got a problem?

After repeatedly asking for help ("Could you help me?" "I don't understand number 10") and not getting any help, the student finally starting asking for the answer, which the group resisted doing:

STUDENT 1: What's number 10?
STUDENT 2: You gotta figure it out on your own.

Frustrated at not being able to solve the problem, the student asked to copy other students' work, which the others refused:

STUDENT 1: Let me copy it.
STUDENT 3: You wish. I'm not working my butt off to let you copy.

The experiences of this student in Unit 1 clearly show that this group had not internalized the norms of helping each other during the first phase of the program. The behavior of this group changed considerably over the next two units. During Unit 2, one student took it upon herself to help the student who had been rejected by the group (including her) during the previous unit. Without waiting for him to ask for help, she explained to him how to find the common denominator (when adding $\frac{2}{5} + \frac{3}{10}$) and persisted until he admitted that he understood what to do:

STUDENT 2: OK. Multiples . . . 10, 5 . . . No, 2. OK, 10 times 1 is 10. 10 times 2 is 20. OK?
STUDENT 1: Mm-hmm.
STUDENT 2: So 5 times 1 is 5. 5 times 2 is . . .
STUDENT 1: Ah!
STUDENT 2: 5 times 1 is? 5 times 2 is 10. We already have 10 here.
STUDENT 1: Oh, OK.
STUDENT 2: You stop. And your answer is 10. You get it?
STUDENT 1: Yeah, that's it.

She carried out the same kind of explanation to help him convert $\frac{2}{5}$ to $\frac{4}{10}$ and again asked whether he followed what she had done: ("You know how to do it?"). On a subsequent problem, when the student asked for help ("If you help me"), she agreed with no hesitation or reluctance ("Yeah, I'll help you"). Between Unit 1 and Unit 2, then, this group seemed to understand and accept the importance of helping each other.

By Unit 3, Group 4 seemed to make even more progress in understanding the desired norms for behavior. In contrast to the other groups, they made repeated references to the need to explain to each other and the need to understand how to solve the problems. Several students declared that they were confused ("I don't understand. Help" "I don't get this") and asked others to explain ("Explain, you dip"). But the difficulty that this group had with the content (converting percentages to decimals) seemed to interfere with their ability to give elaborated explanations. In the following example, one student struggled to give an explanation of why 10% (or 25%) is the same as 0.10 (or 0.25), and the student being helped had a difficult time understanding the explanation. It was clear, however, that one student was trying to explain and the other student was trying to understand:

STUDENT 2: The 10% . . . you just do the 10% per hundred. And this 1 and 0 is . . . decimal is 1 . . . hundredths. It's 10 hundredths.

STUDENT 1: You don't make sense.

STUDENT 2: OK, see? 10%. OK, let me get a different one. You'll understand better with this one. OK. This one's better. 25%. The decimal is 25 hundredths.

STUDENT 1: You know how she [the teacher] was doing that thing with the dimes? I don't understand the thing she was doing.

STUDENT 2: See you put this one there. Yeah, you put this one there. And then you move, wait . . . OK. There are 2 zeroes. And there . . . OK, there are 2 zeroes here, OK?

STUDENT 1: Yeah.

STUDENT 2: And there are 2 numbers. And then there's . . .

STUDENT 1: Is it 0.15 for this one?

STUDENT 2: Yeah. So how'd you do that?

STUDENT 1: I don't know.

This example shows the importance of taking the subject matter into account when interpreting students' behavior. This group was clearly aware of the importance of explaining and understanding but their difficulty with the subject matter prevented them from carrying out high-level explanations.

Differences Between Teachers

This section describes differences between the two teachers as evidenced by the groups in their classes. Groups 1 and 2 were taught by Teacher A and Groups 3 and 4 were taught by Teacher B. Students in Teacher A's groups participated more and had more equal participation among group members than did students in Teacher B's groups. The amount of verbal interaction in Groups 1 and 2 (Teacher A) was much greater than that in Groups 3 and 4 (Teacher B). Across the three units, the average number of utterances in Teacher A's groups was 520, 275, and 454, whereas the average number of utterances in Teacher B's groups was 267, 61, and 196. The rates of student participation in Teacher A's groups were much more equal than were the rates of student participation in Teacher B's groups. In Teacher A's groups, all students contributed to group discussion with the least verbal student contributing between 10% and 20% of the utterances in the group. In both of Teacher B's groups, in contrast, one student made little or no contribution to group work or group discussion. The low-participating member (a Latina in both groups) contributed no more than 4% of the utterances in the group. Because teachers set the context for learning and, consequently, set the tone for student behavior, it is likely that teacher behaviors facilitated or inhibited student exchange of explanations about content. The teacher behaviors discussed next may account for differences in student participation between Teacher A's and Teacher B's groups.

Holding Students to the Group's Norms by Actively Monitoring Group Work.
Teacher A insisted that students work together and made early and frequent references to the norms. She demanded that the students adhere specifically to the norms of working together, of both understanding and learning, of the need to help one other within the groups and of the importance of explaining. In closely monitoring group work, Teacher A noted that several students in Group 1 were working ahead of Miguel, the low-ability student in the group, and she intervened:

TEACHER A: Why don't you wait for Miguel to catch up?

This question may have underscored the importance of working together because later on the students themselves noted that Miguel needed to catch up:

STUDENT 1: OK, let's wait for Miguel, he's going to catch up so we can all do #3.
STUDENT 2: Wait for Miguel.

Teacher A would respond only to questions posed by the group, not to individual students' questions. This required the students to use one another as resources before they asked the teacher for help:

TEACHER A: The director is supposed to talk to me.

Teacher B, on the other hand, interacted with groups around the custodial and mechanical aspects of group work. At the end of her demonstration of how to solve a sample problem, she told the class that she would "come around and check to see that you are practicing them [the social skills]"; she reminded the students to use social skills when they worked together. When she did visit the group, she focused on the mechanisms that had been set up to encourage the students to work together (e.g., each signing one another's paper to indicate that everyone had done the work together and had the same answer) rather than on whether or not they were actually working together on the problems or on the mathematics they were learning:

TEACHER B: You people can start on that since you're already done with your class work. Just make sure that every one agreed and signed one another's papers. And what else do you need to do on your paper?
STUDENT 1: Oh, our number.

TEACHER B: And what else?
STUDENT 1: And our team name.

Similarly, the students also focused on group work mechanics, such as making sure they each signed one another's completed work. The low-ability student, Jackie, a Latina, was not included in the group's work except as needed to sign her name. In Unit 1, Jackie did not verbally participate but was referred to once when she was needed to sign her name:

STUDENT 1: Jackie, (sign) here, that's all.

In Unit 2, Jackie did not participate verbally and she was not addressed by others or referred to by others. In Unit 3, her participation again concerned only the mechanics of group work and with getting an answer so the group's work would be finished:

JACKIE: He's the engineer. He's supposed to raise his hand. What was the answer for number 21?

Insisting That Students Help One Another.   Teacher A insisted that students help one another and that they give explanations to one another. Teacher B, in contrast, did not prompt students to help each other or to give explanations but concentrated on the mechanics of the group assignment. Teacher A refused to answer questions from individual students and referred them back to their group:

STUDENT 1: Ms. A, is this right? Come here.
TEACHER A: Check with them [your teammates].

Teacher A coached the class using language that students had used in helping and explaining. When she overheard students make statements referring to helping and explaining, she repeated what they said as an example for other students:

TEACHER A: Did you hear what she said? "I will explain it to you but you can't copy it."

When a student asked for an answer instead of an explanation, she said:

TEACHER A: You can't do that. She needs to help you.

And to the student who was about to help, Teacher A suggested a way to begin:

TEACHER A: Maybe you can show her what she has to do.
TEACHER A: Show him how to—write it down here for him.

Working in groups is sometimes frustrating for all participants, particularly when one student needs help frequently or is shy or uncomfortable about asking for help over and over again. Teacher A again provided counsel in solving a likely stumbling block by suggesting a way around the problem, namely, that the student ask a different student for help:

STUDENT 1: Trying to do it myself.
TEACHER A: Aren't we supposed to be here to help each other?
STUDENT 1: I asked for help, no one ever listens.
TEACHER A: There are three other people in this group.

She also encouraged students to help by noticing and commenting on it:

TEACHER A: Good Allan. You're helping him a lot.

Using Time Well. The teachers also differed in their use of time. At the beginning of the period, Teacher A tended to ask general leading questions to encourage students to verbalize both the principles and procedures for solving the problems. She put the class in the role of helper and put herself into the role of the help receiver. This modeled the helping she expected the students to do when they worked together. After having demonstrated an example problem, Teacher A set the groups to work together for the rest of the period. She then walked around the room and monitored their work. For the most part, Groups 1 and 2 completed classwork during class and sometimes were able to begin their homework.

Teacher B, on the other hand, described the principles and procedures of the example problem herself and then asked the class for answers. This took a long time because she called on a number of students to give answers and because she demonstrated as many as seven problems. By the time the class had worked through the example problems, much of the period was over. This gave groups in her classes less time to work together. The urgency of finishing work may have decreased the students' likelihood of working together for several reasons. First, students hurried to finish at the end of the period and felt pressured to copy answers:

STUDENT 2: Let me copy it.
STUDENT 1: You wish. I'm not working my butt off to let you copy.
STUDENT 3: We didn't do anything. We are going to get F's.

Second, answers became more valuable than explanations because students were often still working together as the teacher was giving end-of-the-period directions:

TEACHER B: Number 3 (Student 3's paper) goes on top. Engineers, staple the work together.
STUDENT 1: Hurry up!
STUDENT 2: What's number 22?
STUDENT 1: 22 is 6.4%.
STUDENT 3: No, let her explain it.
STUDENT 1: Shut up.
STUDENT 3: You're always slow. Gawd.
STUDENT 4: What's number 27?

Third, higher ability students sometimes first worked alone to complete the assignment and then, if there was time, would help others:

STUDENT 1: Somebody needs help? I'm finished. OK, I'm smart.

DISCUSSION

Conditions of Effective Help Receiving

The results of this study confirmed two of the major conditions that need to be met for help that students receive to be effective for learning: (a) the help received must be elaborated explanations and (b) the student receiving the help must actively use the explanation to try to solve problems for himself or herself. Furthermore, this study showed that the first condition, receiving elaborated explanations, was a prerequisite for the second condition, applying the help received. Receiving elaborated explanations was not sufficient for learning, but was necessary for carrying out further constructive activity on the problem and future problems. These results help clarify the weak and inconsistent relations found in previous research between receiving explanations and achievement. As in many previous studies (see Webb, 1989, 1991), the majority of correlations between level of help received and achievement in the present study were nonsignificant. But level of help received was highly correlated with level of activity after receiving help, which was strongly related to achievement. Without knowing whether and how the learner applied the help received, it would be impossible to predict whether receiving elaborated explanations would be beneficial for learning.

The importance of applying the help received is consistent with the active role of the learner in Vygotsky's view of the social interaction between more-capable and less-capable persons (Tudge & Rogoff, 1989). In collaboration with more-capable persons, and with support from them, less-capable persons practice the skills they are being taught until they become internalized and can be performed without support. The activity of the learner after receiving an explanation is also likely to be a central component of the negotiation between peers in Piagetian collaborative settings. To learn from a peer, it is not sufficient merely to listen passively to an explanation of a conflicting view. It is also necessary to determine the nature of the inconsistencies between one's view and another's view, decide which parts of one's own view may be erroneous or incomplete, and change one's own view accordingly.

This study looked at the level of activity of work carried out by students after receiving explanations, mainly defined by the completeness of their work and the degree of independence from others, but did not distinguish between different kinds of activity at the same level. An important question is whether some kinds of high-level activity would be more beneficial for learning than other kinds of high-level activity. Due to the low frequency of high-level activity in this study, we were unable to address this question. Explaining to another person, for example, with the intent to teach or help that person may be more effective than verbalizing what one has learned simply to demonstrate mastery or carrying out work without much verbalization. Durling and Schick (1976), for example, found that vocalizing to a peer who was also learning the task at the same time produced greater concept attainment than vocalizing to the experimenter who had already mastered the task. Their results, combined with the work of Bargh and Schul (1980; see also Benware & Deci, 1984) showing that persons studying to teach others learned more than persons studying to learn the material for themselves, suggest that the benefits of giving explanations to others involve cognitive restructuring and not just cognitive rehearsal. This work suggests that explaining to others with the intent to help them learn or understand one's own perspective, as may occur when resolving social and cognitive conflicts in a Piagetian setting or when trying to help others learn in cooperative or collaborative group settings, may be more effective than the explaining that the less-capable person is asked to carry out to demonstrate understanding in a Vygotskian pairing.

It is possible that the consistent beneficial effect of giving explanations shown in previous research is related to the intent to teach. In much of the research showing positive correlations between giving explanations and achievement, giving explanations was coded in the context of one student helping another (Webb, 1989). The relative effectiveness of explaining with the intent to teach and explaining with the intent to demonstrate one's own competence is an important question for further research. If it is found that the intent to teach makes explaining more effective for the explainer, this could be designed into instructional programs designed to promote high-level explaining.

Implications and Questions From This Study

The instructional program implemented in this study was effective in encouraging explanations—students who received three phases of instruction in communications skills, helping behavior, and explaining skills engaged in more high-level explaining than students who had received only two phases of instruction. Even though the program did not provide explicit instruction in carrying out constructive activity, students receiving the full program also engaged in more constructive activity than students receiving only the first two phases. Although the program seemed to be effective, the results raise a number of questions for further research and suggest some possible implications for practice. These are discussed next.

Promoting High-Level Explaining and Constructive Activity. This study used a few specific strategies to encourage students to give high-level explanations (primarily skits for students to role play about the difference between an explanation and only the answer, and Pairs-Check in which students took turns playing the role of coach to give other students explanations) and used no explicit strategies to encourage constructive activity after receiving help. Although students did give some high-level explanations and did carry out some constructive activity, they did not always do so. Additional strategies might be incorporated into an instructional program to make it more powerful (see chaps. 4, 6, and 7 for examples).

Responsibilities of the Help Seeker.   This study investigated the kinds of help that students received and the behavior of students after receiving help. It did not examine help seeking in detail. As mentioned earlier, Nelson-Le Gall (1981, 1985; Nelson-Le Gall et al., 1983) described multiple antecedents for receiving help, including being aware that one needs help, being willing to seek help, identifying someone who can provide help, and using effective strategies to elicit help. The only students analyzed in this study were those who asked for help or made errors that indicated a need for help. Some students were clearly aware that they needed help (they asked questions), whereas others were not aware that they needed help (they made errors but did not know that they were wrong). De Lisi and Golbeck (chap. 1, this volume) provide an interesting analysis of how children become aware of a gap in their understanding and their response to that awareness. An interesting question for further research is whether students who are aware of needing help are more receptive to receiving explanations and carrying out further activity than are students who have their errors pointed out by others.

There was no way in this study to identify students who were aware that they needed help but who were unwilling to seek it. However, the fact that some groups had a silent or near-silent low-achieving student is strongly suggestive that some students were unwilling to seek help. The intensive analyses showed that groups with a silent student did not welcome the student into group discussion but instead expected that student only to copy the group's work, and expressed resentment at having to involve the student in group work. The group's attitude and behavior may be traced to that of the teacher: This teacher put groups under time pressure by giving them only a small portion of class time to work together, either was not aware that some students were being excluded from group discussion or failed to intervene to prevent it, and focused on group management issues (e.g., signing each other's papers regardless of whether they worked together). The time pressure and the focus on group mechanics likely added to the social pressures not to seek help: Individuals knew that groups would not be receptive to their asking for help, and groups discouraged such participation. In the instructional program implemented in this study, classes did discuss and post a chart of help-seeking behaviors. However, it is likely that the time pressures imposed by this teacher undermined help seeking.

The classroom discussions of help seeking in this study focused mainly on the kinds of questions to ask other students (e.g., specific rather than general). Although recognizing that one needs help was mentioned as the first step in help seeking (e.g., Say to yourself "I don't understand how to calculate the sales tax"; Farivar & Webb, 1994), there was no discussion of the metacognitive strategies students might use to gain such an awareness, such as self-testing or comparing their work with that of others. In fact, in this study, when students' answers disagreed, they were much more likely to insist that the other students were wrong than to question their own understanding. Instruction and practice in help seeking, then, should include an explicit focus on metacognitive strategies.

Group Composition and Group Size. When students are put into groups for instruction, teachers must make decisions about assignment to groups. Following recommendations by cooperative learning researchers (e.g., Cohen, 1994a; Miller & Harrington, 1990; Slavin, 1986), teachers in this study were directed to form heterogeneous four-person groups that were as balanced as possible according to gender and ethnicity and that included a high-ability, a low-ability, and two middle-ability students. As seen earlier in the discussion of specific groups, one teacher's groups (Teacher B) each had a nonparticipating student (a low-achieving Latina), whereas the other teacher (Teacher A) formed groups in which all students participated, regardless of their gender, ability level, or ethnic background. Status characteristics (Berger, Rosenholtz, & Zelditch, 1980; Cohen, 1982; Cohen, Lotan, & Catanzarite, 1990) may have operated to suppress the participation of some students in Teacher B's classes but not Teacher A's classes. It is possible that the behaviors and attitudes of the teachers played a large part in reducing or accentuating the usual effects of status on student behavior: Teacher A worked hard to establish the norms of working together, helping, and explaining in her classrooms' groups, whereas Teacher B emphasized completing the work and obtaining correct answers in a short amount of time and rarely addressed helping and explaining with individual groups in her classrooms. The lack of participation of low-status students in Teacher B's classrooms blocked their access to the benefits found in this study of receiving explanations and carrying out subsequent constructive activity.

In addition to creating a climate in which participation of all students and help giving and help receiving are encouraged, teachers need to be aware of how group compositions can accentuate or diminish status differences. Because status is often relative (Cohen, 1994b; Cohen et al., 1990), the same student may have lower status in some groups than in others. Following Miller and Harrington's (1990) recommendations to form groups so that status characteristics are less salient to group members and to ensure that one person does not have low status on multiple characteristics simultaneously, a low-ability, Latina female could be assigned to a group with other Latina females instead of to a group of Anglo and Asian males, for example. Interviewing students about their perceptions of their role and functioning in the group may also help reveal relationships among students that teachers need to take into account when assigning students to groups. It is important for teachers to know the social and cultural context in the classroom and school and use this information thoughtfully when forming groups.

This study used groups of four. The fact that Teacher B's groups had a nonparticipating student suggests that groups of four may sometimes be too large for students to work together effectively. Groups of three might make it easier to help one another and may make it less likely for one person to withdraw from the group. Some previous studies found more equal participation in smaller groups than in larger groups (comparing groups of size two, three, and four), but the results are inconsistent (see Webb & Palincsar, 1996). Future research should compare the quality of helping behavior and the equality of participation in groups of different sizes. Teachers may also be able to gauge whether a particular group would function more effectively with three, rather than four, students.

The Role of the Teacher.   When students are working together in groups, the teacher takes on a new kind of role, that of monitor, coach, facilitator. The teacher must be active in this process, needs to check in with groups, must monitor progress and interaction, and must insist that group work standards are kept. As necessary, the teacher can model good helping behavior, give examples, and observe whether targeted skills, such as explaining, are being practiced (see Wood & Yackel, 1990; Yackel et al., 1991).

It is essential for teachers who facilitate group work to be persistent in their observations and have "eagle eyes" to ensure that all group members are involved and that no one is left out. The teacher must continually be aware of what is going on in all groups and help insure that all students are accepted in their groups, feel included, and feel safe to take risks during group work. However, the teacher must let the students do the work, falter as they learn, and persist through the rough spots.

How teachers manage time is a key factor in how students work with one another and whether they have time to work together. Teachers need to allow students time to develop strategies for working together and for solving classwork problems, time to attempt several ways to solve problems, and time to explain the work and ensure that everyone understands. When teachers do too much talking, students rush through work and some are silenced.

The Academic Content of Group Work.   This study showed that students sometimes found it difficult to learn how to carry out the targeted helping skills and deal with difficult new mathematical content simultaneously. This was particularly the case when students were learning how to give explanations at the same time as they were trying to convert numbers between percentages and decimals, a topic that was difficult for them. The implication is that when students are first learning how to work together, how to ask for and give help and how to explain to one another, they should develop and practice these behaviors with relatively familiar content so that they are not grappling with the content at the same time that they are trying to learn how to use helping skills.

Much of the material that groups worked on in this study came from a traditional mathematics curriculum and textbook with a heavy emphasis on mathematical procedures. The problems assigned as classwork, which usually had well-defined procedures, did not always require participation by all students in the group. Groups could obtain a high grade on classwork by having the most competent student in the group solve the problems and then dictate the solutions to the other students (see Hastie, 1986; Laughlin & Ellis, 1986). Although this practice clearly went against the desired norms for group work and helping behavior, it did occur in some groups. To maximize the participation of all members of the group, Cohen (1994b; Cohen & Cohen, 1991) recommended that groups be given complex tasks with ill-structured solutions that cannot be completed very well by a single individual and that require the combined expertise of everyone in the group. In the context of this study, alternatives to the procedural problems that students were asked to solve may be problems with more than one answer and with multiple paths to the solution. In contrast to artificial problems devoid of context (e.g., find 25% of 32), for example, students could carry out mathematics in the context of a real application such as calculating the percentage that each homeroom contributed to the school's holiday food drive, calculating how many families of various sizes the food will feed, and packing the foods for real families. Such activities would necessitate rich discussion, active participation by all students, and a range of skills.

In conclusion, this study showed that students can learn to help one another and how to ask for help. Students can ask targeted questions, give explanations, teach one another, and learn how to learn. Throughout the study, students showed awareness of the importance of giving and receiving help, especially explanations, and of the benefits of working together. Their acceptance of this new way of learning and working was not seamless, it developed more strongly in some groups than in others, but it was apparent nevertheless. Teachers can step back, out of the role of classroom director, and let the students use these new skills.

ACKNOWLEDGMENTS

This study was supported in part by a grant from the Academic Senate on Research, Los Angeles Division, University of California. However, all opinions in this article are those of the authors.

We are grateful to Jerold Kantor, Chris Iwasa, Sandy Nonhof, Jack Hinds, and Colleen Nakamura for participating in this project.

CHAPTER SIX

Designing Collaborative Contexts: Lessons from Three Research Programs

ANNEMARIE SULLIVAN PALINCSAR
University of Michigan

LESLIE RUPERT HERRENKOHL
University of Washington

Following 4 months of daily experience working in small groups, we asked sixth-grade students to evaluate the advantages and disadvantages of working with other people versus working alone. We were fascinated with the responses, especially with the responses to the probe regarding the advantages of working alone:

"You would not have to prove anything to anyone except yourself"

"You wouldn't have to convince anyone"

"You will be able to use your own ideas all the time"

"Nobody to disagree and nobody to argue with"

"You don't have to explain your ideas to someone"

We were impressed with the pattern that emerged from the children's responses; more than 90% of the 44 children responding noted in some fashion that the challenge of working with others is the challenge of achieving consensus. This was in stark contrast with the children's responses to this same question before they embarked on this 4-month adventure with group work. At that time, their responses were more diverse and spoke to issues of privacy, getting more work done, getting work done more quickly, and getting full credit for your work and ideas. What impressed us about the children's reflections after working in small groups is that they captured the essence of collaboration—convergence, or the construction of shared meanings for conversations, concepts, and experiences (Brown & Palincsar, 1989; Roschelle, 1992). Furthermore, their comments reflect the challenges inherent in collaborative activity.

As O'Donnell and King (see Conclusion, this volume) suggest, *peer learning* refers to a host of learning experiences with a diverse array of purposes. In their review of contemporary approaches to peer learning in classrooms, Webb and Palincsar (1996) referred to 12 structural approaches to peer learning, including, for example, peer tutoring, forms of cooperative learning (e.g., jigsaw and teams, games, and tournaments), peer response groups in writing, and student-led book clubs. The emergence of so many peer-based forms of learning in classrooms is, in part, a reflection of evolving constructivist views of the learner with the concomitant perspective that learning occurs as individuals interpret their experiences in particular contexts, including through interactions with others. Furthermore, the most prominent contemporary theories of learning, including sociocognitive conflict (derived from the work of Piaget and his disciples), and sociocultural (derived from the work of Vygotsky and his disciples) and motivational theories all speak to ways in which peer interaction can promote learning and cognitive development (see chaps. 1 & 2, this volume).

In this chapter, we are interested in peer learning that is designed to promote collaboration; specifically, we explore three instructional contexts that were designed to promote collaboration among children. We begin by drawing distinctions between collaborative and cooperative learning. The hallmark of collaboration is that thinking is distributed among the members of the group. The group shares cognitive responsibility for the task at hand. All members of the group work on the same aspect of the problem at the same time and the group members are encouraged to externalize their thoughts as they work through the problem. Furthermore, the participants are asked to come to agreement among themselves before proceeding to a new problem (cf. Taylor & Cox, 1997).

Whereas there are certain forms of cooperative learning that can occur without collaboration, collaborative learning is generally assumed to subsume cooperation (cf. Chan, Burtis, & Bereiter, 1997). Although relatively little has been written about collaborative—as opposed to cooperative—learning among peers, the sense emerging from the literature is that the essence of collaboration is convergence, or the construction of shared meanings for conversations, concepts, and experiences. Roschelle (1992) argued that convergence is achieved through cycles of displaying, confirming, and repairing shared meanings. The iterative nature of the interactions leads to the joint use of meanings, meanings for which there are shared understandings. This process of achieving convergence can also be considered the attainment of intersubjectivity, which Trevarthen (1980) defined as "both recognition and control of cooperative intentions and joint patterns of awareness" (p. 530). We agree with Matusov (1996) that consensus is not the only outcome of achieving intersubjectivity; nonconsensus is just as important and interesting an outcome. What is compelling in the collaborative process are the ways in which the participants coordinate their contributions in joint problem-solving activity to arrive at both agreement and disagreement.

In addition to their focus on collaboration, each of the three contexts that we discuss represents research that has been conceptualized from a sociocultural perspective. We characterize this perspective in the next section.

APPLYING SOCIOCULTURAL THEORY
TO COLLABORATIVE LEARNING

From a sociocultural perspective, cognition itself is a collaborative process (see Rogoff, 1998), and the purpose of inquiry regarding cognitive development is to examine the transformation of socially shared activities into internalized processes (see John-Steiner & Mahn, 1996). The role of social processes as a mechanism for learning is usually identified with Vygotsky, who suggested, "The social dimension of consciousness is primary in time and in fact. The individual dimension of consciousness is derivative and secondary" (p. 30, cited in Wertsch & Bivens, 1992). From this perspective, mental functioning of the individual is not simply derived from social interaction; rather, the specific processes revealed by individuals can be traced to their interactions with others.

Wertsch (1991) proposed three major themes in Vygotsky's writings that elucidate the nature of the interdependence between individual and social processes in learning and development. The first theme is that individual development, including higher mental functioning, has its origins in social sources. This theme is best represented in Vygotsky's "genetic law of development":

> Every function in the cultural development of the child comes on the stage twice, in two respects: first in the social, later in the psychological, first in relations between people as an interpsychological category, afterwards within the child as an intrapsychological category. . . . All higher psychological functions are internalized relationships of the social kind, and constitute the social structure of personality. (Valsiner, 1987, p. 67)

From this perspective, as learners participate in a broad range of joint activities and internalize the effects of working together, they acquire new strategies and knowledge of the world and the cultures in which they are participants. Typically, this tenet has been illustrated examining the interactions of more and less knowledgeable others; for example, children and their caregivers or experts and novices. Illustrative is the cross-cultural research of Rogoff (1991), who studied the supportive contexts in which Mayan children acquire knowledge and strategies:

> The routine arrangements and interactions between children and their caregivers and companions provide children with thousands of opportunities to observe and

participate in the skilled activities of their culture. Through repeated and varied experience in supported routine and challenging situations, children become skilled practitioners in the specific cognitive activities in their communities. (p. 351)

Perhaps as a consequence of these research contexts, contemporary critics of a sociocultural perspective argue that it is a *transfer of knowledge* model (e.g., Cobb, Wood, & Yackel, 1993). However, scholars of this perspective argue that this interpretation is simplistic and misinterprets the transformative nature of internalization that has been described by sociocultural researchers. In our description of the three contexts we explore in this chapter, we address the ways in which coconstruction, rather than simple transmission, occur and we speak to the design of collaborative group work to promote coconstruction.

The second Vygotskian theme that Wertsch (1991) identified is that human action, on both the social and individual planes, is mediated by tools and signs. Semiotic means, or sign systems, including "language; various systems of counting; mnemonic techniques; algebraic symbol systems; works of art; writing; schemes, diagrams, maps and mechanical drawings; all sorts of conventional signs and so on" (Vygotsky, 1981b, p. 137) are important in the higher mental functions of human beings. From this perspective, the researcher studying collaboration is interested in the extent to which these sign systems both facilitate the coconstruction of knowledge in groups and become the means that are internalized to aid future independent problem-solving activity. Leont'ev (1981), a colleague of Vygotsky, used the term appropriation to characterize this process:

> [Children] cannot and need not reinvent artifacts that have taken millennia to evolve in order to appropriate such objects into their own system of activity. The child has only to come to an understanding that it is adequate for using the culturally elaborated object in the novel life circumstances he encounters. (quoted in Newman, Griffin, & Cole, 1989, p. 63)

It is in this sense that the process of collaboration is at the same time the product of collaboration. In the description of the three contexts, we pay special attention to the semiotic means that are featured across these contexts.

The third theme that Wertsch (1991) proposed from Vygotsky's writing is that the first two themes are best examined through genetic, or developmental, analysis:

> To study something historically means to study it in the process of change; that is the dialectical method's basic demand. To encompass in research the process of a given thing's development in all its phases and changes—from birth to death— fundamentally means to discover its nature, its essence, for it is only in movement that a body shows what it is. Thus the historical study of behavior is not an auxiliary aspect of theoretical study, but rather forms its very base. (Vygotsky, 1978, pp. 64–65)

Hogan and Tudge (chap. 2, this volume) outline the four levels of genetic analysis that Vygotsky pursued, all of which are interwoven: phylogenetic, cultural–historical, ontogenetic, and microgenetic. Through the use of genetic analyses it is possible to examine the complex interplay of mediational tools, the individual, and the social world as well as understand the process of internalization. We focus on the microgenetic level of development in our representations of the three contexts, given that the data that we collected reflect a brief period of time in the lives of classrooms and students. The first of the three contexts we describe is Reciprocal Teaching, which we discuss for the purpose of identifying lessons learned from this program of research and the ways in which this research influenced the design of the other two contexts (Collaborative Problem Solving and Cognitive Tools and Intellectual Roles) described in this chapter, both of which were intended to enhance children's ability to engage in scientific problem solving. We chose to organize our discussion of each of the three programs of research in terms of three features: the support of interactive patterns, the nature of the problem space, and the process of creating a shared social context. These are features that our experiences suggest are particularly useful to designing and evaluating collaborative learning contexts.

THREE CONTEXTS FOR COLLABORATIVE LEARNING

Reciprocal Teaching

Reciprocal teaching was designed as an educational intervention to be used with students who demonstrate significant disparities between their ability to decode text and to comprehend text (Brown & Palincsar, 1989; Palincsar & Brown, 1984, 1989). Typically, the participants in reciprocal teaching have fallen below the 35th percentile on standardized assessments of comprehension. Reciprocal Teaching features guided practice in the use of four strategies designed to promote understanding of text. The students and teacher take turns leading discussions about shared text. These dialogues are structured using four strategies. Specifically, before reading the text, the group generates predictions regarding the content that they expect or hope to read about given the topic of the passage. Following the reading of the initial portion of the text, the discussion leader raises questions about the content of the text. The group discusses these questions, raises additional questions, and in the case of disagreement or misunderstanding, rereads the text. Whereas the questions are used to stimulate discussion, summarizing is used to identify the gist of what has been read and discussed and to prepare the group to proceed to the next segment of text. The third strategy, clarification, is used opportunistically for the purpose of restoring meaning when a concept, word, or phrase is unfamiliar to someone in the group or is a source of confusion to the group. Finally, the discussion leader proposes new predictions for the upcoming text, based on prior knowledge of the topic of the text, personal questions regarding the topic, or based on clues that are provided in the text itself (e.g., embedded questions). This leads to the selection of a new discussion leader and the reading of the next portion of text.

The research on reciprocal teaching has generally been conducted in the areas of reading and listening comprehension instruction by general, remedial, and special educators. Typically, the instruction has been conducted in small groups (averaging six to eight) for a period of 20 to 25 days. To determine the outcomes of this instruction, students completed comprehension measures that assessed recall of text, as well as the ability to draw inferences, state the gist of the material read, and apply information encountered in the text to a novel situation. Based on the performance of students not experiencing comprehension-related difficulties, we determined that the criterion indicative of success with these assessments was the attainment of a score of 75% to 80% correct on four out of five consecutively administered assessments. Using this criterion, approximately 80% of primary (Palincsar, Brown, & Campione, 1993) and middle school (Palincsar & Brown, 1984, 1989) students were determined to be successful. Furthermore, these gains were observed to be maintained for up to 6 months to a year following instruction.

In addition to the frequent measures of comprehension, which were independent of the passages used in the instruction, and were administered during the reciprocal teaching instruction (daily for the upper elementary and middle school students and every other day for the primary students), we audiotaped and transcribed each day of instruction and then analyzed the dialogues over intervals of time (e.g., every 5th day). In this manner, we were able to capture both the development of the groups as well as the concomitant changes in the comprehension performance of the individual participants in the groups.

In the next section, we want to propose critical features of reciprocal teaching by drawing on a decade of reciprocal teaching research and literally hundreds of conversations with teachers engaged in reciprocal teaching dialogues. We organize these features in terms of the support of interactive patterns, the nature of the problem space, and the view of learning as acculturation.

The Support of Interactive Patterns

Rogoff, Matusov, and White (1996) argued that to promote collaboration there must be the development of an intersubjective attitude—a commitment to find a common ground on which to build shared understanding (Crook, 1994; Rommetveit, 1974). Reciprocal teaching's dialogic nature and the explicit goal of making sense of the text provide the context for this interaction. Furthermore, the specific strategies used to scaffold the dialogues both invite alternative views of the text as well as encourage the participants to achieve consensus regarding the text. For example, the questions and predictions students raise in the course of reciprocal teaching dialogues may be relatively unconstrained by the text as they represent not only what the students have identified as information acquired in the course of reading the text, but also include issues that students perceive as related to the text, assorted recollections that have been triggered by their reading, or wonderings that may, in fact, never be addressed in the text. In contrast, when the students are summarizing or clarifying the text, they are asked to come to agreement regarding issues such as the "big ideas" in the portion of text under discussion, and they are asked to use the text to support their interpretations.

The relationship of the strategies to the process of developing an intersubjective attitude became clear early in the reciprocal teaching research program. Initially, rather than begin the dialogues with questions of the text, followed by summaries, clarifications, and predictions, children were first invited to clarify what they found confusing. Typically, the children would identify isolated "hard words." This led to a fragmentation of the text and of the conversation, with the teacher being viewed as the sole authority in the group, the translator of difficult words. When the order of the strategies was transposed, the participant structure changed to the extent that there was a sharing out of the process of making sense of the text. Furthermore, it was determined that hard words were actually less problematic and clarifications turned to the bigger ideas in the text that had emerged in the course of generating questions and summarizing the text.

An additional feature of reciprocal teaching that promotes the development of an intersubjective attitude is the expectation that every participant in the group will be responsible for leading the dialogue and will receive the assistance necessary to do so. It is this feature of reciprocal teaching that places significant demands on the teacher. First, teachers play an important role in making clear the expectation that the group observes this social structure. Second, the teacher is actively engaged in enabling all members of the group to be productive participants. This activity of *scaffolding* (Wood & Middleton, 1975) involves an elegant interplay between teachers and students, demanding that, during instruction, teachers are analyzing students' thinking and constantly making decisions about how to advance student understanding while respecting and building on current understanding (Palincsar, 1986, 1998a). As a form of collaborative learning, we have been intrigued with students' ability to provide scaffolding for one another. Frequently, we have observed ways in which students whose zones of proximal development may overlap more with one another than with an adult teacher's have very effectively provided supportive assistance to one another. For example, in the process of helping a peer to make sense of a confusion in the text, children construct metaphors, drawing on action heroes, computer games, song lyrics, and other contemporary popular media about which adults may know very little.

The Nature of the Problem

The nature of the problem clearly influences the activity of constructing meaning and promoting opportunities for attaining consensus. In reciprocal teaching, the nature of the problem is defined both by the demands of the text as well as the purposes for reading the text. The relation between the problem and the demands of the text became quite clear to us when we introduced reciprocal teaching at the first-grade level. At this level, we were confronted with the challenge of finding text that was worthy of discussion. The types of text available to young children often place a priority on controlling the vocabulary or rendering the text highly predictable. Whereas these are important attributes of text when the goal is to enable young children to read with fluency, they are not necessarily attributes of text that lends itself to rich conversation. Hence, rather than use text that was designed to support independent reading, we turned instead to children's periodicals that had short informational articles and engaging narratives with interesting plot structures (e.g., surprise twists) that were read aloud by the teacher.

The nature of the problem is also a function of how the text is being used. One use is simply to figure out what the text is about, and in the initial studies of reciprocal teaching this was the primary purpose. Students read disconnected texts and little reference was made across texts. A second use of the text is to enhance one's understanding of a specific topic or domain of knowledge. For example, the reciprocal teaching dialogues with the first graders (Palincsar et al., 1993) were used to learn simple science concepts related to animal survival themes, such as protection from the elements and protection from enemies through camouflage and mimicry. These themes were represented across the texts used in the dialogues and gave rise to interesting outcomes. For example, there were now opportunities for children to bring the shared knowledge that they were developing to the dialogues. There were multiple occasions for referencing earlier texts and discussions. In addition, there was greater clarity regarding the purposes for discussing the meaning of the text to the extent that the children and teachers focused more of the discussions on how new information in the stories was advancing what the children already knew about the topic at hand.

Brown and Campione (1994) illustrated how Reciprocal Teaching dialogues have become a core participant structure in their Communities of Learners classrooms, where students are engaged in problem spaces that include the development of complex reasoning, argumentation, and explanation as they engage in research.

The Process of Creating a Shared Social Context

The process of learning to engage in collaborative learning is, in many respects, a process of creating a shared social world. For the children and teachers "trying on" reciprocal teaching dialogues, this has often meant cultivating a new pattern of instructional discourse in the classroom; the pattern may be new to the extent that the activity of reciprocal teaching engages children and teachers in making their thinking public as they apply the strategies to understanding the text. It may be different to the extent that the children are called on to share their own expertise and knowledge in making sense of the text, and to assist one another in making sense of the text. Perhaps the change is greatest to the extent that final authority for coming to consensus regarding the meaning of the text rests with the group and not solely with the adult member of the group.

Clearly, teachers' experiences with introducing reciprocal teaching dialogues vary—in part—as a function of the ways in which this form of dialogic collaboration reflects or departs from their prior experience, and, of course, their beliefs about teaching and learning. There are similar issues for older students as well. One example that leaps to mind is the seventh grader who, when she was the dialogue leader, wanted to write her questions down and show them only to the teacher, rather than contribute them to the dialogue. Her reasoning was that if she said them aloud, everyone would know what to study as they read the text.

In contrast to the other two contexts that we describe in this chapter, the teacher's role in this process is prominent and sustained in reciprocal teaching dialogues. Although the teacher is consciously attempting to cede more responsibility to the students for leading and sustaining the dialogue, this occurs through a process in which the teacher is initially engaged in instruction, explaining the use of the strategies and modeling their appropriate use relative to the demands of the texts. Over time, the active teaching on the part of the teacher is reduced to coaching, at least until such time as the group reaches an impediment in the dialogue or the text poses challenges that exceed the group's ability to proceed.

Thinking about learning as a process of creating a shared social world has been useful to thinking about the nature of the changes that one can anticipate over time when instituting reciprocal teaching dialogues in a classroom. Initially, the dialogues are rough and stilted. The strategies drive the dialogues and what is celebrated is the production of a question or the refinement of a summary. Teachers are initially surprised at how dependent the group is on their support. In addition, the strategies are quite salient; for example, the wording of a question receives considerable attention, whereas identifying main ideas in the text receives less attention. Over the course of time, the discussions are increasingly focused on the meaning of the text; that is, the strategies are used flexibly, the dialogue becomes less routinized, and the conversation becomes more free-ranging.

In the next section of this chapter, we proceed to a second collaborative learning context, one designed to promote conceptual understanding in science. Following a description of this context, we use the same three features—supporting interactive patterns, the nature of the problem, and the view of learning as creating a shared social context—to reflect on lessons learned in this program of research and to contrast this collaborative context with reciprocal teaching.

COLLABORATIVE PROBLEM SOLVING IN SCIENCE (CPS)[1]

This program of research was conducted over a 4-year period and was designed to enhance the scientific literacy of sixth graders. Our definition of scientific literacy includes (a) the ability to apply scientific knowledge or concepts in principled ways; (b) facility with the language of science to enable the interpretation and production of spoken and written text; and (c) given the inherently social nature of scientific activity, collaborative skills that promote constructive social interaction (Palincsar, Anderson, & David, 1993).

Three features are useful to describing the CPS program. The first is the subject matter, which was the study of the particulate theory of matter as applied to understanding states of matter and changes of state, as well as other physical changes such as dissolving substances and making and separating mixtures. The subject matter was presented in the curriculum via benchmark lessons in which the students read and discussed information regarding, for example, the relation between temperature and the movement and arrangement of molecules and then engaged in small-group activity in which they were asked to apply the information toward the solution of a problem. To illustrate, in exploring the relation between temperature and changes of state, the students conducted investigations of why popcorn pops. During the course of the 10-week CPS program, nine problems were posed for the small groups to solve. Students were typically asked to independently generate solutions to the problems posed before meeting in their small groups to increase the expectation that everyone would come to the table with something to contribute to the group's effort.

To support the students' interactions in the small-group activity, there were two additional features of the CPS program. First, the students were introduced and coached in the use of explanations as they engaged in their problem solving; specifically, they were informed that explanations should include (a) identification of the substances that were involved in the problem, (b) descriptions of what was happening to the substances (drawing on observations of the data they had gathered), and (c) descriptions of what was happening to the molecules of the substances (drawing on what they knew regarding the movement and arrangement of molecules). Coaching occurred both through whole-class discussion of various explanations that children had provided, as well as though the use of feedback regarding the explanations that the students generated in their individual and small-group work.

Finally, there were four social norms that were introduced to the students. Although the researchers generated these norms, the students were asked periodically throughout the instruction to identify the specific ways in which they were

---

[1] The Collaborative Problem Solving in Science research was conducted in collaboration with Charles Anderson, science educator, from Michigan State University.

experiencing interactions that were supportive of these norms. The four norms with accompanying activities identified by the students follow. The first was to contribute to the group's efforts and help others contribute; the students identified the activities promoting this norm to include sharing resources, discussing ideas, and taking turns with different jobs. The second norm was to give reasons for our ideas, which the students associated with saying ideas in more than one way if they were not understood, and providing examples that would communicate one's ideas. The third norm was to work to understand others' ideas by restating ideas, asking questions when ideas were unclear, and giving everyone time to think. The final norm called for students to build on one another's ideas, a process the students suggested was aided by comparing others' ideas to one's own, explaining reasons for disagreeing with ideas, and acknowledging when someone had a good idea.

The research that we discuss in this chapter was conducted in two middle school sixth grades, composed of students from diverse socioeconomic backgrounds. A total of 21% of the students were from ethnic groups traditionally underrepresented in the pursuit of science. The students were placed in groups of four, and were heterogeneous with regard to science achievement as determined by teacher nomination, as well as the results of the conceptual pretests (described later). Because we were interested in the interactions of the group members over time, the membership in the groups remained constant. In each class, there were two case study groups selected. All of their small-group activity was videotaped. In addition, we collected and reproduced all of their written work. Finally, the case study students were interviewed several times weekly regarding the nature of their experiences in their small-group activity.

Before presenting a few of the lessons learned about peer collaboration in this context, we present a brief summary of the outcomes of this approach. Conceptual measures were administered on a pre- and posttest basis to students in the CPS classrooms, as well as students in the same school who were studying a unit on matter and molecules that was the previous version of this curriculum and did not include the collaborative problem-solving activities (Palincsar, Anderson, & Ford, 1998). The conceptual measure was a paper-and-pencil test consisting of 30 open- and close-ended questions that assessed the students' understandings of the scientific concepts that were targeted in this matter and molecules unit (e.g., states of matter and changes of state, and molecular explanations for processes such as evaporation, distillation, and crystallization). For example, one question read, "Two students were arguing about how they could treat dirty rain water so that they could drink it. Gerry suggested pouring the water through a coffee filter. Pat said, 'I still wouldn't drink that water.' With whom do you agree and why?" Whereas there were no significant differences on the pretest measures across the students in the experimental and control classes, there were significant differences in the posttest results, with the experimental students attaining significantly higher scores on the posttest conceptual measures. These gains were realized by both male and female participants, and held true across achievement levels; that is, there were significant pre- to posttest differences among the students in the CPS classes, regardless of gender or initial achievement levels. The gains demonstrated by the case study groups were representative of the gains made across the groups in the experimental classes.

We also conducted a qualitative analysis of the responses to the pre- and post-measures for the experimental and control students and learned that the differences in the outcomes of these two groups were largely a function of shifts in the experimental group from macroscopic explanations (that focused on describing the processes at an observable phenomenological level) to molecular-level explanations, as well as increased accuracy, complexity, and completeness in providing scientific interpretations of the phenomena that were presented in the conceptual measures. These were encouraging findings, although they were tempered by two findings that were less pleasing: (a) The gains for the experimental children who were identified as members of groups traditionally underrepresented in science were not comparable to the gains of the other experimental students, even though they performed comparably to the other students on the pretest measure (although we have to be cautious here given the small sample size); and (b) we had hoped to see even greater qualitative differences in the kinds of explanations that children in the experimental classes were providing on the posttest conceptual measures. As we examine CPS in terms of three features that were used to examine reciprocal teaching, we return to the successes and shortcomings suggested by the outcomes of the conceptual measures.

The Support of Interactive Patterns and Norms

Perhaps the most useful way of discussing how interaction was supported in the CPS curriculum is to consider the domain-specific nature of the tools and language that were used in this context. Contemporary cognitive and social approaches to science learning highlight the use of specialized language (Lemke, 1990) and the ability to reflect on one's explanatory knowledge (Chi, Bassok, Lewis, Reimann, & Glaser, 1989) to achieve deeper conceptual understanding of scientific phenomena. However, research conducted by King (1990b and chap. 4, this volume) indicates that students do not spontaneously generate productive questions or explanations without support. The support provided in the CPS context (by the teacher and through the structure of the activity) was modeling and guidance in the use of observation, macroscopic description, and molecular description in generating explanations. In this regard, the precise use of language in the course of generating, sharing, and refining explanations was designed to be both a process and a product in the CPS context. The pre- and post-measures mentioned earlier suggest that students in the CPS curriculum did indeed learn to generate more accurate and complete explanations.

However, to evaluate the extent to which the enhanced ability to generate explanations was a consequence of repeated experiences working in a group to co-construct scientific understanding, we need to consider the other two features: the nature of the problems and the issues related to the social context.

The Nature of the Problems

We observed a set of design principles in relation to designing the problems in the CPS curriculum (see Anderson, Palincsar, & Kurth, 1996). A first principle was that the problems afford students the opportunity to explore scientific concepts that have broad explanatory power in making sense of the world. A second principle was that students have the opportunity to refine their understandings of concepts over time. Hence, determining the fastest and slowest ways of dissolving a substance and investigating how to grow large and small crystals engaged students in different explorations of the relations between the nature of the substance and other variables, such as temperature, motion, and time. In addition, the problem design was informed by the research on conceptual understanding of matter and molecules; for example, it has been determined that students confuse dissolving with disappearing (Berkheimer, Anderson, & Blakeslee, 1988); hence, problems were included in the curriculum that would engage students in the process of examining evidence regarding the presence or absence of the solute in the solvent.

Bruffee and Leveson (in press) suggested that we consider the nature of tasks used in collaborative problem solving in terms of being "knowledge-authorizing"; they suggested that it is only with activities that are knowledge authorizing that students create the tools that are necessary to solve the problem, construct scientific knowledge, and renegotiate their own conceptions. Although Bruffee and Leveson do not elaborate on what knowledge authorizing tasks actually entail, our experiences with CPS have revealed interesting dimensions that might put some flesh on this notion. We found, for example, that when there is too much complexity to the problem, most of the group's attention is focused on the procedural aspects and less time is devoted to the scientific warrants and explanations. On the other hand, when there was insufficient complexity, the exchanges were primarily ritualized uses of explanation applied in a post hoc manner. To illustrate, we draw on transcripts of one group engaged in two problem types. In the first problem, the students are generating their solution to getting sugar out of a tea bag without opening the tea bag. Drawing largely on their experiential knowledge of tea bags, they agree that they will immerse the tea bag in water:

1. RUBIO: You know what we can do, put it in boiling water and it will come out.
2. ERIC: Yeah. You can eat it.
3. RUBIO: And it's just like tea.
4. ERIC: No! dah . . . , it's a tea bag.

5. RUBIO: We need boiling water.
6. TED: Or hot water.
7. RUBIO: O.K. We got to put it in boiling water.
8. CHARLES: Or warm water, it doesn't have to be boiling, just hot water. My mom
             just gets water from the faucet.
9. RUBIO: O.K. We need hot water.

In the remainder of this discussion, which lasts another 5 minutes, and in the course of actually carrying out the activity, there is no mention of what is happening to the sugar at either a macroscopic or molecular level, despite the fact that the discussion regarding the temperature of the water clearly has the potential to be of value in thinking about the dissolving process. It is not until the group is hurrying to complete their lab sheet that any mention is made of an explanation for their choice of solution:

1. RUBIO: We have to say something here about what's happening to the sugar
             and what's happening to the molecules . . .
2. TED: The water will break up the sugar and then dissolve it
3. RUBIO: Into?
4. TED: Then to just dissolve it, just say it dissolves . . .

In contrast to this ritualized use of explanation, and a very skimpy explanation at that, 2 days later this same group is considering the challenge of designing a "slow race" to dissolve a cube of sugar. Dissolving a cube of sugar turns out to offer a bit more complexity to the group members, who begin early in their deliberations to discuss what they know about molecules in the dissolving process:

1. CHARLES: Put the sugar cube in a cube of ice! That way the molecules of the
            sugar and the molecules of the ice cannot mix together.
2. RUBIO: Yeah, but the rule is you have to dissolve the sugar . . . you just have
            to do it slow . . . If the molecules don't ever mix, the sugar won't ever
            dissolve.

In this brief exchange, the students are applying what they have learned about the relation between temperature and the movement of molecules, the process of dissolving, and the process of making mixtures at a molecular level, to evaluate and select an appropriate solution to the problem at hand.

As we examined the nine problems in the CPS curriculum, we were struck by the dynamics between the nature of the problem space and the interpersonal relationships of the students. The task must invite negotiation (cf. Cohen, 1994b); if the problem space is too constrained, this is unlikely to happen. If, on the other hand, the limits of the problem space are too ambiguous, then the students once again turn to the authority of the teacher.

In Anderson et al. (1996), we described a design framework that emerged from the CPS research and has been useful to our thinking about the construction of problems that promote collaborative activity in science. The framework suggests attending to four interrelated scientific practices: (a) techniques, through which students engage in inquiry in which they are trying to make reliable and accurate observations; (b) observations, through which students are recording, comparing, and communicating about the phenomena in the inquiry; (c) patterns, through which students are seeking to make rules or generalizations that characterize what they have observed; and (d) explanations, through which students are developing arguments using models or theories to make sense of the patterns they have observed. In the final collaborative problem-solving context that we discuss in this chapter, these design principles emerge not only in configuring the problem space but also in supporting the students' interactions. Before proceeding to discuss that context, we turn to the social issues that emerged in the CPS program.

The Process of Creating a Shared Social Context

With regard to the CPS program of research, it may be more accurate to speak of the process of recreating a shared social context. There were many features of this curriculum that were novel and challenging for the students. For example, interviews with the students indicated that, although they were accustomed to small-group work, they were not accustomed to working in small groups for the purpose of achieving consensus. The comments of the sixth graders, with which we began this chapter, reflect some of the impressions regarding this process. Blunk (1996) conducted a dissertation study in which she examined the students' perspectives on the small-group activity in CPS, using frequent interviews and written reflections. A finding that emerged quickly and repeatedly is that a number of students, especially females, were uncomfortable with the idea of challenging one another's ideas and placed greater value on keeping the peace. For example, in one interview, Elizabeth explained that the group proceeded with a plan against most of the member's better judgment, "just to cheer her up" (in reference to one of the group participants). Hence, although argumentation may be important to the activity of scientists (see Kuhn, 1993, and the section on CTIR in this chapter), sixth graders are hard at work on their own agendas, related to both acquiring status in one's group and seeking solidarity and interpersonal connection in this context.

Furthermore, the challenge of negotiating opportunities for participation in this collaborative activity is even more significant for students who hold a relatively low-status position in the classroom community. In Anderson, Holland, and Palincsar (1997), we recounted the experiences of one young student, Juan, who, despite his competence with the conceptual material and his interest in being a participant in the group work, was repeatedly frustrated in his efforts to assume his place within the group. Similar observations regarding the thorny issues that arise when considering the relations between cognitive and social processes in collaborative learning contexts were made by O'Connor (1998), who closely studied sixth-grade students in mathematics classes over a 2-year period. Her research revealed ways in which ideas were often subordinated to social processes that arose from past interactions among students, suggesting that learning opportunities were filtered through complex interpersonal contexts. Specific phenomena documented by O'Connor include discounting or dismissing individual contributions and resistance to the spirit of the entire enterprise.

Research of this nature suggests that educators interested in the use of collaborative learning need to attend to the development of task requirements and accountability systems that balance attention to the quality of products and performances with attention to the quality of learning processes for all members of a group. In the next and final approach to peer collaboration that we treat in this chapter, special attention is paid to the tools and language of argument structure and the scaffolding of young students' efforts to engage in scientific argumentation.

THE USE OF COGNITIVE TOOLS AND INTELLECTUAL ROLES (CTIR) IN FOURTH-GRADE SCIENCE

This research project evolved from observations of the implementation of a new science program at an urban science and technology magnet school (pre-K through Grade 6). The main purpose of this project was to design a classroom environment that would promote student engagement and collaboration. As teachers in this school implemented their science program, they encountered a number of challenges. The science program was designed so that it had three distinct parts to every lesson: (1) introduction—a brief teacher-directed orientation to the activities in a unit; (2) small-group work time—approximately 30 minutes devoted to group work, with each group completing a different activity and each student in a group assuming a group role such as facilitator or reporter; and (3) reporting—group reporters presented results of their activity to the whole class.

This tripartite organization allowed a rich set of opportunities to emerge in the classroom, but teachers repeatedly described the third component, reporting, as a problematic time in the lesson because, in the words of one teacher, the students would "go on snooze control." Students were not paying close attention to the reports of their classmates. Although cooperation during small-group work was taking place, collaboration at the level of constructing and discussing scientific ideas together as a whole class was not happening spontaneously in the classrooms

In order to address the challenge of creating a classroom environment that invites collaboration among students at the level of constructing and discussing ideas, two theoretically motivated strategies were developed. These strategies were informed by some of the guiding principles involved in reciprocal teaching and CPS. In reciprocal teaching, the focus is on guiding students to use strategies that expert readers employ spontaneously. In CTIR, the emphasis is on strategies that scientists use in formulating explanations of phenomena. Therefore, the first strategy offers students a set of cognitive tools that allow them to examine the similarities and differences that emerged as a result of comparing their small-group science activities.

These tools were developed through synthesizing literature that discussed the nature of scientific knowledge and the tools and processes that characterize scientific discussions. In particular, the work of Kuhn (1992, 1993) and Duschl (1990) was used, as these researchers emphasized the central role that arguing plays in science. Kuhn (1992, 1993) suggested that both children and adults have a tendency to conflate theories and evidence and therefore construct insufficient arguments. Duschl (1990) discussed what he called the "rational feedback mechanisms of science" (p. 53). He suggested that there are two mechanisms of change in science that operate through a feedback system. Specifically, new theories can be generated from existing data or from new data. Implicit in both of these important mechanisms is the notion that theories and evidence must converge in order to develop a viable scientific model. These perspectives emphasize the need to engage children in metacognitive practices designed to explicitly differentiate and coordinate theories with supporting evidence. In addition, instruction regarding the linguistic characteristics of science talk and writing, particularly explanations (Halliday & Martin, 1993; Lemke, 1990), was central to the development of a set of cognitive tools.

As a result of this emphasis on coordinating theories with evidence, three strategic steps were developed to guide students in developing explanations about scientific phenomena. These steps include (1) predicting and theorizing, (2) summarizing results, and (3) relating predictions and theories to results. These three steps comprised a set of cognitive tools that were used to guide students during the completion of their science activities. These cognitive tools allowed the students to share a common focus regardless of the activity that they completed.

The second strategy employed to encourage student collaboration involved the transformation of the cognitive tools into a set of audience roles that would guide students in assuming responsibility for questioning and discussing during whole-class reporting. Again, this idea of cognitive role taking was based on the success of role taking in reciprocal teaching. Many studies have underscored the traditional recitation pattern of schooling (Cazden, 1988; Lemke, 1990; Mehan, 1979). Because the reporting sessions were not designed to be conducted in a teacher recitation format (Reddy, 1994), it was assumed that these audience roles would offer guidance to students as they entered a participant structure that may have been unfamiliar to them. Cooperative learning programs frequently emphasize the importance of small-group roles (Cohen, 1994a), yet they do not discuss the importance of orchestrating whole-class conversations by using the same role-taking technique. In addition, most cooperative learning programs assign important procedural roles (e.g., facilitator, materials coordinator) during group time but neglect to give students roles that guide them to engage intellectually with the ideas that they generate as they complete their activities (exceptions include the research conducted by King, O'Donnell, Webb, & Farivar, reported in chaps. 4, 5, and 7, this volume). As a result of these observations, the cognitive tools mentioned earlier were devised to provide a focus for students during small-group time. To carry this intellectual focus into the whole-class reporting sessions, student audience members were assigned roles that corresponded to the cognitive tools. Thus, some audience members were responsible for checking the reports for predictions and theories, others were responsible for the summary of findings, and some were responsible for determining if the reporter discussed the relation between their group's prediction, theory, and findings.

To investigate the impact of these two strategies on student engagement and collaboration, a small-scale project was conducted in conjunction with the science facilitator at the school (Herrenkohl & Guerra, 1998). Two classes of 12 students each were formed such that they did not differ on sex, race, or standardized test scores. The science facilitator at the school was the instructor for both classes, with instruction focusing on a balance and building theme. The lessons were organized such that whole-class introductory comments, small-group activities, and whole-class reporting sessions occurred every day. At the beginning of the intervention study, students in both classes were introduced to the three strategic steps (i.e., predicting and theorizing, summarizing results, relating predictions and theories to findings) to guide them in constructing scientific explanations during their small-group work time. These tools provided the framework for discussion in both classes throughout all three segments of each lesson. In addition, during the whole-class reporting segment in one of the two classes, student audience members were each assigned an intellectual role that corresponded to one of the three strategic steps (Class 2). In the other class, no special roles or instructions were given to the audience members (Class 1). This design made it possible to examine the impact of cognitive tools alone and cognitive tools combined with intellectual roles.

Analyses of transcribed classroom discussions during the whole-class reporting time revealed significant differences between Class 1 and Class 2. Students in Class 2, who were instructed in the use of the cognitive tools and audience roles, were more engaged in discussion and in building scientific explanations as a whole class. Students in this group were more likely to ask questions of other students; monitor their own comprehension of the ideas presented by others; share responsibility for negotiating, defining, and distributing the cognitive work among classroom members; coordinate theories and evidence; and challenge one another's explanations (Herrenkohl & Guerra, 1998). In addition, students in Class 2 supported one another to articulate their perspectives, thereby demonstrating and promoting further development of important "dispositions" toward learning (Barrell, 1995; Herrenkohl & Wertsch, in press).

These findings suggest that providing a set of tools to guide students in constructing scientific explanations is not sufficient to ensure high levels of engagement and collaboration. To deeply engage students with the cognitive content and with other participants in the classroom, they need to be given roles with concomitant rights and responsibilities.

In the next section, some features of the project that allowed a smooth transition between the design of the intervention in theory and the actual classroom application are discussed in terms of the support of interactive patterns, the nature of the problem space, and the view of learning as acculturation. Class 2 examples are offered, given that the combination of cognitive tools and intellectual roles proved more successful in promoting collaboration among students.

The Support of Interactive Patterns and Norms

To support students in working collaboratively to establish shared understanding in their classroom, the cognitive tools were not presented and defined by the teacher alone. The students contributed their perspective on each of the three strategic steps as well. This provided the starting point for conversations to begin in the classroom. Although the teacher offered a good deal of support to the students at the beginning of the intervention, gradually students took on the responsibility for guiding each other. The meaning of the three strategic steps was revisited and renegotiated repeatedly throughout the intervention. For example, at first the distinction between prediction (i.e., "what you think is going to happen") and theory ("why you think that is going to happen") was difficult for the students to remember and put into practice. Although they were capable of defining these terms, they had more difficulty when they tried to apply these concepts to specific activities. In addition, their knowledge and practices with regard to predicting and theorizing shifted as they progressed through the intervention. What began as more of a process of guessing and offering a reason to support the guess shifted to a more scientific notion of predicting based on a theoretical stance.

The audience roles further contributed to the need to share meanings of the three strategic steps as "common knowledge" (Edwards & Mercer, 1987) within their classroom. Without a shared understanding regarding what would constitute a satisfactory prediction, theory, and so forth, reporters and audience members would be unable to communicate their ideas clearly to one another. Early on in the intervention, the teacher carefully supported students in the audience to ask questions of the reporters.

In the following example taken from the very first report given in Class 2, the teacher supports the students as they attempt to make sense out of both the content being presented and the demands of the audience roles. In this example,

Raul is reporting for his group. Qing and Steve are members of this group. All the other students who speak were members of other groups who have been assigned audience roles. Raul is just finishing his report when the teacher interjects and offers support for students in the audience to begin questioning Raul.

1. RAUL: Steve um picked out some weight it was 39 weights and we couldn't match his exact weights so we put 40 weights and I said it was gonna balance because they were two very close numbers but it didn't balance, um . . .

2. STEVE: I said it was gonna balance too.

3. TEACHER: OK, why don't I stop you right here, who um Rosie, you have the card that says predicting and theorizing.

4. ROSIE: Yup.

5. TEACHER: Did you understand Raul's prediction and his theory?

6. ROSIE: Well . . .

7. TEACHER: If you did, tell me.

8. ROSIE: Just a little bit because he says that he thought that it will balance.

9. TEACHER: Um hum.

10. ROSIE: Because they were two closest numbers and then it didn't balance, I know why it didn't balance because maybe it, for example if we put one 40 grams on number five and 30 grams on number six, which one it will balance I don't even know.

11. TEACHER: But did you did you understand his prediction, you heard the I think part, you heard that?

12. ROSIE: Well.

13. TEACHER: Or do you think he could say it a little bit, do you think the group could say it a little bit better? Raul, I'm not hangin' you out to dry, you're the first guy up here — you've got the hardest job.

14. ROSIE: I don't remember.

15. TEACHER: You don't remember, OK who had that part here [meaning the audience role of checking predictions and theories], Olivia was supposed to be doing this and Carson was supposed to be doing this, and

16. STEVE: Carson's sick.

17. TEACHER: And neither one of them are here right now.

18. STEVE: Carson's sick, that's why.

19. TEACHER: Would it be all right if I took on this role?

20. CHILDREN: Yeah.

21. TEACHER: It would be all right?

22. CHILDREN: Yeah.

23. TEACHER: Well then I'm going to say, Raul could you please read me just the prediction?

24. RAUL: I think that it will balance the first number, you see I said I think it will balance and I was explaining why I thought it was gonna balance, and OK [Qing points to Raul's notebook and whispers something to him].

25. TEACHER: OK OK and Qing is telling me that that was the prediction right there, right?
26. RAUL: Um hum.
27. QING: And then he was telling why.
28. TEACHER: And why is the what?
29. RAUL: Why is the
30. QING: Balance
31. TEACHER: The theory?
32. RAUL: Yeah.
33. TEACHER: Theory, OK, so it is there.
34. RAUL: I think it will balance is my theory.
35. TEACHER: OK, so there is a prediction there and there is a theory, OK who was doing summarizing findings and results.

In this example, we see that the teacher takes on the role of mediator and assists the audience members in attempting to monitor their own understanding of Raul's presentation. This is particularly the case with Rosie. The teacher attempts to determine if Rosie heard and understood Raul's prediction and theory. In Turns 8 and 10, Rosie indicates that she understands "just a little bit." In addition, after Rosie offers her understanding of what Raul said, she presents another example as a way to demonstrate that she knew why the balance scale did not balance for Raul's group. In this example, Rosie expresses her own thoughts but in so doing indicates that she does not necessarily understand how she should be functioning in her role as an audience member. It is not necessarily her place to offer theories at this point, it is her job to try and understand the prediction and theory presented by Raul. In Turn 11, the teacher attempts to refocus Rosie's efforts by asking once again if she understood Raul's prediction. As it becomes clear that Rosie doesn't understand Raul's perspective completely (Turn 14), the teacher attempts to find another student with this audience role. When she is unable to find someone due to one child's absence and the other's brief trip to the lavatory, she asks the students if they would mind if she took on the role. Once the students agree that the teacher can take on this role, she models how a question could be formulated in the event that Raul's prediction was not clear to her (Turn 23). Throughout the rest of the conversation, the teacher is able to help the class establish that Raul has presented both a prediction and a theory. In Turns 28 to 35, the teacher establishes that theories offer reasons to account for predictions. One interesting aspect of this piece of transcript is that although it appears that Rosie did understand Raul's report, she is unable to function in her role of audience member. This finding mirrors the finding in the CPS research that children need time to become comfortable with these ways of interacting, because they are not necessarily familiar or natural within the context of the classroom. In addition, this example illustrates the crucial role that the teacher played in guiding students to assume the roles of listener, critic, questioner, and commentator.

As the students became more familiar and comfortable with their roles, their role taking was regulated by themselves or other students. In the next example that took place on Day 5 of the intervention in Class 2, there is a qualitative shift in the kind of support that is needed for the students. The teacher takes on the role of moderator of the conversation rather than key player as the students assume responsibility for questioning and supporting each other to articulate their perspectives clearly. In this example, Rosie and Olivia are reporting for their group with other students taking on the audience roles. This excerpt of transcript begins with Steve interrupting the girls as they are in the process of giving their report and trying to fix the demonstration that they brought to the front of the room.

1. STEVE: What was the theory? I didn't hear the theory, I didn't hear nothin'.
2. OLIVIA: I'll tell you our theory in a minute. [Olivia and Rosie continue to try to fix their demonstration for the class. There is a short verbal exchange between them.]
3. TEACHER: I think your audience has some questions.
4. ROSIE: Yeah can we get some questions now?
5. QING: Did you put the thing over here or here or here or here?
6. RAUL: What's the theory. I didn't hear a theory.
7. STEVE: I just said I just said what's your theory?
8. TEACHER: What was the theory, ok, what was the theory?
9. QING: I heard it.
10. TEACHER: You heard it?
11. QING: Yeah.
12. TEACHER: You wanna try repeating it?
13. CHILD: You heard a theory?
14. QING: I thought I heard in [she points to Rosie], I thought it will balance, that's what I heard, is that right? [Rosie nods yes.]
15. QING: Haaaaa. [Qing motions success by clapping her hands together. Rosie is smiling at her.]
16. CHILD: Prediction.
17. RAUL: That's the prediction.
18. TEACHER: Ok, you thought
19. RAUL: That's the prediction, that's not the theory.
20. DENISE: Why they thought it would balance.
21. RAUL: Yeah, why they think it will balance.
22. STEVE: That's the prediction. [A number of students start talking at once all agreeing that this is the prediction, not the theory.]
23. OLIVIA: And I thought that it would we thought it would balance because I mean
24. STEVE: We want your theory.
25. OLIVIA: Because it was right in the center because see like right now it's staying like that alone and [inaudible]
26. TEACHER: It's still not clear to you [meaning the class] yet.
27. RAUL: Well, you're [meaning Olivia] saying, well you're saying that your

theory is that if they're even on the same if they're even on each side then it will balance.

28. TEACHER: Is that your theory? Equal distance apart?
29. OLIVIA: Yeah, our theory is that equal dis dis dis ditnance [Olivia stutters on the word distance. In the background Steve and Denise are carrying on their own side conversation regarding predicting and theorizing.]
30. RAUL: Distance.
31. TEACHER: Distance.
32. OLIVIA: Of the parts will make it balance.
33. TEACHER: Yeah, that's her theory. Is that
34. RAUL: Ok, I'm satisfied.

The example stands in contrast to the first on many levels. First, Steve initiates a question based on his audience role prior to the time that the reporters have finished their report. This indicates a far greater degree of regulation of the conversation on the part of the audience members. Steve is anticipating his job of checking predictions and theories and initiates a premature question as a result. It is also interesting to note that the students in this example remind one another of the meaning of prediction and theory. In Turn 14, Qing states what she heard as Olivia's and Rosie's theory. Many students quickly comment that what Qing has represented as a theory is really the prediction (Turns 16–22). In this case, it is not the teacher who is defining the terms for the students, rather it is the students who are working together to remind Qing that she has confused their agreed on definition of prediction and theory. This stands in direct contrast to the first example, where the teacher differentiates predictions and theories for the students. The final point of interest takes place in Turns 26 through 34. In this portion of the conversation, Raul represents or revoices (O'Connor & Michaels, 1993) Olivia's theory and attempts to come to an understanding of her perspective. In the process, he coconstructs this perspective with her (Turns 29–32), offering assistance when she stutters on the word *distance*. The most telling comment, however, occurs in Turn 34, when Raul indicates that he is satisfied with his understanding of Olivia's perspective. He commands control of the conversation and indicates when he is finished questioning, again in quite a different manner from the first example.

A final strategy for facilitating collaboration involved allowing students to nominate themselves for participation in the conversation. Both Phillips (1972) and Au and Mason (1981) noted that the physical and social organization of the classroom can impact students' willingness and ability to participate in the classroom. In both studies, when students had access to controlling their own entry into the conversation, they were more likely to engage with others. In cases where teacher nomination was required, students felt less comfortable participating. Allowing audience members to ask question of reporters supported the student audience members in nominating themselves for participation in the process.

The Problems

There were two main contexts that provided very different opportunities for student problem solving. The first involved the actual completion of the small-group activities. During this time, students worked in groups of four to complete a given problem. Students cooperated to complete the activity using the three strategic steps as a guide and then used chart paper to prepare some supporting materials for the reporter to use when presenting orally to the class. This context allowed students to focus on presenting their problem from the perspective of using the three strategic steps with teacher supervision but not necessarily direct teacher guidance.

The second problem-solving opportunity occurred when students in the audience assumed the role of examining reports for the inclusion of the three strategic steps. In this context, students were not asked to apply the three strategic steps to a problem themselves, they were asked to examine another group's representation and determine if all steps were included and if they understood what the group was saying. In this context, the teacher acted as a facilitator and guide at first and later as more of a conversation moderator (see previous examples).

These two problem-solving contexts allowed students to practice many thinking skills. They were first creators of predictions and theories, summarizers of results, and relaters of predictions, theories, and results in the small-group context. Then as audience members, they were required to listen and evaluate their understanding of others' perspectives under the expert guidance of the teacher and other tools that bridged both contexts.

Students participated in these problem-solving contexts with the extensive support of linguistic tools such as activity cards, charts that displayed the three strategic steps, chart paper representations used by reporters during reporting time, a "theory chart" that became a collective representation of all the theories offered by small groups during the unit, and a "questions chart" that outlined the kinds of questions that students could ask when they assumed their audience roles. The theory chart became a crucial resource for the students to use when completing their activities and while questioning reporters. Because theories were added to the chart each day, students could derive their group theory by examining the chart and recalling the context in which another group presented that theory on a previous day. There were cases when theories developed on one day by one group were appropriated by another group the following day. For example, weight and distance theories were used frequently by groups to account for why a balance scale tipped to the right, tipped to the left, or balanced. Then, on Day 5 of the intervention in Class 2, one group introduced the first theory that accounted for both weight and distance at the same time. They argued that "you can double the distance on one side (of the balance scale) to double the weight on the other" (see Herrenkohl & Guerra, 1998). This theory was used by several groups on Day 6 and it continued to be a pivotal theory that ultimately prompted the students to develop the multiplicative rule of torques. In addition to functioning as a support for groups while they completed their activities, the chart also served an important function during reporting. Audience members used the theory chart as a point of reference for asking reporters to clarify their theory by relating it to the ones already included on the chart (see Herrenkohl & Wertsch, in press). Finally, similar to the CPS curriculum, in which the particulate theory of matter was a centerpiece of the discourse, this problem context lends itself to working toward a deeper understanding of a pivotal theory, regarding the role of density in floating and sinking. Areas of inquiry in which there are no single pivotal theories (an example being the nature of light) will pose additional interesting challenges for the curriculum designer.

The Process of Creating a Shared Social Context

As was true with reciprocal teaching and CPS, creating a shared set of classroom values that established understanding others' perspectives as an important aspect of participation was crucial to the successful implementation of the cognitive tools and the intellectual audience roles. Constructing such a classroom community required patience, time, and collaboration among all classroom members.

During reporting time, the teacher frequently monitored audience member understanding and attempted to establish if the students were satisfied that the reporter addressed all three steps in a manner that they understood (see previous examples). There were numerous examples of students supporting other students in taking on roles that were particularly difficult for them. In one instance, a child who did not like to be a reporter finished her report and received spontaneous applause from her classmates (see Herrenkohl & Wertsch, in press). There was an ethos of respect for others' ideas and a realization of the importance of the contributions of all classroom members. This does not mean that the classroom functioned smoothly at all times. There were tense moments of working through the important distinction between challenging people versus challenging ideas. These distinctions tied the community together and identified it as a lively and intellectually stimulating environment where both debate and consensus were welcomed. In spite of all of this, there were still a few students who were more shy and reluctant to participate until the intervention program was almost completed. These students did participate, however, and in future projects, increasing the duration of the intervention would be warranted.

CONCLUSION

The three programs of research discussed in this chapter span a decade and a half. In some respects, the story of the development of these three collaborative learning contexts reflects the maturation of inquiry regarding collaborative learning. When we began the research on reciprocal teaching, the principle question was whether participation in these dialogues would provide an appropriate context in which students might acquire ways of interacting with text that reflected the ways in which skilled readers interact with text. The focus was on the strategies as means of supporting students' interactions with text and the extent to which the students' participation in these learning dialogues would influence their acquisition of these strategies and their independent learning from text.

Interest in reciprocal teaching as a form of peer collaboration emerged from patterns of findings regarding the relation between the quality of the interactions between teachers and children, as well as among children, and the nature of the learning that occurred. For example, children who participated in groups that were heterogeneous with regard to comprehension ability attained competence more quickly than children in groups that were homogenous. These patterns raised questions about how collaboration occurred in the context of the dialogues, and in turn, how collaboration influenced cognitive development.

Both the CPS and CTIR programs of research exemplify the increasing interdependence of research on collaboration and research that is domain specific. Specifically, these research programs made salient the semiotic means or tools that would both aid the coconstruction process in scientific problem solving and become the means by which students engage in future scientific problem-solving activity. As Webb and Farivar report in chapter 5 of this volume, it appears as though it is not sufficient to simply engage children in higher level reasoning activity, such as generating explanations, but it is also necessary to teach ways of supporting explanations that are specific to the cognitive demands of the domain in which students are working. The intersection between the design of collaborative contexts and the study of domain-specific reasoning and problem solving continues to be an area ripe for study.

Another focus of inquiry, reflected particularly in the CTIR program, is the question of structuring group activity so that responsibility is shared, expertise is distributed, and there is an ethos of building on one another's ideas. Contributing to our understanding of this issue is research regarding the kinds of knowledge-building processes that are likely to promote learning in collaborative groups. For example, Chan et al. (1997) demonstrated that learning was fostered when groups treated new information as something problematic, when students sought connections among diverse pieces of information; in short, when students engaged in talk that was interpretive in nature rather than simply descriptive. The CTIR research illustrates one viable means of engaging students in knowledge-building discourse in a fashion that also attends to the distribution of responsibility for learning. The research reported by King (chap. 4, this volume) and Teasley (1995) also advance our understanding of these issues.

Finally, the development of these three programs of research illustrates the ways in which transforming school practices must be considered, not just in terms of different teaching methods but also in terms of different cultural systems—representing different educational, social, and communicative norms and priorities. In contrast to the majority of the early research on reciprocal teaching, the CPS and CTIR research programs were conducted at the classroom level, raising a host of complex issues that address the culture of the classroom. New sets of issues emerged that demanded attention, including the individual histories of children and how these histories influence their subsequent experiences working with others, the collective history of the members of a classroom, the norms in a classroom regarding listening to one another, persisting in the solution of problems, explaining one's own solution to others, trying to make sense of one's partners' solutions, and attempting to come to consensus. No matter how smart we become about the domain-specific and knowledge-building issues identified here, until we understand more fully how to socialize students into new ways of dealing with peers as intellectual partners, it is unlikely that this research will make much of a difference in the real-world experiences of teachers and students.

CHAPTER SEVEN

Structuring Dyadic Interaction Through Scripted Cooperation

ANGELA M. O'DONNELL
Rutgers University

One of the perspectives on peer learning described in the introductory chapter of this book is a cognitive–elaborative perspective. According to this perspective, peer learning focuses on the cognitive processing of participating individuals during interaction. The anticipated benefits that may occur during peer learning accrue to the individual as a result of deeper processing of material and elaboration of knowledge structures. Peer interaction can provoke deeper processing of material by individuals by promoting the use of explanations, the generation of alternative examples and analogies, or by requiring participants to entertain other perspectives on material. Such opportunities, and responses to them, can prompt a deeper processing of information, an elaboration of existing cognitive structures or a restructuring of prior knowledge.

In this chapter, I first describe a particular peer learning technique, *scripted cooperation,* that reflects a cognitive–elaboration perspective. Scripted cooperation is a highly structured peer learning technique. It requires that participants play particular cognitive roles. The rationale for a such highly structured approach to peer interaction stems in part from the potential pitfalls inherent in unstructured groups. One of the key concerns in using peer learning in classrooms is the degree to which interactions among participants should be structured by the teacher or other authority (O'Donnell & O'Kelly, 1994). This chapter addresses this issue by first describing scripted cooperation, considering the potential pitfalls in unstructured interaction in some detail. I examine the research on scripted cooperation, suggesting ways in which the use of scripted cooperation can limit the occurrence of certain kinds of negative processes, and describe some of the limitations of this approach.

SCRIPTED COOPERATION

In scripted cooperation, pairs of students work with one another on an academic task. Many cooperative techniques (e.g., Learning Together; Johnson &
Johnson, 1994) require that students play specific roles. However, relatively few
techniques require that the prescribed roles involve specific cognitive activities.
Scripted cooperation differs from this general trend by requiring that participating students engage in specific cognitive activities. King's work on reciprocal
questioning also differs from this general trend (King, 1992b; King & Rosenshine, 1993; chap. 4, this volume). One of the central features of scripted cooperation is that the interactions among participants (usually two people) are
structured by a script. A *script*, as used in this context, is analogous to a theater
script. Participants are asked to play specified roles (listener and recaller) and
they are asked to play these roles in a particular order. Two key assumptions are
made with respect to scripted cooperation. First, the use of scripted cooperation
will prompt the use of cognitive processes by participants that might otherwise
not occur. For example, during scripted cooperation, students explicitly engage
in error detection when they might not routinely do so. Second, the use of
scripted cooperation can limit the occurrence of negative social processes that
may impede group functioning and achievement. For example, students are required to alternate roles in scripted cooperation. In unscripted dyads, students
often assume a single role and maintain that role throughout a study period. In
addition, the use of a script can provide opportunities for students to model
strategic learning behavior for one another and to learn from that modeling.
   Scripted cooperation can be used with a variety of tasks but is illustrated here
with a text-processing task. Two participants work together to acquire information from a text. The text is broken into sections and both partners read the first
section. Both partners put the material away and one partner assumes the role
of recaller while the other partner assumes the role of listener. Without referring to notes or the material itself, the recaller provides a summary of the material read. The listener's task is to detect errors, identify omissions, and seek clarification of specific issues. The listener also works from his or her memory of the
task. Both partners then work together to elaborate on the material and make it
more memorable. This cycle of reading, recalling, listening, and elaborating is
repeated for each section of the text. At the end of the text, partners review the
material. Oral summarization facilitates the organization of information and
perhaps, the triggering of metacognitive experiences (Spurlin, Dansereau, Larson, & Brooks, 1984; Yager, Johnson, & Johnson, 1985). Comprehension monitoring often takes a subsidiary role during a knowledge-acquisition task. In
scripted cooperation, the explicit designation of the role of the listener as an active monitor of accuracy and understanding ensures that metacognitive activity
is a part of the process. Elaborative activities facilitate the acquisition and reten-

tion of information (Reder, 1980). The alternation of roles in the script provides partners with the opportunity to benefit from cross-modeling or imitation of strategies and guarantees participation opportunities (Spurlin et al., 1984). Both partners have the opportunity to rehearse, elaborate, and engage in specific metacognitive activities. All of these activities are known to aid text-processing comprehension (O'Donnell & Dansereau, 1992).

Earlier chapters in this book (see De Lisi & Golbeck, chap. 1, and Hogan & Tudge, chap. 2, this volume) draw attention to potential limits of collaboration that might result from differences in the developmental status of participating peers. Effective unstructured interactions require participants to be skilled in the deployment of cognitive and social processes. This chapter provides an overview of research findings related to the use of scripted cooperation and delineates both the benefits and limitations of this technique.

A ROLE FOR STRUCTURE

Few cooperative learning techniques specify the cognitive activities that participants might engage in or delineate roles within groups that are related to such activities. Negative consequences can result from a failure to attend to such issues (see O'Donnell & O'Kelly, 1994). In many unstructured group interaction settings, some students are ignored and others dominate interaction. The work of Noreen Webb and colleagues (1989, 1992; Webb & Farivar, chap. 5, this volume) demonstrates that participation in elaborated verbal behavior is linked to high achievement. If some students are unable to access such cognitive opportunities (e.g., explaining, answering questions, making suggestions) within a group, they are less likely to benefit from the interaction. When teachers use groups as an instructional strategy, the failure of students to participate in the interactions of a group is linked to negative achievement outcomes (Cohen, 1994b).

Furthermore, most of the published research on cooperative learning stems from a motivational perspective and operates from the assumption that good interaction results from motivated students. However, if students do not bring the appropriate cognitive skills to the group activity, group interaction can be ineffective.

The question that lurks beneath all considerations of any form of cooperative learning is the question of "Who benefits?" Webb's (1992) work shows that all students do not necessarily benefit from small-group activities. In some cooperative learning techniques, the intended beneficiary is unclear. In certain techniques (e.g., TGT, STAD; Slavin, 1986), all participants are expected to benefit. The degree to which anyone benefits from peer learning arrangements depends on a whole host of factors. One of the key factors that determines the kinds of outcomes possible, and for whom, is the degree to which the teacher structures the interaction of the peers in a group.

Unstructured Interaction

Many implementations of peer learning involve the use of small groups that are unstructured. Goals may be provided for students that direct them to "work together" to solve problems, react to one another's work, or complete other tasks. In such groups, students are not provided with training in how to work together and are not directed to play specific roles with respect to the assigned task. Even when students have substantial practice in peer learning, they may not include all members of their groups in their interactions (Cohen, 1994a, 1994b).

Both Piagetian and Vygotskian perspectives on the potential benefits of peer interaction (see De Lisi & Golbeck, chap. 1, and Hogan & Tudge, chap. 2, this volume) can be drawn on to support the idea that unconstrained interaction among participants is preferable to structuring interaction. Damon and Phelps (1989) suggested that collaboration among peers is possible only when collaborating peers are equal in power, mutually respectful, and at similar levels of cognitive development. Under such conditions, peers engage in sharing of knowledge and perspectives and can acquire new understandings. From a Vygotskian perspective (see Hogan & Tudge, chap. 2, this volume), cognitive growth occurs through the scaffolding of the less experienced or competent individual by the more experienced or competent individual. Scaffolding of the learner's knowledge requires that the more competent individual be sensitive and aware of the individual's current performance levels and be skilled in extending the possible competence of the individual in the supportive interaction. These kinds of interactions would seem very difficult to structure as they can vary enormously in both content and form from individual to individual. Cohen (1994b) also noted that less structure promotes more conceptual growth on the part of students.

Less structured environments would also seem to support more intrinsically motivated behavior (Reeve, 1996). Increased structure in classrooms tends to be associated with efforts at control. External control can reduce intrinsic motivation in students (Deci & Ryan, 1985). Environments that are less structured can provide students with opportunities for autonomy and control, key components of intrinsically motivated behavior. In one study, students who perceived their classrooms to be more supportive of autonomy reported higher levels of intrinsic motivation and perceived cognitive competence (Ryan & Grolnick, 1984, cited by Dembo & Eaton, 1997). However, the effective use of control by students depends on a variety of factors such as prior knowledge in a domain or prior experience with the materials or tasks available (Williams, 1996).

It is not clear that students can ever be totally unstructured in their interactions in the classroom, because although they may receive little instruction in how to interact from their teachers, the tasks on which they work will constrain interaction (e.g., Howe, Tolmie, Greer, & MacKenzie, 1995). Howe et al. showed that, in the context of 8- and 10-year-old children learning about heating and cooling, tasks that facilitated testing of ideas and prompted the generation of summary rules were superior to tasks that had only one of these elements. In assembly tasks such as building a model, for example, the linear ordering of the assembly of necessary pieces will be a major determiner of the kinds of interactions that occur. In such circumstances, discourse often involves giving directions about where to place things. Webb and Farivar (chap. 5, this volume) illustrate the influence of task on the types of communication that occur during group interactions. Howe et al. (1995) also showed that the task structure can have an important influence on conceptual growth in the physics understanding of young children when engaged in peer collaboration. Despite these results, relatively little is known about how to structure tasks to promote effective collaboration. Some would argue that it is impossible to derive any general principles about promoting collaboration and that any understanding of the effects of peer collaboration can only be very local.

Effective interaction in unstructured contexts would seem to be less likely when the tasks are relatively routine, when the groups are heterogeneous with respect to ability, or when the task is highly contingent (Doyle, 1983). There are well-documented links between the amount and kind of communication that occurs in small groups and subsequent student achievement (Ross & Raphael, 1990; Webb, 1989, 1991). Students who explain more in a group benefit most from the group interaction (Webb, 1992). In particular, those students who give elaborated explanations derive the most benefit (Webb, 1989). In Ross and Raphael's (1990) study of two classrooms, discussions about the substance of the tasks assigned were strongly correlated with achievement.

Not all students, however, participate effectively in unstructured interaction. Mulryan (1992) examined the behavior of fifth- and sixth-grade students working in small groups on mathematical tasks. High achievers were more on-task than low achievers who were often minimally on-task. Reasons for student passivity were varied. In addition, Mulryan found evidence of negative social processes such as social loafing. Debilitating social processes were well described by Salomon and Globerson (1989). They delineated the potential negative impact on team performance of processes. Included among such difficulties are the diffusion of responsibility among group members, social loafing, and the "sucker effect." Social loafing occurs when one or more members of a team allow others to do most of the work. The sucker effect occurs when one or more group members realize that they have been taken advantage of by others and their reaction to this realization is usually very negative, resulting in either sabotage of the group's efforts or disengagement from the task One outcome of negative social processes is to limit the participation of individuals, as occurred in the Mulryan (1992) work.

The potential for derailing effective group process can be seen in the following excerpt of a transcript taken from Kalustian (1994). A group of four third graders was given a bag of money and asked to find out the total amount of money in the bag.

C: Ok, check how many?—I was thinking of . . .
M: That one, that one.
W: Shut up, butt-head.
M: Oh, let's put some . . .
W: Shut up, butt-head.
M: . . . in the plate and see how much we have . . .

Student M is task-oriented but student W reacts with hostility to M's effort to contribute to the task. W interrupts M with a very direct and derisive comment but is ignored and makes a second effort to interrupt but is again ignored. It is evident that W will learn little from this task. This segment of transcript was taken from the initial period of the students working together and did not suggest a promising interaction. These early indications of less than optimal interaction were subsequently confirmed in later interactions as shown in the piece of the same transcript that follows:

M: 8, 9, 9 and 8 . . . how much it is . . . 17, right?
C: Yeah, that's what I did.
M: Yeah, then you carry the 1, that's 9 and 9 is 18.
W: *She wrote, "Oh, W . . . , I like you."*
M: Carry the 1, is 2 . . . $2.89.
A: *You like her too?*
M: $5.00 it says there.
W: *No.*
M: is 2 dollars 80 . . . 89 cents.
C: 89 cents?
W: *You like, you like Andrea?*
M: Wait and that's a . . . 4 minus 2 equals 2.
W: *She lives downtown.*
M: And 10 minus 7 is 3.
C: Ok.
M: So, erase the answer, just erase 8 and a 7 . . . that's it.
A: *I don't want her phone number. I hate . . .*
W: *You goin' crazy. You'all crazy.*
A: *Like this. Me and J . . . we the only people that Andrea likes.*
M: And then write 13 cents.
A: *She don't like you.*
M: Wait, you don't have to write the cents.
C: Ok, I gotta go.
W: *Then why'd she always looks at me?*

The four-person group has essentially become two interacting dyads. One dyad, M and C, are task oriented, working out a problem that required them to determine which of two shopping lists was cheaper, although C has little to contribute. The other dyad, A and W, are totally disengaged from the task and are discussing which girls like them. The task-oriented dyad maintains focus despite the distractions provided by the other dyad. It should be noted that the children did have training in how to work in groups and were encouraged to come to agreement on problem solutions. However, problems can be detected in the early stages of this interaction. Student W did not work on the assigned task, thus self-selecting to be "alternatively involved" (Mulryan, 1992).

Why do some students not interact effectively or appropriately? One possibility is that students may have different goals for participation. Proponents of motivational perspectives on cooperative learning (Johnson & Johnson, 1992; Slavin, 1992) emphasize the importance of developing shared goals and interdependence among students. Students sometimes self-select not to be involved. They are often excluded, however, or conditions in the group develop in such a way that it becomes impossible for them to participate effectively. Mulryan (1992) described six categories of passive students: (1) the discouraged student, (2) the unrecognized student, (3) the intellectual snob, (4) the unmotivated student, (5) the intentional loafer, and (6) the alternatively involved. In Mulryan's study, explanations for passivity include references to both social and cognitive processes. These processes are often inseparable in natural interaction. Mulryan identified only 8 students out of a total of 48 (17%) who were persistently passive. This number does reflect a substantial number of children who are not likely to benefit (academically) from the group interaction. Mulryan noted that other children did little to include their passive classmates.

Status and Participation

Social and cognitive processes intertwine when status becomes differentiated in a group. Status differentiation means that some students in a group are recognized by group members as having high status, whereas other students are recognized as having low status (Meeker, 1981). When students are recognized as having high status, they behave and are treated differently in a group than students with low status. High-status students have more opportunities to talk, answer questions, and control discussion. Low-status students often say little, are dependent, and are often ignored. We know from Webb's (1992) work that most students who do not actively participate do not learn. Exceptions to this are high-achieving students who seem to learn effectively from observation (Webb, 1992).

One source of explanation for differentiated participation in small groups is expectation states theory and its derivative, status characteristics theory (Berger, Cohen, & Zelditch, 1972; Berger, Rosenholz, & Zeldtitch, 1980). According to these theories, power and prestige structures emerge quickly in groups and status becomes differentiated. An expectation state develops between two people in which each person has an expectation (high [H] or low [L]) for his or her competence for the task and an expectation related to the competence of the other individual. The expectation state experienced by an individual is the result of these expectations. It can be HH (both people are expect to have competencies),

LL (neither person will be effective), HL (the individual has positive expectations for him- or herself and low expectations of the other), or LH (the individual has low expectation for him- or herself and positive expectations for the other). These various expectation states are expected to influence interaction. For example, a person with an LH expectation state might be expected to defer to the other person who is assumed to be more competent and thus has higher status in the group. A person with high status is one who is assumed to have competencies necessary to the task. In contrast, a person with low status is assumed not to have competencies necessary to contribute to successful task completion. Ability connected to the task at hand is the most powerful status characteristic and dominates all other influences (Dembo & McAuliffe, 1987; Zelditch, 1985).

Status influences participation rates in important ways. Group members with high status dominate interaction. They say more, give more explanations, initiate more actions, and have the power to ignore others. For example, in the segment of transcript included previously, Student M successfully ignored Student W's insults, a reaction that could lower W's status in the group. Low-status students in a group, in contrast to the high-status students, say little, defer to those with higher status, and may be ignored. They have few opportunities to explain their ideas and are often in the role of help seeker. Student W tried very hard to have others pay attention to him but was unsuccessful.

Webb's (1989, 1992) work clearly demonstrated the importance of explanation as a predictor of individual achievement arising from group activity. Webb and Farivar (chap. 5, this volume) also demonstrate that teaching children to solicit and profit from help is not an easy task. Low-status students in small groups would seem to be greatly at risk of not having access to the opportunity to engage in those behaviors that are clearly associated with achievement.

It is important to note that the original expectation states theory and status characteristics theory were developed and tested in laboratory conditions (Meeker, 1981). The emergence of status characteristics and the consequent negative effects on interaction and quality of communication were therefore demonstrated in very artificial circumstances. In some instances, students performed tasks with partners they did not even see. Such experimental conditions allowed researchers to make specific predictions. One problem with generalizing from this kind of work to natural settings is that information about status is not available to people in natural contexts in the discreet, sequential manner in which it is made available in the laboratory. Cohen and Roper (1972), Cohen and Lotan (1995), and Lockheed, Harris, and Memceff (1983) examined the role of status in natural settings and provided support for the important role that status plays in classroom interaction.

The primary status characteristic in the classroom is ability. Status is acquired in a group if one is understood by one's peers to have competencies that are relevant to the task. The typical tasks in classrooms involve literacy and numeracy, and students skilled in these areas are readily identified by both students and teachers. Teacher behavior (e.g., praise, responses to student answers, level of questions asked) can contribute to signaling competence (Cohen, 1994b). Teachers can also have effects on minimizing the consequences of perceived lack of status. Cohen and Lotan (1995) examined the relation of status and achievement in 13 classrooms whose teachers had participated in a program designed to assist teachers in minimizing the role of status. Classroom teachers who actively assigned competence to students had classrooms in which there was little relation between students' status ratings and their academic achievement. In two classrooms in this study, significant correlations between students' status scores and their academic achievement were found. Teachers in these classrooms did not assign competence to low-achieving students very frequently.

Characteristics of individuals other than ability can also play a role in the determination of status. In situations in which there is no directly available information about the relative competence of group members, other characteristics of the individual may be used to make inferences about competence. Such characteristics include those that can distinguish among individuals, such as gender, race, or ethnicity (McAuliffe & Dembo, 1994). These characteristics are diffuse status characteristics because they can be used to distinguish among people, and inferences about one's expected competence may be made based on one's standing on the variable of interest. Assumptions may be made about one's competence for a task even though there is no necessary relation between the salient characteristic and achievement. For example, whether one is a male or female student may be used to make inferences about expected competency for mathematics, even though there may be no reason to assume any relation between sex and the particular achievement under investigation.

Gender can operate as a diffuse status characteristic (Lockheed et al., 1983). In a study of fourth- and fifth-grade children, Lockheed et al. found that girls were perceived as less competent than boys, although there were no differences in behavior as a function of gender. Webb (1984, 1985, 1991) demonstrated that the kind and amount of verbalization in a group is associated with the distribution of gender in a group. Children working in four-person groups behave differently depending on the balance of boys and girls in the group. When girls outnumber boys, they tend to defer to the boy. When boys outnumber girls, the boys ignore the girl. Under such conditions, it is unlikely that students will persist in their efforts to be involved. It is also unlikely that all students will benefit from the interaction. In a laboratory study of group interaction, Pugh and Wahrman (1985) found clearly differentiated behavior in groups as a function of gender. Women deferred to men more frequently than the reverse, and men were less influenced by women's contributions in a group.

Other variables can serve as diffuse status characteristics. Cohen and her colleagues provided evidence that race operates as a diffuse status characteristic, with Caucasian children being accorded more status than non-Causasian children (Cohen, 1982; Cohen, Lotan, & Catanzarite, 1990; Cohen & Roper, 1972).

Caution should be used in interpreting these results as reflective of current conditions in classrooms, as the profile of classrooms has changed significantly since the early 1980s.

The implication of race and gender acting as diffuse characteristics is that communication and participation in groups may be influenced by one's race or gender. Opportunities to participate effectively may be denied to specific individuals solely on the basis of these characteristics.

The operation of negative social processes such as those outlined by Salomon and Globerson (1989) are problematic for many reasons. First, they may result in negative affect in the groups. Second, negative social processes that result from status differentiation can result in inequalities in opportunities to participate. Such inequalities in participation may result in unequal opportunity to learn. Social processes limiting interaction, however, are not the only potential problem in unstructured groups. Even when all participants are well disposed toward one another, students may be unskilled at the tasks required by the complexities inherent in less structured situations. Meloth and Deering (1992, 1994) demonstrated that students working with specific strategies outperformed students whose motivation for the task was enhanced by the use of incentives but who were not provided with training on strategic learning. Motivation is a necessary but insufficient condition for adequate performance. King's work (chap. 4, this volume) shows that strategic learning can enhance the quality of the cognitive activities of students.

Less structured situations can be distinguished from more structured ones in the degree of interpersonal and cognitive coordination required by participants. Groups that consist of members who are heterogeneous with respect to ability are unlikely to meet the conditions necessary for effective collaboration described by Damon and Phelps (1989). Furthermore, it would seem that students need a tremendous amount of assistance in learning how to provide help or benefit from help given (Webb & Farivar, 1994; chap. 5, this volume). Webb (1989, 1992) delineated the conditions necessary for help. The effectiveness of help provided depends on the timeliness of the help, the relevance of the help given to the student's need, the amount of detail or elaboration provided, whether the help provided is understood by the student, and whether the student who received help has an opportunity to use the help (Webb, 1992). Help giving is a complex task (see Webb & Farivar, chap. 5, this volume). Even adults are not always proficient at providing useful help (Radiszewka & Rogoff, 1988).

The difficulties in offering effective help can be seen in the segment of transcript that follows, the same four-person group that provided the previous transcript (Kalustian, 1994) is computing how much a set of items on a shopping list cost.

C: 14, 15, 16, 17.
W: countin' corny.
A: Yes, you should count.
M: It's not good to count with your fingers. You're already in third grade.

A: Yeah, you should just count 'em with your mind.

W: Boom shockalocka that one. We agree? We agree that it is $2.13?

Student M reacts to Student C counting on her fingers and reprimands her. Student A suggests an alternative strategy, "count 'em with your mind." It is unlikely that Student C could benefit from this suggestion, particularly as Student W successfully changes the subject. Even when students are aware of the need for an alternative approach to a problem, they may not be able to guide another student's behavior. Webb and Farivar (chap. 5, this volume) show the importance of teaching students to provide help effectively.

King (chap. 4, this volume) demonstrates that children can learn to provide better questions to one another, and this in turn yields better explanations. This work, in conjunction with that of Webb and Farivar (chap. 5, this volume) strongly suggest that children can learn to engage in appropriate cognitive and social behaviors but will require extensive support in doing so.

Negative social and cognitive processes in groups can quickly negate the potential benefits from interaction. Such processes seem more likely to occur in unstructured groups than in structured ones. Participants report experiencing social anxiety when asked to work in groups (O'Donnell, Dansereau, Hall, & Rocklin, 1987). O'Donnell et al. (1987) showed that unstructured pairs reported higher levels of social anxiety than did structured pairs. When there is no particular social or cognitive structure, participants must organize the situation, which can open up opportunities for negative social processes. These kinds of effects are not always found in unstructured groups. Ross and Raphael (1990) described the interactions in a class in which the students were responsible for making decisions about how to conduct their groups. Interactions in these groups (student structured) were of higher quality than in a comparison class. The teacher in the unstructured class was very experienced in the use of cooperative learning.

Many approaches have been taken to reducing the possibility of negative social and cognitive processes in groups. These efforts include extensive training in social skills (Johnson & Johnson, 1994), in giving and using explanations (Webb, 1992; Webb & Farivar, 1994, chap. 5, this volume), or providing strategies or scripts for interaction (Meloth & Deering, 1994; O'Donnell & Dansereau, 1992). Most of these techniques have been successful in improving performance. The remainder of this chapter provides a more detailed description of one approach —scripted cooperation—to promoting achievement through peer learning while minimizing the risk of negative social or cognitive processes.

RESEARCH ON SCRIPTED COOPERATION

Scripted cooperation is a learning methodology in which the roles played by the interacting partners and the processing activities in which they engage are specified. These activities include overt summarization, error detection, elaboration, and review, and are known to aid text processing and comprehension.

Research on scripted cooperation has examined (a) the development of effective scripts, (b) the role of task characteristics, (c) the role of individual differences, and (d) the cognitive and affective outcomes that result. More recent work (e.g., O'Donnell, 1996; Stern, 1996) examined the role of reward in the context of scripted cooperation. A more detailed review of much of this work is available in O'Donnell and Dansereau (1992). In the sections that follow, I briefly summarize the research on the effects of scripted cooperation on achievement and the evidence related to the success of scripted cooperation in minimizing negative cognitive and social processes.

SCRIPTED COOPERATION AND ACHIEVEMENT

The basic goal of scripted cooperation is to increase achievement by having students perform cognitive activities that they might not otherwise do. In addition, scripted cooperation is expected to reduce the incidence of negative group processes because of the size of the cooperating unit (dyad) and because of the explicit requirement to alternate roles.

Effects of the Scripts

The script (described previously) is designed to promote a number of information-processing activities that are known to facilitate the acquisition of information. The results of work on the effectiveness of externally provided scripts show that, in general, students learn more when they generate their own scripts (O'Donnell & Dansereau, 1992; Rewey, Dansereau, Skaggs, Hall, & Pitre, 1990). Exceptions to this general finding, however, can be found (O'Donnell et al., 1987).

The majority of the results associated with scripted cooperation are positive, and scripted cooperation has been used successfully with a variety of kinds of material. Scripted cooperation was successfully used in high school mathematics (Berg, 1993). Students were trained in collaborative skills before the introduction of scripted cooperation. Berg recorded the discussions of a subset of interacting dyads and found that students did adhere to the script, remained predominantly on-task, and were successful with the academic content. When off-task discussion occurred, it was usually short-lived.

When students generate their own strategies for interacting on a text-processing task, they may include elements of the scripted cooperation (e.g., breaking the text into smaller units or asking themselves questions about the material). However, Stern (1996) found that 1st-year college students were less likely to use more productive learning strategies than were the more advanced students. They were more likely to use a read, reread strategy when asked to generate their own methods for studying in pairs. Students may uncover the utility of the particular elements of the script independently, but direct teaching of the script can be very helpful.

Some of the research on scripted cooperation was conducted to evaluate the contribution of specific activities to the overall effectiveness of the script. Evaluations of separate components of the script have verified the value of the various components of the script. Overt verbalization is a key element of the script (Lambiotte et al., 1987; Spurlin et al., 1984). The role of the listener is essentially a passive role. However, the simple directions to students to attend to their partners' summaries promotes *active listening*, which results in improved performance over students who are merely asked to listen (Spurlin et al., 1984). Pairs of students who use a cooperative script appear to be more metacognitive about their study task than students who work alone (Hall, Dansereau, O'Donnell, & Skaggs, 1989). They detect errors more accurately and with greater frequency than individuals.

Scripted cooperation is also characterized by the explicit use of elaboration. Elaboration involves reorganizing or restructuring information and connecting new information to old information by the use of imagery, analogy, and other techniques. Pairs of students tend to gravitate toward use of elaboration in comparison to individual students. Kelly and O'Donnell (1994) compared individual versus dyadic search of a hypertext stack on course-relevant material. Search in the stack was facilitated by allowing students to click on concepts of interest and select further information about the concept (e.g., example, definition, analogy). Dyads chose more elaborative information (e.g., selecting "analogy") than did individuals who most frequently chose "definition" as an extension of a concept in which they were interested.

Because elaboration is time-consuming and effortful, the frequency with which participants engage in elaboration is important. This issue was addressed in O'Donnell et al. (1985). Frequent elaboration was effective for expository information but not for procedural information in which detailed steps of a procedure were outlined. One of the implications of this study is that the cognitive activities embedded within a script must be modified in response to specific task characteristics. Although scripted cooperation has positive effects, the effective use of this technique is not as simple as it might first appear. Complex interactions with task, individual differences of students, and incentive structure are also found in this research.

Differences in Scripts. Although a prototypical script was described, different scripts have different effects. Lambiotte et al. (1987, 1988) conducted a set of studies in which they compared the effects of cooperative teaching scripts and cooperative learning scripts. In a cooperative teaching script, students do not share the same material with their partners. In a cooperative learning script, both partners have the same material. The difference in access to material is coincident with different emphases on kinds of processes required. For example, the degree of metacognitive activity experienced by students seems to depend, in part, on the nature of the script they are using. Students report engaging in more metacognitive activity when using a cooperative teaching script than when using a cooperative learning script (Lambiotte et al., 1987).

Furthermore, variations in scripts result in variations in student outcomes (Lambiotte et al., 1988), presumably as a function of the differences in processes promoted by the various scripts. Children who used a cooperative teaching script in which they were instructed to teach one another outperformed students who used scripted cooperative learning on a test of reading comprehension (Rottman & Cross, 1990). Scripts can vary in the emphasis they place on different component activities. Students who emphasized the metacognitive activity in the script performed better on an immediate task than students who emphasized elaborative activities (e.g., explicitly linking the information to prior knowledge). The reverse was true for a transfer task (Larson et al., 1985). Different tasks require different kinds of processes, and scripts must be adapted accordingly. For example, procedural text has very little redundancy, and strategies that are oriented toward identifying main ideas may be ineffective with such text.

Effect of the Task

The task itself is a key influence on interaction in peer learning groups. The task and the tools available for completion of the task facilitate coordination among group members (Lebeau, 1998). The use of scripts that promote helping behaviors with an unfamiliar task reduced the expressed anxiety and incidence of self-deprecatory statements by participants (O'Donnell, 1986). A single script does not work for all tasks. Modifications to the prototypical script described earlier are necessitated by the particular characteristics of specific tasks or desired outcomes. Most of the work in scripted cooperative learning has concentrated on text processing of academic information, and the assessment of cognitive outcomes from that work has concentrated on accuracy and amount of recall. Descriptive information is usually of an expository or narrative nature. Procedural information provides detailed descriptions of steps involved in completing a procedure.

Descriptive and procedural information are best acquired using different kinds of scripts. In a series of experiments, the efficacy of a variety of scripts in promoting learning and performance of concrete procedures was examined. This work is described in detail in a number of publications (e.g., Lambiotte et al., 1987, 1988; Larson et al., 1985; O'Donnell, Dansereau, Hall, et al., 1990; O'Donnell, Dansereau, Hythecker, et al., 1988; O'Donnell, Dansereau, Rocklin, et al., 1988). These experiments together demonstrated a number of findings. First, the results show that procedure learning differs in some respects from academic learning, and scripts must be tailored to the specific kind of information found in texts. Second, scripted cooperation is effective with learning procedural information, and students who use scripted cooperation outperform those who use their own strategies. Third, learner-generated scripts can be effective for immediate task performance but not for retention of the procedure. Fourth, various scripts that differentially support help seeking may be more appropriate for certain individuals than others. Finally, the cognitive activities of participants can be effectively manipulated by the scripts. The importance of the interactions between tasks and scripts was highlighted in these experiments. In addition, the need to tailor scripts to individual differences was also evident in this research.

The tailoring of the prototypical script according to task demands was illustrated by Zuber (1992). Zuber extended the work on scripted cooperation to the area of mathematics, adapting the prototypical script described earlier for the task of solving word problems in fifth-grade mathematics. The script was altered as follows. Pairs of students read the problem and one partner explained to the other what the problem asked. The role of the partner was to again seek clarification; the problem was re-explained (when necessary). Both students solved the problem alone and then compared solutions and solution strategies. Scripted dyads in this research completed more problems and completed them more accurately than did the unscripted dyads in each of 3 weeks of this study. These differences did not reach statistical significance. However, scripted dyads reported significantly more positive attitudes to working with their peers than did the unscripted dyads.

BENEFITS OF SCRIPTED COOPERATION

The research conducted with scripted cooperation shows positive effects. Pairs of students who use scripted cooperation generally (but not always) perform better than students who work in pairs but without the benefit of a script or students who work alone. But does the use of a script limit the types of problems that might occur in an unstructured context?

Scripted Cooperation and Affect

Students who use scripted cooperation generally report liking their partners and are positive about working in groups (O'Donnell et al., 1987; O'Donnell, Dansereau, Hythecker, et al., 1988; Zuber, 1994). In one study (O'Donnell et al., 1987), students worked on an initial task in scripted or unscripted dyads. Participants in both kinds of dyads reported liking their partners. They were then assigned to a new partner for an unscripted completion of a second task. Students who had completed the first task in scripted dyads reported liking their second partner. Those students who had two experiences in unscripted dyads reported strong dislike of their second partner. The emergence of this type of negative affect in groups could be very deleterious to group productivity.

Zuber (1992) also found that scripted dyads liked working in pairs, although their achievement did not differ from those students who worked in unscripted dyads. When the script allows support for help seeking, students report positive attitudes toward the task and their partners. Apparently, scripted cooperation can result in positive affect outcomes.

Participation

One of the problems described in relation to unstructured groups was the possibility of differential participation as a result of status differentiation in the group. The negative effects of status differentiation arise from the emergence of status distinctions and the use of participation to both reflect the emerging distinctions and to maintain them. In scripted cooperation, students must participate, irrespective of whether status distinctions emerge.

Holtz (1994), in a reanalysis of data from O'Donnell (1986), specifically examined the occurrence of status differentiation as a function of the kinds of scripts used. This analysis is limited in many respects and its description here is illustrative rather than conclusive. Participants in the study in question learned to administer an intravenous infusion. The task used here is not isomorphic with the kind of task described by the scope assumptions underlying status characteristics theory (Meeker, 1981). In the purest expression of the theory, the task on which people work is one in which the participants have shared goals, and the judgment of performance quality is made by the participants. Although the situation analyzed here is not entirely appropriate as an application of status characteristics theory or expectation states theory, it does provide an opportunity to examine some of the effects of scripts on behaviors relevant to the theory.

Dyads in the cooperative groups alternated between the roles of performer and listener. The performer actually performed a segment of the procedure and the listener observed the performance and critiqued it. As with other scripted cooperative techniques, the partners alternated roles. Three cooperative scripts were used: (a) prompting; (b) planning; and (c) no-prompting, no-planning. In the prompting group, the performer was permitted to seek feedback during performance of the procedure. In the planning group, the performer first verbally rehearsed the segment of the procedure to be performed and received feedback, then performed the procedure and again received feedback. In the no-planning, no-prompting group, the performer simply completed the portion of the procedure and received feedback from his or her partner following performance.

A Coding System for Status.   A coding system was developed for the purpose of identifying the relative status of partners in dyadic interaction. Only verbal behavior was coded. The verbal behaviors selected for coding were consistent with those identified by Meeker (1981) as being associated with high or low status in group situations. Expectation states theory (Berger et al., 1972) predicts that individuals of high status receive opportunities to act (e.g., answer questions), perform (e.g., give explanations), receive positive evaluations, and are successful at influencing the outcome of the disagreements. In contrast, low-status members grant more action opportunities (e.g., seek help), display fewer task performances, receive more negative evaluations, and demonstrate less ability to influence the group. Verbal behaviors coded as indicators of high status (coded as +1) included reassuring oneself, self-direction, directing partner, providing explanations, and receiving compliments. Low-status behaviors (coded as −1) included self-criticism, denial statements, information seeking, and other help-seeking behavior. A total status score (high status + low status) was computed for each participant. Dyads whose members had different scores were coded as having differentiated status and dyads whose partners had equal scores were considered to have undifferentiated status. Of the 51 dyads available, 40 were considered to be differentiated, with only 11 equal status dyads.

Status differentiation was not equally distributed across the three scripted groups: 35% (6 of 17) of the dyads in the planning group were judged to have equal status members, in comparison to 23% (4 of 17) in the no-planning, no-prompting group, and 6% (1 of 17) in the prompting group. The prompting script is closer to unstructured interaction than the other two scripts. Students are allowed to seek help, although they are instructed not to provide unsolicited help. These instructions were not always followed.

As status becomes differentiated in an unstructured group, the behavioral differences between high- and low-status members are developed, maintained, and amplified. Scripted cooperation requires alteration of roles, which limits one of the primary effects of status differentiation: unequal participation.

Bobier (1997) examined differences in help-seeking and help-giving behavior in scripted dyads by reanalyzing videotape data from O'Donnell, Dansereau, Hythecker, et al. (1988). The three groups in the O'Donnell, Dansereau, Hythecker, et al. (1988) study were scripted cooperative groups. The scripts used in the three groups varied in terms of the degree of structure imposed. In one group, students alternated roles, with one person performing part of the procedure of administering an intravenous infusion while the other person watched. In the second group, students verbally planned the entire procedure (alternating roles in the planning phase) before proceeding to perform the procedure. In the third group, one partner planned a section of the procedure, received feedback, and then proceeded to perform that section of the procedure before exchanging roles. In all groups, students in the role of performer were permitted to ask their partners for assistance.

For each dyad, four types of behaviors were coded: (a) help was sought—help given, (b) help sought—request ignored, (c) help offered—help accepted and (d) help offered—help rejected. In unstructured groups, one might expect to find higher incidence of more negative behaviors such as a student's request for assistance being ignored or an offer of help being rejected. These behaviors are also more likely to emerge in groups in which status differentiation has occurred. Significant group differences were found on only one measure, help sought—request ignored. Participants in the prompting group (the group most like unstructured dyadic interaction) ignored their partners' requests for assistance significantly more that did participants in the two groups that used some kind of planning.

Taken together, the results presented by Holtz (1994) and Bobier (1997) suggest that dyads that are closer than comparison dyads to being unstructured are more likely to differentiate status and to engage in negative social behaviors that may result in cognitive costs. These data are very preliminary and further work is needed to test hypotheses that emerge from these initial analyses. It is also important to note that the dyad is the simplest unit of cooperation and it is the one that maximizes the possibility of equal interaction (Webb, 1992). If status differences emerge even on unfamiliar tasks and help seeking is ignored in dyadic interaction, one can only assume that these negative processes are exacerbated in groups that are larger.

LIMITATIONS OF SCRIPTED COOPERATION

Scripted cooperation can promote achievement and positive attitudes to both the tasks and the partners involved. It has also been used successfully with different age groups, although the majority of the work on scripted cooperation has been conducted with college students. Scripted cooperation can also reduce the incidence of the negative behaviors that may emerge in unstructured settings.

Perhaps the major limitation of scripted cooperation is that it is limited to specific tasks. These tasks are most frequently acquisition tasks. Because progress through a task is scripted, there is little room for innovation on the part of the students, except in the elaboration phase of the script. This limit on spontaneity may make scripted cooperation entirely unsuitable for accomplishing outcomes related to higher order thinking. Cohen (1994b) noted that structured interaction is helpful when the learning task involves factual recall, understanding of the assigned reading, or application of procedures and concepts in a relatively routine manner. She suggested that the beneficial effects may be due to the fact that the use of scripts can raise the level of discourse and that students are drawn into participation. The implication then is that the use of scripts will not facilitate more conceptual skills. King's work (chap. 4, this volume) shows that the use of scripts can raise the level of discourse, equalize participation, and also enhance the quality of questions asked by children and the quality of the responses provided. It may be that scripts can usefully scaffold conceptual development but may need to be specifically designed to do so.

CHAPTER EIGHT

A Fish Called Peer Learning: Searching for Common Themes

SHARON J. DERRY
University of Wisconsin–Madison

Each chapter in this section is a valuable and interesting contribution to research and theory on peer learning environments. Yet, despite a common theme, the conceptual space encompassed by this body of work is broadly diverse. The objects of study within this space represent many variations on the theme of *learning together,* serving to emphasize the seemingly infinite number of ways in which peer learning environments can be conceptualized and designed. The five chapters about which I am asked to comment are therefore not easily clustered for analysis, comparison, or generalization of findings, for their subjects of concern and their theoretical orientations are neither alike nor unique with respect to one another. Rather, they overlap, much like the multidisciplinary scales in Campbell's (1969) "fish scale model of omniscience." My commentary therefore endeavors to characterize the nature of the five chapters assigned to me as individual fish scales, then follows up by suggesting directions and motivations for organizing, as it were, the fish as a whole.

RESEARCH ON DESIGNED VERSUS NATURAL INTERACTION

One cross-cutting theme of these chapters is designed versus natural peer interactions. Chapter 7, by O'Donnell, directly addresses this issue, pointing out that both Vygotskian and Piagetian theory provide arguments against artificially constraining interaction that occurs naturally when peers work together. Nevertheless, only Chapter 3, by Person and Graesser, examines natural interactions, those found in peer tutoring. Although their research was limited to the mathematics domain, it suggested that natural interactions between peer tutors and their less advanced students are flawed in many ways. Students who tutored followed a limited and unsophisticated script, and students who received tutoring did not use active learning strategies that would have enabled them to take better advantage of available help. Nevertheless, peer tutoring was often reasonably effective despite all its flaws. The authors believe that learning benefits were derived from tutor-initiated conversational moves (e.g., hinting, prompting, splicing) that were used to help negotiate impasses in student performance or understanding. This picture of untrained peer tutoring is quite valuable, for it should enable instructional designers to build on a foundation of expected natural strengths and weaknesses when creating learning environments that resemble peer tutoring in problem solving.

That untrained interaction can be improved through scripting and other forms of designed intervention is a major assumption of all other chapters in this section. *Scripting* is used broadly here to describe methods of scaffolding either the form or content of peer interactions. The preponderance of evidence indicates that peer learning can often be enhanced by various methods that impose constraints on, or provide affordances for, the discourse within learning groups. Gaining control over discourse was the explicit purpose of Alison King's experimental designs for developing higher order thinking, described in Chapter 4. Students were given written guidance and prompts for structuring peer questioning, group problem solving, and tutoring. Although details are not supplied by the chapter itself, King cites published experimental studies showing that this structured guidance fostered particular patterns of discourse among students engaged in peer learning tasks. Presumably these discourse patterns represented externalizations of good higher order thinking and learning processes (based on normative theoretical models of good thinking found in various cognitive literatures), inducing students to carry them out enhanced learning. King's discourse-prompting techniques were effective for both problem-solving and reading-comprehension tasks. Even young students were able to engage in high-level discourse when scaffolded in this manner.

The contribution by Webb and Farivar (chap. 5) is the most complex and comprehensive discussion of both theory and research and is notable for reporting new analyses in detail. Their chapter begins with an excellent conceptual discussion of why peer interaction is believed to benefit both those giving and those receiving instruction. In their framework, both givers and receivers have responsibilities that might not be carried out spontaneously. Students who "teach" must respond to cues that a peer needs help, providing adequate explanations tailored for the particular need. Peer learners must be able to recognize when help is needed and explicitly ask for it, then follow through by engaging in appropriate constructive learning activity.

Webb and Farivar investigated whether middle school students' abilities to help and receive help could be improved through training, and whether this training would produce improvements in arithmetic problem-solving performance. They offered students four activity-based instructional units for building class cohesion, general communication skills, ability to provide and receive help, and ability to explain for use in otherwise unstructured groups. Employing an experimental design that lagged control classes behind experimental ones, the authors tested the effects of providing more versus less helping-skills training.

One instructional unit—on giving explanations—appeared to increase both level of help giving and constructive problem-solving activity. However, students supplied fairly low levels of help overall and did not appear to improve over time with training, although nonisomorphism of problem tasks across units made trend analysis difficult. The best predictors of achievement were pretest performance and the extent to which constructive activity following help was maintained over subsequent problems. This tendency to sustain constructive behavior was predicted by level of constructive activity immediately following receipt of help, which was in turn predicted by the level of help received. Hence, an interesting theoretical model was derived, linking achievement to giving and receiving help and to training. Another notable finding from a detailed qualitative analysis carried out with four groups was that teachers' mentoring styles made a big difference in the success of group learning.

Although there is much to admire in their well-planned study and analyses, it is also possible to see specific aspects of their research that might have limited its power, some of which are noted by the authors themselves. For example, their selection of problem-solving tasks was dubious. Not only were the tasks nonequivalent across units, preventing trend detection, some tasks were probably too simple to require use of the trained helping skills. Other uncertainties are raised by coding systems used for scoring levels of help and constructive activity, which ignored the semantic content of verbalizations and were not tied to a theory of discourse or problem-solving behavior. Hence, the scoring probably captured some superficial features of student dialogues but ignored some important deeper ones. Also, the training itself was not tied to the mathematics domain and did not provide much support for understanding mathematics concepts. If the necessary mathematical understandings were not already present within groups, students were unable to benefit from the helping skills. In this regard, the Webb and Farivar approach can be contrasted with those reported in chapters by King and by Palincsar and Herrenkohl, who tied their interventions to theories about good thinking within the task domains in which students engaged.

In Chapter 6, Palincsar and Herrenkohl provide an overview of three research programs: (a) reciprocal teaching, (b) small-group collaborative problem solving in science, and (c) an attempt to promote productive whole-class discussion in fourth-grade science. Each program was discussed in terms of three design issues: (a) how student interaction was scaffolded; (b) design of tasks, conceptualized as delineating problem spaces; and (c) how acculturation was encouraged though activities and procedures designed to promote group norms for good thinking. For example, the learning goals for Collaborative

Problem Solving in Science (CPS) included the ability to engage in argumentation using scientific concepts and evidence obtained from students' observations. Interaction patterns were supported by providing heuristic scripts that served to guide students' thinking and observations during problem solving. Problem space design involved creating "knowledge authorizing" tasks, problems that were neither too complex nor too simple, could be understood in terms of broad explanatory principles, provided opportunities for examining evidence, and so forth. Finally, attention to acculturation took the form of mentoring and training that aimed to help students become comfortable with argumentation processes required for reaching group consensus.

O'Donnell's review of scripted cooperation in Chapter 7 provides an excellent conclusion for the preceding chapters, as three of these (chaps. 4, 5, and 6) describe ways of structuring interaction and cooperation in designed environments, and one (chap. 3) provides foundational knowledge on natural scripts that occur in nondesigned peer tutoring. Chapter 7 also offers many insights as to why collaborative learning is not always successful. Although O'Donnell acknowledges that good arguments for nondesigned peer learning environments are made in the developmental literature, she cites ample evidence that negative cognitive and social processes occur frequently within these environments and that many of these occurrences are related to unequal status among students. The transcripts within Chapter 7 and other chapters in this volume illustrate how lower status students become less involved through processes in which they may voluntarily opt out of discussions or be treated with disrespect or excluded by others. Although additional research is needed to refine methods, structuring the interaction among peers by the use of various scripts or prompts represents one of the most promising categories of instructional design techniques for promoting productive learning interactions while countering negative processes related to status.

The chapters reviewed illustrate that various types of scripted or structured interaction can be employed with different types of learning tasks—ranging from procedural job skills to reading comprehension. From the research and theory cited in Chapter 8, it is known that learning-task characteristics are an important determinant of effective design of peer learning interactions. Nevertheless, there is currently no widely accepted theory of tasks associated with the peer learning community, much less instructional principles that specify how scripts should be designed or adapted in accordance with specific task characteristics. Work in this area appears to be needed.

PEER LEARNING AS A DIVERSE MULTISCIENCE

To the extent that the chapters just described are representative, peer learning researchers share the common goals of understanding the nature of effective peer interaction and finding instructional formats that promote it. Also, scripting or structuring discourse or interaction is viewed as an especially useful, flexible, and promising instructional device for scaffolding student interactions. Other interests within the community are designs for promoting classroom acculturation and attention to learning task characteristics as a basis for guiding design. Yet, despite common interests, researchers differ from one another in many interesting ways, including research methodology, the ages of students studied, sizes of groups studied, the types of tasks and subject domains examined, and the specific designs and approaches to peer learning that are being researched and promoted. Many theoretical differences are evident as well. For although the chapters in this group are grounded in cognitive theory, broadly defined, they do not employ a common language or bibliography or common viewpoint regarding peer learning.

The studies discussed by King in Chapter 4 are grounded in the literature of educational psychology. King's theoretical discussion of discourse-mediated peer learning represents a synthesis of cognitive information-processing perspectives—on such topics as explanation-based learning, elaboration, questioning, and problem solving—with developmental perspectives on social knowledge construction. Webb and Farivar ground the work reported in Chapter 5 in the developmental tradition, blending Piagetian and Vygotskian approaches together. The work reported by Palincsar and Herrenkohl (chap. 6) is grounded explicitly by an extended discussion of their sociocultural perspective, derived from Wertsch's (1991) interpretation of Vygotsky and other Soviet thinkers. However, several theoretical ideas from information-processing psychology, such as the problem space conceptualization of task design, are very central to their work. Moreover, this chapter introduces an important cognitive literature on argumentation that traditionally is only loosely associated with either of their other frameworks. The developmental viewpoint is also prominent throughout an early discussion in O'Donnell's (chap. 7) contribution. However, much of her later argument counters that viewpoint, blending language from the fields of sociology with social and motivational psychology. Unfortunately, Chapter 3 (Person and Graesser) does not reveal its theoretical orientation, although the work references a literature on tutoring that has largely employed an information-processing approach. Their work has some basis in Grice's (1975) conversational theory, and a discussion of how these ideas blend with information-processing psychology to provide a theoretical perspective would have been a welcome addition.

Although most chapters in this collection are theoretically rich, the overall picture is theoretically messy, which is why I now turn to what can be said about the fish called peer learning. It is clear that a cognitively based design science for collaborative instruction is a promising and viable goal. Yet, putting these chapters together in a collective volume brings into focus that such a science does not yet exist. Each chapter represents a research program that is somewhat of a specialty unto itself, overlapping significantly with others, but representing an emerging personal theory, methodology, and problem interpretation that is rich in its own right but significantly attached to a single program of research. To the extent that it is difficult to integrate findings, induce fundamental principles, or develop a common conscience from a research space so unscripted and diverse, it is the broader research agenda that suffers. Of course this is not a condition unique to the peer learning community, but rather a phenomenon of social science in general. Nevertheless, organizational frameworks for cutting across individual programs, perhaps derived by multidisciplinary teams involved in peer learning, would appear to greatly benefit the larger programmatic effort. Efforts such as this volume and the RISE conference associated with it are important in their contribution to cross-program interaction.

TOWARD A THEORY OF TASKS

A common theory of tasks would be useful to the peer learning community, for several reasons. First, task characteristics are often acknowledged as important determinants of group interaction (e.g., O'Donnell, DuRussel, & Derry, 1997; O'Donnell, chap. 7, this volume; Palincsar and Herrenkohl, chap. 6, this volume), and are sometimes implicated in explanations of unexpected or inconclusive findings. For example, in the study reported by Webb and Farivar, nonisomorphism of problem tasks across units gave rise to interpretation problems related to trend analysis. Second, lacking a theory of task characteristics, we are left with many unanswered questions about the generalizability of seemingly important findings. For example, do Person and Graesser's observations of novice math tutors generalize to a family of tasks, stretching perhaps to nontutoring environments outside of mathematics? Finally, the chapter by O'Donnell discusses at length the importance of considering task characteristics in designing interventions, such as cooperative scripts for peer learning. But with no cross-cutting theory of tasks, how can principled rules for adapting cooperative scripts to different tasks be devised?

Declarative, Procedural, and Other Learning Goals

A primary task-defining characteristic is the task's goal. Because school tasks are usually learning assignments, they have been historically characterized in terms of their desired learning outcomes. A theory for describing learning outcomes and the conditions under which they could be accomplished was developed by Gagné (e.g., 1977), and for many years it served to guide instructional design in military and industrial settings (Derry & Lesgold, 1996). Perhaps a similar universal system could support designers and researchers of peer learning environments. That such a need exists is indicated by the apparent requirement for authors in these chapters to categorize their tasks and learning outcomes in various ways in order to discuss their work.

For example, at one point in Chapter 7, O'Donnell characterizes learning tasks as either declarative (acquiring knowledge that) or procedural (acquiring knowledge how), then frames thoughts about designs for scripted cooperation in terms of these learning goals. In proposing that different script designs would be appropriate for different task types, O'Donnell also speaks of "academic tasks," and discriminates between such categories as conceptual and higher order learning tasks.

In fact, Gagné's theory historically made very similar distinctions. For example, Gagné distinguished various types of skill learning from verbal learning goals and identified concept recognition as one type of skill. Gagné's learning outcomes were listed taxonomically and each was associated with a set of recommended conditions that needed to be met in designs of instruction for that task type. This taxonomy was very useful to teachers and instructional designers when instruction was needed for tasks that could be typed according to this taxonomy. It was also useful to researchers, because it enabled them to characterize their work as generalizing to a class of tasks.

Then why is Gagné's work less favored today? A major argument is that today's instructional tasks often represent complex performances that require flexible use of both declarative (verbal) and procedural (skill) knowledge, in unpredictable combinations. Conducting scientific research or developing engineering designs are examples of complex tasks that are neither declarative nor procedural in nature, but that are increasingly valued in schools and beyond. The instructional designs of Palincsar and Herrenkohl, described in Chapter 6, are excellent prototypes of the modern trend in science education toward situating learning goals within complex tasks, believed to represent authentic learning contexts. Such complex goals cannot be categorized as one type of learning or another unless they are broken down into highly specific subskills that are taught separately. Such task analyses help to define prerequisite skills needed for higher level complex performances, but instruction that promotes mastery of these skills in isolation from one another is currently controversial (e.g., Derry & Lesgold, 1996). Hence, the declarative–procedural distinction, along with other psychological distinctions such as those that have historical roots in Gagné's taxonomy, have some usefulness for a science of peer learning, but this usefulness is limited. Their value is most obvious when the goals of learning can be clearly and uniquely typed.

Higher Order Learning Goals

A theory of tasks would need to discriminate between higher and lower order learning outcomes and identify forms of higher order learning. King's peer learning scripts do not seem intended to help students acquire task or subject matter knowledge per se; rather, subject knowledge is viewed more as a stimulus and vehicle for accomplishing higher social and developmental goals, including capacity for self-regulated learning, social knowledge construction, and intelligent, analytical thought.

From King's viewpoint, good instructional designs are those that encourage sophisticated levels of discourse in peer learning groups. King believes that good peer learning discourses have properties that encourage development of higher order learning outcomes. Hence, tasks in King's approach involve achieving particular discourse patterns applied to appropriate content, where the discourse can be viewed as a mediator for (King's view) or externalization of (my view) thinking processes, which are the major goals for student development. A science of learning tasks from this perspective would likely resemble a taxonomy of normative discourse patterns tied to particular content domains. For example, I could imagine a set of "critical investigative discourse structures" for use with science laboratory exercises. A science of design would involve the development and use of scripts and other forms of scaffolding to bring discourse about selected content to life and structure it in desirable ways. Ultimately, such external scaffolding would need to disappear, leaving internalized mental structures to support future discourses, both internal and external, in natural settings.

The Problem Space

Palincsar and Herrenkohl employ the concept of problem space to describe their thinking about task design. According to information processing theory, problem spaces include the following components: (a) a goal; (b) a starting state, the conditions that exist at the task's beginning; and (c) various possible steps that students might take to get from a starting state to a goal. For example, in reciprocal teaching, the goal for reading might be to enhance students' understanding about evolution. The steps necessary for acquiring understanding would be found in the reciprocal teaching procedure itself, but its exact implementation would vary depending on the students' starting knowledge and reading ability and on the demands of the text.

Problem spaces must be based on "knowledge-authorizing" tasks, that is, they must be suitable tasks for accomplishing the learning goals. For example, the goals of CPS were scientific literacy, defined to include (a) ability to apply scientific knowledge in principled ways, (b) facility with the language of science, and (c) collaborative skills that promote social knowledge construction. Hence, the objective of task design was to create problems that afforded collaborative discussions that had as their purpose the interpretation of observed phenomena using scientific principles. If the demands of the problem space were either too great or too small given the students' starting abilities, the task did not function as a suitable platform for achieving the desired learning goals.

Possibly for convenience, Palincsar and Herrenkohl treat the issue of problem-space design as related to, but separate from, the problems of structuring interaction and supporting classroom acculturation. That is, their discussion implies that there are three separate but interconnected steps in instructional design for peer learning: planning problem spaces, designing interaction, and building classroom norms. However, the promoting of particular interaction patterns and the scaffolding of cultural norms are highly interrelated to each other and to the problem space itself. Normative patterns of classroom interaction merely add constraints and affordances to problem spaces and hence are a large part of what defines and shapes them. I do not believe this is a trivial point because it suggests that a key to successful peer learning design may be to meld cultural norms, discourse patterns, and tasks into a seamless, unified problem space. I do not believe that the problem spaces in the chapters I reviewed were always thus unified. For example, a "disconnect" may have existed between the mathematics tasks and the discourse patterns in the Webb and Farivar study. A unified problem space for peer learning should constrain and afford discourse such that desired norms and cognitive processes are enacted during problem solving without cognitively overloading students. These enactments should be internalized as knowledge outcomes, so that they continue after artificial constraints and affordances (e.g., scripts) are withdrawn.

The ideal problem space for group learning is of course difficult to achieve in real classroom settings where students exhibit many different entering characteristics. It is especially difficult to achieve when the desired knowledge outcomes for students are strong performances in authentic, complex problem spaces, such as those represented by the science classrooms described by Palincsar and Herrenkohl. The classroom designs described in the chapters I reviewed are all laudable efforts in exactly the right direction that make various degrees of headway toward creating ideal problem spaces for group learning. Of course, none of these efforts were entirely successful, and it is instructive to speculate why.

In some ways, King's approach comes closest to representing the seamless, unified problem space. Her scripted discourse patterns implicitly embody cultural norms, define the learning task, constrain the problem space, and represent the learning goals. If learning is successful, presumably norms and patterns and new performance capabilities are left behind when scripts are faded. There is a pleasing simplicity to this approach because it does not overload students' working memories with multiple goals and forms of training. A greater concern for transfer, task authenticity, and fading of scripts would take this interesting approach even further in my opinion.

The Task in Peer Learning: A Summary

Inevitably, there is a problem task in peer learning designs—something that students "do" in order to learn together. Moreover, tasks must be carefully chosen and carefully designed if successful peer learning is to occur. But the relation between what task students perform together and the desired learning outcomes of that task activity varies from program to program. In O'Donnell's program, acquiring the skills of correct task performance is the major desired learning outcome of collaborative group work. In other programs (e.g., King, chap. 4, and Webb and Farivar, chap. 5, this volume), the task functions more as a vehicle for practicing and internalizing higher order communication skills that are the major goals of instruction and that presumably will facilitate later performance on a range of tasks. In still other programs (e.g., Palincsar and Herrenkohl, chap. 6, this volume), the task functions as a rich context for exploring the domain in ways that will uncover and illustrate key explanatory principles. It also is intended to afford development of collaborative practices that are normative for the domain's culture.

These three scenarios require different ways of thinking about tasks in the context of peer learning design. The first scenario represents a case in which particular performances, such as job tasks, must be acquired. A likely aim of design in this case would be to script or otherwise support group interaction so as to maximize the learning efficiency and (importantly) minimize the likelihood of negative group interactions due to status characteristics. A theory of tasks might supply a taxonomy of task categories tied to group-based instructional methods associated with each taxonomic category. This approach might extend the historical foundation laid by Gagné and others for design of individualized instruction, but would not work well for highly complex tasks that require higher order thinking skills.

The second scenario represents the case in which higher order thinking skills are the main instructional goals. If such skills are viewed as discourse structures that can be enacted on the social level and internalized as thinking strategies, a theory of tasks would likely supply a taxonomy of important discourse patterns with their associated content or problem contexts. Such an approach would extend the work of King.

The third scenario is related to the second but is more complicated in that tasks must be both authentic and knowledge authorizing. That is, tasks must help shape complex problem spaces that encourage students to explore, observe, and discuss phenomena, not only for the purpose of inducing principles about those phenomena, but also for the purpose of participating in the culture of a domain. A theory of tasks in this scenario might build on the design concepts found in the Palincsar and Herrenkohl chapter. It would need to provide guidelines for creating unified problem spaces that scaffold desired student practices and processes while minimizing negative interactions and avoiding student overload.

ARGUMENTATION AND
SOCIAL KNOWLEDGE CONSTRUCTION

The five chapters in this section both explicitly and implicitly reveal common understandings of several theoretical accounts of how peer interaction fosters knowledge construction. One viewpoint held in common is the Piagetian constructivist position, which assumes that learning occurs when new data are assimilated to prior knowledge structures, perhaps updating them, or when new data are accommodated by prior knowledge structures, causing them to be modified. From this well-known viewpoint, the cognitive conflict that may occur during peer interaction is a driving force behind construction of new knowledge, as it forces students to accommodate differences between their beliefs and those of others.

Similarly, the information-processing view, implicitly accepted throughout these five chapters, also assumes that new knowledge results from integrating incoming information with prior knowledge, through processes such as elaboration (similar to assimilation) and reconstruction (similar to accommodation). A related social cognition perspective, represented primarily in the chapter by O'Donnell, characterizes group knowledge construction as the "degree to which information, ideas, or cognitive processes are shared, and are being shared, among the group members and how this sharing of information affects both individual- and group-level outcomes" (Hinsz, Tindale, & Vollrath, 1997, p. 43). The sharing of information is affected by group characteristics such as the distribution of prior knowledge and the status of individual members.

Another common perspective on knowledge construction is represented by sociocultural theory, discussed in several chapters in this volume. From this viewpoint, knowledge resides within cultures and is negotiated by them through practices that involve discourse and other forms of semiotic mediation. A mentorship model of social interaction accounts for development, which is viewed as the gradual appropriation of cultural norms, language, and other cultural tools by new members. It is due to this theory that classroom acculturation has become a major theme in these chapters and throughout the peer learning community.

A fifth way to think about knowledge construction is from the perspective of reasoned argument, discussed briefly by Palincsar and Herrenkohl (chap. 6). Although this view has not yet been influential in the peer learning community, it has important implications for research and practice because it suggests that other theories are incomplete in an important way. Within this framework, a distinction is made between knowledge construction based on nonreasoning or faulty reasoning, and knowledge construction that results from attention to reasoned argument. In a discourse based on reasoned argument, students mobilize evidence to support their beliefs, weigh different beliefs in terms of evidence, and question beliefs that cannot be adequately supported. When new beliefs are acquired or old beliefs are altered based on critical evaluation of reasoned arguments, a preferred form of knowledge construction has occurred.

This viewpoint implies a strong relation between argumentation skills and ability to benefit from collaborative learning, regardless of theoretical perspective. From the Piagetian and information-processing perspectives, peers must not just challenge one another and reconstruct their prior knowledge to reach consensus by accommodating the views of others. They must do so in terms of a normative model of good argument that weighs available evidence and reasons before accepting a course of action or adopting a belief. From the social cognition perspective, the sharing of knowledge must include the sharing of reasons and evidence for beliefs, and speakers' arguments, rather than their status characteristics, are the objects of attention. From the Vygotskian perspective, classroom norms must embody and support the processes of good argumentation, and mentors within the culture must model and scaffold it.

Argumentation skills are not easily acquired, however, and merely scaffolding them in the context of peer learning environments that have other instructional goals may not provide sufficient support for learning them. Argumentation has two aspects—form and content—representing two types of knowledge that students must possess in order to perform. Knowledge of argument form involves understanding the components of argument, including their interrelations. As a minimum, arguments have at least one premise, or supporting evidential statement, and one conclusion. Arguments also often include stated and unstated assumptions, counterarguments, and complex chains of reasoning involving many premises and multiple conclusions. There are various rules pertaining to argument evaluation. For example, one strong premise or many weak premises can support equally good arguments. Many reasoning fallacies can be caused by failure to distinguish between invalid and valid argument *forms*.

A second aspect of argumentation, and possibly a more difficult one, is argument *content*. Content skills involve understanding the nature of evidence and how it can be used to support conclusions. Unhappily, there is ample and growing evidence that many adults and students in mainstream American culture cannot or will not reason with evidence (Halpern, 1996; Kuhn, 1991). For example, Kuhn found that many members of professional, lay, and student populations have difficulty supporting their opinions and beliefs with reasons, and some are even opposed to doing so. For example, Kuhn's participants were asked questions such as, "Why do children fail in school?" After sharing their causal theory (e.g., lack of parental support), participants were asked what kinds of evidence they might give to support their belief. The following segments are from three interviews (Kuhn, 1991). The interviewer's words are parenthesized and in italics, and each participant was asked the following: *If you were trying to convince someone else that your view is right, what evidence would you give to try to show this?*

1. What evidence will I give? I'll just talk about it. *(Like you just did?)* Yes, just talk about it.

2. I wouldn't really give them evidence. I would just try to convince them that was the reason why. *(How would you do that?)* I'd keep at it, you know, keep telling them that, yes, this is the reason, this is the reason. If it ends up that he doesn't believe me, or whatever, it ends right there.

3. I would not try to give any evidence. I only . . . when it comes to kids, I work by my good instinct, and I would say there are sometimes parents who are totally tuned into their children will know more than the professional. . . . If you live with your child day in and day out, and if you can stand outside that circle and be objective, as well as subjective when you must be, you know what's happening. . . . *(Is there anything someone could say or do to prove that what you've said is what causes school failure?)* I would go by my life experience. Everybody has life experience. I'm not trying to push my views on anyone else. I think my views are very liberal. That's what gets me through. But, no, I'm not going to go toe-to-toe with anyone. It's not important to me. (pp. 82–83)

The forms of discourse illustrated above were from a small group of participants who argued on the basis of "nonevidence" (Kuhn, 1991, p. 81). The segments illustrate the problem that students may not understand what evidence is. Kuhn's work also documented many other types of fallacious arguments.

Within specific domains of study, such as science or history, what is accepted as evidence may be culturally determined and should be regarded as an important aspect of the domain as taught. However, there appears to be a general scientific and mathematical conceptual base pertaining to evidential reasoning that is generalizable to many cultures and domains. This general conceptual base is what allows us to draw valid parallels among various courses of study that focus on argumentation—rhetoric, forensics, scientific method, statistical reasoning, critical thinking, as examples. Evidential reasoning, even in everyday situations that are not obviously mathematical, often requires good intuitive understanding of such statistical and scientific concepts as control, correlation, covariation, replication, probability, deduction, induction, and hypothesis testing. Many psychologists and educators (e.g., Abelson, 1995; Konold, 1989; Kuhn, 1991; Tversky & Kahneman, 1971) believe that theories of statistics and probability provide normative models for good everyday reasoning. Typical reasoning fallacies, such as sterotyping individuals on the basis of group memberships or believing in lucky streaks, represent violations of probability laws.

Furthermore, formal training in statistics is known to improve students' ability to reason evidentially (Nisbett, Fong, Lehman, & Cheng, 1987). Training in critical thinking that focuses on both argument form and content, including the statistical and scientific aspects of evidence, has improved performance on measures of reasoning ability (Halpern, 1996). That students' argumentation and reasoning skills can be improved through instruction grounded in the context of small-group problem solving has also been suggested by two recent studies conducted by my research group: one a 3-week unit taught in middle school social studies, science, and mathematics classes (Derry, Levin, Osana, & Jones, in press); the other a semester-long intervention for freshman education majors (Derry, Levin, Jones, Osana, & Peterson, 1998).

In the middle school study, students in experimental classes heard four presentations on argumentation and basic statistical reasoning concepts (e.g., control, replication, and correlation), then utilized these ideas to carry out mentored, small-group activities. The main small-group activity was to use available materials to research and develop argumentative presentations about a proposed bill for government regulation of the vitamin industry, which was in the news at the time. Students within groups played roles that encouraged them to argue opposing perspectives. For example, some students represented the vitamin industry, whereas others represented the Food and Drug Administration. Groups presented their arguments in class at a mock legislative hearing.

Assessment tasks and scoring procedures were developed to measure students' ability to reason about evidence provided in court cases inspired by a popular television show. These tasks represented a theory-based, far-transfer assessment design. Performance on counterbalanced forms of the task was measured both prior to and after the instructional unit, and the performance and gains of students in experimental classes was compared with that of students in comparison classes that did not participate in the program. To the extent possible, statistical analyses adjusted for the lack of random assignment of classes to treatment. In brief, analyses indicated that the instructional program did appear to develop students' ability to reason evidentially about complex authentic problem situations that differed substantially from tasks used during instruction.

In another related study, Derry et al. (1998) designed and evaluated a semester-long course in statistical reasoning that was offered to freshman education majors. In conjunction with readings and lectures, this course utilized mentored small- and whole-group problem-solving activities to promote the idea "that the purpose of statistics is to organize a useful argument from quantitative evidence, based on a form of principled rhetoric" (Abelson, 1995, p. xiii). For example, students learned about experimentation by working in research groups to conduct experiments with Wisconsin Fast Plants, and by presenting their research findings at a class "conference."

Evidence of student growth was obtained from pre- and postcourse interviews of 16 students. Interview tasks and scoring were designed to measure students' ability to reason with statistical evidence from everyday sources, such as news reports. Both quantitative and qualitative analyses indicated that students made meaningful gains in their ability to reason evidentially about everyday issues. However, the authors discussed how broader institutional contexts were not supportive of course norms and may have limited course effectiveness.

Most of the peer learning designs described in the chapters under discussion were significantly dependent on students' capacity to construct and understand arguments. The dialogues of explaining and using help described in the chapter by Webb and Farivar often resembled argumentation, as did tutoring sequences reported by Person and Graesser, and the questioning and tutoring discourse structures reported by King. For example King's students were asked to provide elaborated responses—such as explanations, justifications, and rationales—to question starters. However, generating good justifications and rationales would have required the ability to generate argument. Only Palincsar and Herrenkohl explicitly designed their environments to scaffold argument form and content.

Because argumentation processes may be a necessary condition for productive peer interaction, and because such processes are unlikely to occur naturally in previously uninitiated groups, instructional designs for peer learning should always give consideration to the need for argumentation skills. However, given the importance and complexity of argumentation, a school-wide, or even culture-wide commitment to this instructional goal may be necessary for sufficient impact. Many different kinds of efforts can contribute to an overall school culture that is supportive of collaborative learning. Treating statistical reasoning as a form of literacy in mathematics and social studies, encouraging formal debate in classes and through extracurricular activity, teaching rhetoric in English, and offering elective course in critical thinking are just a few of the many possibilities. Many more opportunities exist around the family dinner table.

COLLABORATIVE LEARNING: CONCLUDING COMMENT

Peer learning as a science of practice is not embodied within any one scholar or research program. Rather, it forms a "multiscience" (Campbell, 1969) characterized by many specialized research programs that overlap like fish scales in terms of their theories, methods, techniques, and goals. A challenge for peer learning researchers will be to work together more often and to develop better organizing frameworks to facilitate their own cross-program collaboration. One potential multidisciplinary task is to build a more unified, common theory of knowledge construction that incorporates current thinking on evidential argument. Another is building a theory of collaborative tasks and instructional methods. That proponents of peer learning may be working against predominant cultural norms, which do not strongly support the use of reasoned, evidential argument in everyday living, is yet another reason for researchers to work and learn together more often and more effectively. So a collective competence can more readily emerge. So a peer learning agenda can move swimmingly ahead.

PART III

Implications of Peer Learning
for Teaching and Teacher Education:
Overview

The final section of this book addresses the complexities for teachers in supporting effective peer interaction. Three areas of difficulty with respect to teachers' knowledge of peer learning are addressed in this section: (a) the role of the teacher in the effective implementation of peer learning in classrooms, (b) the problems in preparing preservice teachers to effectively use peer learning as part of their instructional repertoire, and (c) the issues involved in the professional development of in-service teachers to initiate peer learning in their classrooms. Together these chapters contribute to our understanding of the important role teachers play in the effective use of peer learning in classrooms and the critical need to help teachers develop the necessary skills.

Marie Cooper, I.H.M., delineates the choices that teachers must make with respect to peer learning (chap. 9) and like Derry (chap. 8), calls attention the importance of the task. The stance that the teacher adopts with respect to the students, activities, and tasks in their classrooms is critically important. Other chapters in this section suggest that teachers are currently rather ill-equipped to make such choices. Meloth and Deering (chap. 10) note that teachers may not effectively support cognitive processing on the part of collaborating students.

Woolfolk Hoy and Tschannen-Moran (chap. 11) and Almog and Hertz-Lazarowitz (chap. 12) describe the complexities involved in preparing teachers for their roles in classrooms in which students work together or shifting their roles in existing classrooms. The absence of theoretical models of groups as cognitive systems exacerbates the difficulties in altering existing beliefs about how learning occurs.

CHAPTER NINE

Classroom Choices
From a Cognitive Perspective
on Peer Learning

Marie A. Cooper, I.H.M.
Immaculata College

At all levels of schooling and across the curriculum, instructors seeking to guide their students into more robust, accessible, versatile, and transferable learning, opt with growing frequency to implement peer learning in their classrooms. More than 20 years ago, the government's Coleman Report (Coleman, 1973) suggested that collaborative activities are the most effective means for initiating adolescents more fully into academic culture. Empirical evidence from the ensuing 2 decades of research and testing (e.g., Brown & Palincsar, 1989; Heller, Keith, & Anderson, 1992; Thornton & Sokoloff, 1990; Webb, 1989, 1991) supports this trend, giving teachers hope of greater conceptual and procedural gains for their students, closer match of instructional techniques to a variety of student learning styles, greater enjoyment of the learning task, and a stronger persistence in learning.

Peer learning does hold promise in all these areas, but it is not a panacea, and positive results are not automatic. Assured outcomes demand rigorous examination of goals, intelligent and informed planning of an implementation strategy for accomplishing those goals, an alert eye to the dynamics of the process, and a means of evaluating outcomes clearly and without prejudice. The stance of the teacher within the process, the design and maintenance of the classroom environment, and the choice of task and dialogue stand as pivotal in the work of creating a match between goals and an implementation strategy that makes possible the attainment of these goals. These aspects of implementation are strongly linked: A specific choice in one area sets parameters for the others. Inadequate reflection on any of the three will limit student gains and may create far-reaching problems (Hoadley, Hsi, & Berman, 1995). In this chapter, I first provide an overview of the cognitive perspectives on peer learning that are constructivist in nature. In the second part of the chapter, I consider key classroom choices that must be made in order to promote learning.

ROOTS OF PEER LEARNING

Constructivism

Cognitive perspectives on peer learning are diverse (as reflected in this volume, for example), growing as they do from multiple traditions in the study of learning. As an instructional technique, peer learning arises from the conviction that students can assist one another to build their own understanding, integrate new learning into existing cognitive structures, and adjust those structures as needed. It is, then, a manifestation of the constructivist paradigm for education (see De Lisi & Golbeck, chap. 1, this volume). Whereas there is no single view of education that can claim to be the principal constructivist view, there are commonalties to all that wear the label (Matthews, 1994). Essential to the constructivist view is the idea that each learner must build his or her own knowledge, interpreting new experiences and assimilating them into existing cognitive frameworks, adjusting the frameworks as necessary when they come into conflict with phenomena encountered, or with the interpretation of those phenomena by others, as met in social discourse (Clancey, 1994; Resnick, 1989; von Glasersfeld, 1989; De Lisi & Goldbeck, chap. 1, this volume). The constructivist teacher provides the student with techniques for learning and an environment rich in phenomenological and social experience, empowering the student to take control of his or her own learning, and making the student's only limitations those of his or her own biology (Anderson, 1983).

This insistence that students must build their own knowledge does not mean that they cannot learn from material presented by an instructor, but only that such presented information must be processed by the student, interpreted, and assimilated to his or her own mental structures (Resnick, 1989; Vygotsky, 1962). A genuine constructivist educational environment is not an unstructured discovery zone, but a highly structured physical and social environment that provides a wealth of information and experience to the learners (Resnick, 1989). The instructor has a critical role in providing well-planned experiences to confront students' naive or incorrect concepts, in initiating students into the culture and conventions of the field of study, and in equipping students with appropriate tools and the opportunity to develop procedural competence (Driver, Asoko, Leach, & Mortimer, 1994).

The important role of the student's striving for understanding is underscored by McDermott's (1997) word of caution to teachers, especially to teachers of science, about merely providing information as opposed to facilitating learning. The expertise and excitement that teachers hold for their subject matter is generally an outgrowth of long, arduous, and sometimes tedious struggle in their own careers as students. In the effort to call new classes of students to expertise, and to share their own wonder and enthusiasm, many teachers work diligently to save students the very struggle that brought them the insights they treasure. Carefully designed presentations organize and subdivide difficult topics into manageable bits, relieving the students of the need to carry out the same processes, often limiting the degree of reflection and reorganization that may mediate a deeper understanding and fuller integration of new learning. Such simplification may actually reinforce naive or false understandings (Koschmann, Myers, Feltovich, & Barrows, 1994). Moreover, the passive learning model represented by teachers' extensive work in presenting material so thoroughly pre-analyzed gives learners a false picture of science as a culture, encouraging the view of science, or any knowledge base, as a set of immutable facts. Students learn much about the nature of science and the scientific enterprise by the manner in which they learn science (Bruffee, 1993; Dewey, 1933). When students construct their own scientific understanding as the fruit of their own struggles, they may develop a truer picture, and build a stronger understanding, of both the targeted concepts and the overarching scientific field of those concepts, as well as a more positive attitude toward science, learning, and their own abilities. Three expressions of constructivism are considered next: (a) situated cognition, (b) cognitive apprenticeship, and (c) activity theory. These approaches share many of the features of constructivism described earlier but differ in ways that can influence classroom choices of tasks, materials, evaluation systems, and the roles to be adopted by teachers and students.

Situated Cognition

New knowledge must be constructed by the learner, and the strength and truth of that construction depends on the prior knowledge to which it is linked and the accessibility of that knowledge. In addition, knowledge is heavily influenced by the situation in which it is acquired (Resnick, 1989). In the situated cognition model of constructivist educational theory, instructional events are designed with a view to embedding the acquisition of concepts within some realistic and meaningful task. These tasks are generally conducted in a social context with the teacher providing guidance. Student involvement in these tasks gives students a more realistic picture of the components of expertise in a given domain, practice in higher order thinking skills, and the ability to apply new knowledge in a variety of problem-solving contexts, and in the manner of experts (Brown, Collins, & Duguid, 1989).

Whereas more radical proponents of constructivist educational theory consider knowledge as stored in the environment rather than in any internal cognitive structures, and reconstructed by individuals each time it is used, others consider the logical conclusion of this view, the constant individual reconstruction of everything, including constructivism, by each learner (Cobb, 1994) to be extreme if not absurd. A middle ground may be found in the work of Pea (1985, 1993), which considers intelligence as distributed across the social and physical environment. Although not denying that an individual has mental representations, Pea viewed intelligence as something that is accomplished, not a static possession.

Pea believed intelligence to be distributed as well across both the symbolic and physical tools available in the learning environment. Once students are enculturated to the use of these tools, they are able to externalize more complicated reasoning processes, making them clearer and diminishing the likelihood of error. These tools can include literary works, art, recorded reenactments, the symbolic structure of algebra or calculus, or the variety of measuring instruments found in a typical instructional lab. They serve as repositories and extensions of the students' cognitions, but also bring with them, and make available to the student, the intelligence of their designers.

In the process of learning, students can extend and amplify their own memories and cognitive abilities by externalizing them in the environment. When the externalization considered is across the social group, Pea's theories reflect a growing belief among social scientists that meaning is a negotiated entity, established in the interaction between partners (Hogan & Tudge, chap. 2, and Palincsar & Herrenkohl, chap. 6, this volume; Vygotsky, 1962). A recent study (Heller et al., 1992) lent weight to this belief in its finding that students working in structured cooperative groups consistently solve more difficult problems than the most able individual in the group can solve independently, and that this gain transfers well to individual problem solving on tests. Considerable research confirms the effectiveness of cooperative learning in well-structured groups, at all levels of academic progress, and a constantly growing body of literature offers recommendations for the judicious implementation of cooperative tasks (e.g., Brown & Palincsar, 1989; O'Donnell, chap. 7, this volume; Webb, 1989, 1991).

Cognitive Apprenticeship

The process of cognition, then, is inextricably linked to its physical and social context (Resnick, Salmon, Zeitz, Wathen, & Holowchak, 1993). When this situated knowledge is firmly embedded in significant and authentic activity, the learning process can be greatly enhanced. Because of the similarities between this shared, mentored activity in realistic situations and more advanced levels of traditional craft apprenticeship, such an instructional practice has come to be known as cognitive apprenticeship (Brown et al., 1989; Collins, Brown, & Newman, 1989; Resnick, 1989).

In the more traditional craft apprenticeship, students learn physical skills and procedures under the tutelage of a master. The immediate nature of feedback encourages the apprentice's growing skill in error detection and correction of his or her own work. In application of the apprenticeship model to cognitive tasks, this feedback loop retains its importance, and requires the design of external tasks that model the internal process of systematization of new knowledge. This systematization, coupled with immediate feedback and the presence of the instructor as guide in meaningful and realistic activities, models expert patterns of learning and working and facilitates the development of metacognitive skills (Collins et al., 1989).

The implementation of the cognitive apprenticeship model is in close agreement with Vygotsky's (1962) view that learning occurs always at the zone of proximal development, one step beyond or, in some cases as noted by Hogan and Tudge (chap. 2, this volume), one step behind the student's current equilibrium state. The multiple support structures of the model make the transition from current state to new conceptual and procedural knowledge a more seamless and confident one.

Activity Theory

Activity theory, a derivative of Vygotsky's theories on cognitive development delineated by Leont'ev (Donato & McCormick, 1994; Fishbein, Eckart, Lauver, VanLeeuwen, & Langmeyer, 1990), encompasses, integrates, and extends the cognitive theory presented thus far. Activity theory examines the physical environment, social interaction, and learning task, and interweaves the three with a theory of learning that has strong implications for the classroom choices that determine the effectiveness of peer learning.

In Leont'ev's view, each educational experience consists of an objective or goal and a set of strategies or activities for progress toward that goal. A feedback loop persists between the student's activity and cognition, with adjustments to both sides in the course of the student's interaction with the environment, and with the reciprocal relations among learner, task, environment, social structure, and activity noted by Salomon (1993) in his elaboration of distributed cognition. This theory meshes well with the cognitive apprenticeship model, the authentic tasks serving as the activities. Social interaction performs an important function here, focusing the activity, refining the cognitive gains from the activity, preventing overautomatization of tasks, and triggering metacognitive operations. All activities and strategies are strongly linked to student goals, and an insufficient goal (passing a quiz, getting through a chapter) may in turn weaken the strategy employed and diminish the focus on the activity (Bereiter & Scardamalia, 1989). Well-structured peer negotiation can help to clarify and reinforce goals, maintain proper focus, increase feedback, and raise cognitive and metacognitive awareness and motivation (Cuseo, 1989).

Applications of Theory to Classroom Choices

A number of important principles emerge from the consideration of constructivism in general and from the specific expressions of constructivism embodied
in situated cognition, cognitive apprenticeship, and activity theory. These include the notion that knowledge is personally constructed, and that activities in
which understanding can be constructed must be authentic and based in the
learner's experience. Support for cognitive activity is necessary and discussion of
the activity is also important. These principles have important implications for
classroom practice.

A number of recommendations have been made for the implementation of
constructivist learning techniques to classroom settings. Arons (1990, 1993), examining the learning patterns of physics students, synthesized a number of
these recommendations in his listing of relevant modes of inquiry for students.
Arons's prescriptions are applicable to instruction in all the sciences and, with
little modification, have validity in other areas of study as well. According to
Arons, the observation of phenomena and the abstraction of concepts from
these observations are vital. The process should always proceed bottom-up,
from the concrete to the abstract, especially in light of the difficulty students experience in trying to apply concepts acquired in their abstract form to unfamiliar
concrete settings (Vygotsky, 1962). Redish (1997) added that, optimally, phenomena planned for learning activities should be anchored in the student's real
and immediate experiential world. New knowledge is most efficiently acquired
in a known and understood context. A note of caution: The most carefully
planned activity or investigation, without summative discussion of the activity
as a follow-up, is not enough to alter students' prior understandings (Johsua &
Dupin, 1987). Accommodation of inadequate cognitive frameworks requires of
learners both dissatisfaction with their existing structures and an encounter
with intelligible and plausible alternatives (De Lisi & Goldbeck, chap. 1, this volume; Gorsky & Finegold, 1994). Research indicates that the discussion process
at two levels mediates this change: within the smaller, more immediate peer
group and then again in the larger group of the full class (Thornton & Sokoloff,
1990). This dual interaction leads students to reflect on, reorganize, and refine
their thinking in negotiation within the smaller group and then provides an au-
dition for the thinking of others that may facilitate further extension and refinement of concepts. Interviews conducted as part of one study of introductory
undergraduate physics students suggest that students reap a triple benefit in this
process: clearer, more efficient understanding of course material; a clearer understanding of the work patterns of professional scientists; and a sense of confidence and poise (Cooper, 1995).

Cooperative and collaborative learning techniques offer much to the process
of cognitive reorganization. Studies have shown a wide variety of cooperative
or collaborative activities to have cognitive and metacognitive benefits. Design-

ers must give careful attention, however, to the forms of interaction among members of the group. Webb (1991) suggested that consistent efforts be made to connect new work to students' prior knowledge and that students must be free to seek help and encouraged to provide it when others request help. Webb and Farivar (chap. 5, this volume) provide an extensive analysis of the role of help seeking and help giving in cooperative groups.

One recommendation from the diverse applications of constructivist education underlies the others: The student bears primary responsibility for his or her own learning. Peer learning helps students to accomplish the learning task within a group setting of shared intelligence. Can this be effectively accomplished in real classroom situations?

CLASSROOM CHOICES

The choice to incorporate peer learning experiences into an educational program commits the instructor to a challenging task. Peer learning represents a major shift in focus from what is being taught to what is being learned, and transfers the responsibility for knowledge acquisition, organization, and implementation from the teacher to the student. It will also necessarily change the requirements for the environment in terms of material resources needed and the kinds of tasks selected. The role adopted by the teacher when using peer learning will depend in part on the environment and tasks required. The choices to be made by a teacher with respect to these factors will constrain or extend the potential roles played by the teacher.

Environment

In discussing the optimal environment for implementation of peer learning in the classroom setting, one does well to reflect on the levels of environment that may have an impact on the students' learning. The physical setting for any learning is important and, if carefully considered, fades from direct consciousness while lending subtle support to the activities within. Within that physical setting, the role of technology is gaining increasing prominence and can serve as amplifier and organizer of students' cognitive activities (Pea, 1985) or can provide distraction from the tasks at hand (Koschmann et al., 1994). The social environment for learning is also a powerful influence on the process and can be a predictor of the success of the outcome. The nature of conversation and response to questions and requests for help carry special strength here (Webb, 1989, 1991; Webb & Cullian, 1983). The nature of social interactions within the physical and technological environment is the foundation for a local culture of learning, and that culture is an agent of change in the behavior and mental functioning of the developing learner. An instructor planning to incorporate peer learning into students' learning experiences cannot disregard the elements of environment.

Physical Environment. Peer learning designed to engage students' cognitive frameworks does not need an elaborate physical environment. Two or three students working at problems or jointly developing a report in a corner of the room may be engaging in highly effective peer learning activities, applying and reinforcing higher order thinking skills. However, a well-planned physical environment can strongly support the endeavor.

Certainly, an environment designed to encourage peer learning requires the space for students to interact without disturbing, or being disturbed by, others. In some cases, especially in the laboratory sciences, it is advisable to design a space in which one type of interaction, perhaps dyadic, may spontaneously evolve to a larger grouping, for instance, a group of four, as the students or the teacher find such a change necessary. By locating two dyadic tables closer to each other than to other groups in the room, the instructor encourages regrouping, and students easily seek the larger groups when greater interaction would prove helpful (Cooper & O'Donnell, 1996). The use of carpeting and wheeled chairs in the classroom, although not necessary, minimizes noise and makes the shift so simple and inconspicuous that it quickly becomes an automatic response to the need for more collaboration. Carpeting and wheeled chairs are especially useful when the chosen form of collaboration centers on an investigative activity.

One element of classroom arrangement that frequently eludes the conscious attention of those designing learning space is the placement of the instructor's desk. Cuban (1982), a historian of educational reform, noted that even in classrooms believed by teachers to be student-centered, the teacher's desk is often front and center, signaling the true focus of the classroom. The vital and multifaceted role of the instructor is without question, but something as simple as the movement of a desk to the side of the room can send a message to the students that the work and the responsibility for their learning is their own.

Social Environment. The encouragement of an atmosphere of respect and trust is essential to the successful implementation of peer learning (Andrews, 1992; Chan, 1988; Webb, 1989). Students must know that they are safe to express their thoughts, opinions, and misunderstandings. Dialogue will occur on three levels and must be safeguarded at all three: within the small group; in the larger, summative group; and between the groups and the instructor. Pea (1985, 1993) reminded us that intelligence is accomplished in the interaction of persons within an environment and with the artifacts of a given culture. The most complete learning is built in partnership, the outcome of shared authority and responsibility, with no one partner bearing full authorship (Cole, 1991; Lave, 1988; Salomon, 1993).

Elsewhere in this volume, Webb and Farivar offer the results of research into the structure of peer learning groups, the nature of dialogue within groups, and their influence on students' learning and self-esteem. The case for explanations requested, given, and received within a peer group has been well documented (see Webb, 1989). Later in this chapter, the modeling of metacognition and self-monitoring skills within teacher–student dialogue is noted. Whole-group discussion can be especially useful in clarifying and reorganizing thought and for modeling and giving the opportunity for practicing expert modes of thought. As a strong learning strategy, however, whole-group discussion is frequently overlooked, or bypassed as unnecessary, to the detriment of learning.

When students are asked to explain their problem-solving processes, several things happen. They are forced to think about the salient features of the problem (Berardi-Coletta, Dominowski, Buyer, & Rellinger, 1995; Berry & Broadbent, 1984). This awareness of the salient features of the problem is essential to the transfer of problem-solving skills from a single problem to others of its type (Stein, Way, Benningfield, & Hedgecough, 1986). In the student's effort to explain the procedure that he or she followed and the reasons for the various steps of the procedure, there is a triggering of metacognitive awareness. The student must think about his or her thinking (Berardi-Coletta et al., 1995). Berardi-Coletta and colleagues (1995) presented strong evidence that it is this metacognitive triggering that results in enhanced skill and increased efficiency. The explanation of reasoning is essential to the process. A simple description of procedural steps, without the demand for explanation of reasoning, fails to produce lasting change because it involves only information currently in working memory, neglecting connection with the broader knowledge base (Ericcson & Simon, 1984). The organization of thought, critical thinking skills, and growing self-confidence mediated by student explanation is lost, or at least greatly diminished, when solutions are demonstrated exclusively by instructors. Modeling is valuable, even essential, but practice and individual appropriation of the competencies involved demand student presentation. To develop an environment in which the kinds of cognitive activities just described can occur, the nature of the task assigned to a peer learning group must be carefully considered.

TASK

Earlier in this chapter, the importance of environment was discussed in terms of distributed cognition. The task assigned to a peer learning group is a vital part of the more general environment within which peer learning occurs. Salomon (1993) suggested that it is within activity that cognitions are most effectively shared. In accord with Leont'ev's (1978) activity theory and elaborating on Pea's (1985, 1993) notion of distributed cognition, and even Bandura's (1978) reciprocal determinism, Salomon (1993) noted that "individuals' input, through their collaborative activities, affect the nature of the joint, distributed system. This, in turn, affects their cognitions so that their subsequent participation is altered, resulting in altered joint performances and products" (p. 122). Collaborative interaction on cognitively appropriate activities, then, is a spiraling transformational process, marked by a dynamic reciprocity at every turn.

Activities appropriate to promoting cognitive growth are as varied as the competencies they are designed to support. Researchers and practitioners promote the use of small-group discussions, collaborative laboratory investigations (Laws, 1991, 1997; Thornton & Sokoloff, 1990), structured group problem solving (Heller et al., 1992; Phelps & Damon, 1989), problem-based learning (Koschmann et al., 1994), jointly authored papers (Chan, 1988; Duin, 1984), group presentations (Scott & Heller, 1991), and even joint tests (Robinson & Schaible, 1995). Guiding principles, however, are consistent across curricular boundaries. Whatever the activities chosen, it is imperative that both the task and the processes needed for the completion of that task be carefully planned so that students' energies are focused principally on higher order thinking skills such as evaluation, synthesis, and application (Berry & Broadbent, 1984; Cuseo, 1989). Especially useful are activities that encourage learners to formulate explanations and opinions, and to test them against the views and understandings of others (Hoadley et al., 1995; Koschmann et al., 1994). Prediction–revision tasks, explanation, abstraction, and summarization all serve these functions well. Inadequately planned activity and dialogue structures within a peer learning framework can lead to poor communication, unequal responsibility, unreflective group thinking, and the implementation of simple tasks that do not engage students' cognitive structures (J. Anderson, Reder, & Simon, 1996; Hoadley et al., 1995).

Tasks that encourage robust, transferable learning must be open-ended and interpretive and fully integrated into an overall instructional plan (Bruffee, 1993). The use of peer learning techniques for closed-ended, result-focused tasks may reinforce earlier learning but does little to encourage new understandings. Such uses promote the view of group activities as busy work, limiting its effectiveness not only in the current instance, but in later, more wisely chosen applications (Cohen, 1990; Phelps & Damon, 1989). On the other hand, careful planning of the task and the interconnections of activities, alert monitoring of dialogue, and strategic probing help students use higher order thinking skills more consistently (Cuseo, 1989), reflect on their thinking, and develop more expert patterns of learning (Chi, Feltovitch, & Glaser, 1981; Hake, 1995; Walker, 1987).

Tasks are most truly and effectively peer learning tasks if they are structured for negotiated production of some cognitive product. Tasks that require division of labor eliminate the *guided stimulation* and *qualitative scaffolding* that undergird cognitive gains in peer learning (Salomon, 1993). In joint production, students have the opportunity to observe and internalize modeled processes. In the appropriation of shared processes, individuals are able to continue the collaboration even in the absence of their peers (Salomon, 1993).

Some areas of the curriculum are well suited to particular activities. In language-linked courses and social studies, well-planned group writing projects offer more benefits to the student than simple growth in writing skill. The negotiation necessitated by work within a group facilitates semantic webbing, gives practice in the evaluation and organization of gathered information, models the coherent structuring of that information, and offers reflection on the development of a knowledge base (Andrews, 1992). The group can act as a respectfully critical audience for individual writing as well, honing the novice writer's presentation style with an immediacy and absence of threat less achievable in traditional assignments. The feedback of peers in the negotiation of a final product helps students gain a sense of authority over their own writing. This, in turn, may lead to a greater motivation to write (Chan, 1988). The recent use of computer networking allows for the continuation of the process even outside class. In the Andrews (1992) study cited, students reported support and growing self-confidence as their greatest gains.

In mathematics at any level, the power of peer learning lies not in its potential for drill and practice of fundamental concepts but in the opportunity it affords to emphasize concrete, context-embedded problem solutions. Such problem solving promotes transfer of abstract mathematical concepts to real applications (Deering, 1994; Koschmann et al., 1994; National Council of Teachers of Mathematics, 1989). Information-rich problem structures (Heller & Hollabaugh, 1992; Heller et al., 1992) are particularly useful here. Applicable in both mathematics and science, an information-rich problem is a problem relevant to current instructional material and grounded in a student's experience outside school. In contrast with textbook problems, such a problem tells a story and, like most problems in the real world, has both more and less information than is needed for its solution. More measures and facts are present than are pertinent to the solution task, and information that can be deduced from common knowledge, or easily found in reference sources, is absent. Students must, as they will in real situations, determine what information they need, select what is useful in the problem, and find or recall the rest. Negotiation in such a task helps reorganize thinking, promote metacognition, structure the process, give a student a sense of the genuine applicability of the abstract concept, and bolster confidence.

Joint solution of problems affords students the opportunity to develop a tolerance for uncertainty vital to genuine scientific pursuit (Dewey, 1910). A trust in the process developed by practice gives students the freedom to explore possibilities. Working alone, one is more likely to aim for certainty as quickly as possible, missing the critical skills gained in reflectively wrestling with ideas.

As suggested earlier, a special difficulty exists in long-held erroneous or naive understandings of scientific principles. Such false cognitive frameworks are best confronted in collaborative settings that follow multiple applications with discussion and explanation. Single applications may be memorized by students as exceptions to the understandings that have served them well throughout their lives. Applications in diverse activities may trigger reflection, generalization, and finally, conceptual change (McDermott, 1997). Resnick (1989) noted that learning occurs in interpreting experiences and information, not simply in recording them. Again, care must be taken that the final stage of any collaborative activity promotes generalization, reflection, and abstraction.

TEACHER STANCE

The importance of the environment and the tasks that are part of that environment is very clear. The role of the teacher in developing and maintaining this environment (including the selection of a task environment) is crucial. The importance of the teacher is paradoxically juxtaposed with an increased responsibility for learning on the part of the student. It is not an opportunity for the instructor to step back and let things happen. At best, such an attitude would guarantee that very little would happen on the cognitive level; at worst, it could result in cognitive loss for the student. Hogan and Tudge (chap. 2, this volume) caution planners of educational programs that the zone of proximal development exists not only beyond the learner's current knowledge state but behind as well. Without wise choices and thoughtful guidance, students can replace newly acquired competencies by earlier, less successful strategies and less accurate understandings that remain more familiar and comfortable. Careful planning, inconspicuous observation and evaluation, and prescribed adjustment are essential if new learning is to move forward with any degree of consistency.

In any successful implementation of peer learning techniques, the teacher plays a number of vital roles as (a) developer of an educational program; (b) model of the expert learner; (c) coordinator of activities; (d) mentor, Socratic interlocutor and metacognitive trigger; and finally as (e) an evaluator. The fulfillment of these roles carries benefits for both teacher and student, but it demands time, discipline, and dedication.

Teacher as Developer of an Educational Program

Any successful educational program demands of planners and instructors that they be aware of and embrace three theoretical perspectives: (a) a theory of the desired student knowledge state, (b) a theory of the student's entry state, and (c) a theory of the process of transition from one to the other (Glaser, as cited in Gelman & Greeno, 1989). Peer learning provides teachers with the opportunity for ongoing evaluation and adjustment of all three (Andrews, 1992; Cooper & O'Donnell, 1996). Involvement of students in peer learning activities frees teachers for reflective observation of individual groups, evaluation of the cognitive dynamics of the groups, and adjustment of tasks for the optimum learning experience of all students. The teacher must plan the tasks and the tools, and guide the nature of the dialogue of groups within the environment so as to enhance the development of conceptual and procedural competencies (Gelman & Greeno, 1989). All of this requires considerable time, reflection, and individuation on the part of the teacher. Meloth and Deering (chap. 10, this volume) note that practicing teachers find it hard to do these activities, and Woolfolk Hoy and Tschannen-Moran (chap. 11, this volume) note the difficulty in preparing preservice teachers to manage groups effectively. The effort carries benefits, however, for both student and teacher. Added to the cognitive benefits to the student discussed elsewhere in this chapter and this volume, the direct interaction between teacher and student that informs planning greatly adds to the teacher's satisfaction (Andrews, 1992; Cooper & O'Donnell, 1996) and gives students a greater sense of partnership with instructors in the learning process (Cooper & O'Donnell, 1996).

Teacher as Model

The explicit modeling of learning and problem-solving strategies for the student is important to the student's appropriation of expert procedures (Collins et al., 1989; Heller & Hollabaugh, 1992). Within the peer learning environment, opportunities for such modeling exist both in whole-group activities and in direct interaction between the teacher and individual groups. Students given the chance to see how an expert approaches a learning task, a problem-solving task, and a presentation task, followed by time to reflect on the approach and discuss and apply expert methods in realistic, relevant settings, have a greater likelihood of applying those methods more consistently outside the instructional setting. It is impractical for teachers to expect that students will make the transition from novice to expert strategies without explicit instruction.

In one implementation of a modeling–collaborative problem-solving program for introductory physics students (Heller & Hollabaugh, 1992; Heller et al., 1992), students collaborated in strongly structured groups on the solution of information-rich problems after observing the expert analysis and solution of similar problems. The nature of the groups and roles within the groups as well as the nature of the problems and problem-solving tasks is discussed later in this chapter. Students of all ability levels showed significant gains in their ability to analyze and solve problems within the groups and successfully transferred those skills to independent problem solving.

Teacher as Coordinator of Activities

The immediate application of new knowledge to a number of related activities challenges erroneous and naive conceptions, enhances student organization of concepts, and encourages transfer (Koschmannn et al., 1994; McDermott, 1997; Reif & Allen, 1992). The teacher who can orchestrate activities with common characteristics promotes students' organization and interconnection of concepts and increases the likelihood of accommodating a greater proportion of students with diverse learning styles and strategies (Koschmann et al., 1994). Student questions asked during the implementation stage of learning, rather than in the acquisition stage, are more effective (Fishbein et al., 1990). During implementation of activities, students become aware of what they need to understand to carry out their tasks, and so their questions are motivated and focused, and the very act of asking is a characteristic of control over their own learning. If the social environment has been well-established and maintained with an atmosphere of acceptance and mutual respect, and dialogue is carefully monitored, responses to the questions help students make cognitive gains as well as gains in self-confidence (Webb, 1991).

Teacher as Mentor and Socratic Interlocutor

Gorsky and Finegold's (1992, 1994) caution bears repeating here. The most creative investigative task, the most spectacular demonstration, may be remembered, but is not likely to change student's erroneous or naive conceptions until that student reaches a sense of dissatisfaction with his or her understanding and sees the conclusion of the investigation as a plausible replacement. Open-ended questions asked by the teacher during the implementation stage of learning can set up the cognitive disequilibrium needed to eliminate naive understandings and misconceptions (Hake, 1995), guide organization, and trigger metacognition. The teacher who can monitor student progress and plan activities so as to facilitate active questioning may help students' growth toward effective organization, increased metacognition, and motivation for continued learning.

The teacher in a peer learning environment has a unique opportunity for direct interaction with students. The teacher in such an environment is an expert, a member of a culture of learning who invites students to active membership in the culture. This mode of interaction with the students was mentioned earlier as cognitive apprenticeship, and it gives the teacher the status of mentor and guide. Within this role, the teacher exercises two principal functions: as model of Socratic interaction, and as shaper of dialogue. Socratic dialogue is a cognitively powerful manifestation of the position of the teacher as mentor characterized primarily by the posing of probing questions. Teachers who consistently ask "what if?" and "why do you think that?" of students promote the cognitive disequilibrium that triggers new thinking and creative ideas. In one study of introductory college physics students working within a collaborative, computer-supported classroom, students explicitly noted that this mentoring was important and of value to them (Cooper & O'Donnell, 1996). Students, working in dyads on laboratory investigations and problem-solving exercises, had access to their professor and two teaching assistants who circulated through the lab as students worked. Although students appreciated the chance to ask questions of the instructors, they stated clearly, consistently, and without solicitation in interviews that one of the most important aspects of the class for them was that the instructors asked them probing questions as they worked. The questions were always open-ended. Some asked students to explain their reasoning; some asked students to predict what would happen if certain characteristics of the investigation were changed; some asked for supporting evidence for statements. Students explained to the interviewer that these questions led them to consider their work from a different point of view, led them to think more deeply, and helped them relate the laboratory experience to the more direct instruction, the problem solving, and their reading. These same students tended to ask more open-ended questions of themselves and others as the semester progressed, thus internalizing the modeled learning strategy.

Teachers model format and acceptable patterns of dialogue for peer–peer interactions as well. Webb's extensive studies of group interaction (1989, 1991; Webb & Cullian, 1983; Webb & Farivar, chap. 5, this volume) consistently pointed to the essential nature of mutual respect within the learning dialogue and the importance of receiving reflective answers to one's questions. The teacher may choose to assign specific dialogue tasks to students within a group as an aid to focusing conversation (Heller et al., 1992) or simply offer examples and well-timed suggestions to students in the course of their work. Whatever the instructor's choice, dialogic interaction may promote a student's learning, confidence in his or her ideas, and enjoyment of the learning process when conducted with focus, care, and respect.

Teacher as Evaluator

Finally, throughout the process, in the contact between teacher and student characteristic of the peer learning environment, the teacher has a unique opportunity to probe students' understandings while they are fluid and to make corrections at opportune moments. Meloth and Deering (chap. 10, this volume) pointed to the importance of these interventions. Testing here is not merely an end-state tool but truly a diagnostic tool facilitating strategic curricular adjustment. Moreover, the dialogue affords a reflective observation of the students' thinking that gives a clearer picture of the nature and extent of understanding than is possible with more fixed evaluative tests that put time and distance between the students' response and the teacher's evaluations. If a teacher is truly to follow Glaser's (see Gelman & Greeno, 1989) prescription to know the beginning state of the student, the desired end state, and transition strategies, Socratic dialogue gives a truer picture of entry-level understanding and intermediate states than the most well-thought-out paper test or overt behavior in a laboratory setting. Dialogue provides the opportunity for a clearer picture of covert cognitive processes, which often remain hidden behind more obvious observable behavior (Winn, 1990). Whereas cognitive and procedural competency are strongly linked, it is possible that students follow correct procedures for incorrect reasons, masking essential misunderstandings, schemata that are at the heart of the cognitive viewpoint.

A misunderstanding is easier to probe and correct at the time of its expression. Moreover, in direct interaction, one may correct that misunderstanding by steering the student's thinking through strategically asked questions, triggering cognitive dissonance and encouraging metacognition. Such benefits are not possible with written tests, and dialogue is not limited by the time delay that is unavoidable in paper tests, laboratory reports, papers, and exercises. Formative evaluation, then, becomes in this setting a more fluid and immediate technique allowing for finer and quicker adjustments of task for optimum learning. This ongoing evaluation does not supplant more fixed summative tests at regular intervals, but it does inform and extend their usefulness.

THE ROLE OF TECHNOLOGY IN PEER LEARNING

Teachers today have the advantage of access to varied technology that can support their work in collaborative or cooperative classrooms. Technology may serve as a method for distributing and amplifying intelligence within a learning environment (Pea, 1985, 1993) and assist both teachers and students in that environment. Technology, in the form of computers or advanced analytical tools, may serve as a way for students to use the tools of their intended cognitive culture (Brown et al., 1989). The well-planned and carefully structured use of interactive computers in peer learning may serve as a mediating tool for learning activity, providing more opportunities for students, engaged in active social construction of learning (Pea, 1993). Current use of the computer in education extends far beyond its original function as a tool for programmed reinforcement to an instructional instrument that is a part of the total learning environment.

The integration of computers into the educational environment has been a growing phenomenon over the past 30 years. At all levels of schooling, computer-integrated learning systems (ILS) have been developed and implemented with varying results. Early implementations used computers for drill and practice, but they have been found to have a stronger impact on new learning, particularly for better students (Hativa, 1994). Students in an ILS environment tend to spend more learning time actively engaged (Worthen, VanDusen, & Sailor, 1994). Evidence shows the ILS to have strong affective outcomes for both students and teachers, to encourage persistence, and increase motivation and self-esteem (Adams & Shrum, 1990; VanDusen & Worthen, 1994).

Originally considered a tool for individualizing learning, the ILS has shown its strongest effects in a collaborative setting (Cox, 1992; Koschmann et al., 1994), providing learners with both cognitive and metacognitive support (Hativa, 1994; Mevarech, 1994). Interaction that occurs when the ILS tasks are set within a peer learning environment encourages students to refine their ideas in interaction with others and to restructure and organize their thinking in formulating explanations to partners. Palincsar and colleagues (Palincsar, Anderson, & David, 1993) demonstrated the power of collaborative problem solving in helping students develop a clearer understanding of the nature of science and scientific work. There is evidence that integrating this collaborative interaction into a computer-based format enhances the effects of both the collaboration and the integrated technology (Cox, 1992). In its use as an educational tool within a learning environment based on the principles of situated cognition, and more particularly of cognitive apprenticeship, the computer serves as an effective tool for reorganizing mental processes, helping students develop appropriate hierarchical structures for new knowledge (Pea, 1993). Such guidance in organization is not easy to accomplish in the context of a traditional educational setting.

Studies over the past decade have shown positive results in the use of computer tools in the classroom, and these initial successes encourage teachers to implement the tools. Judiciously used within a collaborative framework, computers can help strengthen higher order thinking skills (Hativa, 1994), increase time spent in active engagement (Worthen et al., 1994), promote the cognitive disequilibrium that helps displace naive understandings (Gorsky & Finegold, 1994), encourage metacognition (Hativa, 1994; Mevarech, 1994), and strengthen and refine communication (Hoadley et al., 1995). The list is not exhaustive. Within particular disciplines, further benefits are claimed, and some evidence has been gathered for the claims. In writing, for example, the use of electronic mail within a class gives students the opportunity for a respectfully critical peer audience, and skills can grow dramatically (Koschmann et al., 1994). In the sciences, the use of computer tools can enhance students' understanding of the nature of the scientific process (Cox, 1992; Thornton & Sokoloff, 1990). Care must be taken that the tools serve the instruction.

One of the first instances of collaborative, interactive, computer-based learning in secondary and postsecondary science was Thornton and Sokoloff's (1990) implementation of the Universal Lab Interface and its accompanying *Tools for Scientific Thinking*. The program provided bottom-up investigation and generalization, mediated by peer negotiation and guided by Socratic dialogue. Evaluation of student outcomes for initial pilots showed highly significant gains of the experimental group over students participating in the more traditional lecture format. In the first experimental dissemination of the program among other local schools, however, outcomes for some classes and some schools failed to corroborate the encouraging first results. The class pattern called for a summative whole-group discussion as a follow-up to each investigation. Some teachers, concerned about time, seeing the students' excitement and involvement in learning, and hearing the quality of their small-group discussions, dropped the whole-group summary discussions in favor of continued activity within the smaller group. Each case of disappointing results was tied to a neglect of summative discussion, and each case of encouraging results was linked to their maintenance. A second study (Cooper, 1995; Cooper & O'Donnell, 1996) informally reinforced these findings and suggested the further investigation of student presentation and critique of problem solutions and explanations.

An additional use of technology in peer learning is to support teachers' adoption of the complex roles required by peer learning environments. Almog and Hertz-Lazarowitz (chap. 12, this volume) describe a professional development program that depends on technology to assist teachers in learning the skills necessary to play the roles required in a complex technology-rich environment.

Although technology can be used to implement key principles from constructivist learning approaches (e.g., social nature of learning, the active construction of knowledge by the learner) a number of cautions are warranted. Implementation of technology cannot be carried out for the optimum use of the technology but rather for the maximum benefit to the student (Koschmann et al., 1994). Glaser's rule is the best measure (Gelman & Greeno, 1989): All instruction must be based on the initial state of the student, the desired end state, and the best transition from one to the other. Otherwise, the computer can be a very expensive distraction. A second area of care follows from the first: Any computer-based activities must have valid purpose grounded in sound educational theory. Students must see the need for the activities if they are to have any value (Doolittle, 1995). The use of computer-based problems and investigations anchored to the real-world interests of the students and the avoidance of simple drill exercises can promote genuine involvement and promote higher gains.

Salomon (1993) also cautioned that more specialized and advanced cognitions, frequently found in college science programs, do not distribute well and thus it may not be possible to share expertise, even when there is technological support for such exchanges. As an individual's level of expertise increases, there develops a depth, a breadth, and an automaticity of both cognitive and procedural competencies that is the possession exclusively of the individual. This expertise remains, at least to some extent, internal and inaccessible to others, both because it is the result of the extensive and specific knowledge characteristic of experts (Chi et al., 1981; Walker, 1987) and because the expertise of others is essentially different.

CONCLUSION

In general, the implementation of a peer learning program focused on cognitive gains requires the same type of spiraling reciprocity mentioned earlier in the context of activity theory. In the progress of an effective program, cognitive goals, tasks, and verbal interactions serve as the elements of the reciprocity loop, with formative evaluation enabling the transition from one to the other and classroom choices setting the framework within which all proceeds. Careful attention to physical and social environment, teacher stance, and activity make of the three an almost invisible but powerful support for learning.

Essential throughout is the shift in focus from what is being taught to what is being learned. In a study of an introductory physics program that employs peer learning within an integrated technological environment (Cooper, 1995), the investigator found students to be very much aware of this shift. When asked the greatest strength of the program, a number of students considered it to be the shift of responsibility for learning from teacher to student, whereas a number of others found the same characteristic to be the program's most difficult aspect. However it is viewed, when students take responsibility and an active role in their learning, they begin to develop a notion of what it means to know and how knowledge is acquired (Bereiter & Scardamalia, 1989), a good start toward ongoing learning throughout life.

Doolittle (1995) summarized recommendations of many researchers in setting out a number of principles for effective implementation of peer learning at any level. Among his principles are the use of whole and authentic activities, the creation of a need for what is to be learned, the choice of tasks that necessitate interaction and negotiation and can only be successfully completed in collaboration with others, monitoring of progress, encouragement of self-explanation and group discussion, and the careful maintenance of a social environment in which students can securely test their thinking. Encouragement of refinement and self-evaluation by groups augments the students' development of responsibility for learning and the tools for successfully assuming that responsibility (Mink, 1992).

A Caution

Implementing an educational change is relatively easy. It engenders enthusiasm, an air of excitement that helps diminish the negative effects of initial obstacles. Maintaining an innovation, changing one's fundamental stance with respect to the process of instruction, is far more difficult (Mason, 1971; Tobias, 1990, 1992a, 1992b). Research has shown a strong persistence of methods and attitudes already familiar and comfortable (Cuban, 1982; Tobias 1990). In many cases, teachers willing to risk working with a new method are the very teachers who are most successful, and are acknowledged as such, in their traditional techniques. Enduring the awkwardness, the new and intensive work patterns, and the sense of shifted control can be especially difficult. If students must learn to tolerate uncertainty, so must instructors. It is tempting, when the implementation becomes difficult or time intensive, or when results are slow in coming, to revert to what is best known or to create a hybrid of traditional and innovative program that may carry the weaknesses of both and the strengths of neither. The instructor who can avoid this temptation may offer students benefits that will last a lifetime.

CHAPTER TEN

The Role of the Teacher in Promoting Cognitive Processing During Collaborative Learning

MICHAEL S. MELOTH
University of Colorado, Boulder

PAUL D. DEERING
University of Hawaii

In this chapter, we describe the nature of productive collaboration and how teachers may contribute to the promotion of effective collaboration by the roles they play. We believe that the quality of students' discussion during group activities is an important and underexamined component of the collaborative learning process. We believe that three aspects of the teacher's role in the classroom can inform our understanding of how peer collaboration contributes to student learning: instruction provided to students prior to group work, the teacher's monitoring practices during group work, and the teacher's beliefs about learning and collaboration.

Subsumed under *peer collaboration* are the various, specific cooperative learning approaches (Johnson & Johnson, 1994; Kagan, 1989; Slavin, 1995), the more loosely defined peer work groups (Graybeal & Stodolsky, 1985; Webb, 1989), and reciprocal teaching (Brown & Palincsar, 1989). We believe that there are general issues regarding how students collaborate and how their teachers structure such collaboration that transcend the boundaries of these various approaches. Thus, we use the term *peer collaboration* or *collaborative learning* to include all of these approaches, and we use *cooperative learning* or *reciprocal teaching* only to refer specifically to approaches identified as such by their proponents. We focus our discussion toward understanding the teacher's role in peer collaboration in natural classroom settings where teachers and students must attend to and deal with a multiplicity of demands.

Collaborative learning has been studied extensively over the past 3 decades. The results of this work show that students generally learn more via collaborative learning approaches than through traditional, teacher-directed instruction (Johnson, Maruyama, Johnson, Nelson, & Skon, 1981; Slavin, 1995). This research base offers a sound rationale for employing some form of collaborative instruction across numerous learning contexts.

Despite these benefits, however, we believe that the teacher's role has been weakly conceptualized and underutilized in the collaborative learning paradigm, particularly within the cooperative learning approaches (Johnson & Johnson, 1994; Kagan, 1989; Slavin, 1995). These approaches often emphasize managerial, organizational, or facilitative roles for teachers in encouraging peer group collaboration. Indeed, there are strong theoretical and intuitive rationales for this view of the teacher. Most cooperative learning programs stem from theories from social and organizational psychology positing that groups function most effectively when they are interdependent, autonomous, and self-directed (Schmuck & Schmuck, 1992). Johnson and Johnson (1992) emphasized the importance of positive interdependence, a condition under which group members recognize that they cannot succeed unless all of their group members are successful. Students, therefore, will strive to help others learn and get good grades. Autonomy and self-direction characterize cooperative learning groups' freedom from direct teacher supervision, and their ability to decide how, and in some cases, what, to study or work on (Cohen, 1994a; Kagan, 1989). Positive interdependence, autonomy, or self-direction are unlikely to be developed if an outside authority exerts too much control over the student groups in a classroom.

Teachers are viewed by cooperative learning theorists (Cohen, 1994a; Johnson & Johnson, 1994; Kagan, 1989), and often view themselves (Prawat, 1992), as wielding a great deal of power and control. As such, it can be difficult for them to delegate responsibility for learning to students and it can be difficult for students to accept it. Therefore, if groups are to learn through peer collaboration, they must view their group as a primary source of information, support, and assistance. The teacher's role, then, is to help ensure that this occurs. Collaborative learning approaches are seen by many teachers and theorists as an appropriate response to the overly directive nature of much classroom instruction. Teachers frequently dominate instructional interactions and limit the kinds of activities that can promote development of complex knowledge and skills (Brophy & Good, 1986; Durkin, 1978–1979; Fisher et al., 1978; Goodlad, 1984; Shuell, 1996). Thus, much of cooperative learning's appeal lies in overcoming the passivity and powerlessness that characterize students in so many classrooms.

Cooperative learning theorists do not call for the outright elimination of teacher-directed instruction, and they do agree that instruction should be provided before students work together and that teachers should monitor groups so that they can accomplish their tasks. Yet, it remains unclear how teachers can best facilitate productive collaborative interactions. In the following sections, we explore the role of teachers in collaborative learning. We begin by describing our view of what productive group interactions entail. We then examine issues of instruction and of peer group interactions. Finally, we take a rather sharp turn to explore teachers' beliefs about the nature and value of collaborative learning and how these beliefs can have subtle, and not so subtle, effects on practice. In these discussions, we examine what research has said over the past 2 decades, including some of our recent studies. In addition, we propose further research that can provide a richer understanding of the teacher's role in collaborative learning and, by extension, a more comprehensive theory of why and how collaboration helps children learn.

PRODUCTIVE COLLABORATIVE INTERACTIONS

The quality of group interactions is a logical starting point for any discussion of the workings of collaborative learning (Cohen, 1994a). Like many others, we believe that these interactions are most beneficial when they are targeted toward the improvement of students' cognitive and metacognitive processes (Brown & Palincsar, 1989; Webb, 1989). These interactions not only make students smarter, they also provide them with evidence of success, all of which can have a positive effect on motivation and self-esteem (Ames, 1981; Johnson, Johnson, & Holubec, 1990; Stipek, 1988).

Like Cohen (1994b), we find that the cooperative learning paradigm has not adequately examined students' verbal discourse in naturalistic classroom settings, particularly when it comes to sharing task-related information in a manner that contributes to learning. This paradigm, as some have noted (Bossert, 1988–1989; Cohen, 1994b), has also not adequately examined the kinds of task-specific talk that may be beneficial to learning. Instead, the paradigm has typically treated students' group interactions as something that will "take care of itself" if the proper structures for accountability, tasks, and group skills training are implemented. When general guidelines for group talk are encouraged (e.g., "Listen to the ideas of others" and "Make sure you ask good questions"; e.g., Johnson & Johnson, 1994; Kagan, 1989; Slavin, 1995), there may be little or no follow-through on implementation. Although Johnson and Johnson (1994) and Kagan (1989) offered guidelines about how to promote desirable social and affective group interactions, neither they nor their colleagues directly addressed cognitive or metacognitive discussion content. In our examination of more than 100 studies of cooperative learning published between 1980 and 1992, fewer than 5% investigated group discussion content.

The few studies that focused on collaborative group communication confirm the importance of discussion. Webb (1989) reviewed 19 studies in Grades 2 through 11 that examined verbal interactions in peer work groups during math and computer instruction. She found strong associations between group interactions and individual student achievement. She found that giving high-level elaborations, or explaining one's thinking about a problem, was strongly associated with higher student achievement. A significant, but weaker positive effect on achievement was found for receiving high-level elaborations, and the effect was significant only if the assistance was conceptually and temporally close to a need of the recipient. Finally, Webb found that a student's encountering difficulty but not receiving any help was strongly associated with lower achievement.

Webb's (1989) research offers crucial insight into the "black box" of students' group interactions. Recipients of help benefit only moderately from it, and only under fairly restrictive conditions (but see Webb & Farivar, chap. 5, this volume). Students learn significantly more in groups if they provide high-level elaborations, but they do so infrequently. Our examination of the studies in Webb's review indicates that 12.3% of all statements (range = 6.2%–19.3%) were high-level elaborations. In our studies of the talk in collaborative group interactions among elementary school students, we found results similar to those of Webb (Deering & Meloth, 1993; Meloth & Deering, 1992, 1994). The cognitive and metacognitive levels and the focus of groups' discussions were positively correlated with student cognitive and metacognitive learning outcomes.

In sum, our work (Deering & Meloth, 1993; Meloth & Barbe, 1992; Meloth & Deering, 1992, 1994) and that of Webb (1989) offer two important insights about small group learning: (a) task-related talk about facts, concepts, strategies, and thinking is very important to students' learning; and (b) high-level talk occurs with low frequency when left to emerge "naturally" or as a by-product of cooperative learning structures. Although somewhat dismaying, these conclusions suggest direct intervention to facilitate quality discussion in student groups, as is addressed in the following section.

Students are not likely to engage in the kinds of task-specific discourse that can lead to learning complex information unless they receive clear and explicit assistance, either in advance of group work or during cooperative discussions (Cohen, 1994b). Additionally, tasks that encourage rich task-specific discourse are usually ill-structured ones, that is, they are open-ended and lend themselves to a variety of different answers or a variety of different paths to a solution. These tasks, although good for cooperative interactions, are not necessarily easy to construct and outcomes from them are not easy to assess. Furthermore, these kinds of tasks may result in nonproductive behavior by participants (see O'Donnell, chap. 7, this volume), and those students who have come to depend on tasks with clear, straightforward solutions actively resist tasks that involve some degree of ambiguity and risk (Marx & Walsh, 1988). Constructing tasks that offer an optimal degree of ambiguity is a delicate balancing act. If tasks are too ambiguous, students spend all of their time simply trying to figure out what the goal may be and little time actually discussing how they might go about accomplishing the task. When tasks are unambiguous, accomplishing the task may require little discussion. Just as important, without careful analysis of ambiguous, ill-structured tasks, it can be difficult to adequately assess students' learning. Teachers must determine whether student learning is best facilitated by having groups generate and discuss a list of potential solutions or by having individual students support his or her own solution path? How much and what kinds of instruction should be given before groups begin? Should students be provided with a list of possible solutions or should they be encouraged to generate their own list? Must these solutions and any supporting arguments be recorded so the teacher, who may be working with other groups, can later evaluate students' learning?

We need to further examine how teachers can more effectively organize, implement, and monitor cooperative discussions that can lead to complex learning in classroom settings. Insight into the kind of verbal discourse that is likely to lead to improved learning can be found in studies, both in naturalistic and laboratory settings, that "script" discussions so that group members focus their attention on specific task content and use specific cognitive and metacognitive strategies during these discussions. The scripts used in reciprocal teaching (Brown & Palincsar, 1989; Palincsar & Herrenkohl, chap. 6, this volume) include assigning roles and requiring specific kinds of verbal discourse. Students are designated either as a group leader or as a member of the group, with leadership changing every few minutes or at the beginning of each day's discussion. It is assumed that leading the discussion requires the use of a variety of different strategies and skills, most of which are associated with listening comprehension, such as analyzing the quality of each group member's contributions and restating information offered by others. Verbal discourse is scripted in two ways. First, a set of robust comprehension strategies (usually, but not limited to, clarification, inference, question generation, and summarization) is identified by the teacher, who then encourages students use these strategies as they read and discuss expository text. Second, students are also required to elaborate, support, justify and explain how they arrived at a particular conclusion or opinion.

Others (Cohen, Lotan, & Leechor, 1989; Ehrlich, 1991; Johnson & Johnson, 1985) structure interactions through combinations of specific roles (e.g., facilitator, recorder, reporter) and written instructions or guidelines. There is some disagreement about whether assigning roles and providing written guidelines enhances productive collaborative discussions. For example, Hertz-Lazarowitz (1989) suggested that doing so reduces the likelihood that students will develop the kinds of autonomous, self-directed learning skills that are essential for successful peer interactions. At the same time, studies have shown that such scripting can be beneficial (see O'Donnell, chap. 7, this volume). Scripting is particularly beneficial when it is conceptually tied to the desired learning outcomes and directly assessed by outcome measures. For example, Johnson and Johnson (1985) encouraged students to use rather elaborate guidelines to focus "constructive controversy" about a sensitive issue. Zack (in Cohen, 1994b) assigned students the role of facilitator to help the focus group discussions, whereas

Ehrlich (1991) asked the group help the group's reporter fill out a special worksheet that the reporter would then prepare for presentation to the whole class. Meloth and Deering (1992, 1994), using a variation of reciprocal teaching, provided the group leader with "think sheets" to use when guiding group discussion. Finally, in studies reported by O'Donnell and Dansereau (1992), dyads are provided highly structured scripts under tightly designed laboratory conditions to guide discussions involving specific thinking strategies. In all of these cases, scripting interactions resulted in positive learning outcomes. The role of the teacher in promoting productive interaction is critical. Two primary ways in which teachers can influence the interaction of group members are in the instruction provided before group interaction and in the monitoring of group interactions.

THE TEACHER'S ROLE IN PROMOTING EFFECTIVE COLLABORATION

Instruction and Collaborative Learning

The collaborative learning paradigm, in particular cooperative learning, has largely overlooked the potential of the familiar tool of direct instruction as a means to enhance the effectiveness of students' group work. Slavin (1995) argued that cooperative activities are intended to replace independent seatwork and therefore should generally be preceded by some form of direct instruction. There are a few collaborative learning approaches that do provide some insight into the ways in which instruction might be used to facilitate productive cooperative interactions. Slavin and his colleagues offered a substantial description of the kinds of direct instruction that can be used to support two cooperative learning approaches: Team Assisted Individualization (TAI) in mathematics (Slavin, Leavey, & Madden, 1984; Slavin, Madden, & Leavey, 1984) and Cooperative Integrated Reading and Composition (CIRC) in literacy (Stevens, Madden, Slavin, & Farnish, 1987). In both, Slavin called for teacher-directed lessons to be conducted with small, similarly-achieving groups of students, to be followed by individual and group practice of the lesson's content and skills in heterogeneous groups, and finally, individual, level-specific tests. The two programs successfully promote student achievement in comparison with traditional methods. Results associated with these programs suggest the potential of carefully focused instruction directed at helping students make the most of their group work. Slavin, however (1989–1990), found that despite his recommendations that detailed instruction be provided prior to peer group interactions, many teachers continue to believe that cooperation is a substitute for instruction, and not that instruction is an important prerequisite for cooperation.

Other approaches to collaborative learning also demonstrate that instruction prior to group discussions is beneficial. For example, in reciprocal teaching (Brown & Palincsar, 1989; Palincsar, 1992), teachers remain with a single student group during its entire discussion, participating as often as needed to ensure that students discuss and use information effectively. It might seem that with the teacher's ongoing, intensive participation in group discussions, the need for prior direct instruction would be reduced or unnecessary. However, Palincsar (1992) concluded that students' learning in reciprocal teaching is enhanced by prior instruction focused on important lesson content. It stands to reason then that if prior instruction is important even when the teacher participates directly in peer group discussions, it ought to be all the more significant when students work together with only minimal teacher intervention, as in cooperative learning.

Our studies reveal that prior direct instruction in collaborative learning contexts can be quite varied and often very brief. In one study, we examined instruction in six elementary classrooms as teachers presented lesson information and monitored collaborative group interactions (Deering & Meloth, 1993; Meloth & Deering, 1990). Overall, the group activities were quite creative and interesting: One fourth-grade class was discussing how to transform Aesop's fables into a puppet show to be given to the school's second-grade classrooms, and a sixth-grade class was discussing how theme, plot, and character contributed to their understanding and enjoyment of *The Outsiders*. In all the classrooms, students worked diligently on their tasks with minimal disruption. However, group discussions included very few statements about what was being learned from the activities, with a preponderance of comments focused on procedures and materials. Two factors stood out to explain this distribution of discussion content. One was that prior direct instruction on what was to be accomplished in these classrooms was very brief, lasting from 1 to 5 minutes, and focused primarily on procedures, such as who handles which materials. Almost completely missing was information about what students were to learn, as well as how the instruction was connected to the group activities. The second factor we noted was that the kinds of tasks assigned for group work were quite consistent with the kinds of discussion elicited: Tasks that were more procedurally complex were associated with a high proportion of procedural discussion, and cognitively rich tasks elicited more academically focused discussions (Deering & Meloth, 1993).

We found similar results in another project (Deering, Meloth, & Sanders, 1994; Sanders & Meloth, 1997), where we spent a full year observing and interviewing six elementary teachers and their students as they used collaborative learning during literacy instruction. Patterns similar to those described previously emerged, with little, if any, direct instruction related to cognitive and metacognitive processes that would help students learn in peer groups. In another study of 12 elementary classrooms using cooperative learning for literacy instruction, all participating teachers had recently completed a course focusing on the approaches of Kagan, Johnson and Johnson, Slavin, Aronson, and Cohen (Meloth & Barbe, 1992). Again, the teachers provided little substantive information about the cognitive goals of their lessons or of the group activities. Additionally, although students worked together actively and nondisruptively, their conversations did not frequently include substantive information about their tasks.

In order to test whether direct instruction on process could influence the quality of students' group discussions, we conducted two quasi-experimental studies of collaborative learning in elementary school classrooms during literacy instruction (Meloth & Deering, 1992, 1994). We hypothesized that instruction prior to group work would affect students' discussions and learning, and further, that instruction focused on key lesson content would prove more efficacious than a rewards-based cooperative learning approach (Slavin, 1995). In both studies, we conducted baseline observations of group work and found similar, low proportions of discussion oriented toward substantive task content across all classrooms. Subsequently, one set of classrooms in each study, the *reward condition,* was provided moderate instructional and curricular support for promoting talk about important task content, plus training in implementing a cooperative learning team reward structure (Slavin, 1995). Much greater instructional and curricular support was provided the second set of classrooms, the *strategy condition,* but no reward structure was used. The intervention-phase results revealed that the proportion of group discussion about important lesson content remained relatively constant in the reward classrooms but increased significantly in the strategy classrooms. Additionally, students' comprehension and metacognition in the strategy classrooms increased significantly over that of the comparison group students. Although the effects of instruction and curriculum cannot be disentangled in these studies, they support the contention that prior instruction on process can influence students' group discussions, and that the two are associated with learning gains. Based on the results from our studies (Meloth & Deering, 1992, 1994) and from others (Rosenshine & Meister, 1994; Rosenshine, Meister, & Chapman, 1996; Pressley, El-Dinary, & Brown, 1992; Shuell, 1996), we suggest that instruction must serve to enhance productive collaborative discourse.

Characteristics of Instruction That Can Promote High-Level Discourse. First, instruction must be a natural precursor to peer group activities, not a stand-alone lesson that has little apparent connection to the information to be used and learned when students work together. Instruction must help students recognize the specific cognitive (and where appropriate, the metacognitive) goals associated with the lesson so that they are aware of them during collaborative discussions. Without such information, students are left to their own interpretations of the goal, interpretations that may not match their teacher's intended goals (Marx & Walsh, 1988). This mismatch can result in inefficient, purposeless discussions or discussions that focus on information that will not help them learn what the teacher intends them to learn.

Second, instruction must focus on the cognitive and metacognitive strategies that students can use in pursuit of learning the lesson's important content. There are two sets of necessary strategies: content and collaborative. Content strategies refer to those that are associated with using and understanding the lesson's content, regardless of whether students will work under individualistic conditions or in collaboration with their peers. Without some information about how to direct and regulate their thinking, it is unlikely that all students will do so with a high degree of frequency or success. Instruction should also inform students about the particular collaborative strategies that can help all group members learn content specific to the lesson. The kinds of strategies to be used, of course, depend on the specific goals or expected learning outcomes of individual lessons. Some lessons may be better learned if students frequently draw and discuss inferences from text, whereas others may involve the use of summaries to help students monitor their progress. If so, students should know this, yet we know from past research that such information is not always communicated to students, regardless of whether they engage in independent seatwork or cooperative activities (Pressley et al., 1992; Roehler & Duffy, 1991).

Third, instruction must provide students with an understanding of the specific means of collaboration that should help all group members improve their understanding. The means of collaboration include the requisite general social skills, such as being a good listener, asking for help when needed, and so on, that are identified in descriptions of collaborative learning programs (Cohen, 1994a; Johnson & Johnson, 1994; Slavin, 1995). In addition, students should be taught about the kinds of discourse that should aid learning, such as how to generate good questions, when to elaborate on one's assertions, and when to explain how one arrived at a particular conclusion or opinion. Studies of peer group discourse have demonstrated quite convincingly that such talk is an essential ingredient for learning (Cazden, 1986; Palincsar & Herrenkohl, chap. 6, this volume), yet like information about strategy use, this information is often infrequent in instruction (Pressley et al., 1992).

In sum, research on the role of direct instruction in collaborative learning contexts is in its infancy, at best. However, there is evidence to suggest that when teachers provide instruction prior to group activities, it is often too brief and vague to have much impact (Deering & Meloth, 1993; Deering et al., 1994; Meloth & Deering, 1990). The studies that have examined the effects of prior direct instruction on productive collaboration are starting to build a case for such instruction to be an important part of the collaborative learning process, one that merits much further investigation (Meloth & Deering, 1992, 1994; Slavin et al., 1984; Stevens et al., 1987; Webb & Farivar, 1994).

Monitoring Group Interaction

Like instructional recommendations found in many collaborative learning programs, recommendations regarding monitoring of cooperative groups tend to focus more on the organization and management of group behaviors and activities and less on how teachers can support the acquisition or use of cognitive and metacognitive processes. A part of most recommendations is that teachers should keep their participation in groups to a minimum on the assumption that doing so will help the group become more interdependent, autonomous, and self-directed (Cohen, 1991). Teachers are encouraged to monitor the group's on-task behavior, intervene to teach collaborative skills, and provide task assistance only where necessary. This view of the teacher is more like a consultant who helps improve effective group functioning than an instructor who contributes information or scaffolds students' learning.

Cohen (1991, 1994a) went a step further in her recommendations for monitoring. Concerned that teachers delegate substantial authority to student groups, she recommended minimizing monitoring statements that prompt task completion and those that teach information students should have known prior to or because of group work. When such statements are provided, Cohen observed a reduction in cooperative behaviors and communication among group members and, therefore, less learning. Thus, she recommended that teachers stimulate students' thinking by providing a group with brief comments and questions and then moving away so that students can continue their discussions. Cohen maintained that this quick-response teacher role communicates to students that they are the ones most responsible for their learning and that they are trusted to conduct their discussions effectively.

The limited monitoring practices recommended by cooperative learning theorists may help students work together with a minimum of disruptions, and this is likely to satisfy many. However, what remains unaddressed is how teachers can recognize when students are communicating information effectively. To do so, teachers need to be aware of the connection among the lesson's cognitive goals; the activities they have designed to meet these goals; and the kinds of content knowledge, metacognitive strategies, and verbal interactions they anticipate will help students learn from the task. They must keep all this in mind as they observe, interpret, and possibly intervene in group interactions. This is a very complex task. Unfortunately, we find little specific discussion of the complexities of monitoring, particularly as related to students' cognitive and metacognitive processes.

Standing in stark contrast with the strategies recommended by Cohen (1994a) and others is reciprocal teaching (Brown & Palincsar, 1989; Palincsar & Brown, 1984). One of the key components of this approach is its prolonged and strategic teacher monitoring of group interaction. Rather than abdicating most monitoring to the student groups as in cooperative learning, reciprocal teaching calls for the teacher to scaffold group interactions, such that a delicate balance is maintained between students' emerging competence (i.e., knowledge of task content) and task complexity. The teacher must help the group through modeling comprehension strategies, steering the discussion, and providing other interjections so that all members will succeed at constructing meaning from text, and internalizing literacy strategies. The teacher may gradually decrease her or his level of participation as students become competent at initiating and sustaining discussions, or may choose to select tasks that are increasingly complex. Such strategic monitoring ensures that students are constantly challenged and provides the opportunity for teachers to capitalize on unanticipated ideas or difficulties that arise. The consistent gains in cognitive and metacognitive outcomes found in studies of reciprocal teaching (Brown & Palincsar, 1989; Palincsar & Brown, 1984) suggest that its high-profile approach to monitoring bears further investigation across the collaborative learning spectrum.

Meloth (1991) compared reciprocal teaching and cooperative learning in literacy instruction over a 16-week period. Two sixth-grade teachers, one regular education and one special education, jointly provided instruction in reciprocal teaching to one classroom and instruction in cooperative learning to another. Both classes were provided the same pre-group-work instruction, focusing on the knowledge and skills they would be learning or refining during collaboration. Students in the reciprocal teaching classroom were placed into four heterogeneous groups. While teachers worked with one set of groups, the remaining two completed assignments collaboratively or read silently. In the cooperative learning classroom, students worked in six heterogeneous groups, with brief teacher monitoring practices similar to those recommended by the cooperative learning paradigm (Cohen, 1994a; Johnson & Johnson, 1994), plus group rewards for achievement and project completion (Slavin, 1995). Greater achievement, metacognitive skills, and motivation were found for the reciprocal teaching students. In addition, when they engaged in group discussions without the teacher, these contained more detail regarding task content than those in the cooperative condition. These findings suggest that the prolonged, strategic teacher monitoring of groups in reciprocal teaching can have substantial impact on student learning and discussion content, and that the latter effect is durable. These issues bear much further investigation.

A middle ground between reciprocal teaching's prolonged monitoring of groups and the more indirect monitoring approach of cooperative learning is suggested by another of our studies (Meloth & Barbe, 1992). In this study, a total of 180 peer group discussions across 15 elementary classrooms were examined for teacher monitoring statements and ways in which students changed their discussions in response to these statements. In our original analysis, monitoring statements were frequently nonspecific and concerned mostly with task progress, for example, "You guys are doing OK?" or "How's this group doing?" Just 20% of all specific monitoring statements were oriented toward important task content. This finding could be interpreted in two ways: It might indicate that groups were functioning smoothly and there was little need for teachers to provide them with very much cognitively oriented information, or it might indicate that students needed such assistance but teachers did not provide it. From our examination of the data, both conditions occurred, although the latter was far more common. For example, teachers often moved quickly from group to group, completing the interaction in 5 seconds, a span of time that does not seem sufficient to accurately assess, much less respond to, a group's need for scaffolding of complex literacy knowledge. Additionally, when teachers asked questions about students' thinking, such as, "What kinds of ideas were raised in this group?" they frequently accepted irrelevant responses. At other times, teachers made statements such as "Bring up some of the implications of the discovery of crude oil," and then moved to another group before determining if the present one could respond to the directive. Many could not, and as a result, ended up talking about literal, surface-level content or engaging in off-task discussions until the teacher returned, a time span that could exceed 10 minutes.

To shed further light on the issue of monitoring, we reanalyzed data from the Meloth and Barbe (1992) study to focus on instructional exchanges between teacher and students. These were defined as interactions where teachers provided a group with five or more statements about understanding task content, using communicating effectively, or both. Instructional exchanges occurred more frequently in four of the classrooms, yet groups within them did not evidence any more dependence on the teacher. For example, they were no more likely to turn immediately to the teacher when they encountered difficulty. Instead, the student groups actively attempted to make sense out of their task and often succeeded. When they did not, they sought teacher help. As an example, the following exchange occurred in one third-grade classroom discussing their observations of the weather. Students had kept independent records of weather patterns for nearly 3 months and were currently engaged in summarizing their observations for a group report. To help them, the teacher provided some guide sheets to focus their discussions:

JUAN: What can we do to, um summarize, ah, this, these different observations? We can start with . . .

DARCY: There's just too much, three months of stuff, it's impossible to do it.

KEVIN: No it's not, we just have to figure out a way to do it. We have a week.

JUAN: But where can we start? The (guide sheet) says to list three or four ways to summarize our observations. What's one way?

BRIAN: Hey, hey, I got it, how about, ah, no, that wouldn't work.

JUAN: What? What wouldn't work? We got to . . . Tell us.

DARCY: Here's a way. Why don't we each redo our graphs to make them more alike and then . . .

KEVIN: We can compare them and then . . .

The teacher then appears at the group's table and poses a question without apparently having heard students' discussion. She also interrupts a student's explanation of their discussion:

TEACHER: Looking at your weather charts, do you see any kind of a pattern from last week?

DARCY: No, all are charts are kinda different but were thinking . . .

TEACHER: Do you know what the first category is for, the one titled "Percent of Clouds"?

DARCY: Yeah.

TEACHER: Why don't you begin by focusing on that.

The teacher then leaves the group. Despite her suggestion and her failure to listen Darcy's explanation, the group returned to its conversation:

BRIAN: Do you think we should talk about that category or what (Kevin) said?

JUAN: Let's try Kevin's idea and if that doesn't work, we'll do the category.

As this example indicates, students were beginning to agree about a starting point and continued with the idea of how to more easily compare each student's data before deciding on what to put in their report. Although the teacher did not ask students to explain what they were considering, students appeared to have a enough confidence in their approach that they were undeterred by the teacher suggestion

These transcripts also revealed that teacher participation in a group does not seem to reduce productive discussion by the students, even when the teachers provided specific instruction when they sensed that the group needed information or guidance. For example, one fourth-grade teacher approached a group, listened for about 15 seconds, and determined that the group was focusing on irrelevant information. The following exchange occurred:

TEACHER: Ok, here's what I really want you to think about. What do you think are the big differences between wolves, coyotes, and dogs? I know that wolves and coyotes have very strong relationships with others in their packs, but I wonder if dogs are the same way or if, because we domesticated them, they are more different than similar to coyotes and wolves. What do you think, Brenda, you have two dogs at home, don't you?

BRENDA: Yeah, my dog follows us around and barks when someone comes to the door so . . .

TEACHER: So do you think this is what wolves and coyotes do? Bark when a stranger comes near their territory?

BRENDA: Yeah.

TEACHER: (speaking to the group) So, what do you think my next question to you will be?

TODD: Does this mean dogs might be more like wolves?

TEACHER: Excellent. Why do you think that is a logical question?

The teacher engages in a few similar exchanges and then leaves the group. The very next student exchange is the following:

DIANE: We need to talk about how dogs are different, more than that they come in more different sizes.

BRENDA: But sizes count because they indicate people bred them to be different.

CARL: My dog retrieves ducks if my father shoots 'em. Let's see a wolf do that!

In this example, the teacher took the opportunity to provide a brief minilesson by posing a question and modeling her thinking when answering it. She then immediately turns the responsibility for thinking over to students, who return to their conversation by examining the relevance of different kinds of dogs as well as a rational for why different characteristics distinguish them from wolves and coyotes. Although Carl's comments draw a brief laugh from his group mates, his point is well taken, retrievers' characteristics separate them from wolves. Other observed contributions from teachers that appeared to help conversations included stopping by a group, giving a brief, direct explanation of a key concept, and then moving on to another group. Other times, teachers would listen for a few moments, determine what problem students' were experiencing, spend a minute or two explaining what they were to learn, and provide a few examples of how the group could locate or apply the information. At no time did these exchanges seem to reduce the quality of conversations and in many cases enhanced the ideas shared among group members.

Not all of the instructional exchanges in the four classrooms were effective, and the exchanges in the remaining classrooms were not always ineffective. However, effective exchanges had three elements in common, all of which encouraged students to communicate their ideas and to support these ideas with explanations and elaborations. First, teachers provided information, often by modeling their own thinking that they believed would help students focus or refocus on important lesson goals. Second, teachers used information from the activity to contextualize the how and why of effective communication, model the process with a student, or provide explanations. Such minilessons appeared to help students make the connection between the process (communication) and product (what was to be learned). Third, teachers asked few questions during these exchanges and instead got to the point quickly and efficiently. Importantly, rather than reducing interdependent, autonomous, self-directed learning, these instructional exchanges had a powerful, facilitative impact on many group discussions: Cooperative behaviors increased and students shared more task-related information than they had prior to such exchanges. These findings would appear to contradict Cohen's (1991, 1994a) concern that teacher participation in group discussions may reduce group autonomy and self-directed learning. It should be recognized, however, that our observations occurred over brief periods of times (3–5 weeks), a period of time that may be too brief to reveal whether such monitoring practices encourage students to become overly reliant on teacher assistance during peer group discussions.

In sum, monitoring of groups appears to be a very important and complex component of collaborative learning. It seems that the quality of instructional exchanges, not the existence or length of the exchanges per se, is what make them effective. Thus, cooperative learning proponents' recommendation that monitoring be as brief as possible may be missing the point. Rather, monitoring should be as long as necessary so that students are provided with information that will help them engage in productive and informative discussions. Additionally, teachers must know when to step in and when to leave a group alone. They must also know whether a few simple comments or statements of encouragement are needed, or if more detailed instruction is required. Further, it appears that teachers should provide questions and comments in reference to the problems that students are currently experiencing.

Teacher Beliefs

We turn now to a quite different issue that can have a strong impact on productive collaborative interactions—teachers' beliefs about their role as teachers and the role that cooperation should play in learning. These beliefs drive whether teachers attempt to utilize peer collaboration and how they use it to foster learning. There are a variety of terms related to teacher beliefs (Clark & Peterson, 1986) that all refer in one way or another to teachers' knowledge about the purpose of schooling, appropriate roles for themselves and students, and the nature of knowledge acquisition. For this chapter, the distinctions among the terms are unimportant, so the terms *beliefs* and *belief systems* are used interchangeably.

The issue of teacher beliefs is quite a departure from the earlier discussions of productive interactions, instruction, and monitoring. We include it, however, because of the growing evidence that despite the growing use of collaborative learning in U.S. classrooms, many teachers seem to hold beliefs that are incompatible with or contrary to current understanding of effective peer group interactions. Our concern can be encapsulated as the following: It is not enough to know how to implement collaborative learning tasks, teachers must also have a conceptual grasp of the theory or theories that underlie collaboration so that they can use the method thoughtfully and effectively. The ability to use collaborative learning without a sufficient grasp of how it works is analogous to the long-standing concern in education about students who can perform a task without really understanding it.

Woolfolk Hoy and Tschannen-Moran (chap. 11, this volume) provide a very insightful discussion of teacher beliefs and much of their discussion will not be repeated in this chapter. It is important to recognize, however, that many teachers appear to hold beliefs reflecting a transmission view of teaching and an absorptionist view of learning (Palincsar, Stevens, & Gavelek, 1989; Prawat, 1992; Rich, 1990). It was this belief system that Goodlad (1984) so consistently observed with teachers lecturing (transmitting) and students enduring (ostensibly absorbing). Transmissionist beliefs are instilled in future teachers during their years of experience as passive students, are strongly supported by the broader culture (Buchmann, 1989; Flory, 1991), and are quite resistant to change (Buchmann, 1989).

Despite its prevalence, however, transmissionism conflicts with the learning perspectives of the majority of the proponents of collaborative learning, which is itself a highly popular educational approach and even a belief system (Bossert, 1988–1989). None of the collaborative learning theorists espouse the passivity inherent in transmissionism, and more importantly, most conceive of learning as a dynamic, social, and inexact process. For example, Johnson and Johnson (1985) found that student learning is enhanced through academic controversy, in which "facts" are open to dispute, and are not simply commodities to be absorbed. Bayer (1990) and other collaborative learning proponents (e.g., Brown & Palincsar, 1989; Palincsar et al., 1989) endorsed a constructivist perspective, maintaining that peer collaboration

> promotes cognitive development and the use of critical thinking strategies. Individual group members faced with conflicting viewpoints attempt to clarify, analyze, synthesize, speculate, and evaluate the conflicting points of view as they work their way toward resolution. . . . Cognitive development occurs, then, through incorporation of others' viewpoints into our own thought processes. (p. 12)

Clearly, this conception of learning as an unpredictable grappling with ideas is a far cry from a view of knowledge as fixed, bound, and transmittable.

The conflict between the common transmission perspective and the uncertainties of collaborative learning leaves many teachers with a dilemma in reconciling the two. How can one cover or transmit essential content while still using one of the highly popular collaborative learning approaches? Linda Anderson's (1989) work suggests that the resolution of such dilemmas is important, noting that unless teachers at least understand, if not agree with, the theory underlying an instructional method, they are unlikely to engage in the subtle actions that can make it successful. Additionally, teachers must believe that the method will help them meet their responsibilities or they are unlikely to continue to use the method over time. Unfortunately, there is considerable evidence that teachers often do not sustain even moderate changes in instruction once they complete staff development courses, much less the major changes involved in collaborative learning (Feiman-Nemser, 1990; Richardson, 1994; Sparks & Loucks-Horsley, 1990).

Rich's (1990) work affirms that teacher beliefs are an important and challenging area for collaborative learning. He found that many teachers entered his cooperative learning staff development workshops with little confidence that the approach could improve students' academic knowledge and skills. Even after intensive efforts aimed at demonstrating that cooperative learning can enhance achievement, many of the teachers left unconvinced and, consequently, failed to implement it. Rich attributed this to a lack of congruence between teachers' beliefs about schooling and their entering perceptions of cooperative learning. Most appeared to believe that acquisition of academic skills best occurs through more direct forms of instruction and independent practice. Cooperative learning was viewed as a means to improve social skills and self-esteem, a goal of far less importance to them. Rich also suggests that the perceived incompatibility between teachers' beliefs and cooperative learning sometimes results in passive (and not so passive) acts that sabotage its implementation. Doing so, of course, provides teachers with even more evidence that cooperation cannot meet their academic goals and therefore reinforces their use of other instructional methods, such as direct instruction.

Palincsar et al. (1989) also investigated the link between teachers' beliefs and their approaches to collaborative learning, with similar findings. They interviewed 25 teachers not trained in any formal collaborative methods regarding their beliefs about the nature and value of collaborative learning. Virtually all mentioned that they used collaboration because it helped students become more actively involved in learning and provided opportunities to build confidence, obtain peer approval, and improve social skills. The teachers rarely mentioned the cognitive benefits of collaboration. When probed, they reported that collaborative groups were most useful for drill and practice, but not for the development of new knowledge or in-depth exploration of ideas. Some, mostly first-grade teachers, also expressed doubts that students possessed knowledge and skills that could be productively shared with peers.

Our findings in studies throughout this decade were similar to those of Rich (1990) and Palincsar et al. (1989), with teachers' beliefs regarding the cognitive benefits of collaborative learning approaches to be relatively inchoate (Deering et al., 1994; Meloth & Sanders, 1991). Like our colleagues, we also found teachers to universally extol the social and affective benefits of collaborative learning.

In one study, Meloth and Sanders (1991) interviewed 40 in-service and 20 preservice teachers regarding their beliefs about cooperative learning. Half of the in-service teachers had received training in cooperative methods, whereas the other half used such approaches but had received no formal training, and the preservice teachers had studied cooperative approaches in their teacher education program. Despite the teachers' differences, the findings were remarkably consistent across the three groups. All mentioned that cooperative learning was an effective means to improve social skills and achievement in general. However, fewer than half in each group mentioned that cooperative learning could enhance complex knowledge and skills, and only three from the entire group mentioned that it might improve thought processes or recognition of multiple points of view. Only 10 teachers, all from the trained in-service group, believed that cooperative learning could be used to introduce complex content. In fact, half of the teachers noted that they would be uncomfortable entrusting essential content primarily to cooperative approaches. Interestingly, whereas all the teachers spoke of the social benefits of cooperative learning, only three mentioned that it would help more competent students recognize and appreciate the contributions of low-achieving students. All mentioned the importance of social skills training and grouping strategies, although there was little interest in reward structures. What was clearly missing from their endorsement of collaboration was any commentary on how students might enhance the cognitive quality of their discussions, and how teachers might monitor and intervene as needed.

We found quite interesting results regarding the changing of teacher beliefs in the study cited earlier where we observed the six elementary classrooms during a year of collaborative learning literacy instruction (Deering et al., 1994). The first semester of the project was an inquiry into the teachers' beliefs and the relation of those beliefs to their instruction and students' verbal reports of learning. After 1 semester, we shared tentative findings with the teachers and introduced concepts from social constructivist learning theory and instructional research (Brown & Palincsar, 1989). We then collaborated with the teachers to develop agendas for instructional refinement. During the second semester, we found the teachers to more explicitly address cognitive and metacognitive content in their lessons and to express greater interest in such content in interviews. Interestingly, students' liking for their collaborative lessons increased, although there were no other discernible changes in the teachers' instruction. As one teacher expressed, the project helped her to see collaborative learning's potential benefits and her and the students' roles within it in a whole new light: "You know, I'm really starting to pay attention to what the kids do when they work together! They really *teach* each other! I never noticed how much they do that before!" (Deering et al., 1994, p. 12).

Further illumination on how teacher beliefs can shape what is constructed as cooperative learning was offered by a 2-year ethnographic study conducted by Deering (1992). The focal teacher in the study was a middle-aged male, new to teaching after a successful career as a business entrepreneur. He held beliefs about learning that were classically transmissionist, extolling the importance of memorization and repetition in eighth-grade mathematics. In addition, his views on cooperation were quite reflective of his business background:

> In the real world most of the time you don't sit in isolation in your job. And if you are presented with, you know, R and D work or whatever . . . you usually have a group or a team that will help solve that problem. . . . So, that's where I see it is going to be a real big benefit . . . because they learn to work together. . . . [I use group competition] because it's part of our society. It gets them really excited and I don't think it hurts them a bit. (p. 241)

Students in this class were required to compute group members' quiz and test averages in order to determine which teams qualified for rewards, similar to Slavin's (1995) Student Teams Achievement Divisions (STAD) approach. Unfortunately, the business-like team record sheets were so complex that students had little success deciphering them. Consequently, the incentive system that leveled the playing field between high- and low-achieving students held little meaning for the students. On hearing of the term competition, they competed within their teams to control the worksheets and other academic materials, processes that disadvantaged the low-achieving students. Peer collaboration was actually a rarity in this classroom. Thus, the teacher's beliefs, and also his relative inexperience, interacted with students' predisposition toward individualistic competition, to produce a version of interactions that facilitated little cooperation and limited learning opportunities.

Work by Stodolsky (1984; Graybeal & Stodolsky, 1985) and Ross and Raphael (1990) further demonstrated that there can be great variation in what is constructed as *collaborative learning* or *cooperative learning* across different contexts. It stands to reason that much of this variation may be related to individual teachers' beliefs, as found by Deering (1992) and as suggested by a large body of general research on teacher beliefs (L. Anderson, 1989; Clark & Peterson, 1986). This alone suggests that much greater attention should be paid to teachers' beliefs regarding collaborative learning. Still more support for the importance of research into teacher beliefs can be gathered from the studies that found teachers overlook or downplay the potential cognitive benefits of collaborative learning (Meloth & Sanders, 1991; Palincsar et al., 1989; Rich, 1990).

The research reviewed here suggests that researchers and teachers have completely different approaches in mind when they speak of *cooperative* or *collaborative learning:* Researchers envision processes to facilitate students' cognition and metacognition; teachers tend to think of means to enhance social and affective development, or even business competitiveness. Without arguing about whose vision is the "right" one, it seems essential to bring teachers' beliefs to the foreground in our research into the workings of collaborative learning.

CONCLUSION

We proposed that student cognition has, in general, received too little attention from the collaborative learning paradigm, and particularly from cooperative learning theorists. Further, we suggested that three areas that can influence student cognition have received similarly cursory attention: the role of direct instruction in preparing for discussion, teacher monitoring of groups, and teacher beliefs about collaborative learning. Examining the relations among these issues can offer insight into how the paradigm came to be where it is, as well as where it might go next.

Cohen (1991) referred to collaborative learning as *complex instruction,* a term that seems particularly apt in reference to the research reviewed here. For teachers, collaborative learning, particularly cooperative learning, can present a myriad of paradoxes. Teachers have been called on to stop dominating the classroom via transmission instruction and to turn over a great deal of control to students working in cooperative groups. However, they have been offered only minimal guidance as to what their new role ought to be, other than teachers or monitors of social skills, selectors of activities, and perhaps organizers of cooperative task or reward structures. In addition, the paradigm has generally offered only global insights into student learning, mostly as comparisons on achievement tests with the transmission approach. Little attention has been paid to the quality of students' cognitive and metacognitive processes, nor to how group interactions are associated with them. Lacking this, there has been little attention to how direct instruction and teacher monitoring of group processes might facilitate productive, cognitively rich group discussions. In sum, the paradigm has called for a teacher-as-manager who must attend to social and motivational issues but not much to the traditional cognitive or academic realm.

It is not surprising that teachers often believe that collaborative learning's chief benefits are social and affective. It is further unsurprising that many teachers apparently give up on such approaches, because they have been offered so little guidance on how to scaffold effective group work through the familiar tools of direct instruction and monitoring of students. Fortunately, each of these areas has begun to receive attention by researchers.

It is clear that beliefs can have a tremendous impact on whether, for how long, and especially, in what manner, teachers employ collaborative learning approaches. Fortunately, there is evidence that teachers can develop richer belief systems that include cognition as an important aspect of collaborative learning. This appears to be especially true regarding staff developmental approaches that model collaboration rather than transmission (Deering et al., 1994; Good et al., 1991; Richardson, 1990; Sanders & Meloth, 1997). Much further research is needed to explore the links between teacher beliefs and their approaches to collaborative learning, and ways their thinking about collaborative learning might be further enriched.

There is substantial empirical support for the commonsense notion that students' group discussions have great impact on their learning, with cognitive discussion content being associated with greater cognitive and metacognitive gains (Meloth & Deering, 1992, 1994; Webb, 1989). Furthermore, there is ample evidence to suggest that cognitively oriented discussion does not often emerge naturally in collaborative groups or as a result of social or motivational structures (Deering & Meloth, 1993; Meloth & Barbe, 1992; Meloth & Deering, 1992, 1994; Webb, 1989). Fortunately, there is also evidence that teachers can have impact on the quality of students' group discussions. Two means by which they have been able to do so are prior direct instruction (Meloth & Deering, 1992, 1994; Palincsar & Brown, 1984; Slavin, Leavey, et al., 1984; Slavin, Madden, et al., 1984; Stevens et al., 1987; Webb & Farivar, 1994) and careful monitoring of student group work (Brown & Palincsar, 1989; Meloth & Barbe, 1992; Palincsar & Brown, 1984).

It is clear that research into the teacher's role in facilitating cognitive and metacognitive gains through collaborative learning is in its infancy, or perhaps childhood. Much further research is needed into each of the areas reviewed. We need to know more about the kinds of group discussions that are most facilitative of cognitive and metacognitive gains. We need to know much more about how direct instruction, monitoring of groups, and perhaps other instructional components can contribute to high-quality group discussions. These areas all call for a much richer, more developed, and more complex way of thinking about the teacher's role in collaborative learning contexts. Teachers can change their thinking about collaborative learning, and now collaborative learning researchers must change their thinking as well, to include more attention to student cognition and the teacher's role in its facilitation. Teacher preparation programs must provide better training for preservice teachers in using peer learning effectively. (Woolfolk Hoy & Tschannen-Morgan, chap. 11, this volume). In-service professional development must also address the effective use of groups, perhaps emulating the model of professional development described by Almog & Lazarowitz, chap. 12, this volume).

CHAPTER ELEVEN

Implications of Cognitive Approaches to Peer Learning for Teacher Education

ANITA WOOLFOLK HOY
MEGAN TSCHANNEN-MORAN
The Ohio State University

Our goal in this chapter is to examine how teacher education can prepare beginning teachers so that they develop expertise in cooperative methods, particularly cognitive approaches to peer learning, as they gain experience in teaching. Today, at least one course in most teacher education programs advocates peer learning. Yet, these increasingly popular approaches are very complex and challenging to apply effectively, especially for prospective and novice teachers. We explore the current state of teaching and learning to teach, asking what prospective teachers should learn and how they should learn it, by focusing on four topics. In section one, we consider the role that peer learning might play in schooling and teaching in the future. Next, we develop a framework that could guide teachers' application of peer learning approaches. In the third section, we examine how prospective teachers might learn to use this framework and what gets in the way of such learning. Finally, the last section of the chapter explores the larger issue of professional development in the complex environment of teaching.

VIEWS OF SCHOOLING, TEACHING, AND TEACHER EDUCATION

Kenneth Howey (1996) recently surveyed the reforms and restructuring efforts in K–12 schooling to analyze the views of teaching, learning, and learning to teach assumed in those efforts. See the Appendix for a full listing of the commonalties he identified across these reforms. Prominent in Howey's conclusions is the notion that reformed schools in the future will depend on learning communities or cohorts remaining together across multiple years. Cooperative learning structures will be central features of classrooms, learners will be interdependent, and group accountability and collaboration will characterize learning. Teachers will be expected to collaborate with parents, administrators, and each other. Cooperative learning structures and approaches are seen as valuable; interdependence, reciprocal learning, and learning communities are mentioned often as desirable features of teaching and learning (see also Almog & Hertz-Lazarowitz, chap. 12, this volume).

Standards for teacher licensure and certification reflect the ideals captured in the previously mentioned reform agendas. Most current standards, such as those of the National Association of State Directors of Teacher Education and Certification, and the National Council for Accreditation in Teacher Education, include expectations that new teachers will know how to use different teaching methods to develop critical thinking and problem solving and that cooperative learning will be an important strategy in the teacher's repertoire.

The goal of many educational reforms and standards today is "teaching for understanding." What does this vision of teaching require? Teacher education curriculum specialists suggest that new teachers be prepared to use cooperative learning to teach for understanding. School reformers, licensing organizations, and teacher education curriculum specialists agree that understanding is the goal of K–12 teaching and that collaborative–cooperative learning is an important avenue to reach this goal. Thus, the ability to incorporate collaboration and cooperative learning into teaching is seen as an important outcome of teacher preparation.

USING PEER LEARNING: A PROBLEM-SOLVING MODEL

Many teachers using cooperative learning techniques, not just beginning teachers, are doing so without an adequate conceptual framework to guide them through the complex array of decisions necessary to take advantage of peer learning. Teachers often understand cooperative learning as a method or set of procedures but do not have a clear sense that different activities fit different goals and are likely to encourage different learning outcomes. They lack the tools to assess the capabilities and challenges of their students and identify appropriate strategies to match their learning goals with the unique characteristics of a given group. Once a group learning process is underway, teachers often are ill-equipped to understand the underlying causes of the difficulties that arise and do not have an arsenal of remedies to address particular problems, based on their underlying causes. Finally, teachers are not taught mechanisms for post-instruction evaluation, to assess new information gained about the group, what progress was made, and what new goals are now feasible. Teacher educators themselves also may lack a conceptual framework and thus are unable to communicate it to preservice teachers.

In order to organize the considerations involved in planning, implementing, and assessing peer learning, we propose a five-part framework: group characteristics, goals, getting there, guiding the process, and gazing backwards–glimpsing ahead (see Table 11.1). The overarching purpose of the framework is to help teachers design peer learning situations in which the quality of communication and interaction supports learning (Cohen, 1994b; King, chap. 4, this volume; Meloth & Deering, chap. 10, this volume, Palincsar & Herrenkohl, chap. 6, this volume; Ross & Raphael, 1990; Webb & Farivar, chap. 5, this volume). Whereas there is a certain sequence to these five elements, they should not be seen as steps to be followed in order but rather as processes that may be revisited as needed.

Group Characteristics

The maturity of the group as a group—how well members know each other, their comfort with one another, and their ability to work constructively together —affects the goals that the group can attain and the activities they can accomplish to reach those goals. In addition, the maturity and developmental level of individuals within the group, and the assets and liabilities each student brings to the group process, affect both goals and processes.

In planning for a peer learning experience, a teacher needs to consider the developmental issues and needs typical of children at the age being taught. For example, children in fifth grade may be receptive to new intellectual challenges, whereas by seventh grade, social and emotional concerns may dominate and need to be addressed before energy and attention can be devoted to cognitive challenges. Beyond what is typical, however, teachers must be aware of the developmental level of their particular group of children. This may be an unusual group of ninth graders who are comfortable with themselves and with each other, who are motivated and ready to be challenged intellectually. Or it may be a group with particularly high levels of interpersonal tension, difficulties in communication, and other factors that make cooperation difficult.

If social skills are lacking, then direct teaching of those skills may be required. Skills such as encouraging, asking for and giving help, or monitoring voice level may be improved with instruction (Webb & Farivar, chap. 5, this volume; Swing & Peterson, 1982) but may take extensive teaching and modeling over a period of time. More sophisticated communication skills (e.g., checking for understanding, checking for agreement) can be added as more basic skills are mastered (Webb & Farivar, 1994). Teachers need to have a sense of the continuum of social and cognitive skills for students at their grade level, how to diag-

TABLE 11.1
A Problem-Solving Model for Peer Learning

Stages	Principles and Considerations
Group characteristics	What is the cognitive development of the group, the span of achievement levels in the group, and the group's readiness for new challenges?
	Is the social and emotional maturity of the group adequate for the kinds of activities planned?
	If skills, classroom norms, or attitudes are lacking, then steps need to be taken to address the deficits, either through direct instruction or activities that will encourage development.
Goals and tasks	Teachers need to have a basic continuum of social skills and affective processes that are age appropriate for the students in the class.
	Teachers need to have a continuum of cognitive development in mind for individuals and the group as a whole.
	The teacher needs to be able to mesh these two developmental processes so that they build on one another.
	Teachers must have an awareness of the purposes for various peer learning strategies and the potential problems in each.
Getting there	In assigning students to groups, teachers must be sensitive to issues of status, achievement level, gender, race, ethnicity, and special needs and yet be aware that assigning group members by "category" may encourage the students to continue to think of one another as members of a category rather than as individuals.
	If the task is collaborative seatwork or a routine task, then constraining the dialogue through narrow roles may be productive. If the task is ill-structured and more cognitive in nature then a more open exchange and elaborated discussion will be more productive (Cohen, 1994a, 1994b).
	If the learning goals include complex, higher order thinking, and the group tasks are ill-structured, strategies that encourage questioning, explanation, challenge, elaboration, exchange, and critical thinking may be valuable.
	In making decisions about incentive structures, teachers need to be aware of the potential for unanticipated consequences such as goal displacement (focusing on rewards rather than learning) or negative impact on the motivation of some students. In many cases, it is helpful to structure in individual accountability as well as group assessment.
Guiding the process	As group activities begin, teachers can revisit the decisions made during planning to make adjustments if necessary and gather information for reflection and future planning.
	Teachers must be willing to adapt their role according to the needs of the situation and the group.
	Teachers must have a sense of what is a productive level of conflict and when an intervention is necessary to get the process back on track.
	Teachers should be aware of typical problems in peer learning and intervention strategies to address those problems.

Continued

TABLE 11.1 *(Continued)*

Stages	Principles and Considerations
Gazing backwards and glimpsing ahead	Teachers need a conceptual framework, a way of thinking about what happened, to assess what new information was gained during the process.
	Teachers need to understand that peer learning strategies can inhibit rather than enhance learning and need to be prepared to deal with these potentially dysfunctional aspects.
	The problem-solving model is circular. The evaluation of one peer learning activity begins the process of setting goals and planning for the next.

nose where a particular group of students falls on that continuum, and what are reasonable next steps or goals. In addition, classroom norms of cooperation need to be established (Webb & Palincsar, 1996).

Teachers must also be aware of the intellectual capabilities of the students in a group. In planning for peer learning, a teacher should be aware of whether there is a wide or narrow span of achievement levels in the group—this may affect the assignment of students to groups. Is the task likely to be relatively easy or more difficult for the students? A teacher whose goal is to concentrate on developing group process may choose a task that is relatively easy for the students, whereas a teacher who has mature, well-functioning groups may choose a more cognitively challenging task. Special challenges such as the inclusion of children with special needs and those with specific learning disabilities, or students with behavior difficulties or language difficulties add to the complexity of understanding the needs of a particular group of children. Principles and considerations related to group characteristics are presented in Table 11.1.

Goals and Tasks

Not all peer learning techniques are designed for the same purposes. Teachers who are not clear about their own goals and who are unaware of the specific purposes of different peer learning techniques may be perplexed when one approach seems to work whereas another fails, and they have no clear way of sorting out the causes for the success or failure.

Strategies for peer learning can serve two general purposes: affective or cognitive development. In the affective realm, for example, cooperative learning techniques may be used to foster the social cohesion of the group, promote social skills and teamwork, ease tensions, and teach tolerance of people from different backgrounds or with different abilities (Slavin, 1995). Cooperative learning techniques also may be used to enhance motivation, encourage an individual or group to put forth greater effort, and persist in the face of setbacks or difficulties (Kagan, 1994; Slavin, 1995). Cognitive approaches, on the other hand, are designed to provide opportunities for review or practice of skills, to exchange questions and explanations in order to enhance learning of cognitive objectives, or to enhance the quality of students' thinking and problem solving about a particular subject (O'Donnell & O'Kelly, 1994). Although cognitive and affective goals are distinct, they are to some extent interdependent. It may be that certain affective issues need to be addressed before cognitive objectives can be effectively pursued (Miller & Harrington, 1993). Principles and considerations related to goal setting are presented in Table 11.1.

Getting There

Once teachers know something about the characteristics of a group of students and have set some realistic and achievable goals, they must structure a process for achieving those goals. Many interrelated and complex decisions are required including designing the groups' tasks; selecting learning strategies or structures; and determining the size of the groups, how students will be assigned to groups, what instructions and resources will be provided, as well as what kinds of rewards or incentives will be offered, if any, and how student progress will be assessed. Problem solving around each of these issues involves balancing a great many contingencies and conditions.

Deciding which peer learning strategy to employ is by no means a simple undertaking. Which technique will be most productive depends on the nature of the task and the goal the teacher hopes to achieve (Good & Brophy, 1994). Tasks for cooperative groups may be more or less structured. Highly structured tasks include work that has right answers—drill and practice, applying routines or procedures, answering questions from readings, computational or algorithmic mathematics, and so on. Ill-structured tasks have multiple answers and unclear procedures, requiring problem finding and higher order thinking. Ill-structured, complex tasks are more likely to be true group tasks; that is, they are likely to require the resources (knowledge, skills, problem-solving strategies, creativity) of the whole group to accomplish, whereas highly structured tasks often can be accomplished just as effectively by individuals. These distinctions are important because ill-structured, complex, true group tasks appear to require more and higher quality interactions than routine tasks, if learning and problem solving are to occur (Cohen, 1994a; Cohen & Arechevala-Vargas, 1987).

Highly Structured Review and Skill-Building Tasks. A relatively structured task such as reviewing previously learned material for an exam might be well served by a structured technique such as STAD (Student Teams Achievement Divisions; Slavin, 1986, 1995), in which teams of four students compete to determine which team's members can amass the greatest improvement over previous achievement levels. The use of recognition or extrinsic rewards can enhance motivation, effort, and persistence under these conditions, and thus increase learning. If the task is collaborative seatwork or a routine task, then constraining the dialogue through narrow roles, especially roles that focus attention on the work to be accomplished, also may be productive.

Ill-Structured Conceptual and Problem-Solving Tasks. If the task is ill-structured and more cognitive in nature, then an open exchange and elaborated discussion will be more helpful (Cohen, 1994b; Ross & Raphael, 1990). Thus, strategies that encourage extended and productive interactions are appropriate when the goal is to develop higher order thinking and problem solving in ill-structured situations. In these situations, a tightly structured process, competition among groups for rewards, and rigid assignment of roles are likely to inhibit the richness of the students' interactions and interfere with progress toward the goal. In these instances, the use of rewards may well divert the group away from the goal of in-depth cognitive processing. When rewards are offered, the goal often becomes achieving the reward as efficiently as possible (Webb & Palincsar, 1996). The size of groups will also have an impact on the kind and quality of interactions in the group. Groups of four or fewer are more likely to give all participants a chance to contribute, ask, and explain.

Social Skills and Communication Tasks. When the goal of peer learning is enhanced social skills or increased intergroup understanding and tolerance of differences, the assignment of specific roles and functions within the group might facilitate communication (Cohen, 1994b; Kagan, 1994). In these situations, it can be helpful to rotate leadership roles so that minorities and females have the opportunity to demonstrate and develop leadership skills and all group members can experience the leadership capabilities of each individual (Miller & Harrington, 1993).

Group Composition. The composition of the group affects participation rates, particularly participation in cognitive activities that are most strongly linked to achievement (O'Donnell & O'Kelly, 1994). Achievement levels, status, race, ethnicity, and gender may influence students' participation within a group. Academic status is the most powerful of the status characteristics in the classroom, but peer status—perceived attractiveness or popularity—can also have an impact on group interactions. Students with high status may tend to dominate a group, whereas low-status students may well be excluded from making equal contributions (see O'Donnell, chap. 7, this volume).

To overcome status effects and nonparticipation, teachers can use strategies such as assigning a true group task that requires wide participation, giving low-status students access to information or resources vital to the group, or emphasizing instructions that highlight the importance of different kinds of contributions. Because girls or students of color may be overshadowed in groups where they are outnumbered, it can be helpful to form groups with even distributions of male and female or majority and minority students. Assigning students to groups based on gender or racial differences, however, may perpetuate students' inclinations to relate to each other on the basis of these classifications. Rather than isolating minority students across groups in an obvious attempt to have different categories of students in every group, it may be better to assign students based on interests, skills, or other characteristics that give students common ground (Cohen, 1994a; Miller & Harrington, 1993). For example, if the group task will require drawing, the class artists could be equally distributed across groups.

Assessment. Assessment is another potentially thorny issue. Teachers need to be aware of the ways that group assessment can provide disincentives as well as incentives for participation. For example, when scores on an assignment or exam are averaged for a group score, students who have loafed are rewarded whereas hard-working students are punished. Students may feel resentful when their grades are jeopardized by an unmotivated or underachieving student, especially when the students see that they have even fewer resources than the teacher for dealing with the problem individual.

Slavin (1995) recommended reward interdependence along with individual accountability in situations where cooperative learning is used to motivate more capable students to help less-able peers on a collaborative or collective-seatwork task. However, Cohen (1994b) noted that reward interdependence does not appear to be necessary for achievement when students are motivated to complete a challenging and interesting group task that requires everyone's contribution for a good outcome.

There is no single best way to assign students to groups, or one perfect order of goals. Over the year, teachers have the opportunity to try out a number of groupings. The closer teachers attend to issues and the more ways they have to think about the dynamics in the group, the more likely it is that they will make sensible choices. Tailoring the goals and structures for cooperative learning is vital to its success. Principles and considerations related to "getting there" are presented in Table 11.1.

Guiding the Process

Group characteristics, goals, and getting there provide a rough framework for planning peer learning experiences. But even with the best planning, "the wild lies in wait" (Shulman, 1995)—unanticipated dynamics are bound to emerge as the activity unfolds. Teachers must respond or repair when interactions do not go as expected (Webb & Palincsar, 1996). In addition, as groups progress, the teacher needs to be willing to relinquish some control to the students, while not relinquishing all guidance of the process (Miller & Harrington, 1993).

Once the learning activity is underway, the teacher has the opportunity to revisit the first three phases in the decision-making process to determine whether midcourse adjustments are necessary. In moving around the room, sampling segments of dialogue from various groups, the teacher can ask, "Have I accurately gauged the cognitive and affective abilities of these students (group characteristics)? Is the task more difficult for them than was anticipated? If so, do the difficulties arise from problems with social or cognitive skills?"

Next, how do the students understand the goal of the activity, and are their goals in keeping with the teacher's goals? For example, in one examination of group learning, the teacher's goal was for the students to engage in "thinking scientifically," but for the students, the goal of maintaining status relationships within the group took precedence (Meloth & Deering, chap. 10, this volume; Palincsar & Herrenkohl, chap. 6, this volume). This became clear only as the activity unfolded over several days.

Finally, a fundamental consideration determining whether students are moving productively toward the learning goals (whether they are getting there) is the quality of the interaction in the groups. In monitoring the group work, the teacher needs to notice both the quantity and the quality of interactions taking place (Cohen, 1994b; Meloth & Deering, chap. 10, this volume). Do the processes unfolding support learning, or are problems developing that will interfere with achieving the goals of the activity? Students fail to participate for a variety of reasons (Mulryan, 1992). Each peer learning technique has its own set of potential pitfalls. Teachers must monitor group interactions to detect these problems and develop strategies for dealing with them.

For a structured cognitive activity, one remedy for these problems is to add individual accountability to group interdependence in the design of group activities and assessments. However, for less structured tasks, giving attention to the underlying causes of students' nonparticipation and changing classroom norms may be required (Cohen, 1994b; Weinstein, 1996). Students may need to be taught skills that are unfamiliar to them.

The level of conflict in a group, in particular, is an issue that requires careful attention. Bearison, Magzamen, and Filardo (1986) suggested that the relation between conflict and productivity is curvilinear. Too little conflict may indicate passivity and less than full participation on the part of some students, whereas too much conflict can be counterproductive in reaching group goals. Teachers must judge whether the level of conflict is productive, and if not, intervene — either to increase or decrease the conflict in the group. It may be helpful just to ask some focused questions to get the students back on track or it may be useful to give a directive, a reminder, or quick answer and then move on. In some situations, it may be most fruitful to send complaining students back to their group to work out problems for themselves. The teacher also needs strategies for intervention when things completely break down. In these cases, it might be helpful to abandon the task temporarily, ask students to reflect on their functioning as a group, and engage in problem solving to address the difficulties that have arisen (Johnson & Johnson, 1988).

In reviewing the choices made during the first three phases of the problem-solving process (group characteristics, goals, and getting there) and noting how the choices are affecting the groups, the teacher begins gathering information for the final phase—reflecting on the experience. By continually monitoring the interactions taking place in the group, being sensitive to level of conflict and noting whether progress is being made toward the goals, the astute teacher will be able to adapt his or her role according to the needs of the group, and guide the group toward enhanced thinking and increased productivity (see Table 11.1).

Gazing Backward and Glimpsing Ahead

It is not necessary to have all the strategies and remedies defined in advance. What is necessary is having a way of learning from the experience, in order to fine-tune the goals and structures for future sessions. As peer learning progresses and when projects end, teachers need ways to think about what happened and derive implications for next steps. A teacher who does not use post-instructional time to take note of the dynamics—what went well and where there were difficulties—has lost an opportunity to hone the process and to gather information about what may be productive groupings for more cognitive tasks for the future.

Teachers also need to assess their own participation in the activity (see Meloth & Deering, chap. 10, this volume). Were my directions clear enough so that students knew what to do? What information was missing? Did I adapt my role to changing group needs and intervene in a way that was helpful? Did my plans provide the time and resources needed by the groups to be productive? What problems could have been foreseen and how could they have been avoided? How has the group progressed and what are the next steps the group is now ready to face? A problem-solving model of peer learning must also include attention to the ways that peer learning can go astray or be misapplied.

What Can Go Wrong.   Group interactions can impede learning and reduce rather than improve interpersonal attraction. McCaslin and Good (1996) listed several disadvantages of group learning:

- Students often value the process or procedures over the learning. Speed and finishing take precedence over thoughtfulness and learning.
- Rather than challenging and correcting misconceptions, students support and reinforce misunderstandings.
- Socializing and managing interpersonal relationships may take precedence over learning.
- Students may simply shift dependency from the teacher to the "expert" in the group—learning is still passive and what is learned can be wrong.

- Status differences may be increased rather than decreased. Some students learn to loaf because the group progresses with or without their contributions. Others are even more convinced that they are helpless to understand without the support of the group.

Using the Problem-Solving Frame for Reflection. Teachers need a framework, a way of systematically considering what has happened and why, so that they can take constructive action to respond. Without such a framework, the teacher may have a sense that things went poorly or things went well, but no notion of why and how to adapt the process in the future. By starting with only a few procedures and some simple strategies for preventing or responding to problems, then analyzing the results using the problem-solving model we have proposed here to organize new thinking and experiences, teachers can enrich their understanding over time. In this way, peer learning can be more than a method, it can be a powerful and flexible set of teaching approaches for a variety of student learning goals. Table 11.1 summarizes the problem-solving stages developed earlier.

PREPARING PROSPECTIVE TEACHERS FOR PEER LEARNING

We propose to use the problem-solving stages described earlier in a more general way to think about preparing prospective teachers to use peer learning.

Group Characteristics

Perhaps the most important characteristics to consider in teacher education are prospective teachers' entering beliefs about teaching, learning, and learners. In learning to teach, what prospective teachers already know determines to a great extent what they will learn and remember in teacher preparation programs:

> By the time prospective teachers come to our educational psychology courses, they almost surely have constructed deep and powerful implicit models of learning based on many thousands of hours of being taught. And why is this important? Because research in cognition and education shows time and again that mental models organize how students learn what is taught in a domain and are quite resistant to change via instruction. (Strauss, 1996, p. 18)

Thus any consideration of how to prepare teachers to use peer learning must begin with an understanding of prospective teachers' knowledge about teaching and learning (Howey & Zimpher, 1996). What do those learning to teach "know" about teaching?

Beliefs About Teaching and Learning. Initially, prospective teachers' knowledge about teaching may be limited to what they have learned by being students

—Lortie's (1975) "apprenticeship of observation." The work of Anderson (1994), Borko and Putnam, (1996), Brookhart and Freeman (1992), Calderhead (1996), Hollingworth (1989), Holt-Reynolds (1992), Kagan (1992), McLaughlin (1991), Morine-Dershimer (1993), Pajares (1992, 1993), Strauss (1993, 1996), Weinstein (1989), Weinstein, Woolfolk, Dittmeier, and Shanker (1994), Zeichner and Gore (1990), and our own experiences suggest that the following beliefs are characteristic of many prospective teachers:

Teaching is
- telling—in clear and interesting ways.
- directing—leading activities.
- engaging students—getting their attention, arousing curiosity, selling ideas, connecting with students' interests, being creative.
- nurturing—helping students feel good about themselves as they develop social skills—affective goals are more important than cognitive objectives.
- an interpersonal skill that involves being fair, kind, flexible, and loving.

Learning to teach is learning
- to do—strategies, activities, events.
- to be—a good, kind, caring, nurturing person (although most prospective teachers feel they already possess these qualities).

Teaching is effective
- if teachers are knowledgeable (so they can tell clearly), creative, interesting (being funny or witty helps here), organized, directive, and caring.
- when learning doesn't happen, differences are due in large part to the students' home background or teacher's failure to be clear and interesting.

In seeming opposition to some of these beliefs, are the notions—often held by the same prospective teachers—that learning should be "hands-on," that making lessons relevant to students' interests is the key to good teaching, and that caring about and respecting your students will virtually eliminate discipline problems. "Creative, real-life" activities that involve important content will lead directly and almost automatically to learning that content (Putnam & Borko, 1997).

Related to these beliefs and perhaps the most common assumption that we encounter in perspective teachers is that *traditional* teaching is bad whereas good teaching requires being different or surprising. It may be the case, they believe, that there is no one best way to teach, but there is a worst way, and it is the way of the traditional teacher.

Beliefs About Cooperative Learning. There is some evidence that cooperative learning is viewed by many practicing teachers as a means to improve social skills, peer relations, confidence, and self-esteem or to provide drill-and-practice.

Direct teaching and independent practice are viewed as more appropriate strategies for academic outcomes and the development of new knowledge (Meloth, 1991; Meloth & Barbe, 1992; Meloth, Deering, & Sanders, 1993; Palincsar, Stevens, & Gavelek, 1989; Rich, 1990). How do preservice teachers view cooperative learning? There is little work on this subject and much is needed. A recent query to the American Educational Association Division of Teaching and Teacher Education listserve asking how programs prepare prospective teachers for cooperative learning received no responses. Our experience suggests that many prospective teachers have been exposed to cooperative learning, either before or during college, but their encounters most often have been with structures and strategies that emphasize motivation, peer relations, and social skills. Experience with effective, well-designed, and monitored groups that foster cognitive goals is rare. Our students are more likely to report being the one in the group who "did all the work" or feeling "grouped out." Many teacher education professors attempt to model different strategies including cooperative learning, but capture the form more than the substance. In these instances, prospective teachers seem to develop a resistance to the approach, based on their limited exposure.

Taking Beliefs Into Account. Prospective teachers' beliefs about teaching and learning are built over years of school experiences and can be highly resistant to change. It is through the lens of these strong beliefs that students in teacher preparation programs make sense of and value their classes and field experiences (Putnam & Borko, 1997). Studies of teacher education programs and classes that intentionally attempt to confront and change prospective teachers' beliefs about teaching and learning reveal both the problems and the possibilities of this endeavor.

It appears that successful programs encourage students to discuss the beliefs that guide their thinking and actions, pinpoint the differences between those beliefs and the perspectives that their professors want them to consider, and analyze the advantages and limitations of thinking with and acting on their current beliefs. In addition, their professors respect their students' beliefs and use them to evaluate research-based principles (Borko & Putnam, 1996; Holt-Reynolds, 1992; Hollingworth, 1989; Ross, Johnson, & Smith, 1991). But even researchers who report some success in affecting prospective teachers' beliefs about teaching and learning also express skepticism that these changes will persist or will actually influence actions (Bird, Anderson, Sullivan, & Swindler, 1992). It is possible that prospective teachers learn a new vocabulary for describing existing beliefs without actually making fundamental changes.

Frank Pajares (1993) suggested several approaches to challenging beliefs. Some class activities should be designed to create cognitive conflict. Using this conflict, teacher educators can help students identify their own beliefs and explore why certain beliefs resist change. All beliefs should be examined and challenged, not just those that conflict with the beliefs of the teacher educator or the education curriculum. Concept maps, metaphor analysis, debates, and dialogue journals are possible ways to help students become aware of their own beliefs and the beliefs of their peers. We found that asking students to analyze teaching and learning in popular films such as *Dead Poet's Society, Dangerous Minds,* or *Stand and Deliver* helps bring underlying beliefs to the surface and can spark challenges and productive conflict about "good" teaching. Johnson and Johnson's (1988) structured controversy process could be used to explore conflicts and to model cooperative learning as well.

Prospective teachers can be encouraged to "try on" ways of interacting or teaching that conflict with their beliefs, as long as the outcomes are likely to be positive and not simply confirming of the beliefs. Often change in behavior precedes change in belief (Guskey, 1989; Rokeach, 1968). Clearly, asking people to make changes in their fundamental beliefs about teaching and learning is bold and perhaps a bit arrogant. The tension between challenge and support—between assimilation and accommodation, between program elements that are consistent with students' current understanding of teaching and elements that question and undermine those conceptions—is a tension that must be tolerated and cultivated.

Goals

What should teacher educators' goals be in relation to peer learning? Mary Kennedy (1988) described four different views of professional knowledge that underlie teaching expertise and that can suggest goals for teacher preparation programs. The views emphasize either technical skills, principled knowledge, critical analysis of teaching problems, or deliberate action based on the skills, knowledge, and analysis. This fourth view of expertise incorporates the first three and adds the element of making choices for specific situations and then enacting the choices (Anderson, Blumenfeld, et al., 1995; Kennedy, 1988). Each view of professional knowledge suggests possible goals related to peer learning.

Skills. What skills must teachers master to use peer learning? If we return to the problem-solving model, there are skills related to establishing groups, planning goals and tasks, monitoring interactions, assessment, handling problems situations, and reflecting on progress. Prospective teachers might study and practice the following skills:

- Design specific routine or procedural group tasks to follow up direct instruction, for practice or review, or to reinforce the learning of explicit content
- Create higher order thinking, ill-defined group tasks that require problem finding and problem solving

- Specify and teach roles for students in groups that encourage the kinds of interactions needed for the learning expected—for example, group facilitator roles for ill-defined tasks where exchange, probing, examination of ideas, and justification of positions are valuable and more structured roles for routine or procedural tasks where motivation, practice, and persistence are keys to learning
- Model the appropriate roles for students
- Establish group composition that encourages participation, taking into account the task, maturity of the group, and the abilities and needs of individuals
- Provide appropriate teaching and instructions so that groups have clear focus and understand how to accomplish the task
- Avoid communicating that the point of the group is to follow steps or procedures
- Use extrinsic rewards, when appropriate, in support of positive interactions and learning
- Monitor and evaluate interactions to determine if productive exchanges are occurring
- Intervene to further learning or to prevent management problems
- Use systems to observe group progress and apply insights to improve peer learning in the next attempt

Principles. The problem-solving model we proposed is an interrelated set of principles and considerations about peer learning that can be used for organizing the concepts and relationships that are important in peer learning. It is especially crucial for prospective teachers to have a conceptual frame for peer learning to counter their likely entering beliefs that (a) group work is useful mostly to develop social skills and motivation, (b) a few people end up doing all the work in groups, or (c) cooperative learning is a set of procedures or steps.

This last belief may be reinforced by teacher educators themselves. Often, it seems, methods that should be understood conceptually as sets of interrelated principles are turned into skills—transformed into a series of steps and or a set of roles. Most educational psychology textbooks, for example, have sections on the various cooperative learning strategies (STAD, Jigsaw, Learning Together, Group Investigation, Scripted Cooperation, etc.) and perhaps a description of research on the effectiveness of various methods (e.g., Biehler & Snowman, 1997; Gage & Berliner, 1991; Slavin, 1997). Writing this chapter led the first author to expand problem-solving considerations for cooperative learning in the seventh edition of *Educational Psychology* (Woolfolk, 1998). The goal is to move beyond the procedures and roles to help prospective teachers understand the theories of learning underlying cooperative approaches. One step toward preparing teachers to use cooperative learning would be to present the topic in a conceptual rather than a procedural way.

When teachers fail to understand the theory underlying a particular method, they are likely to misapply the method or abandon it when initial problems occur (C. W. Anderson, 1989; Meloth et al., 1993; Richardson, 1990). Thus, relating cooperative learning to different theories may help prospective teachers develop a conceptual understanding of cooperative learning. Different cognitive theorists highlight different aspects of group work as critical for learning. For example, theorists who stress a cognitive-elaboration perspective point to the value of group discussion in helping participants rehearse, elaborate, and expand their knowledge. Peer learning strategies that encourage cognitive elaboration involve small (two to four person) heterogeneous or homogeneous groups exploring, reviewing, and rehearsing skills and knowledge, and in the process, reorganizing or integrating information (O'Donnell & O'Kelly, 1994).

Alternatively, advocates of a Piagetian cognitive-developmental perspective suggest that as children engage in dialogue with others at different developmental stages and attempt to explain and justify their point of view, they will begin to move toward a higher level of development (see De Lisi & Golbeck, chap. 1, this volume). Peer learning strategies consistent with this theoretical perspective involve small (two to four person) groups, perhaps made up of students who are similar in many ways but at different cognitive developmental levels, exploring different perspectives, sharing understandings, and challenging ideas (O'Donnell & O'Kelly, 1994).

Theorists who favor a Vygotskian cognitive-developmental perspective on learning and development suggest that social interaction is important for learning because higher mental functions such as reasoning, comprehension, and critical thinking originate in social interactions and are then internalized by individuals. Children can accomplish mental tasks with social support before they can do them alone. Thus, cooperative learning provides the social support and scaffolding that students need to move learning forward (Hogan & Tudge, chap. 2, this volume; Tudge, 1990b). Peer learning strategies consistent with this theoretical perspective involve dyads in which one student is more knowledgeable about the task. The focus often is skill development or explanation of concepts (O'Donnell & O'Kelly, 1994).

Having a grasp of principles of cooperative learning and their relation to theories of learning will not guarantee that a beginning teacher will use the approach productively or even that every situation that might arise is covered by the model. We agree with Anderson, Blumenfeld, et al. (1995) that "although knowledge of principles can be useful, such knowledge is always probabilistic and applicable to many but not all similar situations. Practitioners must be adept at understanding nuances of situations in order to determine when a principle really is applicable" (p. 147).

Analysis: Situating Principles in Practice. Kennedy's (1988) next view of knowledge reminds us that prospective teachers must know more than skills and principles. They must be able to identify, critically analyze, and ultimately solve problems of practice. In relation to peer learning, this could mean analyzing cognitive and social strengths and weaknesses of individual students in order to form groups, analyzing the interactions of a group to judge the level of thinking of participants, or deciding whether peer learning is an appropriate strategy for achieving particular academic or social objectives. Teacher preparation programs seldom focus on analyzing the quality of interactions in peer learning groups, for example. Again, there are few teaching materials—audio, video, or written examples of peer learning—that depict productive interactions and cognitive learning. One source of authentic interactions is transcriptions of dialogue in cooperative groups available in published research, for example, the dialogues of Juan and his peers attempting to learn science in a small-group setting (Anderson, Holland, & Palincsar, 1997).

A number of teacher educators recommend the use of cases to develop analytical capabilities and to situate teaching skills and principles in practice (Doyle, 1990; Kennedy, 1988; Leinhardt, 1990; Putnam & Borko, 1997; Sykes & Bird, 1992). Putnam and Borko (1997) suggested that case teaching is particularly promising for exploring problems of pedagogy and for grounding theoretical ideas about teaching and learning in slices of classroom life. Both cases of problematic teaching situations and cases of exemplary teaching could be helpful in developing prospective teachers' knowledge of peer learning. Through analysis of problem cases, prospective teachers practice framing issues, generating alternative solutions, making choices about actions, and considering the implications of their choices (Putnam & Borko, 1997). Video and hypertext cases might allow students to explore the complexity of cooperative learning by analyzing different tasks, goals, group compositions, strategies, and interactions—noting how changes in one of these dimensions affect other dimensions.

The limitation with analysis, as Kennedy (1988) noted, is that practicing teachers cannot end with generating and evaluating alternatives—they must act. Here, a second kind of case, samples of exemplary teaching, might be necessary to provide images of action (Leinhardt, 1988, 1990). We return to this idea shortly.

Skills, Principles, and Analysis in Action. Kennedy's (1988) last view of knowledge draws on the work of such educators as Dewey (1904/1965), Schwab (1978), and Schon (1983, 1987) and adds to critical analysis the ability to take deliberate action:

> Successful deliberate action requires a body of experiences on which to draw, the ability to conduct mental experiments, the ability to critically evaluate their outcomes, and the ability to revise one's definition of the situation if not satisfied

with the solutions the mental experiment yielded. In addition, it requires a highly developed sense of purpose, for purpose is the criterion against which both ideas and actions are judged. Professional educators must not only provide their students with these things, but also do so in a way that transforms the students into thinkers capable of deliberation and deliberate action. (Kennedy, 1988, p. 149)

To consider how prospective teachers might develop the capacity for deliberate actions in planning, guiding, and assessing peer learning, we move to the next considerations in our problem-solving model—getting there and guiding the process.

Getting There and Guiding the Process

Rather than viewing most teacher preparation courses as opportunities to learn skills and principles that will be applied later in teaching, many teacher educators and standards boards are calling for preparation that situates the learning of skills and principles in real-life teaching contexts (cf. Anderson, Blumenfeld, et al., 1995; Darling-Hammond, 1994; Goodlad, 1994; Guyton & Rainer, 1996; The Holmes Group, 1996; Leinhardt, 1988; Shulman, 1990; Putnam & Borko, 1997). The question is, "How?"

Putnam and Borko (1997) concluded that "there is not just one way, or even one best way, to situate teacher learning in practice. Rather there are different ways to situate learning, each suited particularly well to different components of teacher learning" (p. 1290). Writing about educational psychology and teacher preparation, Anderson, Blumenfeld, et al. (1995) suggested that one key to situating the learning of prospective teachers in practice is to design better tasks for teacher education students.

Doyle (1983) defined tasks as the products students are asked to create, the resources provided, and the kinds of thinking that students are expected to apply in order to produce the outcomes using those resources. Tasks determine what academic content students will encounter, what they will do with that content, and how they will think about it. Tasks have a particular subject focus and also involve certain cognitive operations such as memorize, infer, classify, and apply, so that as students work on a task, they are learning content and practicing operations. Anderson, Blumenfeld, et al. (1995) described five considerations for designing meaningful tasks for teacher education:

1. "A set of tasks should provide multiple representations of key ideas across situations" (p. 152). This might mean designing tasks that allow multiple opportunities for prospective teachers to observe productive and problematic interactions in groups. To do so, however, raises issues of depth versus breadth in coverage and also questions about cooperation across different courses in teacher preparation programs. Can enough time be devoted to peer learning within and across courses, or will students encounter superficial discussions of structures and strategies in several different courses?

2. *"A set of tasks (though not necessarily every task) should feel authentic, representing as much as possible the complexity of teaching without overwhelming students"* (p. 152). The key here is to ask students to take several dimensions into account at once as they make decisions about peer learning, then analyze the possible implications of the decisions. It can be difficult to find the right balance of authenticity, complexity, and pace that allows novices to sort through the issues and practice responses. Some simplifying or slowing down may be necessary. Simulations, microteaching, videotaping, and teaching laboratory experiences can be good initial learning situations, allowing prospective teachers to focus on manageable segments of the design, monitoring, or assessment of peer learning (Howey, 1996).

3. *"Tasks should be designed to help make explicit prospective teachers' beliefs and conceptions, and to engage them in explaining their own beliefs and considering alternative points of view"* (p. 152). Possibilities for accomplishing these kinds of tasks were described earlier.

4. *"Tasks should create opportunities for public interaction among the students and between the instructor and students"* (p. 152). This consideration invites a recommendation to use peer learning in the teacher preparation classes. Certainly many teacher preparation programs include such an element. Yet, unless the planning and execution of peer learning are informed by the kinds of considerations described in this or other models of productive group learning, it is likely that participation in so-called cooperative learning in college classes will be unproductive. Experiences that simply reinforce prior beliefs—that group learning is mostly for social or motivational objectives or that work in groups is just a way to divide the labor (with some people always doing more or less than their share)—will not help prospective teachers understand and use peer learning.

The final consideration in designing tasks described by Anderson, Blumenfeld, et al. (1995) brings us to the next element in our problem-solving model—guiding the process.

5. *"Grading and assessment should be congruent with other considerations"* (p. 152). In guiding the process of learning about peer learning, assessment—in terms of formative and summative evaluation, written and oral comments, and reactions to students' comments and questions—will shape the task, the interaction, and thus the learning. A major factor that affects how students will use a task is how they will be assessed—what is the performance to be exchanged for a grade (Doyle, 1983)? If a goal is to help prospective teachers create thoughtful practices of peer learning, then assessment should focus attention on this task. One option is to set as a major assignment that students develop their own problem-solving model for peer learning. What will they consider and on what basis will they make decisions about goals, groupings, getting there, guiding, and gazing backward? Excellent readings for such an assignment include Cohen (1994b), Good and Brophy (1994), O'Donnell and O'Kelly (1994), Ross and Raphael

(1990), Slavin (1983), Webb and Palincsar (1996), and the chapters on managing group work in Weinstein (1996) and Weinstein and Mignano (1997).

Gazing Backward and Glimpsing Ahead

Much has been written about the value of reflection in teaching. Learning about peer learning seems an ideal focus for teacher educators' self-study. There is great interest and enthusiasm about cooperative learning, as described in the first section of this chapter. Yet, the complexity of the process combined with prospective teachers' entering beliefs about teaching and the ways that cooperative learning is often encountered in textbooks, courses, and workshops all combine to support misunderstandings or limited understandings of cooperative learning. It would be useful to assess what prospective teachers are learning about peer learning from the activities and experiences in the classes and programs. How useful do they find the conceptual framework provided in their college classes? What elements have remained helpful and which parts have been rejected or forgotten? What changes should be made in the framework to respond to the problems of practice? If our students and those of our colleagues are an indication, prospective teachers are learning that cooperative learning is great—until they try it.

DEVELOPING PROFESSIONAL KNOWLEDGE AND ACTION: WHAT IS A GOOD BEGINNING?

Planning, guiding, and evaluating peer learning are complex processes. There are developmental considerations in selecting tasks and in structuring groups. Both tasks and students' interactions should support learning. Some direct instruction along with appropriate monitoring of the groups may be necessary to make the best use of peer interactions for learning. The decisions about the composition of the group have implications for the quality of the interactions within the group and for the kinds of tasks that can be accomplished. Teachers may need to assume different roles at different stages in a group's maturity or to help students accomplish different tasks. Even the best of plans and procedures can unravel and require repair. To complicate matters further, all of these challenges are embedded in the larger complexity of teaching.

Classrooms are complicated, multidimensional places (Doyle, 1986). Furthermore, life in classrooms is simultaneous—everything happens at once. Classrooms are crowded with people, tasks, and time pressures. Many individuals, all with differing goals, preferences, and abilities, must share resources, accomplish various tasks, use and reuse materials without losing them, move in and out of groups, keep track of what is happening, and so on. In addition, actions can have multiple effects. Assigning a student whose English is limited to a group role that requires oral communication may give that student needed practice in speaking but could threaten the flow of action in the group and create management problems.

Because classrooms are public, the way the teacher handles these unexpected intrusions is seen and judged by all. Students are always noticing if the teacher is being "fair." Is there favoritism? Do some groups seem privileged? Finally, classrooms have histories. The meaning of particular teacher's actions or a student's actions depends in part on what has happened before. The 15th time a student arrives late requires a different response from the teacher than the first late arrival.

Anderson, Blumenfeld, and colleagues (1995) added to the list of complexities in teaching that teaching is inherently not only a social but also an ethical enterprise. All choices are influenced by values and all decisions have implications for students. At times, a choice that favors one child or group will disadvantage others. In the realm of group learning, as we have seen, teachers' decisions can affect the statuses and opportunities of students. Can a beginning teacher manage the complexities of peer learning embedded in the larger complexities of teaching? What sort of preparation program will help?

Bringing Order: Simplifying the Complexity

From the Gestalt psychologists to Piaget to modern cognitive views of learning, two insights recur. First, to make sense of situations, humans use what they already know, and second, they impose order on complexity by detecting patterns, seeking predictability, and sometimes creating simplified models (Gardner, 1985). Anderson, Blumenfeld, et al. (1995) suggested the following:

> Indeed, one of the goals of professional education is to help novices impose cognitive order on the rampant complexities of the problems faced by professionals such as designing buildings with limited resources and conflicting needs, or diagnosing an ailment where the symptoms do not fit a clear pattern. Professional education programs are based in large part on educators' ideas about how they can best help novices learn how to frame and simplify their world in order to act responsibly and competently. (p. 147)

In Anderson, Blumenfeld, et al.'s (1995) analysis of professional education programs is an inherent challenge to prepare novices to both think and act—to analyze situations, imposing order in ways that support learning, and then act on those analyses. This challenge is consistent with Kennedy's (1988) description of the knowledge underlying teaching expertise described earlier. But what is a reasonable simplification—a good beginning?

A Simplified Frame. We propose that prospective teachers be given a matrix similar to that in Table 11.2. The matrix could be empty or partially complete. The prospective teachers could fill in sections based on readings, class discus-

TABLE 11.2
A Simplified Matrix for Organizing Peer Learning

Considerations	Social Skills Task: Team Building and Cooperation Skills	Structured Tasks: Review, Practice Facts and Skills	Unstructured Tasks: Conceptual, Problem-Solving, Thinking, and Reasoning
Group size and composition	Groups of 2–5, common interest groups, mixed groups, random groups	Groups of 2–4, mixed ability, high-medium/medium-low, or high-low/medium-medium	Groups of 2–4, select members to encourage interaction
Why assign roles?	To monitor participation and conflict, rotate leadership	To monitor engagement and insure that low-status students have resources to offer, such as Jigsaw	Only to encourage interaction, divergent thinking, and extended, connected discourse, such as debate sides, group facilitator
Extrinsic rewards/incentives	Not necessary/may be helpful	To support motivation, effort, persistence	Not necessary
Teacher's role	Model, encourager	Model, director, coach	Model, facilitator
Student skills needed	Listening, turn taking, encouraging, managing conflict	Questioning, explaining, encouraging, content knowledge, learning strategies	Questioning, explaining, elaborating, probing, divergent thinking, providing rationales, synthesizing
What supports learning? Watch and listen for . . .	Modeling and practice	Giving multiple, elaborated explanations, attention, and practice	Quantity and quality of interactions, using and connecting knowledge resources, probing and elaboration
Potential problems	Unproductive conflict, nonparticipation	Poor help-giving skills, disengaged or excluded students	Disengaged or excluded students, cognitive loafing, superficial thinking, avoiding controversy
Averting problems	Simpler tasks, direct teaching of social skills, team building, conflict resolution skills, discuss group process	Structure interdependence and individual accountability, teach helping and explaining	Structure controversy, assign "thinking roles," allow adequate time
Start small	One or two skills, such as listening and paraphrasing	Pairs of students quizzing each other	Numbered heads together

sions, or field experiences. The matrix could be built across several teacher preparation courses, so that subject-specific considerations in using peer learning could be included as well. As mentioned earlier, this could be part of ongoing or summative assessment in one or more courses. This frame might be introduced one consideration at a time, followed by a simulation exercise. For example, given a hypothetical class, what task would you design in a particular subject? What kind of task is it (social skills, factual, or conceptual)? How would the students in the class be assigned to groups for this task? Why? After practicing designing tasks and making decisions about group compositions, the prospective teachers can be asked if and how they would assign roles. Next, add considerations about rewards and incentives. By adding considerations in each subsequent round of decisions, prospective teachers practice dealing with greater complexity and more authentic situations.

The last row in Table 11.2, "small start," reflects a general issue in using any complex teaching strategy. Initially, expectations for what the teacher can successfully orchestrate should be small and reasonable. As skill and knowledge develop, more complicated procedures can be attempted. The following section describes why strategies such as "numbered heads together" (Kagan, 1994) make sense as starting points.

Reasonable Expectations and Gradual Complications.   Weinstein (1996) described the nightmarish experience of a student teacher who enthusiastically launched into a complicated peer learning strategy with his high school history class. Neither the teacher nor the class had any experience with group work. After a series of disasters, the student teacher concluded, "All in all, these were the two worst days of my student-teaching experience. After reading all those education theorists who say that cooperative learning is such great stuff, I had been real excited, but now I'm not so sure. Maybe if your class were really motivated to begin with, it would work" (p. 170).

Weinstein (1996) noted that the student teacher started by trying the most complicated form of group work with a thoroughly unprepared group of students. One suggestion for this student teacher would be to begin at the beginning—start small. Begin by teaching students how to work in groups and how to cooperate. Focus on one or, at the most, two communication skills. Define, model, explain, and seek student examples of the skills. Have them practice skills—make sure everyone participates. Use a simple, nonacademic task as a group project for practice. See Cohen (1994a), Good and Brophy (1994), or Kagan (1994) for exercises that lend themselves to learning and practicing communication skills.

When moving to use peer learning for cognitive outcomes, again start small by using formats similar to approaches that are familiar to the students. This may mean the beginning teacher simply tells students during a direct instruction lesson to turn to another student and decide on an answer to a question, or sum-

TABLE 11.3
Types of Groupwork: From Simple to Complex

Type of Group	Skills Required	Example of an Activity
Helping permitted Helping obligatory	Ask for help Explain, provide support and encouragement	Using newspapers to learn geography and current events; students help one another but complete an individual worksheet
Peer tutoring	Ask for help, explain, provide support and encouragement	Tutor helps tutee to complete a set of math problems
Cooperative group	Divide group task into individual tasks; coordinate individual efforts to produce final group product	M & M activity; students count the number of candies in individual bags and then pool figures
Completely coop- erative group	Take turns; listen to one an- other, coordinate efforts, share materials, collaborate on a single task, solve con- flicts, achieve consensus	Building a landfill that doesn't leach toxins into the ground; determining a political party affiliation; as a group, decide if hypo- thetical person is Democrat or Republican

Note: Adapted from Weinstein & Mignano, 1997, p. 180 and Weinstein, 1996, p. 74.

marize the key points so far. Kagan (1994) described a structure called *numbered heads together* in which four students—numbered one to four—"put their heads together" to be sure everyone knows the answer to questions the teacher has asked. Then the teacher picks a number and all the students with that number raise their hands or stand up. The teacher calls on several for their answers. This structure is similar to whole-class question-and-answer, so it is an easy transition for students.

Stodolsky (1984) described five different ways that students can work to-gether, from the simplest format, helping permitted, to the most complex and demanding, complete cooperation (see Table 11.3 for a summary of the five types). A reasonable first effort for beginning teachers would be to use helping or tutoring approaches to peer learning before attempting more advanced forms. All the considerations of our problem-solving model could be applied to plan and implement these experiences, but complexity would be lessened in making the decisions. As a sense of efficacy in planning and implementing peer learning strategies developed, more complicated structures, tasks, and goals could be attempted.

Conditional Knowledge: Matching Teaching to Learning Outcomes

We believe there is a more fundamental problem for prospective teachers as they try to use peer learning effectively for cognitive outcomes. They lack an understanding of the connections between teaching strategies and students' learning. When asked to explain why students might learn when they participate in a particular activity or are taught in a particular way, our students have great difficulty explaining the mechanisms of learning and how teaching influences those processes. Explanations are likely to be peppered with descriptions of how the activity is relevant, interesting, authentic, real-life, hands-on, or not boring—descriptions of motivational and affective dimensions of the activity. Few students are able to connect the activity to cognitive processes that lead to learning, and few prospective teachers articulate what they want students to learn in ways that adequately represent academic content or cognitive outcomes. Again, intended learning outcomes are often affective or motivational—positive attitudes, self-esteem, teamwork, following directions.

Without a clear sense of learning outcomes and without an understanding of how teaching affects learning, it is difficult for these novice teachers to recognize dialogue that might support learning in any teaching setting—one-to-one, small group, or whole class. What are good questions and explanations? Prospective teachers do not spend much time these days learning about good explanations because direct instruction has fallen from favor and, as we saw earlier, many prospective teachers agree that traditional teaching (i.e., explaining) is bad. Of course, if teachers do not recognize productive explanations and dialogue, how will they help students learn to give good explanations or have productive dialogues?

Thus, another reasonable expectation for prospective teachers is that they learn to recognize and craft good questions and explanations themselves before expecting them to structure groups and train students to produce this kind of interaction and dialogue. Then there is one last issue—do beginning teachers know the subjects they are teaching well enough to recognize and guide productive dialogue about the subjects?

One Last Complication: Understanding the Subject

How prospective teachers will use peer learning for cognitive ends depends in part on their understanding of the academic subjects they are teaching. Without clear conceptions of organizing ideas and connections in a discipline, it is difficult to pose questions or teach students to pose questions that will foster productive interactions. Without an understanding of how knowledge develops in a discipline, it is difficult to distinguish developing but imperfect understandings from misunderstandings. It is difficult to know when to guide and when to withdraw from discussion. Meloth et al. (1993) made a similar point: To monitor group work effectively, "teachers themselves need to be aware of the connections among the lesson's cognitive goals, the activities they have designed to meet these goals, and the kinds of content knowledge, metacognitive skills, and verbal interaction they anticipate will help students learn from the tasks" (p. 13).

There is probably much to say about the role of teachers' subject matter understanding in using cooperative learning. At present, we know little about this relation except for a few studies suggesting that more knowledgeable teachers tend to use cooperative learning less (Battistich, Solomon, & Delucci, 1993; McCaslin & Good, 1996). As teachers gain greater knowledge and facility with cognitive approaches to peer learning, this may change.

SUMMARY AND CONCLUSIONS

Using peer learning in a classroom context involves a complex set of decisions around a number of contingencies and considerations. In order for beginning teachers to cope with this complexity, they need a conceptual framework, a way of thinking about the decisions they must make. Prior to choosing a method or strategy, teachers must be able to assess the capabilities and challenges in the group they are working with, understand that different processes have different goals, and choose goals that are appropriate to move the group along in both their affective and cognitive development. When goals have been established, teachers must decide on tasks and structures to facilitate those goals, taking into account the unique characteristics of the group and individuals within the group. Once a group process is underway, teachers have a new set of decisions about how to participate in and guide the process. Finally, unless teachers have a means to reflect on the peer learning experience, they will not be prepared to decide on realistic next steps and set future goals. This is indeed a formidable challenge. Beginning teachers need to be encouraged to start small and then to add new knowledge and learning as they gain experience.

Teacher educators will be ill-prepared to communicate a conceptual framework to their students if they do not understand and use such a framework in their own decision making as they plan their courses and programs. Misuse of peer learning strategies in teacher preparation programs may decrease rather than increase the likelihood that students will attempt those strategies in their own teaching. In assessing the characteristics of their group of students and selecting goals, teacher educators need to be keenly aware of the existing beliefs about teaching and peer learning held by their students. They must also choose tasks and structure processes that not only give their students a framework for problem solving about peer learning but also practice in those decision-making and teaching skills. Finally, teacher educators need to give attention to the depth of their students' knowledge in the subject areas they will teach.

Reform movements envision schools in the 21st century that will involve greater levels of cooperation and collaboration. Peer learning strategies provide a powerful mechanism not only to address affective goals in education but also to enhance students' cognitive development; to deepen their understanding of concepts; and to press them to examine, articulate, and elaborate their ideas with greater clarity and rigor. Unless programs that prepare future teachers give them effective means to manage the complex problem solving involved in implementing peer learning strategies, the rich possibilities offered will not be realized and peer learning may be abandoned as just another educational fad. With a conceptual framework to undergird teachers' knowledge of peer learning strategies and guide their decision making, peer learning holds promise to enhance children's thinking and reasoning skills across the curriculum in the century ahead.

APPENDIX A
Commonalties in School Reform Recommendations
Identified by Howey (1996)

Schools	Classrooms	Curriculum	Teaching and Instruction	Learners and Learning
Site-based management and shared decision making	Learning stations and learning laboratories	Themes and interdisciplinary units	Team planning and multi-mode instruction	Active, self-monitored
Considerably expanded parental involvement	Cooperative learning structures	High, clear standards	A focus on inquiry and conceptual learning	Group interdependence and accountability; cooperative learning
More formalized relations with a variety of social service agencies	Cross-age tutoring	Closely coupled, outcomes-based assessment	Attention to personal and social development as well as cognitive learning	An emphasis on the strengths of diversity and heterogeneity
Learning communities or cohorts remaining together across multiple years	Paraprofessional and parent volunteers	Interaction in multiple modes with the "real world."	The use of aides and paraprofessionals	Interaction with the social community and tasks geared toward civic responsibility
Electronic learning laboratories	Hands-on materials	Diminished reliance on texts and inert information	The use of electronic communications	Parent–child learning centers
Job-embedded professional development			A focus on individual and group monitoring or meta-cognitive abilities	Personal computers
Differentiated staffing and team teaching			Attention to beliefs, preconceptions, and misconceptions	Time periods set aside for the enablement of learning communities
Civic activities and rigorous investigation of local issues			Reciprocal teaching and learning by teachers and students	

Teachers as Peer Learners: Professional Development in an Advanced Computer Learning Environment

TAMAR ALMOG
RACHEL HERTZ-LAZAROWITZ
University of Haifa

This chapter presents our vision of the classroom of the future. We describe the kinds of learning and teaching processes that will be needed in such classrooms, and conceptualize a process of building such an environment in a project entitled SELA (the Hebrew initials for Learning Environment with Advanced Technologies). The SELA project provides a model of professional development that was implemented in Israel (Salomon & Almog, 1994, 1996). The project integrated the Group Investigation (GI) model (Dewey, 1909), based on its Israeli adaptation (Hertz-Lazarowitz & Zelniker, 1995), within a teacher peer learning community, using advanced computer technologies. We provide the background for this project and a description of the program. We also discuss the implications of our perspectives for professional development of teachers and how participation in this program influences subsequent behavior in the classroom.

Two major books influenced our perspectives about students and teachers within the school context. One is *Life in the Classroom* (Jackson, 1968), which describes the traditional, unchallenging classroom where students are forced to study irrelevant content. The second book, *Schoolteacher* (Lortie, 1975), presents the teacher as a lonely semiprofessional, closed behind his or her classroom doors. In the past decade, revolutionary movements in schools challenged these images. These evolutions unite two innovations: intelligent computer technology and a social-communal organization of learning and teaching. These two combined trends hold the potential to create new learning and teaching environments of a scope and quality previously unknown in schools.

The first section of this chapter describes the future classroom and the implications of such classrooms for teaching and learning. The second part deals with processes within the future school using our former conception of classroom mirrors (Hertz-Lazarowitz, 1992). The third part of the chapter provides the theoretical background for the new learning setting for teachers, the Teachers' Peer Learners' Community (TPLC). The interweaving of principles derived from the theoretical background of the TPLC is illustrated in the description of a professional development training program that is described in the fourth section of the chapter. In the last part of this chapter, we discuss three general issues: (a) the significance of TPLC in the professional development of teachers in the near future, (b) the implications of key features of the constructivist theory of the actions of the TPLC, and (c) the potential of teachers who experienced the TPLC to transfer their experiences to their schools.

CHANGES IN SOCIETY AND THEIR POTENTIAL IMPACT ON EDUCATION

It is widely agreed that one of the basic purposes of education is to socialize students to be prepared as adults for the world they will encounter. This task is difficult to conceptualize in the near future, because it is hard to predict the needs of society in the future, although it is likely that the following characteristics will influence the learning environment: Rapid and dramatic changes in all dimensions of life, including politics, economics, social and national relationships, the arts and communication (Kennedy, 1993; Naisbitt & Aburdene, 1990; Toffler, 1981, 1990), will revolutionize the definition of knowledge from its acquisition to its construction. The encyclopedic mastery of information that for many generations was necessary in many fields will be replaced by the ability to obtain relevant, meaningful, and challenging information to construct knowledge. Social organizations, including schools, will have to change and respond with a constructivist approach (Vygotsky, 1978) and restructure their thinking, learning, and teaching. With the enormous growth of the knowledge needed in order to function in the society, it will not be possible to keep students and teachers isolated from each other. Cooperative learning within classrooms and teamwork of teachers in the school will be significant and important.

In the future, every schoolchild will be connected to the computer for some goals, so growing engagement with advanced computer and communication technologies will characterize every educated person. Mastering complex and high-level technologies will be essential in order to function effectively as a member of the future task force of the labor market. People will become significant resources for the wealth of future society, and their ability to interact with technology not only as a machine, but also as a knowledgeable partner will be valued. Societies in the future will depend mainly on human capital, which will replace, in its importance, the ownership of raw materials and muscle power.

The growing engagement with advanced technologies in the society of the future will have an additional impact. Technology holds the potential to change and gradually break absolute values, and challenge judgments and certainties of long-standing truth. Enlightened choices allow for more pluralism of values and ideals, because information and knowledge will be less controlled by central agencies (Beare & Slaughter, 1993).

Given this picture, educational systems will have to develop different types of students and teachers. They will have to deal with technological sophistication but also obtain a high level of cognitive abilities and social-moral sensitivities. Cognitive abilities will be directed toward the new meaning of information with an emphasis on applying general learning strategies rather than acquiring information. Students will acquire broad knowledge as opposed to limited knowledge and will be able to connect new knowledge to schemes. Educational systems will set new priorities, planning new processes of learning and teaching, and utilizing and understanding scientific concepts such as the distinction between fact and opinion, understanding theory, raising hypotheses, and setting inquiry paradigms. Interdisciplinary thinking and a connectionist approach to information will become a most significant feature of learning in future society.

This new educational agenda will have to include social and moral qualities where students, teachers, and administrators will work to create the "caring school" (Noddings, 1984, 1995), to protect youngsters from violence and abuse, and to afford them a life secured by quality and equality. Any school change is truly counted only if it reaches the classroom—therefore, in the following section, we describe a few features of the future classroom, which combines the elements of investigation, technology, and moral cooperation.

The Future Learning–Teaching Environment: Six Mirrors

No one can say how exactly the future classroom will look and function, and therefore planning of schools and classrooms for the future is in initial stages. It is clear, however, that changes in any dimension of classroom activity will interact with other dimensions in the classroom (Hertz-Lazarowitz, 1992).

Hertz-Lazarowitz (1992) proposed a model of the classroom that takes into account the richness and complexity of the classroom environment and the intricacies of the interactions between many variables in the classroom. This model consisted of six *mirrors*, a term chosen to portray the view that the dimensions that characterize the classroom are interrelated and reflected in one another: Structure and activities in one dimension have implications for what is possible in another dimension. For example, if the teacher maintains central control of the classroom (the mirror of teacher's instruction), this will be re-

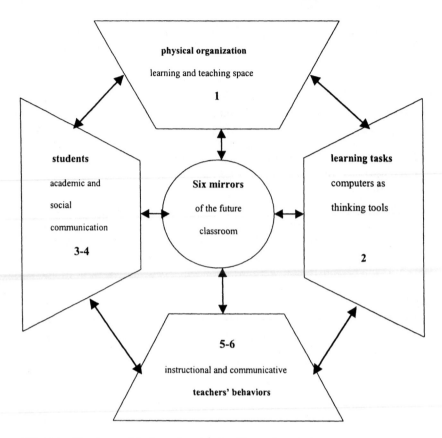

FIG. 12.1.   Six mirrors of the future learning–teaching environment.

flected in students' behavior. The students will be unable to engage in multilateral investigation (the mirror of students' academic behavior).

We claim that technological development, if utilized correctly, has the potential to eventually revolutionize the classroom (Salomon & Almog, in press). In the following paragraphs, we adopt Hertz-Lazarowitz's (1992) characterization of the six mirrors of the classroom to describe an integrative model of the future learning–teaching environment (see Fig. 12.1). This model consists of (1) the physical setting and organization, (2) the structure of the learning task, (3–4) the academic and social communication of the student, and (5–6) the instructional and communicational behaviors of the teacher. These mirrors are interrelated in a systematic way, and cannot be separated when functioning, observing, or studying the learning environment (Hertz-Lazarowitz, 1992).

The Teachers' Peer Learning Community program was designed to prepare teachers for the classroom of the future. The program was developed from this model and in order to appreciate the approach to the TPLC, it is necessary to describe these facets of the future classroom in some detail.

The Physical Organization – The Learning and Teaching Space

The future classroom, with advanced technologies, will be organized in a flexible manner, to meet traditional and innovative organization of learning teams. The physical setting of the classroom will have to accommodate human engineering aspects and computer demands. The classroom will have to become a pleasant and flexible place in which to work. Teachers will give instructions via their computer network, from the teacher's computer to the students' personal computers and vice versa. The classroom will be a decentralized organization with many smaller units (groups or teams) operating simultaneously. This organization of "group of groups" fits the high-technology environment. The possibility of turning a classroom wall into an electronic screen—a display from any computer (teacher's or student's) to a large screen—will allow dynamic presentation of information and products involved in learning projects. The change in instruction and learning will have to be followed by changes in the design and architecture of other rooms and spaces in the school such as teachers' rooms, laboratories, and libraries.

Learning Tasks – Using Computers as Thinking Tools

Teachers, alongside their students, and sometimes following them, are learning to use the computer as a tool to develop skills in thinking and reflection. The computer can help students and teachers organize and carry out efforts of high-level learning and frees them from being busy with simple learning tasks, allowing them to be engaged in more challenging tasks. The computer's power lies in the excitement of access to rich and complex bodies of information, to construct meaningful knowledge by investigation. Peers working together on computer tasks in this regard can enhance the potential of the computer. Learning with smart data banks and advanced computer communication facilitates the exchange of information with other learning teams and with experts beyond the school walls.

Computerized Academic and Social Communication

Open electronic communication with the "outside world" will expose teachers and students to peers from other schools and cultures. Through computer-mediated communication on the information highway, every classroom can become a real-time, online information center. Schools will familiarize their students and teachers with the many services of social institutions like research centers, laboratories, banks, newspapers, stock market information, and various resource centers. Students will be able to interact with online information, for example, in economics classes, to analyze the latest foreign currency data; in citizenship classes, to review last night's public opinion surveys; in sports, to follow the results of the latest games in various states. In these interactive knowledge-seeking contexts, students will master the most significant academic and social skills needed for citizens in the next century: working with on-line information to cooperate and collaborate with other people for actual learning, analyzing, and decision making.

Teachers: Initiators, Producers, and Communicators of Learning

The roles of the teacher are presently undergoing major changes. Whereas teachers' roles were traditionally based on historical definitions—the "sage on the stage"—they will gradually become partners in a community of teachers and increasingly immersed with students as partners for learning—the "guide on the side." The role of teachers as active initiators and actors of the "show of learning and teaching" will be influenced by the metaphor of production and interpretation (Schonman, 1995). Teachers will become producers of new classroom curricula and programs, where new technology and sophisticated teaching materials are an ongoing part. Multidisciplinary teaching, in addition to monodisciplinary teaching, will become a central part of learning in schools, which in turn will require the establishment and cooperation of multidiscipline teaching teams.

The teacher of the future will need to be a skilled computer user and well versed in complex and varied information and knowledge networks. This teacher will also need to be able to guide his or her students to use technology in an enlightened way and not to be consumed by its cognitive shallowness and emptiness. Transforming information into knowledge in a context of moral and ethical dilemmas previously unknown to the teacher could be empowered by working in teams and communities of teachers. The shared vision and responsibilities must meet the demands and challenges of educating our youngsters. The kind of professional preparation needed to develop such teachers will also need to be qualitatively different than what it currently is. In the next section, we describe the theoretical underpinnings of a professional development model that is designed to prepare teachers for the kinds of classroom described earlier.

THEORETICAL BACKGROUND FOR TPLC TRAINING

In the Teacher Peer Learning Community, teachers were trained to create the environment of the future classroom. Teachers were engaged simultaneously in four areas: the cognitive area, the social area, the technological area, and the integration of all three into a contextual domain. The TPLC curricula and activities are presented in detail later in this chapter. The premise of the training program was that teachers would learn best about the complexities of the future classroom by being engaged themselves in an investigative experience with their peers, supported by technology.

Two theoretical sources shaped the construction of the investigative learning environment in the training of the teachers: (a) the concepts and literature of learners' communities, and (b) the theory and process of Group Investigation. In addition, our design of the TPLC curriculum was informed by our analysis of the current relation of teachers to technology. The interweaving of these three areas determined the sequence of activities that the teachers experienced and constructed in their training workshops.

Learners' Communities

The concept of learning in partnership and in communities is rooted in ancient Judaism. *Havruta o mituta* (Companionship or death) is a frequently cited Aramaic maxim coined by Jewish sages. According to the maxim, studying without social interaction is equivalent to death. The *Havruta* type of learning took place in the synagogue or yeshiva, which constituted the communal center of Jewish life. The highest and most valued form of learning is the talmudic *Pilpul*. This form requires learners to argue a point with logic, coherence, and elegance, while being scrutinized by experts hunting for flaws in logic. It was Rabbi Yitzhak Bar-Moshe, author of a pedagogy book (written 130 years ago), who reviewed Jewish pedagogues and proposed that the best way to study the Torah (Bible) was the investigative method of proving a problem, discussing it, posing questions, and providing answers within "the group of significant partners" (Assaf, 1948).

Many centuries later, Dewey (1909, 1927) and the progressive education emphasized the investigative-project approach, where learning activity was conducted in groups, using the classroom and the community as learning sites. GI was a long-standing innovative pedagogy that focused mainly on students' group learning, without creating a parallel of teachers' organization in communal teaching. Recently, the concept of community among teachers, Teacher Learner Community (TLC), was introduced by school change agents. They found that only when the culture of the school changed from the solitary work of teachers to the culture of working in TLC did teachers hold the power to transform schools and classrooms (Hertz-Lazarowitz & Calderon, 1994; Sarason, 1996).

Brown and Campione (1994) characterized learners' communities in terms of six principles. Many of these characteristics are also true for teachers. Communities of learners (either students or teachers) are characterized by (a) active, strategic learning with metacognitive awareness; (b) diversity with respect to abilities, culture, language, and expertise, leading to opportunities for teamwork and collaboration; (c) diversity with respect to "tabs of development," producing "multiple and overlapping zones of readiness" among the participants; (d) multiple roles of teacher, learner, researcher, and expert shared and alternated among all participants, leading to many opportunities for cross-age and peer tutoring in addition to tutorial teaching and coaching; (e) the independence created by distributed expertise; and (f) a commitment to deep substantive content knowledge pursued over extended periods of time in a variety of contexts.

The Group-Investigation (GI) Model

The second major source of influence on the TPLC curriculum was Group Investigation (Hertz-Lazarowitz & Zelniker, 1995; Sharan & Hertz-Lazarowitz, 1980). The GI process was restructured into six stages and revitalized as a main model in the cooperative learning movement in many cultures (Bruce & Weil, 1986; Hertz-Lazarowitz & Zelniker, 1995). Four major features—investigation, interaction, interpretation, and intrinsic motivation—characterize GI. The unique character of GI lies in the integration of these four basic features within a meaningful context of an issue worthy of investigation (Sharan & Sharan, 1992).

Investigation refers to the general orientation toward learning adopted by the teacher and student. When a group of learners is carrying out a group investigation project, it becomes an inquiry community, and each participant is an investigator who coordinates his or her inquiry within the group and class common purpose. Thus, in Thelen's (1981) words, the class is both an inquiry community and a community of inquirers.

Interaction is essential to the successful use of GI. Students and teachers need to learn and practice effective interaction as they work in groups. Peer learning in GI is the vehicle by which students and teachers encourage one another, elaborate on each other's ideas, help each other focus on the task, and confront one another's ideas with opposing points of view. Intellectual and social interaction are the means by which learners rework their personal knowledge in light of the new knowledge gathered by the group in the course of the investigation (Sharan & Hertz-Lazarowitz, 1980; Thelen, 1981).

Interpretation of the combined findings is a process of negotiation between personal knowledge and new knowledge, and between ideas and information contributed by other members of the group. Facilitating the process of interpretation through group interaction is consistent with Dewey's view of education as well as with the constructionist approach to cognition. GI provides learners with the opportunity to interact with others who have investigated different aspects of the same general topic, and who contributed different perspectives on that topic. In this context, interpretation is a social, cognitive, and intellectual process par excellence.

Learner motivation in GI is intrinsic. GI motivates learners to take an active role in determining what and how they will learn. It motivates students and teachers to choose investigation issues that are connected to their own needs, curiosity, experience, feelings, and values, and are relevant to the general community (Sarason, 1996). The decision of the topic for the GI is a social act, which can empower thinking and critical perspectives of the GI participants. A meaningful investigation is an expression of a choice.

The classical GI method as proposed by Dewey seems somewhat naive today, when we foresee the future with its complexity of technological developments and the multifaceted meaning of environments and communities. Still, we argue that its six-stage model is generic enough to guide the process of social investigation in the TPLC and in the classrooms.

The six stages of the GI model are as follows:

Stage 1: Class determines subtopics and organizes into research groups.

Stage 2: Groups plan their investigation.

Stage 3: Groups carry out their investigation.

Stage 4: Groups plan their presentation or feedback.

Stage 5: Groups make their presentation.

Stage 6: Teacher and students evaluate their project.

The process of GI fits the needs of the new learning environment with its advanced technological opportunities and inspired the design of the TPLC. In the new learning environment, investigation can occur over a challenging range through the use of advanced technology, promoting peer interaction, constructing interpretation, and bringing social and moral perspectives to the learning environment.

Teachers and Computers

The new era of technological developments in the last decade, and the rapid absorption of the personal computer, have created new pedagogical challenges for educators to go beyond the use of technology to implement old instructional patterns and begin using technology to reshape the learning environment.

Teachers are often criticized for their ineffective use of technology (Morton, 1996). Those teachers working in the highly computerized classroom of the future must have, in our opinion, personal experience in the day-to-day working use of the computer and its accessories. Beyond this personal experience, teachers of the future classroom should develop a new perspective on computers as an integral part of an environment that is structured to engage students in the learning process. As Morton (1996) defined such an environment, "Computer systems in schools should be viewed as structured learning environments with complex and comprehensive capabilities to access and manipulate information. . . . They should be seen as interactive learning extensions of the children themselves" (p 417).

Teachers are the agents of change to create new learning environments but unfortunately, their training usually was tailored to bringing and integrating computer technologies for the benefit of their students, whereas the teachers themselves and their experiential and meaningful learning was neglected. When a revolutionary vision fails in the school, it is only honest and humble to examine the role of the trainers in this state of affairs. The introduction of computers into schools, by various agencies and professionals, suffered many conceptual and pedagogical faults in its implementation and in the processes whereby teachers were persuaded to buy into it. We need only recall the 1970s and the insistence that teachers learn the programming language BASIC.

At the present time, and in the near future, we must empower the teachers. Being the agents of change, teachers need to be the focus of all efforts of introducing, using, and becoming experts in the new learning environment. Teachers have to become the creators and owners of the new classroom of the future. We have to understand that the new classroom environment with enlightened technology puts the majority of teachers in a context in which they have to unlearn and depart from many old teaching behaviors that were part of their effectiveness as teachers. At the same time, they have to explore and intensively learn new teaching behaviors, in which they are novices and frequently behind their students. This is a complex psychological process, and teachers as well as students have different learning styles and need support systems to accomplish the goals of revolutionizing the meaning of teaching–learning.

In our work with teachers, we realized that most of them have been left behind in terms of their knowledge of technology, and the gap between them and their students is growing. We found that there was little effort to address their particular type of interaction with the computer, and on the basis of our work, we offer a typology of computer users among the teachers and suggestions for empowering them.

The first type is the *anxious computer user*, who has never touched a computer in his or her life and is afraid of working with it. Such users perceive the computer as something complicated, which demands a lot of learning, "not for their own generation." Often, they are attracted to the computer but give up approaching it before they even try. This type is frequent among teachers, but it is possible to correct this psychological state by nonthreatening guidance tailored to the teacher's style and path of learning, and by personal patient guidance.

The second type is the *limited user*. This teacher or person has managed to learn one or two software products (e.g., a simple word processor) and enjoys working with it. They are limited to what they know, afraid to experiment with new fields or procedures. Such users do not have extensive knowledge of the computer's peripheral operations (DOS, Windows) and perceive it as a somewhat more advanced tool than the old tools they knew before. Limited users are conservative, sticking to the same software year after year, not even upgrading their software or computer. Limited computer users can become enlightened (the third type) by being exposed to the various user-friendly software and working in an icon-driven environment.

The third type is the *enlightened user,* who has considerable experience working with computers. These users know the advantages of the computer and perceive it as an enjoyable and creative device. They take an interest in the computer software market and are willing to learn new software by themselves (or with minimal instruction). Such users are less conservative, aspire to broaden their knowledge, are ready to be venturesome with databases, communicate via the Internet, and explore and experiment with computer-related innovations. In the new technological learning environment, these teachers, with the understanding of the intellectual benefits (as users) and the pedagogical benefits (as teachers) of the computer, are the types who will make the difference.

The fourth type is the *computer freak,* who has become addicted to the computer. This type is characterized by an obsessive drive to collect and master software and computer products. They spend long hours linking up to databases and peers, surfing the "highways" of the Internet. The computer freak is found in almost every classroom today; usually it is the student, not the teacher. Often they increase frustration among other classmates who are not such whizzes. Educating teachers to be enlightened computer users is crucial, in our view, for their work in the 21st century learning environment. Thus, working with the different types of teachers was part of the TPLC.

The Curriculum of the TPLC

The intent of the TPLC curriculum was to help teachers prepare for the classroom of the future. In the SELA project, the investigation topic chosen was planning the city of the future. This topic had two phases: studying an existing city—in our case Haifa—where or in whose area most of the participants lived, and then, based on this phase of investigation, planning the city of the future.

In this section, we describe the elements of the TPLC curriculum, provide a detailed description of its implementation, and highlight the general areas of curriculum impact. Table 12.1 presents 11 elements of the TPLC curricula. Teachers in the TPLC program participated in 12 sessions in which they researched and learned new, complex, interdisciplinary topics, using advanced technology (the word processor, multimedia software, and data banks) and worked in cooperative and collaborative working teams.

The TPLC Sequence Of Activities

The sequence of the 12 meetings of the TPLC are presented briefly in the following section. A typical session usually lasted 3 to 4 hours and included the four areas described earlier: cognitive, social, technological, and curricular. Generating questions, clarifying concepts, and working on research are examples of

TABLE 12.1
TPLC—Elements of the Curricula

---

1. *Cooperative learning:* Ways of dividing the class into learning groups; obtaining skills in co-operation and in prosocial behavior such as information exchange, active thinking by exchanging ideas, effective communication, tolerance, openness, sensitivity, and the ability to admit mistakes.

2. *Use of advanced technology:* Learning to use the computer, work with multimedia software and databanks (local and abroad).

Stages of GI with Advanced Technologies

3. *Formulating the topic for investigation and dividing it into subtopics:* Brainstorming, discussing ways of dividing complex subjects into subtopics, defining methods of organizing topics and subtopics hierarchically.

4. *Raising questions for investigation and problem solving:* Arranging the questions hierarchically and according to related topics—exchanging questions with peers; discussing ways of obtaining answers.

5. *Creating and planning work program:* Discussing decisions related to scheduling; division of task work; assigning authority, responsibility, and roles to team members.

6. *Gathering information with advanced computer-network technology:* Academic investigation with various resources and computerized data banks; making judgments about the information; expansion and reduction of information.

7. *Dealing with nontextual information:* Working with maps, tables, graphs, and photographs.

8. *Analysis and comprehension of texts:* Working on academic and scientific literacy. Discussing variety of text structures; strategic reading aimed at formulating questions; abstracting; distinguishing main issues; identifying key terms as a guide for further research.

9. *The writing process:* Working on the model of writing as a process: drafting, reviewing, editing, peer reviewing, and publishing. The final product was a multimedia and written professional product.

10. *Preparing and presenting an oral report:* Working on the structure of the report for the TPLC, and examining in what ways it differs from a traditional written presentation; skill building for a multimedia presentation, emphasizing rhetoric of presentations, and audiovisual devices.

11. *Evaluation:* Working on developing criteria for creating a variety of ways to evaluate each team's multimedia products and subproducts. Evaluation takes place within groups, between groups, and with experts in the community.

---

what we defined as the cognitive area. Helping by mutual explanation, talking and reflecting with peers about mistakes, and taking roles to facilitate group work are some examples of the social area, although these examples also have a cognitive element to them. Defining key terms for searching databases, revising a written text on a word processor, and preparing a multimedia product are some examples for the technological area. Last, but not least, deciding on resources, learning diverse content related to urban life, and planning an interdisciplinary unit are examples of development in the curricular area.

1. Getting to Know One Another. The first session was aimed at getting to know one another and becoming acquainted with the new advanced technology learning environment. An introductory lecture describing the changes that will take place in society and within schools in the near future was presented to the TPLC participants. It was aimed to motivate teachers to participate in an innovative project and to be a part of the educational avant-garde. For acquaintance purposes, the participants created a "visiting card" using a word processor that involved a short self-presentation. The visiting cards were presented in a whole-group activity, which allowed a social and personal investigation into the composition of the group. The teachers began the construction of the TPLC from their own explanation of whether the cards and people actually mirrored the uniqueness of persons and the composition of the TPLC. This activity also served as an introduction to computers and a demonstration of the difficulties in making a "self-abstract" from all the information one possessed. This meeting integrated social, academic, and technological elements.

2. Creating and Investigating an Interdisciplinary Theme. The second session focused on creating an interdisciplinary curriculum for the investigative theme. An introductory lecture about thematic and interdisciplinary curricula, and their growing relevance for education in the postmodern world, was presented. The features of what constitutes a good interdisciplinary subject were discussed. The TPLC agreed that an interdisciplinary theme should be real and of high relevance to the students, the community they live in, and even on the national and international agenda. The theme would require making contact with people and agencies out of schools, be intellectually challenging by encouraging a range of highly academic activities, have considerable accessible valuable information, and include cognitive, academic, and social ingredients. Planning the city of the future seemed to be such a topic

3. Dividing an Interdisciplinary and Complex Topic into Subtopics. The third session challenged the TPLC in designing the units of the theme. Breaking the whole into parts and discerning interdependency among subtopics demanded understanding and elaboration as well as other high-level cognitions. The TPLC went through much brainstorming (Osbom, 1953) about the various features of urban life. Presenting many views and bringing up different arguments while negotiating around conflicts in the group were the TPLC's cognitive ways of constructing an organized and to some extent agreed–on conceptual map to work on the investigation of the topic. The final conceptual map of the theme had eight subtopics. These features of urban life resembled city information indexes or phone books: (a) education; (b) culture and leisure; (c) city services and urban infrastructures; (d) population and religions; (e) building and landscape; (f) transportation; (g) commerce, industry and tourism; and (h) the quality of the environment.

4. Creating the TPLC Teams. The fourth session was structured to systematically create the teams within the TPLC. After some discussion, the TPLC chose to structure itself by maximizing the heterogeneity of the participants in a team using the following variables: sex, ethnicity, religious affiliation, subject-matter expertise, knowledge of computers, and special talents such as graphics, writing, and public speaking.

The team members were then assigned to produce a logo and name of the team by a two-part computer activity. In the first part, each team divided into pairs, in which one member knew how to use Paintbrush—Windows' graphic software (the "teacher")—and the other did not (the "learner"). Every 5 minutes, the roles were reversed, so both the teacher and the learner explained and worked on the computer. Following the pair activity, teams of four designed their logo and name, which became the first part of the multimedia presentation, to be used all through the TPLC training.

5. Choosing the Team Subtopic and Introducing Multimedia Software. In the fifth session, the teams began their process of investigation. Each team listed three out of the eight subtopics presented earlier (Session 3) that they most wanted to research. Efforts were made to ensure that teams were interested in the topic of investigation. If more than one team was interested in the same topic, the team leaders tried to divide the aspects somewhat differently so that all the teams would be satisfied with their selected research topic.

Following the GI model, the group started to plan and construct their work while they utilized many cognitive and metacognitive strategies. Among the strategies used were decision making in relation to organizing information and building dynamic, flexible, hierarchical orders of facts, ideas and associations. Participants came to understand that distinctions can be drawn between top-down or bottom-up thinking, that one can work from the general to the specific or vice versa. This fifth stage was cognitively the most difficult for the teachers and we tried to provide appropriate support.

In the second part of this TPLC session, the teachers were introduced to an Israeli multimedia software by the name of "KNOW."[1] This software is used for planning, building, and analyzing teams' projects based on multimedia resources, and it enables the user (in this case, the team) to import various types of resources such as text, pictures, graphics, videos, animations, and sounds, and then to create hypermedia links between them. The links can be presented graphically as a conceptual map that is built automatically by the system according to the links defined between the resources. It is possible to navigate between the resources without any prior programming knowledge. This navigating capability, along with the conceptual map, makes the software into a tool with enormous learning potential. It supports nonlinear multidimensional thinking; fosters a variety of thinking skills such as organization, sorting, and distinguishing essential from nonessential elements; and encourages students

---

[1] Svivot Company, Olesh, Israel 42855.

and teachers to plan and analyze. This kind of software enables teachers and students to concentrate on complex multidisciplinary problems and also to learn how to use multimedia tools as part of a team effort.

In this new environment, much of the planning of the TPLC was on computer, so the multimedia work accompanied the investigation of each team. Every question, draft, drawing, picture, thought, and piece of information was placed on the team screen—to create the team's computerized and dynamic portfolio. While working, the teams produced and reproduced many concept maps, constantly retrieved data, connected and created new databases, and rethought the organization of the information they collected as they went on with their investigation. One teacher reacted as follows:

> What a difference from what we usually do in the classroom with the computer . . . now I see how it helps me to think and organize my instruction. . . . I never worked with a team on such things, it is a new world for me. . . . I love the fact that I can put so many thoughts into the computer and work on them again and again myself and with a team. . . . I wish we could do it with our students.[2]

6. Raising Questions as a Preliminary Stage in Investigation. This session was devoted to raising and formulating enlightened questions and key concepts as a prerequisite to searching for information and becoming more familiar with the computer. The TPLC experimented with techniques for generating questions (see Table 12.2) to come up with questions that would identify the many subtopics they wanted to study, focus the computerized search for information, and allow the gathering of information from primary and secondary sources on the information highways. The training for raising questions followed GI procedure.

The second part of the session upgraded the teachers' work level with the computer. Each TPLC team was asked to place on the screen their investigation topic, their division into subtopics, and the major questions they wanted to explore on each of the subtopics. The computer products and outputs, prepared earlier via word processor and graphics programs, were imported into the multimedia team screen. At this stage, intensive peer learning took place: Teachers helped each other acquire the knowledge and necessary computer skills for progressing on the GI tasks.

Observing the teams, we saw one pair for over an hour, a 25-year-old religious Muslim male teacher working and helping a Jewish religious female teacher, twice his age, integrate her thoughts into the mode of advanced technology, and at the same time, acquire some basic computer skills. Such teachable segments of time were the essence of the TPLC, where ethnic, religious,

---

[2]The quotations from teachers were collected as part of a research project in which participants were promised anonymity.

TABLE 12.2
Training for Raising Questions:
An Example From "Teams Working on City Roads"

Questions About Roads	Sources of Information
What is the road plan in Haifa?	Maps, atlases
Which highways go in and out of Haifa?	Maps
How many roads are constructed in Haifa every year? What are the general principles for road construction?	Haifa Municipality Department of Building and Transportation, Data bank of the Transportation Authority in Israel
Why are roads built in certain places? What are the economic and social considerations of developing roads?	Department of Public Works, Department of Road Engineering at the Technion, Statistical data bank of Israel
Where are roads placed?	Department of Public Works, Department of Engineering at the Technion
How are roads planned and how are roads authorized? Who plans / authorizes / implements?	Municipal Building Department City Engineer
When were the first roads constructed in Haifa?	Atlas of Haifa and the Carmel
What roads are particularly busy, when, and why?	Police, Traffic Department

and other people's categorizations were overlooked by the participants in their aim of meeting the tasks before them as a community.

7. and 8. Knowing How to "Swim in the Sea of Information." The synergy of working with information and transferring it into meaningful knowledge was the focus of the two following sessions of the TPLC. This challenge was evident in each of the following sessions. In the next paragraphs, we describe three issues: the meaning of getting information and constructing knowledge, the significance of becoming a strategic reader and strategic writer, and working with complex computerized databanks.

1. Getting Information and Constructing Knowledge. Production and construction of knowledge consists of four stages: defining the desired product, obtaining raw data, processing the raw data into structures of knowledge, and representing the knowledge effectively to other people. The TPLC came up with different strategies to maximize efficacy of teachers' work with information brought up by the participants, based on their experience.

One main issue for clarification was the role of the teacher as a professional, occupied with obtaining materials for learning and teaching in this changing world. Strengths and limitations of traditional and nontraditional sources and the differentiation among various types of information—primary and secondary, raw and processed data—were presented and discussed. The TPLC reviewed a great variety of sources for information, such as catalogued and processed information found in textbooks, journals, newspapers, encyclopedias, CD-ROMs and computer software. Still, learning will involve contact with primary sources, such as questionnaires, interviews, observation, databanks of social institutions, many networks, and CMC, which must then be processed by the user. The message that individuals at all levels have responsibility to generate information and construct it for learning is a revolution. New skills are required to obtain and process information in the future.

2. Strategic Reading and Strategic Writing. Strategic reading and strategic writing, which involve metacognitive skills, are now becoming more significant than before (Bereiter & Scardamalia, 1987). Skills needed for strategic reading of an essay were experienced and practiced in the TPLC with scientific material in the form of journal articles or information from the databank. Strategic reading with a partner or in a group was based on the literature of collaborative reading and writing. These stem from such methods as reciprocal teaching (Brown & Palinscar, 1989) and scripted cooperation (O'Donnell & Dansereau, 1992). Writing within a collaborative context was practiced by the TPLC throughout their investigation, with the use of elaborated writing techniques (Hertz-Lazarowitz & Shadel, 1996).

3. Working With Rich Computerized Data Banks. The rich technology environment blends reading and writing while searching for information from computerized data banks. In this TPLC meeting, participants in cooperative groups searched the university data banks for relevant papers on the aspect of urban life that the team was researching. The knowledge of how to work with computer data banks was new to many of the teachers. They liked it and were excited about it. After this session, the TPLC used university and other related data banks frequently and regularly, read papers, and wrote with the multimedia software, as they continued their investigation.

9. Constructing and Evaluating the Team's Multimedia Presentations. In the first half of the session, teams of teachers continued their work and constructed multimedia text-based presentations on their investigative aspect of urban life. The teachers used the cognitive, social, and computer-related skills they had acquired in their presentations. They constructed a feasible work plan leading to the desired product; setting and adhering to a timetable, planning and organizing the teamwork (division of responsibilities and authorities), computerized information search, information processing, asking questions, and using a word processor, graphics, and multimedia software.

In the second part of this session, the TPLC formulated the need to present parts of their product as a midsession team investigation product. A number of objectives for this computer presentation were suggested: setting dates and objectives for peer feedback and evaluation, reviewing where each team was in its work, determining which objectives had already been attained, and identifying which tasks remained to be done—fostering between-team exchange and sharing of information. This process facilitated interdisciplinary perspectives in the research and making room for peer response in order to improve the final presentation. Three forms of presentations were suggested: (a) reporting to the entire group by each team, in order to construct a holistic and panoramic view of all the investigations community; (b) submission of a written and visual report by each team to all the other teams or posting the report on the team's progress board on the walls of the room; and (c) pairing two teams and sharing the product each produced to receive detailed and useful feedback on it.

The TPLC summarized the main criteria for evaluating multimedia presentations. These included the following: Are the questions relevant and focused and do they cover the main issues of investigation? Are the answers to the questions focused, based on knowledge, and enlightening? Is the structure of building the multimedia presentation logical? Is it easy to browse through the content of the display? Are the categories organized in solid hierarchical order? Is the multimedia presentation rich and based not only on texts, but also on pictures, and later in the course, on maps and illustrations? Is the presentation aesthetic? These TPLC evaluation activities helped each team to revise the team presentations while taking into account the other team's feedback.

10. Dealing With Nontextual Information. In this session, the TPLC was exposed to a demonstration of nontextual presentations provided by computer, such as electronic sheet, tables, graphs, bars, and pies. The teachers discussed each of the presentations as a vehicle to coordinate different types of data—continuous data (graph) or noncontinuous data (bars), general picture (graph) versus detailed picture (table)—and to integrate voice, sound, data, and images into one package. We focused on maps as an example of nontextual information. After a short lecture accompanied by demonstrations and exercises about maps as information presenters, we asked the participants to draw a map of the route from their home to school. A teacher from another school tried to find his colleague's route on a real map. One of the teachers said, "It's amazing, I have driven from home to school hundreds of times, yet there is little resemblance between my cognitive map and reality. I realized that just a few details have been stored in memory."

This exercise highlighted the many cognitive challenges and proficiencies needed for drawing and interpreting maps (Almog, 1993). Four proficiencies were analyzed by the TPLC. Participants needed to (a) translate the concrete world into an abstract medium—developing the imagination, (b) translate three-dimensional reality into a two-dimensional map, (c) decide what to include on a map (given the limitation of the scale) by distinguishing the important (for the drawer and for the reader) from the trivial, and (d) translate a medium of vertical projection to horizontal projection—exercising mental rotation in different visual directions. Acquiring proficiency with maps provides practice in looking at reality from different points of view.

11. Haifa: The City Today—Concluding the Subject.   In this session, each team gave its final presentation and the multimedia product of its investigation subject related to Haifa. Two perspectives based on the investigation were presented side by side: (a) the current state of what exists in Haifa urban life in the various subtopics, and (b) the problems and challenges that relate to planning the city in the future. Each team presentation led to a discussion about the topic, and tentative suggestions and conclusions were obtained.

During the process of presenting the multimedia products, we focused on presentations before an audience. We discussed the differences between written and oral presentation and the things worth focusing on in an oral presentation. The presentations were of good quality and the TPLC participants had a feeling of accomplishment. Some teachers commented that this experience was the first time they had the right training and guidance to integrate technology with challenging investigation while working in "real cooperation." One teacher said, "If I had been trained this way a couple of years ago, when they started teaching us computers, I could have reached the sky with my students long ago."

12. Planning the City of the Future—Teamwork and Multimedia Presentations. After the TPLC participants were exposed to nontextual information and especially to maps and images, they incorporated them by working on picture scanning and recording sounds into their multimedia presentations for planning the city of the future. For this activity, teams included between-group experts in different investigation topics. Each new team had experts from four to five groups.

The new intersubject teams started with a brainstorming activity of "what is the city of the future?" Some groups placed it on the moon, some wanted to create it on a desert island. As the discussion went on, and questions and dilemmas were raised, the groups gradually returned to their work on Haifa, the city of today. They created multimedia presentations of the city of the future, and offered educated and creative solutions to the diverse problems they had discovered in their previous investigation of Haifa today. In creating these new presentations, the TPLC participants repracticed the cognitive, social, and technological skills they had acquired in their previous TPLC activities. At this stage, they were able to apply advanced computer techniques of picture scanning and sound recording.

Summary

Four areas of skill were conceptualized and practiced simultaneously in the training for investigation with advanced technology in the TPLC: the cognitive area, the social area, and the technological area; these three areas were integrated within the curricular area, in the context of advanced technology.

DISCUSSION

The significance of using the TPLC for teachers' development is discussed in terms the TPLC as facilitator of teachers' professional development, as a social construct of learning in various aspects, and as facilitator of transfer of learning to actual classrooms.

TPLC Facilitates Teachers' Professional Development

The TPLC provided a context for teachers' development. They learned many instructional behaviors, and enriched both their pedagogical and content knowledge (Shulman & Sparks, 1992). Together with learning new behaviors, teachers had to unlearn old, nonrelevant learning–teaching behaviors (see Table 12.3). Learning and extinction of learning was evident in each meeting of the TPLC. For example, experienced teachers usually know how to plan curricula, design learning tasks, and look for resources for their teaching, but they do it mostly alone.

In the TPLC, teachers learned to do these very same actions in partnership and within advanced new technologies. They worked in multidisciplinary teams

TABLE 12.3
Key Characteristics of Teachers' Peer Learning

Type of Knowledge	Specifics
Professional Development	• Learning versus unlearning instructional behavior • Novice versus expert experience • Understanding the social construction of the Teachers' Peer Learners Community • Designing interdisciplinary curricula • Working with advanced technology • Structured social, cognitive, and instructional reflection
Social Construction of Learning Concepts of knowledge	• Information accessing and processing • Distributed cognition • Constructing a network of ideas within an advanced computer learning environment
Zone of proximal development	• Helping discourse • Instructional discourse • Investigative discourse • Subject-matter mastery

within a community, they had to encounter teachers from other schools, they had to collaborate with different ethnic and cultural groups, they had to design curricula in an interdisciplinary new theme, and all their activities became public.

The most effective mechanism to master each part of the TPLC and all of them together was the construction of a group of experts with unity of purpose. Even though the teachers were novices at many of the skills and constructs embedded in the TPLC, the staff regarded them as mature and expert professionals. Indeed, their investigative conversations and instructional discourse were the source for the quality of the activities in the TPLC.

For many teachers, it was the first time in their careers that they became the actors in the process of learning, not the observers or the managers. The need to use advanced computer technologies gave them a sense of being novice learners, concomitant with a sense of being experts in other aspects of the TPLC context. The technology facilitated and framed mutual exploration and interactive learning and increased helping among the teachers.

Reflection, one of the significant qualities of expert teachers (Berliner 1986; Schon 1983), took place in each segment of the TPLC. Reflection was structured into the TPLC in special segments of time, after certain sequence of activities. The TPLC offered at least three objects of reflection: social processes, cognitive processes, and the interrelations between the TPLC elements. Each such reflection had two different directions: one focused on the here and now and the other on the classroom; we termed the latter *transfer reflection* to differentiate it from actual transfer. We could assess the first in the TPLC context, and the second during the year following the TPLC. An example of social reflection is illustrated next. After planning and preparing their self-presentation in the computerized visiting cards (see Meeting 1), teachers' reflection dealt with themselves as participants, about issues such as the ways they chose to present themselves, as part of their visiting cards, and what one could learn from it. In the reflective discussion, the teachers understood the many elements of the heterogeneous composition of the group, and the fear of presenting them before everybody was discussed (one participant chose to present himself only by his identity number and address).

Only after completing this type of reflection did the teachers move to the second type—transfer reflection—where they focused on their role as teachers performing a similar activity in their classroom. They discussed the content of the activity, the feasibility of doing it in a crowded classroom, and most significantly, the teachers' vision of their actual students in such an activity. The combination of self- and group reflection of the teachers as participants, and the transfer reflection to their classroom, came to a meaningful closure when the teachers realized that the same personal and cultural constructs and processes existed within each group and each classroom.

An example of cognitive reflection is the stage of formulating questions during the first stage of the GI (see Meeting 6). Teachers easily generated a long and ample list of questions for investigation, but when they had to decide what the main questions were, and what was worth investigating, they encountered many difficulties in establishing criteria for making such decisions. Only in the reflection process did they realize that usually, most of their instruction time was devoted to generating activities for themselves and their students, without taking the time to think of the value and meaning of such activities for quality teaching leading to high-level learning. In many other realizations during reflection, teachers saw themselves as unique individuals in the teaching–learning bond.

In the reflection process dealing with computer environment and the TPLC context, many of them moved through the novice–expert continuum in two areas: (a) the computer learning environment, and (b) the orchestration of investigative interdisciplinary teams. With respect to learning about the computer environment, teachers reported being scared and concerned that their students were more knowledgeable than they were. They also expressed concern about managing complex teams investigating complex interdisciplinary topics. The same teachers felt themselves to be experts in many other components of the TPLC, where they could integrate their experience, knowledge, and understanding, based on their professional strengths.

What we learned about professional development through the TPLC context is that for teachers, it seems that it is only possible to change when teachers' areas of novice-level knowledge are embedded in knowledge in which they are expert. Thus, empowerment of teachers should always build on the strength of teachers. This is especially true in regard to complex technologies, where so many teachers are anxious and feel incompetent. Therefore, training for using computer technologies should not be conducted as a separate aspect of teachers' professional development. Another aspect of professional development is that reflection as a major process in the TPLC should be connected to all the dimensions of the new learning environment, and should allow for transfer reflection. As one of the teachers remarked:

> I participated in so many courses on using computer in my teaching, and it did not work for me. The training was so bad and it made me feel dumb. This TPLC was different: I worked with some teachers who knew a lot and helped me, some who were like me in their level of mastering the technology, and some who knew even less than myself, and I could help them. But we all were respected as teachers who knew a lot in other areas, we were not judged as users of technology alone, but rather as educators. Here finally I could really master lots of skills I never believed I would. (see Footnote 2)

TPLC as a Social Construction of Learning

The second significant aspect of the TPLC for the teachers was the enhancement of their ability to construct their own social context. Following Vygotsky's (1978) concepts of constructivist theory, we examined the TPLC in relation to concepts of knowledge and the zone of proximal development (see Table 12.3).

Concepts of Knowledge. Knowledge can be transmitted and transformed in three channels: unidirectional, bidirectional and multidirectional (Sharan & Hertz-Lazarowitz, 1980), and in three patterns of peer interaction: peer tutoring, peer cooperation, and peer collaboration (Damon & Phelps, 1989; Hertz-Lazarowitz, 1989). At the TPLC, teachers applied at least three types of different concepts of knowledge (presented in Table 12.3). In the first one, accessing and processing information, unidirectional transmission of knowledge takes place. Knowledge is passed from one individual to another, and peer tutoring or traditional teaching occurs. With advanced technology, such learning is evident in the acquisition of simple computer skills. As knowledge develops to become elaborated for transmission and production, interaction becomes mostly bidirectional, with some multidirectionality. Such learning is evident in working with databases or generating and selecting topics for inquiry, and requires the form of cooperative peer learning.

As teachers engaged in production of knowledge, for example, in finding the interdependency between tourism, commerce, and education in the city, they were engaged in distributed cognition learning in forms of peer collaboration. Argyris (1982) suggested the concept of action-based knowledge, where teachers have to transfer the knowledge gained at the TPLC to their future actions in the classroom. The transfer of the various types of knowledge cannot be the sole responsibility of one teacher, because teamwork and cooperation are a part of the project in each school. In this way, change is both an individual and an organizational endeavor.

As the interaction among the TPLC members became more elaborated and constructivist, each teacher became a possible source of learning and a potential peer for cognitive development. It was recognized that knowledge was constructed through discussions, inter- and intragroup conflicts, and arguments as members were presenting different opinions and views and networking their ideas. The computer multimedia software (KNOW) facilitates and empowers creative thinking. The TPLC combines the structures of peer tutoring, cooperation, and collaboration (McCarthy & McMahon, 1992), and each member was perceived as a knowing other (Damon & Phelps, 1989). Knowledge was negotiated and constructed in the investigation process, in all mirrors of the classroom: the computer environment; the learning tasks; and the instructional, communicational, social and cognitive elements (presented earlier in this chapter, and in Hertz-Lazarowitz, 1992).

Zone of Proximal Development (ZPD). Peer learning with children relies on the concept of the ZPD (Vygotsky, 1978; see Hogan & Tudge, chap. 2, this volume). Regarding adults, the meaning of this important concept in the constructivist theory is less defined. When teachers interact in peer learning in the TPLC, we may assume that the basic features of ZPD are relevant but that adult ZPD interaction might have additional characteristics. There are at least three features that are common to children and adults. For teachers, there is a difference between actual and potential development, and what can be achieved with (adult) peers is different from what can be accomplished alone; there is an implicit notion of transference of knowledge, shared by either children or adults, that facilitates development (McCarthy & McMahon, 1992).

Newman, Griffin, and Cole (1989) focused on the joint activity in which participants (elementary school children) exercised differential responsibility on a collaborative task by virtue of having different expertise. In the next paragraphs, we delineate four unique areas of adults' expertise that we observed in practice among the teachers in the TPLC. These areas included being expert in the discourse of helping, being expert in creating high-quality instructional discourses, being expert in working with challenging investigative tasks, and finally, being expert at various disciplines while creating an interdisciplinary team (see Table 12.3).

The first area relates to the mechanism of the interactive discourse of helping, by which the teachers exercised their differential responsibilities. Nelson-Le Gall (1992) conceptualized help seeking and help giving in the learning context as a complex and challenging phenomenon, because social-cognitive and cognitive-motivational correlates accompany every act of learning (see Webb & Farivar, chap. 5, this volume). In the TPLC, help seeking and help giving were the most frequently observed interaction (Hertz-Lazarowitz, 1992). Adults, probably more than children, have self-knowledge of the areas where they need help, and can more easily recognize others who can help them. Thus, elements of effective help seeking such as self- and other knowledge, self- and other evaluation, and strategies for help seeking and help giving were part of the interactive behaviors of the teachers. Whereas research shows that children lack the skills of seeking help effectively (Nelson-Le Gall, 1992; Webb & Farivar, 1994), teachers were very effective in helping. The dynamics and continuous negotiation with others facilitates the process of approximation for cognitive development. Thus, helping interactions were a crucial element in the mastery-oriented proximity of different zones of development within the TPLC.

The quality of the instructional learning and teaching discourse was the second area in which the adult teachers were experts. The context of the TPLC fostered effective peer learning by various qualities of discourse. Dialogues were continual, lengthy, creative, and dynamic. More opportunities for dialogue, which included demonstration of competence, modeling, and other discourses of cooperation that "rouse mind to life," as Tharp and Gallimore (1988) demonstrated among children, were in action. This high-quality discourse allowed processes of internalization in knowledge, attitudes, and beliefs to occur.

The structure and content of the investigative tasks of the TPLC, as presented earlier in this chapter, reflected the third area of expertise. The tasks were interdisciplinary in nature, investigative and creative, and therefore generated a high quality of interactive discourse. Teachers brought to the GI process many aspects of their personal and professional lives. These included their experiences, their background in different subject matters, their views and philosophy of life and teaching, their reflection of the processes they experienced, and their cultural and even religious perspectives. The outcomes of their learning as presented in the quality of the TPLC were evident in the oral and written reports of the teachers and in their multimedia productions, and their reflections and summaries about the TPLC experiences were of adult quality.

The fourth element that contributed to the professional growth of the teachers was the fact that teachers were expert in different subject domains. The interactive exploration of geography, history, science, literature, religion, math, and English created a truly interdisciplinary community. In conversations at the end of a school year during which they implemented SELA in their classrooms, teachers noted that the most important elements in the teacher's ability to become a teacher in the new learning environment were twofold: first, to give up centrality as a teacher (toward the students), and second, to give up centrality of subject matter and create an interdisciplinary team.

The TPLC as a Facilitator of Transfer of Learning to the Classroom

The original goal of the TPLC was to develop a group of teachers who would bring this new learning environment into their schools. Thus, the facilitators of the SELA project followed the teachers as they implemented the same investigation topic (the city in the present and in the future), using advanced technologies in their classrooms (Salomon & Almog, 1996). The final section of this chapter describes portraits of different transfer for each school, 1 year after the TPLC training was completed.

In the first school, a religious girls school, four teachers participated in the TPLC. These four teachers (all female) created strong bonds of peer work in the TPLC. Each of them was a type of entrepreneur. They went back to their school, highly motivated to implement the project as faithfully as possible. They combined two classrooms and created two investigative learners' communities, using their 4 weekly hours for the project (the time formerly devoted to traditional computer lessons). Working in TPLC in the SELA project, they created a difference in the school. The students mastered the technology and implemented the investigative process in a learning climate of an exciting happening. The project and these students became the pride of the school. Thus, the transfer and implementation of the TPLC to create a new learning environment was a success story. As one teacher commented:

> I have been teaching at this school for many years; my own daughter graduated from it. This year, while I was teaching with my team in the SELA project, my

daughter began her university education. While I was creating the new learning classroom, my daughter was struggling with simple computer procedures and writing processes at the university. I felt we hadn't taught those things properly before. My 8th-grade girls today can manage many of these skills and activities better than my own daughter. Indeed, she herself came to my classroom and was amazed by the girl's performances, blaming me (her mom), for her low level performance.

In the second school, the team of teachers included three female teachers. In the TPLC, this team did not achieve peer collaboration. The two senior teachers were very involved in the investigation project but were less involved in mastering the advanced technologies. They left work with the computer to the one young teacher. On returning to their school, the same pattern was observed in their classroom as they implemented the SELA project. The investigative process was of a high quality of learning, but the integration with technology was much less advanced. In these classrooms, GI was similar to the earlier learning environment, and the excitement and richness that the technology could bring to the students were neglected. The technology and computers in the classroom served more as tools for writing (word processors) and for development of various simple skills. In general, students experienced less peer-interactive learning in these classrooms. This transfer was partial, covering only one aspect of the TPLC.

One of the teachers reflected on the project in her classroom by saying, "For me, the great contribution of SELA project is the improvement in the social aspects of learning. The GI contributed to the positive social perception of the classroom climate. Even though the technology was not at work most of the year, the project was still a success. . . . Computers are only tools, nothing more."

The third school was an Arab school, from which only two mathematics teachers participated in the TPLC. These teachers were advanced users of the computer and greatly helped other participants. In other areas of the TPLC, they were less involved. On returning to their school, they decided to initiate a similar training for the staff of the school (30 teachers). During the year, this plan was gradually translated into traditional training sessions for computer technology. The in-service training was quite remote from the TPLC notion, but teachers gained two elements of the TPLC: exposure to the computer and overcoming their anxiety, and initial interdisciplinary planning of their own Arab city. The pattern of transfer in this school was an extension of parts of the TPLC. These two teachers did not implement the new learning environment but rather took it upon themselves, with the assistance of the university staff, to bring some of the TPLC messages to all the teachers.

The fourth school had four teachers in the TPLC. When they returned to their classrooms, they were faced with some problems, like the others. However, motivation to cope with initial frustrations was low for this team. These were excellent teachers, very motivated and active in the TPLC, but in their own school they were very busy with other tasks and roles. The pattern of transfer in this school was to reduce the complex and abundant plan of the TPLC project to "technologies." For instance, they used groups in the classroom but composed them poorly. They divided the theme of the city into small subcategories, but the topics they offered or directed the students to work on were not challenging. They avoided technology and used it rarely. The project in this school was a very pale image of what had been planned and resembled traditional teaching.

On reflection on the project in this school, those teachers attributed the limited implementation to external factors: "If I were less busy with other things in the school . . .; my partner was sick a long time . . .; one needs more hours to implement such a project . . .; I thought the students would learn the computer technologies faster . . .; I didn't think the students would need so much help."

From the descriptions of these four schools, we can conclude that the transfer and implementation pattern of the SELA project were of three types: (a) full and successful transfer, in one school; (b) partial transfer of only one element of the project, either in the GI or the technological aspect (Schools 2 and 3); and (c) distorted transfer and misuse of the educational innovation the originators had in mind. Salomon and Almog (1996) present three factors that affect transfer to schools: teacher preparation, teachers' fatigue, and organizational support.

A close examination of the various modes of transfer revealed additional factors: Isolating either technology or the GI process of the TPLC reduced the potential for creating a new learning environment. By partial transfer, teachers did increase some skills, mostly in using computers, but the connection of these skills to creating the classroom of the future did not take place. One important finding of the analysis of the actual implementation of the SELA project in the classrooms indicated that in the schools where teachers continued to work in teams, a high quality of transfer and implementation took place.

In conclusion, a new learning environment for the future classroom can be successfully put into practice from a well-planned theory or vision, when several conditions exist simultaneously: implementation must takes place in all units of the learning–teaching environment. In the project SELA, it includes the TPLC context, GI process, interdisciplinary approach, and mastery of advanced computer technologies. Beside the realization of future vision, the commitment of the school organization and its leadership is essential. The concepts of TPLC and of learners' communities within a school system or a classroom context are not easy to uphold if the school as an organization is not committed to the concept. This chapter outlined a curriculum that holds potential for creating a meaningful model for the classroom of the future, when and if its core vision is cherished.

Concluding Remarks

ANGELA M. O'DONNELL
Rutgers University

ALISON KING
California State University San Marcos

What does it mean to learn with a peer? The chapters in this book include various approaches to describing the processes by which learning may occur among peers and how such processes might effectively be promoted. The role of the teacher in supporting peer learning and the implications of cognitive perspectives on such learning for teacher preparation are also discussed in a number of chapters. Based on the work presented here, we can conclude with some confidence that peer learning situations can effectively support student learning and that much is known about how to promote such learning in groups.

Any discussion of peer learning involves consideration of who is learning, how the role of peers with whom one works can be conceptualized, what it is that peers learn together, what changes as a result of the interaction, and how we can know what occurs in groups or what has been learned. The chapters in this book speak to these questions. The key question underlying many of these others is "why should we worry about the intricacies of interaction?"

The first argument to be made for being concerned with the nuances of interaction stems from practical considerations. Without a theory about why peer learning might work and for whom and on what kinds of tasks, it is hard to imagine an equitable instructional environment in which the learning of all children is promoted. Even if students do not derive the optimal benefits of from peer learning, they may still fare as well as in other forms of instruction, at least with respect to cognitive outcomes. However, poorly conducted peer learning activities can have important negative motivational effects on students, as noted in a number of the chapters in this book. It is also hard to imagine teachers making reasoned and coherent choices about activities, desired outcomes, and peer learning arrangements that are appropriate to their instructional goals without those teachers having a deep understanding of theoretical perspectives on peer learning and an ability to consider alternatives. As Woolfolk Hoy and Tschannen-Moran (chap. 11) note, it is an extremely difficult task to prepare teachers for effective support of peer learning.

The second argument that can be made in support of a concern with the nuances of interaction during peer learning is in terms of advances in theoretical understandings of human interaction in instructional contexts. Who learns, and how the peers with whom one works can be considered are central theoretical issues in peer learning research. Underlying these questions is an age-old question related to the relation between the individual and the environment. Is the peer in a learning system simply another feature of the environment from whom one can learn? Alternatively, is there something about joint action that goes beyond individual cognition, as might be suggested in more sociocultural models of learning? Arguments have been made in favor of the individual nature of knowledge acquisition and representation of knowledge (cf. Anderson, 1990) and in the favor of the social nature of such knowledge acquisition (Brown, Collins, & Duguid, 1989). Precise models of group cognition are not available, although work by Scardamalia, Bereiter, and Lamon (1994) focused on what is learned by a community of learners as represented in a network of knowledge constructed by a classroom of students. Most of the chapters in this book focused on what is learned by individuals rather than focusing on "community knowledge." Paliscar's and Herrenkohl's work on cognitive tools and intellectual roles (chap. 6) comes closest to looking at the broader community of learning in a classroom, influenced as it is by sociocultural theory.

Irrespective of whether we focus on the peers in a peer learning situation as a feature of the environment with whom one interacts or as an extension of one's cognition, what happens to the individual student as a consequence of interaction in a learning environment? Can models of individual cognition account for the effects of such interaction or is there a need for new models of "group" cognition? What does it mean to learn with a peer? Suppose you work with someone and have the opportunity to discuss a topic with this individual. If you come away from such a discussion having learned some new information or with a new perspective on the problem, are these new ideas yours? To what extent do you "own" the knowledge or information? Has learning occurred? Is knowledge individually represented? How influential was the environment? Can the individual perform competently alone after peer learning? The central idea here is a question about individual representation or joint representation and what happens as a function of the distribution of cognition between peers. Salomon (1993) might ask if there is "cognitive residue" from the interaction? Damon (1991) might ask if there is increased functionality? Can a learner only accomplish in the presence of others? There is an underlying tension here between the role of the individual and the role of the environment in influencing

behavior, and this tension has reverberated for centuries with more or less influence being attached to the role of the environment (e.g., Gibson's, 1966, ecological optics; Thorndike's law of effect, 1911) or to the individual (e.g., Chomsky, 1965). Piaget's theory (as described by De Lisi and Golbeck in chap. 2) and
Vygotsky's theory (as described by Hogan and Tudge in chap. 3) provide ways of
describing the intricate relation of environment (including the social environment) and individual cognition.

Two other developments in articulating this relation (individual and environment) include Anderson's (1983) rational analysis of behavior and the description of situated cognition (Brown et al., 1989). Anderson (1983) is most noted
for his work on skill acquisition, which he described as the development of a
series of productions. His analysis of complex cognitive behavior was in terms
of production rules comprised of if–then sequences of increasing complexity.
In his 1990 book, *The Adaptive Character of Thought,* Anderson described most
psychological theory as being conducted at a representational and algorithmic
level of analysis in which mechanisms for implementation are proposed and
used. In contrast, Anderson proposed a rational level of analysis in which human behavior could be described as purposeful and optimal, given the conditions. From this perspective, human behavior is an optimal response given the
context. Contextual cues provide the basis for selecting behavioral responses.
According to Anderson, what is needed is a characterization of the context. To
describe human behavior as optimal marked a departure from the tradition of
cognitive psychology that generally characterized human behavior as flawed.
Anderson's work also departed from tradition by assigning a critical role to contextual cues.

A second development in delineating the interactive nature of the relation
between the individual and the environment is the notion of situated cognition
(Brown et al., 1989). The basic premise of situated cognition as outlined by
Brown and colleagues is that potential for action cannot be fully described independently of the specific situation. Sometimes this is interpreted to mean that
little is transferable from one context to another.

The distinctions between the representational and the situated nature of human cognition are important when looking at the role of peers. If we emphasize
the developmental status of the individual, we may expect the role of peers to
be one of challenging that individual to increase or decrease his or her functionality as a result of peer interaction. The question of who benefits from the interaction is then one of individual development. The implications of Piaget's work
(see De Lisi & Golbeck, chap. 2) for peer learning are partly in understanding
such a role for peers. Some arrangements of peer learning such as peer tutoring
clearly emphasize that the tutee is the intended learner. If the tutor learns in the
process of tutoring, it is a rarely measured outcome. The chapters by De Lisi
and Golbeck (chap. 2) and Hogan and Tudge (chap. 3) both draw attention to the
idea that peers can have negative influences on learning. Hogan and Tudge de-

scribe this possible effect of peers as operating "behind the zone of proximal development."

De Lisi and Golbeck note that the "attainment of educational objectives using peer learning is a joint function of the students' cognitive systems and the particular content area being worked on by the peer team" (p. 36). Students' change in understanding will be enhanced in conditions of mutual respect but perturbations must occur to prompt change. The key role of the task in which children are engaged is underscored in this analysis and as Derry (chap. 8) points out, insufficient attention has been paid to developing a theory of tasks that might provide greater understanding of this important influence. Others, such as Cohen (1994a), also place tremendous importance on the nature of the task in promoting effective interaction, but there is little systematic work on the nature of tasks and their interaction with cognitive processes or support for development of cognitive change.

From a Vygotskian perspective (Hogan & Tudge, chap. 3), the burden of scaffolding the student's developing understanding lies in the skill of the adult or peer within the interactive space of the zone of proximal development. In such an analysis, the task used can provide an observable prop on which to base explanations. Webb and Farivar clearly demonstrate the complexity of effective scaffolding. This point is further emphasized in the chapter by Meloth and Deering (chap. 10).

What remains understudied is the impact of peer learning experiences on subsequent individual learning competencies. De Lisi and Golbeck and Hogan and Tudge report research with conservers and nonconservers and the subsequent performance of the nonconservers. However, within the school context, the issue of the *residue* from peer learning in terms of individual competencies is rarely addressed. In general, the chapters in this book do not speak to this issue either.

What changes for the interactants when they are collectively regarded as a unit as a result of peer interaction? Little is known about joint development, as the unit of analysis of outcome in peer learning study is most often the individual. Even then, transfer to new situations is not often assessed. The work of Hewitt and Scardamalia (1998) suggested that a classroom can be considered as a self-improving system, but we do not have a model of cognition that allows us to consider the cognitive functioning of the entire classroom as a unit (Moore & Rocklin, 1998).

An important current that underlies the consideration of the mechanisms underlying effective peer learning is the issue of measuring effective interaction and outcomes. The chapters at the beginning of this book draw our attention to the importance of not mistaking immediate change in performance as evidence of conceptual change, thus prompting a concern with measurement over time. Measurement of effective interaction is difficult. We know a great deal about the kinds of verbal processes that may prompt effective discourse that is then associated with achievement, but we do not know if these same processes are true across task types. What happens in the silences during task accomplishment? In this book, we focused primarily on cognitive perspectives on peer learning, but measurement of effective process will necessarily have to take into account the social processes that may enhance or mute effective cognition.

There is much that remains to be understood about groups. When we do observe effective interaction, what motivates its continuance? How do we effectively promote productive interaction without undermining the personal goals of participants? We need models of group cognition that allow us to understand how a group interfaces with a task. We also need a greater understanding of how effective teachers model groups and respond to such models so that we can better prepare preservice teachers and in-service teachers to promote effective peer learning and to make theoretically driven adjustments when necessary.

References

Abelson, R. P. (1995). *Statistics as principled argument*. Mahwah, NJ: Lawrence Erlbaum Associates.

Adams, D. D., & Shrum, J. (1990). The effects of microcomputer-based laboratory exercises on the acquisition of line graph construction and interpretation skills. *Journal of Research in Science Teaching, 27*, 777–787.

Almog, T. (1993). *Acquiring proficiencies in terrain navigation and spatial orientation*. Unpublished doctoral dissertation, Department for Education in Science and Technology. Technion, Haifa, Israel. (in Hebrew)

Ames, C. (1981). Competitive versus cooperative reward structure: The influence of group and individual performance factors on achievement attributions and affect. *American Educational Research Journal, 18*, 273–288.

Ames, G., & Murray, F. B. (1982). When two wrongs make a right: Promoting cognitive change by social conflict. *Developmental Psychology, 18*, 894–897.

Anderson, C. W. (1989). The role of education in the academic disciplines in teacher preparation. In A. Woolfolk (Ed.), *Research perspectives on the graduate preparation of teachers* (pp. 88–107). Englewood Cliffs, NJ: Prentice-Hall.

Anderson, C. W., Holland, J. D., & Palincsar, A. S. (1997). Canonical and sociocultural approaches to research and reform in science education: The story of Juan and his group. *Elementary School Journal, 97*, 357–381.

Anderson, C. W., Palincsar, A. S., & Kurth, G. (1996, April). *Design principles for collaborative problem solving in science*. Paper presented at the Annual Meeting of the American Educational Research Association, New York City.

Anderson, J. R. (1983). *The architecture of cognition*. Cambridge, MA: Harvard University Press.

Anderson, J. R. (1990). *The adaptive character of thought*. Hillsdale, NJ: Lawrence Erlbaum Associates.

Anderson, J. R., Conrad, F. G., & Corbett, A. T. (1989). Skill acquisition and the LISP tutor. *Cognitive Science, 13*, 467–505.

Anderson, J. R., Corbett, A. T., Koedinger, K. R., & Pelletier, R. (1995). Cognitive tutors: Lessons learned. *Journal of the Learning Sciences, 4*, 167–207.

Anderson, J. R., Reder, L. M., & Simon, H. (1996). Situated learning and education. *Educational Researcher, 25*(4), 5–11.

Anderson, L. M. (1989). Classroom instruction. In M. Reynolds (Ed.), *Knowledge base for the beginning teacher* (pp. 101–115). New York: Pergamon.

Anderson, L. M. (1994, October). *Reforming our courses and rethinking our roles.* Paper presented at the Annual Meeting of the Midwestern Association for the Teaching of Educational Psychology, Chicago.

Anderson, L. M., Blumenfeld, P., Pintrich, P., Clark, C., Marx, R., & Peterson, P. (1995). Educational psychology for teachers: Reforming our courses, rethinking our roles. *Educational Psychologist, 30*, 143–157.

Andrews, S. V. (1992, February). *Enhancing learning and scholarship in the college classroom: The role of learning teams.* Paper presented at the Annual Meeting of the American Association of Colleges for Teacher, San Antonio, TX.

Arons, A. B. (1990). *A guide to introductory physics teaching.* New York: Wiley.

Arons, A. B. (1993). Guiding insight and inquiry in the introductory physics laboratory. *The Physics Teacher, 31*, 278–282.

Argyris, C. (1982). *Reasoning, learning, and action: Individual and organizational.* San Francisco: Jossey-Bass.

Assaf, S. (1948). *Jewish education sources* (in Hebrew). Tel Aviv: Dvir Publishers.

Au, K. H., & Mason, J. (1981). Social organization factors in learning to read: The balance of rights hypothesis. *Reading Research Quarterly, 17*, 115–151.

Azmitia, M. (1988). Peer interaction and problem-solving: When are two heads better than one? *Child Development, 59*, 87–96.

Azmitia, M., & Perlmutter, M. (1989). Social influences on children's cognition: State of the art and future directions. In H. W. Reese (Ed.), *Advances in child development and behavior, Vol. 22* (pp. 89–144). New York: Academic Press.

Bandura, A. (1978). The self system in reciprocal determinism. *American Psychologist, 33*, 344–358.

Bargh, J. A., & Schul, Y. (1980). On the cognitive benefits of teaching. *Journal of Educational Psychology, 72*, 593–604.

Barrell, J. (1995). *Teaching for thoughtfulness: Classroom strategies to enhance intellectual development.* White Plains, NY: Longman.

Battistich, V., Solomon, D., & Delucci, K. (1993). Interaction processes and student outcomes in co-operative groups. *Elementary School Journal, 94*, 19–32.

Bayer, A. S. (1990). *Collaborative apprenticeship learning: Language and thinking across the curriculum, k-12.* Mountain View, CA: Mayfield.

Beare, H., & Slaughter, R. (1993). *Education for the twenty first century.* London: Routledge.

Bearison, D. J. (1982). New directions in studies of social interactions and cognitive growth. In F. C. Serafica (Ed.), *Social-cognitive development in context* (pp. 199–221). New York: Guilford.

Bearison, D. J., Magzamen, S., & Filardo, E. K. (1986). Socio-conflict and cognitive growth in young children. *Merrill-Palmer Quarterly, 32*, 51–72.

Beilin, H. (1992). Piaget's enduring contribution to developmental psychology. *Developmental Psychology, 28*, 191–204.

Benware, C. A., & Deci, E. L. (1984). Quality of learning with an active versus passive motivational set. *American Educational Research Journal, 21*, 755–765.

Berardi-Coletta, B., Dominowski, R. L., Buyer, L. S., & Rellinger, E. R. (1995). Metacognition and problem solving: A process-oriented approach. *Journal of Experimental Psychology: Learning, Memory, and Cognition, 21*, 205–223.

Bereiter, C., & Scardamalia, M. (1987). *The psychology of written composition.* Hillsdale, NJ: Lawrence Erlbaum Associates.

Bereiter, C., & Scardamalia, M. (1989). Intentional learning as a goal for instruction. In L. B. Resnick (Ed.), *Knowing, learning, and instruction: Essays in honor of Robert Glaser* (pp. 361–392). Hillsdale, NJ: Lawrence Erlbaum Associates.

Berg, K. F. (1993). *Structured cooperative learning and achievement in a high school mathematics class.* Paper presented at the Annual Meeting of the American Educational Research Association, Atlanta, GA. (ERIC Reproduction Services No. ED 364-408).

Berger, J. B., Cohen, B. P., & Zelditch, M., Jr. (1972). Status characteristics and social interaction. *American Sociological Review, 37*, 241–255.

Berger, J. B., Rosenholz, S. J., & Zelditch, M., Jr. (1980). Status organizing processes. *Annual Review of Sociology, 6*, 479–508.

Berkheimer, G., Anderson, C. A., & Blakeslee, T. (1988). *Matter and molecules teacher's guide: Science book* (Occasional paper 121). East Lansing: Michigan State University, Institute for Research on Teaching.

Berkowitz, M., & Gibbs, J. (1983). Measuring the developmental features of moral discussion. *Merrill-Palmer Quarterly, 29*, 399–410.

Berliner, D. C. (1986). In pursuit of the expert pedagogue. *Educational Research, 15*(7), 5–13.

Berndt, T. (1987). The distinctive features of conversations between friends: Theories, research, and implications for socio-moral development. In W.M. Kurtines & J. L. Gewirtz (Eds.), *Moral development through social interaction* (pp. 281–300). New York: Wiley.

Berry, D. C., & Broadbent, D. E. (1984). On the relationship between task performance and associated verbal knowledge. *Quarterly Journal of Experimental Psychology, 36*, 209–231.

Biehler, R. F., & Snowman, J. (1997). *Psychology applied to teaching* (8th ed.). New York: Houghton Mifflin.

Bird, T., Anderson, L. M., Sullivan, B. A., & Swindler, S. A. (1992). *Pedagogical balancing acts: A teacher educator encounters problems in an attempt to influence prospective teachers' beliefs.* East Lansing, MI: National Center for Research on Teacher Learning.

Blatt, M., & Kohlberg, L. (1975). The effects of classroom moral discussion upon children's level of moral judgment. *Journal of Moral Education, 4*, 129–161.

Bloom, B. S. (Ed.). (1956). *Taxonomy of educational objectives: The classification of educational goals. Handbook 1. Cognitive domain.* New York: McKay.

Bloom, B. S. (1984). The 2 sigma problem: The search for methods of group instruction as effective as one-to-one tutoring. *Educational Researcher, 13*(6), 4–16.

Blunk, M. L. (1996). The role of cognitive mechanisms and social processes in cooperative learning. *Dissertation Abstracts International, 57*(3), 1010A. (University Microfilms No. AAI962573)

Bobier, D. (1997). *The effects of scripted cooperation on gender differences in help-seeking behavior.* Unpublished manuscript, Rutgers, The State University of New Jersey, New Brunswick.

Borko, H., & Putnam, R. (1996). Learning to teach. In D. Berliner & R. Calfee (Eds.), *Handbook of educational psychology* (pp. 673–708). New York: Macmillan.

Bornstein, M. H. (Ed.). (1991). *Cultural approaches to parenting.* Hillsdale, NJ: Lawrence Erlbaum Associates.

Bossert, S. (1988–1989). Cooperative activities in the classroom. In E. Rothkopf (Ed.), *Review of Research in Education, 15* (pp. 225–250). Washington, DC: American Educational Research Association.

Botvin, G., & Murray, F. B. (1975). The efficacy of peer modeling acquisition of conservation. *Child Development, 46*, 796–799.

Bovet, M., Parrat-Dayan, S., & Voneche, J. (1989). Cognitive development and interaction. In M. Bornstein & J. S. Bruner (Eds.), *Interaction in human development* (pp. 41–58). Hillsdale, NJ: Lawrence Erlbaum Associates.

Bransford, J. D., Goldman, S. R., & Vye, N. J. (1991). Making a difference in people's ability to think: Reflections on a decade of work and some hopes for the future. In R. J. Sternberg & L. Okagaki (Eds.), *Influences on children* (pp. 147–180). Hillsdale, NJ: Lawrence Erlbaum Associates.

Britton, B. K., Van Dusen, L., Glynn, S. M., & Hemphill, D. (1990). The impact of inferences on instructional text. In A. C. Graesser & G. H. Bower (Eds.), *Inferences and text comprehension* (pp. 53–87). San Diego, CA: Academic Press.

Bronfenbrenner, U. (1989). Ecological systems theory. In R. Vasta (Ed.), *Annals of child development, Vol. 6* (pp. 187–249). Greenwich, CT: JAI.

Bronfenbrenner, U. (1993). The ecology of cognitive development: Research models and fugitive findings. In R. Wozniak & K. Fischer (Eds.), *Development in context: Acting and thinking in specific environments* (pp. 3–44). Hillsdale, NJ: Lawrence Erlbaum Associates.

Bronfenbrenner, U., & Ceci, S. (1994). Nature-nurture reconceptualized in developmental perspective: A bioecological model. *Psychological Review, 101,* 568–586.

Brookhart, S. M., & Freeman, D. J. (1992). Characteristics of entering teacher candidates. *Review of Educational Research, 62,* 37–60.

Brophy, J. E., & Good, T. L. (1986). Teacher behavior and student achievement. In M. C. Wittrock (Ed.), *Handbook of research on teaching* (3rd ed., pp. 328375). New York: Macmillan.

Brown, A. L. (1988). Motivation to learn and understand: On taking charge of one's own learning. *Cognition and Instruction, 5,* 311–321.

Brown, A. L. (1992). Designing experiments: Theoretical and methodological challenges in creating complex interventions in classroom settings. *Journal of the Learning Sciences, 2,* 141–178.

Brown, A. L., & Campione, J. C. (1986). Psychological theory and the study of learning disabilities. *American Psychologist, 41,* 1059–1068.

Brown, A. L., & Campione, J. C. (1994). Guided discovery in a community of learners. In K. McGilly (Ed.), *Classroom lessons: Integrating cognitive theory and classroom practice* (pp. 229–272). Cambridge, MA: MIT Press.

Brown, A. L., & Palincsar, A. S. (1989). Guided, cooperative learning and individual knowledge acquisition. In L. B. Resnick (Ed.), *Knowing, learning, and instruction: Essays in honor of Robert Glaser* (pp. 393–451). Hillsdale, NJ: Lawrence Erlbaum Associates.

Brown, J. S., Collins, A., & Duguid, P. (1989). Situated cognition and the culture of learning. *Educational Researcher, 18*(1), 32–42.

Brown, P., & Levinson, S. C. (1987). *Politeness: Some universals in language use.* Cambridge, England: Cambridge University Press.

Bruce, J., & Weil, M. (1986). *Models of teaching* (3rd ed.). Englewood Cliffs, NJ: Prentice-Hall.

Bruffee, K. A. (1993). *Collaborative learning: Higher education, interdependence, and the authority of knowledge.* Baltimore, MD: The Johns Hopkins University Press.

Bruffee, K. A., & Leveson, D. J. (in press). Why collaborative learning works in teaching science.

Bruner, J. S. (1961). The act of discovery. *Harvard Educational Review, 31,* 21–32.

Buchmann, M. (1989, April). *Breaking from experience in teacher education: When is it necessary, how is it possible?* Paper presented at the Annual Meeting of the American Educational Research Association, San Francisco.

Calderhead, J. (1996). Teachers: Beliefs and knowledge. In D. Berliner & R. Calfee (Eds.), *Handbook of educational psychology* (pp. 509–725). New York: Macmillan.

Campbell, D. T. (1969). Ethnocentrism of disciplines and the fish-scale model of omniscience. In M. Sherif & C. W. Sherif (Eds.), *Interdisciplinary relationships in the social sciences* (pp. 328–348). Xenia, OH: Aldine.

Cazden, C. (1986). Classroom discourse. In M. Wittrock (Ed.), *Handbook of research on teaching* (3rd ed., pp. 432–463). New York: Macmillan.

Cazden, C. (1988). *Classroom discourse: The language of teaching and learning.* Portsmouth, NH: Heinemann.

Chan, C., Burtis, J., & Bereiter, C. (1997). Knowledge building as a mediator of conflict in conceptual change. *Cognition and Instruction, 15,* 1–40.

Chan, C. K. K., Burtis, P. J., Scardamalia, M., & Bereiter, C. (1992). Constructive activity in learning from text. *American Educational Research Journal, 29,* 97–118.

Chan, M. M. (1988, March). *Learning by doing, discussing, and questioning: A collaborative learning course.* Paper presented at the Annual Meeting of the Conference of College Composition and Communication, St. Louis, MO.

Chapman, M. (1988). *Constructive evolution: Origins and development of Piaget's thought.* New York: Cambridge University Press.

Chapman, M., & McBride, M. L. (1992). The education of reason: Cognitive conflict and its role in intellectual development. In C. U. Shantz & W. W. Hartup (Eds.), *Conflict in child and adolescent development* (pp. 36–69). New York: Cambridge University Press.

Chi, M. T. H., & Bassock, M. (1989). Learning from examples via self-explanations. In L. B. Resnick (Ed.), *Knowing, learning, and instruction: Essays in honor of Robert Glaser* (pp. 251–282). Hillsdale, NJ: Lawrence Erlbaum Associates.

Chi, M. T. H., Bassock, M., Lewis, M., Reimann, P., & Glaser, R. (1989). Self-explanations: How students study and use examples in learning to solve problems. *Cognitive Science, 13,* 145–182.

Chi, M. T. H., Feltovich, P. J., & Glaser, R. (1981). Categorization and representation of physics problems by experts and novices. *Cognitive Science, 5,* 121–152.

Chi, M.T.H., & VanLehn, K.A. (1991). The content of physics self-explanations. *Journal of the Learning Sciences, 1,* 69–105.

Chomsky, N. (1965). *Aspects of a theory of syntax.* Cambridge, MA: MIT Press.

Clancey, W. J. (1994). Comments on DiSessa. *Cognition and Instruction, 12,* 97–102.

Clark, C. M., & Peterson, P. L. (1986). Teachers' thought processes. In M. Wittrock (Ed.), *Handbook of research on teaching* (3rd ed., pp. 255–290). New York: Macmillan.

Clark, H. H., & Schaefer, E. F. (1989). Contributing to discourse. *Cognitive Science, 13,* 259–294.

Cobb, P. (1988). The tensions between theories of learning and instruction in mathematics education. *Educational Psychologist, 23,* 78–103.

Cobb, P. (1994). Constructivism in mathematics and science education. *Educational Researcher, 23,* 4–12.

Cobb, P., Wood, T., & Yackel, E. (1993). Discourse, mathematical thinking, and classroom practice. In E. A. Forman, N. Minich, & C. A. Stone (Eds.), *Contexts for learning* (pp. 91–119). New York: Oxford University Press.

Cognition and Technology Group at Vanderbilt. (1993). Toward integrated curricula: Possibilities from anchored instruction. In M. Rabinowitz (Ed.), *Cognitive science foundations of instruction* (pp. 33–55). Hillsdale, NJ: Lawrence Erlbaum Associates.

Cohen, B. P., & Arechevala-Vargas, R. (1987). *Interdependence, interaction, and productivity (Working Paper No. 87–3).* Stanford, CA: Stanford University, Center for Sociological Research.

Cohen, B. P., & Cohen, E. G. (1991). From groupwork among children to R & D teams: Interdependence interaction and productivity. *Advances in Group Processes, 8,* 205–225.

Cohen, E. G. (1982). Expectation states and interracial interaction in school settings. *Annual Review of Sociology, 8,* 109–235.

Cohen, E. G. (1990). Continuing to cooperate: Prerequisites for persistance. *Phi Delta Kappan, 72*(2), 134–138.

Cohen, E. G. (1991, April). *Classroom management and complex instruction.* Paper presented at the Annual Meeting of the American Educational Research Association, Chicago.

Cohen, E. G. (1994a). *Designing groupwork: Strategies for the heterogeneous classroom* (2nd ed.). New York: Teachers College Press.

Cohen, E. G. (1994b). Restructuring the classroom: Conditions for productive small groups. *Review of Educational Research, 64,* 1–36.

Cohen, E. G., & Lotan, R. A. (1995). Producing equal-status interaction in the heterogeneous classroom. *American Educational Research Journal, 32,* 99–120.

Cohen, E. G., Lotan, R., & Catanzarite, L. (1990). Treating status problems in the cooperative classroom. In S. Sharan (Ed.), *Cooperative learning: Theory and research* (pp. 203–230). New York: Praeger.

Cohen, E. G., Lotan, R., & Leechor, C. (1989). Can classrooms learn? *Sociology of Education, 62,* 75–94.

Cohen, E. G., & Roper, S. S. (1972). Modification of status relations in Israeli youth: An application of expectation states theory. *Journal of Cross-Cultural Psychology, 11,* 364–384.

Cohen, P. A., Kulik, J. A., & Kulik, C. C. (1982). Educational outcomes of tutoring: A meta-analysis of findings. *American Educational Research Journal, 19,* 237–248.

Colby, A., Kohlberg, L., Fenton, E., Speicher-Dubin, B., & Lieberman, M. (1977). Secondary school moral discussion programs led by social studies teachers. *Journal of Moral Education, 6,* 90–111.

Cole, M. (1991). On socially shared cognitions. In L. B. Resnick, J. Levine, & S. Teasley (Eds.), *Perspectives on socially shared cognition* (pp. 398–417). Hillsdale, NJ: Lawrence Erlbaum Associates.

Coleman, J. S. (1973). *Youth: Transition to adulthood* (Report of the Panel on Youth of the President's Science Advisory Committee, James S. Coleman, Chairman). Washington, DC: Office of Science and Technology.

Collins, A. (1985). Teaching reasoning skills. In S. F. Chipman, J. W. Segal, & R. Glaser (Eds.), *Thinking and learning skills, Vol. 2* (pp. 579–586.) Hillsdale, NJ: Lawrence Erlbaum Associates.

Collins, A., Brown, J. S., & Newman, S. E. (1989). Cognitive apprenticeship: Teaching the crafts of reading, writing, and mathematics. In L.B. Resnick (Ed.), *Knowing, learning, and instruction: Essays in honor of Robert Glaser* (pp. 453–494). Hillsdale, NJ: Lawrence Erlbaum Associates.

Collins, A., Warnock, E. H., Aeillo, N., & Miller, M. L. (1975). Reasoning from incomplete knowledge. In D. G. Bobrow & A. Collins (Eds.), *Representation and understanding* (pp. 383–415). New York: Academic Press.

Cooper, C. R. (1980). Development of collaborative problem-solving among preschool children. *Developmental Psychology, 16,* 433–440.

Cooper, S. M. A. (1995). *An evaluation of the implementation of an integrated learning system for introductory college physics.* Unpublished doctoral dissertation, Rutgers, The State University of New Jersey, New Brunswick.

Cooper, S. M. A., & O'Donnell, A. M. (1996, March). *Innovation and persistence: The evaluation of the C.U.P.L.E. studio physics course.* Paper presented at the Annual Meeting of the American Educational Research Association, New York.

Cox, M. J. (1992). The computer in the science curriculum. *International Journal of Educational Research, 17,* 19–35.

Crook, C. (1994). *Computers and the collaborative experience of learning.* London: Routledge.

Cuban, L. (1982). Persistence of the inevitable: The teacher-centered classroom. *Education and Urban Society, 5,* 26–41.

Cuseo, J. (1989). Cooperative learning: Why does it work? *Cooperative Learning and College Teaching, 1,* 3–8.

Damon, W. (1977). *The social world of the child.* San Francisco: Jossey-Bass.

Damon, W. (1983). The nature of social-cognitive change in the developing child. In W. F. Overton (Ed.), *The relationship between social and cognitive development* (pp. 103–142). Hillsdale, NJ: Lawrence Erlbaum Associates.

Damon, W. (1991). Problems of direction in socially shared cognition. In L. B. Resnick, J. M. Levine, & S. D. Teasley (Eds.), *Perspectives on socially shared cognition* (pp. 384–397). Washington, DC: American Psychological Association.

Damon, W., & Killen, M. (1982). Peer interaction and the process of change in children's moral reasoning. *Merrill Palmer Quarterly, 28,* 347–367.

Damon, W., & Phelps, E. (1989). Critical distinctions among three approaches to peer education. *International Journal of Educational Research, 13,* 9–19.

Dansereau, D. F. (1988). Cooperative learning strategies. In C. E. Weinstein, E. T. Goetz, & P. A. Alexander (Eds.), *Learning and study strategies: Issues in assessment, instruction, and evaluation* (pp. 103–120). New York: Academic Press.

Darling-Hammond, L. (1994). *Professional development schools: Schools for developing a profession.* New York: Teachers College Press.

Deci, E. L., & Ryan, R. M. (1985). *Intrinsic motivation and self-determination in human behavior.* New York: Plenum.

Deering, P. D. (1992). *An ethnographic study of cooperative learning in a multiethnic working class middle school.* Unpublished doctoral dissertation, University of Colorado, Boulder.

Deering, P. D. (1994, April). *Is "Cooperative Learning" either, both, or neither? Tales from three middle school classrooms.* Paper presented at the Annual Meeting of the American Educational Research Association, New Orleans, LA.

Deering, P. D., & Meloth, M. S. (1993). A descriptive study of naturally occurring discussion in cooperative learning groups. *Journal of Classroom Interaction, 28*(2), 7–13.

Deering, P. D., Meloth, M. S, & Sanders, A. B. (1994, April). *The Cooperative Reading Project: A collaboration with teachers to examine and improve upon cooperative learning in literacy instruction.* Paper presented at the Annual Meeting of the American Educational Research Association, New Orleans, LA,

De Lisi, R. (1987). A cognitive-developmental model of planning. In S. L. Friedman, E. K. Scholnick, & R. R. Cocking (Eds.), *Blueprints for thinking: The role of planning in cognitive development* (pp. 79–109). New York: Cambridge University Press.

Dembo, M., & Eaton, M. (1997). School learning and motivation. In G. Phye (Ed.), *Handbook of academic learning* (pp. 65–103). Washington, DC: American Psychological Association.

Dembo, M., & McAuliffe, T. (1987). Effects of perceived ability and grade status on social interaction and influence in cooperative groups. *Journal of Educational Psychology, 79,* 415–423.

Derry, S. J., & Lesgold, A. (1996). Toward a situated social practice model for instructional design. In D. C. Berliner & R. C. Calfee (Eds.), *Handbook of educational psychology* (pp. 787–806). New York: Macmillan.

Derry, S. J., Levin, J. R., Jones, M. S., Osana, H. P., & Peterson, M. (1998). *Fostering students' statistical and scientific thinking: Lessons learned from an innovative college course.* Manuscript submitted for publication.

Derry, S. J., Levin, J. R., Osana, H. P., & Jones, M. S. (in press). Developing middle school students' statistical reasoning abilities through simulation gaming. In S. P. Lajoie (Ed.), *Reflections on statistics: Agendas for learning, teaching, and assessment in K-12.* Mahwah, NJ: Lawrence Erlbaum Associates.

DeVries, R. (1997). Piaget's social theory. *Educational Researcher, 26*(2), 4–17.

DeVries, R., & Goncu, A. (1987). Interpersonal relations in four-year dyads from constructivist and Montessori programs. *Journal of Applied Developmental Psychology, 8,* 481–501.

DeVries, R., Haney, J., & Zan, B. (1991) Sociomoral atmosphere in direct-instruction, eclectic, and constructivist kindergartens: A study of teachers' enacted understanding. *Early Childhood Research Quarterly, 6,* 449–472.

DeVries, R., Reese-Learned, H., & Morgan, P. (1991). Sociomoral development in direct-instruction, eclectic and constructivist kindergartens: A study of children's enacted interpersonal understanding. *Early Childhood Research Quarterly, 6,* 473–518.

DeVries, R., & Zan, B. (1994). *Moral classrooms, moral children.* New York: Teachers College Press.

Dewey, J. (1965). The relation of theory to practice in education. In M. L. Borrowman (Ed.), *Teacher education in America: A documentary history.* New York: Columbia University, Teachers College Press. (Original work published 1904)

Dewey, J. (1909). *The child and the curriculum.* Chicago: The University of Chicago Press.

Dewey, J. (1910). *How we think.* Boston, MA: Heath.

Dewey, J. (1927). *The school and society.* Chicago: The University of Chicago Press.

Dewey, J. (1933). *How we think: A restatement of the relation of reflective thinking to the educative process.* Boston: Heath.

Dillon, J. T. (1988). *Questioning and teaching: A manual of practice.* New York: Teachers College Press.

Dimant, R., & Bearison, D. (1991). Development of formal reasoning during successive peer interactions. *Developmental Psychology, 27,* 277–284.

Doise, W., & Mugny, G. (1984). *The social development of the intellect.* New York: Pergamon Press.

Doise, W., Mugny, G., & Perret-Clermont, A. N. (1975). Social interaction and the development of cognitive operations. *European Journal of Social Psychology, 5,* 367–383.

Donato, R., & McCormick, D. (1994). A socio-cultural perspective on language learning strategies: The role of mediation. *The Modern Language Journal, 78,* 453–464.

Doolittle, P. E. (1995, June). *Understanding cooperative learning through Vygotsky's zone of proximal development.* Paper presented at the Lilly National Conference on Excellence in College Teaching, Columbia, SC.

Doyle, W. (1983). Academic work. *Review of Educational Research, 53,* 159–200.

Doyle, W. (1986). Classroom organization and management. In M. C. Wittrock (Ed.), *Handbook of research on teaching* (3rd ed., pp. 392–431). New York: Macmillan.

Doyle, W. (1990). Case methods in teacher education. *Teacher Education Quarterly, 17,* 7–15.

Driver, R., Asoko, H., Leach, J., & Mortimer, E. (1994). Scientific knowledge in the classroom. *Educational Researcher, 23*(7), 5–12.

Duin, A. H. (1984, May). *Implementing cooperative learning groups in the writing curriculum: What research shows.* Paper presented at the 25th Annual Meeting of the Minnesota Council of Teachers of English, Mankato, MN.

Durkin, D. (1978–1979). What classroom observations reveal about reading comprehension research. *Reading Research Quarterly, 14,* 481533.

Durling, R., & Schick, C. (1976). Concept attainment by pairs and individuals as a function of vocalization. *Journal of Educational Psychology, 68,* 83–91.

Duschl, R. A. (1990). *Restructuring science education: The importance of theories and their development.* New York: Teachers College Press.

Edwards, D., & Mercer, N. (1987). *Common knowledge: The development of understanding in the classroom.* London: Routledge.

Ehrlich, D. E. (1991). *Moving beyond cooperation: Developing science thinking in interdependent groups.* Unpublished doctoral dissertation, Stanford University.

Eicholz, R. E., O'Daffer, P. G., & Fleenor, C. F. (1989). *Addison-Wesley mathematics* (Grade 7). Menlo Park, CA: Addison-Wesley.

Elder, G. H., Jr., Modell, J., & Parke, R. D. (1993). *Children in time and place: Developmental and historical insights.* New York: Cambridge University Press.

Ellis, S. (1987). *The effects of collaboration on children's instruction: Observations of a Navajo sample.* Unpublished doctoral dissertation, University of Utah.

Ellis, S., & Gauvain, M. (1992). Social and cultural influences on children's collaborative interactions. In L. T. Winegar & J. Valsiner (Eds.), *Children's development within social context: Research and methodology, Vol. 1* (pp. 155–180). Hillsdale, NJ: Lawrence Erlbaum Associates.

Ellis, S., & Rogoff, B. (1982). The strategies and efficacy of child vs. adult teachers. *Child Development, 53,* 730–735.

Ellis, S., & Rogoff, B. (1986). Problem solving in children's management of instruction. In E. C. Mueller & C. R. Cooper (Eds.), *Process and outcome in peer relationships* (pp. 301–325). Orlando, FL: Academic Press.

Ellis, S., & Siegler, R. S. (1994). Development of problem solving. In R. J. Sternberg (Ed.), *Handbook of perception and cognition, Vol 12: Thinking and problem solving* (pp. 333–367). San Diego, CA: Academic Press.

Ericcson, K. A., & Simon, H. A. (1984). *Verbal protocols as data.* Cambridge, MA: MIT Press.

Falk, J. (1980). The conversational duet. *Berkeley Linguistics Society 1980* (pp. 507–514). Berkeley: University of California.

Farivar, S., & Webb, N. M. (1991). *Helping behavior activities handbook.* Los Angeles: Graduate School of Education, University of California.

Farivar, S., & Webb, N. M. (1994). Helping and getting help: Essential skills for effective group problem-solving. *Arithmetic Teacher, 41,* 521–525.

Feiman-Nemser, S. (1990). Teacher preparation: Structural and conceptual alternatives. In W. R. Houston (Ed.), *Handbook of research on teacher education* (pp. 212–233). New York: Macmillan.

Ferrara, K. (1992). The interactive achievement of a sentence: Joint productions in therapeutic discourse. *Discourse Processes, 15,* 207–228.

Fishbein, H., Eckart, T., Lauver, E., VanLeeuwen, R., & Langmeyer, D. (1990). Learners' questions and comprehension in a tutoring setting. *Journal of Educational Psychology, 82,* 163–170.

Fisher, C., Filby, N., Marliave, R., Cahen, L., Dishaw, M., Moore, J., & Berliner, D. (1978). *Teaching behaviors, academic time, and student achievement: Beginning teacher evaluation study (Phase III-B Final Report).* San Francisco: Far West Laboratory for Educational Research and Development.

Fitz-Gibbon, C. T. (1977). *An analysis of the literature of cross-age tutoring.* Washington, DC: National Institute of Education. (ERIC Document Reproduction Service No. ED 148 807)

Flory, M. D. (1991, November). *Limits on the image: The teacher as movie star.* Paper presented at the Annual Meeting of the American Anthropological Association, Chicago.

Forman, E. A. (1992). Discourse, intersubjectivity, and the development of peer collaboration: A Vygotskian approach. In L. T. Winegar & J. Valsiner (Eds.), *Children's development within social context: Metatheory and theory, Vol. 1* (pp. 143–160). Hillsdale, NJ: Lawrence Erlbaum Associates.

Forman, E. A., & Cazden, C. B. (1985). Exploring Vygotskian perspectives in education: The cognitive value of peer interaction. In J. V. Wertsch (Ed.), *Culture, communication, and cognition: Vygotskian perspectives* (pp. 323–347). New York: Cambridge University Press.

Forman, E. A., & McPhail, J. (1993). A Vygotskian perspective on children's collaborative problem-solving activities. In E. A. Forman, N. Minick, & C. A. Stone (Eds.), *Education and mind: The integration of institutional, social, and developmental processes* (pp. 213–229). New York: Oxford University Press.

Fox, B. (1991). Cognitive and interactional aspects of correction in tutoring. In P. Goodyear (Ed.), *Teaching knowledge and intelligent tutoring* (pp. 149–172). Norwood, NJ: Ablex.

Fox, B. (1993). *The human tutorial dialogue project.* Hillsdale, NJ: Lawrence Erlbaum Associates.

Freund, L. S. (1990). Maternal regulation of children's problem-solving behavior and its impact on children's performance. *Child Development, 61,* 113–126.

Furth, H. G. (1978). Children's societal understanding and the process of equilibration. In W. Damon (Ed.), *New directions for child development: Social cognition* (pp. 101–122). San Francisco: Jossey-Bass.

Furth, H. G. (1980). *The world of grown-ups: Children's conception of society.* New York: Elsevier.

Furth, H. G. (1981). *Piaget & knowledge: Theoretical foundations* (2nd ed.). Chicago: The University of Chicago Press.

Furth, H. G. (1987). *Knowledge as desire: An essay on Freud and Piaget.* New York: Columbia University Press.

Furth, H. G. (1996). *Desire for society: Children's knowledge as social imagination.* New York: Houghton Mifflin.

Gage, N. L., & Berliner, D. C. (1991). *Educational psychology* (5th ed.). New York: Houghton Mifflin.

Gagné, R. M. (1977). *The conditions of learning* (3rd ed.). New York: Holt, Rinehart & Winston.

Gardner, H. (1985). *The mind's new science: A history of the cognitive revolution.* New York: Basic Books.

Gauvain, M., & Rogoff, B. (1989). Collaborative problem solving and children's planning skills. *Developmental Psychology, 25,* 139–151.

Gelman, R., & Greeno, J. G. (1989). On the nature of competence: Principles for understanding in a domain. In L. B. Resnick (Ed.), *Knowing, learning, and instruction: Essays in honor of Robert Glaser* (pp. 125–186). Hillsdale, NJ: Lawrence Erlbaum Associates.

Gibbs, J. (1987). *Tribes: A process for social development and cooperative learning.* Santa Rosa, CA: Center Source Publications.

Gibson, E. (1966). *The senses considered as perceptual systems.* Boston: Houghton Mifflin.

Gick, M. L. (1986). Problem-solving strategies. *Educational Psychologist, 21,* 99–120.

Gilly, M. (1990). The psychosocial mechanisms of cognitive constructions: Experimental research and teaching perspectives. In A.N. Perret-Clermont & M. L. Schubauer-Leoni (Eds.), *Social factors in learning and instruction* (pp. 607–621). New York: Pergamon.

Glachan, M. & Light, P. (1982). Peer interaction and learning: Can two wrongs make a right? In G. E. Butterworth & P. H. Light (Eds.), *Social cognition: Studies of the development of understanding* (pp. 238–262). Brighton, UK: Harvester Press.

Golbeck, S. (1998). Peer collaboration and children's representation of the horizontal surface of liquid. *Journal of Applied Developmental Psychology, 19,* 573–594.

Goldman, S. R., Pellegrino, J. W., & Bransford, J. D. (1993). Assessing programs that invite thinking. In H. O'Neill & E. Baker (Eds.), *Technology assessment: Estimating the future* (pp. 199–230). Hillsdale, NJ: Lawrence Erlbaum Associates.

Good, T. L., & Brophy, J. E. (1994). *Looking in classrooms* (6th ed.). New York: Harper Collins.

Good, T. L., McCaslin, M. M., & Reys, B. J. (1991, April). *Improving schools: The need for better curriculum tasks.* Chicago, IL: Paper presented at the Annual Meeting of the American Educational Research Association.

Goodlad, J. (1984). *A place called school: Prospects for the future.* New York: McGraw-Hill.

Goodlad, J. I. (1994). *Educational renewal: Better teachers, better schools.* San Francisco: Jossey-Bass.

Gopnik, A. (1996). The post-Piaget era. *Psychological Science, 7,* 221–225.

Gorsky, P., & Finegold, M. (1992). Using computer simulations to restructure students' conceptions of force. *Journal of Computers in Mathematics and Science Teaching, 11,* 163–178.

Gorsky, P., & Finegold, M. (1994). The role of anomaly and of cognitive dissonance in restructuring students' concepts of force. *Instructional Science, 22,* 75–90.

Graesser, A. C. (1992). *Questioning mechanisms during complex learning.* (Eric Document Reproduction Service No. ED 350 306).

Graesser, A. C., Bowers, C. A., Hacker, D. J., & Person, N. K. (in press). An anatomy of naturalistic tutoring. In K. Hogan & M. Pressley (Eds.), *Scaffolding of instruction.* Brookline Books.

Graesser, A. C., & Person, N. K. (1994). Question asking during tutoring. *American Educational Research Journal, 31,* 104–137.

Graesser, A. C., Person, N. K., & Magliano. (1995). Collaborative dialogue patterns in naturalistic one-to-one tutoring. *Applied Cognitive Psychology, 9,* 495–522.

Graybeal, S. S., & Stodolsky, S. S. (1985). Peer work groups in elementary schools. *American Journal of Education, 93,* 409–428.

Grice, H. P. (1975). Logic and conversation. In P. Cole & J. Morgan (Eds.), *Syntax and semantics: Vol. 3: Speech acts* (pp. 41–58). New York: Academic Press.

Guskey, T. R. (1989). Attitude and perceptual changes in teachers. *International Journal of Educational Research, 13,* 439–453.

Guyton, E., & Rainer, J. (Eds.). (1996). Constructivism in teacher education [Special Issue]. *Action in Teacher Education, 18* (2).

Hake, R. R. (1995, June). *Socratic dialogue inducing laboratories: Do they work?* Paper presented at the Project Kaleidoscope workshop "Revitalizing Introductory Physics," Miami University, Oxford, OH.

Hall, R. H., Dansereau, D. F., O'Donnell, A. M., & Skaggs, L. P. (1989). The effects of textual errors on dyadic and individual learning. *Journal of Reading Behavior, 21,* 127–140.

Halliday, M. A. K., & Martin, J. R. (1993). *Writing science: Literacy and discursive power.* Pittsburgh, PA: University of Pittsburgh Press.

Halpern, D. F. (1996). *Thought and knowledge: An introduction to critical thinking* (3rd ed.). Mahwah, NJ: Lawrence Erlbaum Associates.

Harkness, S., & Super, C. M. (1996). Parents' cultural belief systems: Their origins, expressions, and consequences. In S. Harkness & C. M. Super (Eds.), *Parents' cultural belief systems* (pp. 1–23). New York: Guilford.

Hartup, W. W. (1992). Conflict and friendship relations. In C. U. Shantz & W. W. Hartup (Eds.), *Conflict in child and adolescent development* (pp. 186–215). Cambridge, England: Cambridge University Press.

Hastie, R. (1986). Experimental evidence on group accuracy. In B. Grofman & G. Guillermo (Eds.), *Information pooling and group decision making* (pp. 129–157). Greenwich, CT: JAI.

Hativa, N. (1994). What you design is not what you get: Cognitive, affective, and social implications of learning with ILS—An integration of findings from six years of qualitative and quantitative studies. *International Journal of Educational Research, 21,* 81–111.

Heller, P., & Hollabaugh, M. (1992). Teaching problem solving through cooperative grouping, Part 2: Designing problems and structuring groups. *American Journal of Physics, 60,* 637–644.

Heller, P., Keith, R., & & Anderson, S. (1992). Teaching problem solving through cooperative grouping, Part 1: Group versus individual problem solving. *American Journal of Physics, 60,* 627–636.

Herrenkohl, L. R., & Guerra, M. R. (1998). Participant structures, scientific discourse, and student engagement in fourth grade. *Cognition and Instruction*.

Herrenkohl, L. R., & Wertsch, J. V. (in press). The use of cultural tools: Mastery and appropriation. In I. Sigel (Ed.), *Theoretical perspectives in the development of representational (symbolic) thought*. Hillsdale, NJ: Lawrence Erlbaum Associates.

Hertz-Lazarowitz, R. (1989). Cooperation and helping in the classroom: A contextual approach. *International Journal of Educational Research, 13*, 113–119.

Hertz-Lazarowitz, R. (1992). Understanding students' interactive behavior: Looking at six mirrors of the classroom. In R. Hertz-Lazarowitz and N. Miller (Eds.), *Interaction in cooperative groups: The theoretical anatomy of group learning* (pp. 71–102). New York: Cambridge University Press.

Hertz-Lazarowitz, R.; & Calderon, E. M. (1994). Implementing cooperative learning in the elementary schools: The facilitative voice for collaborative power. In S. Sharan (Ed.), *Handbook of cooperative learning* (pp. 300–317). New York: Greenwood.

Hertz-Lazarowitz, R., & Shadel, B. (1996). Evaluating writing in the cooperative classroom. *Helkat-Lashon, 23*, 205–231. (in Hebrew)

Hertz-Lazarowitz, R., & Zelniker, T. (1995). Cooperative learning in Israel: Historical, cultural, and educational perspectives. *International Journal of Educational Research, 23*, 267–281.

Hewitt, J., & Scardamalia, M. (1998). Design principles for the support of distributed processes. *Educational Psychology Review, 10*, 75–96.

Hinsz, V. B, Tindale, R. S., & Vollrath, D. A. (1997). The emerging conceptualization of groups as information processors. *Psychological Bulletin, 121*, 43–64.

Hoadley, C. M., Hsi, S., & Berman, B. P. (1995). *Networked multimedia for collaboration and communication*. Berkely: University of California at Berkely.

Hogan, D. M. (1996). *The co-construction of social development: A longitudinal study of the relations among social class, parenting, and children's activities*. Unpublished dissertation, The University of North Carolina at Greensboro.

Hollingworth, S. (1989). Prior beliefs and cognitive change in learning to teach. *American Educational Research Journal, 26*, 160–189.

Holt-Reynolds, D. (1992). Personal history-based beliefs as relevant prior knowledge in coursework. *American Educational Research Journal, 29*, 325–349.

Holtz, A. (1994). *The effects of scripted cooperation on the achievement of low status students in dyadic interaction*. Unpublished manuscript, Rutgers, The State University of New Jersey.

Howe, C., Tolmie, A., Greer, K., & Mackenzie, M. (1995). Peer collaboration and conceptual growth in physics: Task influences on children's understanding of heating and cooling. *Cognition and Instruction, 13*, 483–503.

Howey, K. (1996). Designing coherent and effective teacher education programs. In J. Sikula (Ed.), *Handbook of research on teacher education* (2nd ed., pp. 143–170). New York: Macmillan.

Howey, K., & Zimpher, N. L. (1996). Patterns in prospective teachers: Guides for designing preservice programs. In F. B. Murray (Ed.), *The teachers educators' handbook* (pp. 465–505). San Francisco: Jossey Bass.

Inhelder, B., & Piaget, J. (1958). *The growth of logical thinking from childhood to adolescence*. New York: Basic Books.

Jackson, P. (1968). *Life in classrooms*. New York: Holt, Rinehart & Winston.

Johnson, D. W., & Johnson, R. T. (1985). Classroom conflict: Controversy versus debate in learning groups. *American Educational Research Journal, 22*, 237–256.

Johnson, D. W. & Johnson, R.T . (1988). Critical thinking through structured controversy. *Educational Leadership, 45*, 58–64.

Johnson, D. W., & Johnson, R. T. (1992). Positive interdependence: Key to effective cooperation. In N. Miller & R. Hertz-Lazarowitz (Eds.), *Interaction in cooperative groups: The theoretical anatomy of group learning* (pp. 174–199). New York: Cambridge University Press.

Johnson, D. W., & Johnson, R. T. (1994). *Learning together and alone: Cooperative, competitive, and individualistic learning* (4th ed.). Boston: Allyn & Bacon.

Johnson, D. W., Johnson, R. T., & Holubec, E. J. (1988). *Cooperation in the classroom, revised*. Edina, MN: Interaction Book Co.

Johnson, D. W., Johnson, R. T., & Holubec, E. J. (1990). *Circles of learning: Cooperation in the classroom* (3rd ed.). Edina, MN: Interaction Book Co.

Johnson, D. W., Maruyama, G., Johnson, R., Nelson, D., & Skon, L. (1981). Effects of cooperative, competitive, and individualistic goal structures on achievement: A meta-analysis. *Psychological Bulletin, 89,* 47–62.

John-Steiner, V., & Mahn, H. (1996). Sociocultural approaches to learning and development: A Vygotskian framework. *Educational Psychologist, 31,* 191–206.

Johsua, S., & Dupin, J. J. (1987). Taking into account student conceptions in instructional strategy: An example in physics. *Cognition and Instruction, 4,* 117–135.

Kagan, D. (1992). Implications of research on teacher belief. Educational Psychologist, 27, 65–90.

Kagan, S. (1989). *Cooperative learning: Resources for teachers*. San Juan Capistrano, CA: Resources for Teachers.

Kagan, S. (1994). *Cooperative learning.* San Juan Capistrano, CA: Kagan Cooperative Learning.

Kalustian, L. (1994). Peer learning and status characteristics: Potential inequality of cognitive opportunity in problem-solving groups. *Dissertation Abstracts International, 55*(12), 3742A. (University Microfilms No. AAI95–14122)

Kelly, A. E., & O'Donnell, A. M. (1994). Hypertext and the study strategies of preservice teachers: Issues in instructional hypertext design. *Journal of Educational Computing Research, 10,* 373–387.

Kennedy, M. M. (1988). Inexact science: Professional development and the education of expertise. In E. Rothkopf (Ed.), *Review of Research in Education* (Vol. 14, pp. 133–167). Washington, DC: American Educational Research Association.

Kennedy, P. (1993). *Preparing for the twenty-first century*. New York: Random House.

King, A. (1989a). Effects of self-questioning training on college students' comprehension of lectures. *Contemporary Educational Psychology, 14 ,* 1–16.

King, A. (1989b). Verbal interaction and problem-solving within computer-assisted cooperative learning groups. *Journal of Educational Computing Research, 5,* 1–15.

King, A. (1990a). *ASK Your Partner to Think—TEL WHY.*[KC] Unpublished manuscript and materials, California State University San Marcos.

King, A. (1990b). Enhancing peer interaction and learning in the classroom through reciprocal questioning. *American Educational Research Journal, 27,* 664–687.

King, A. (1991). Effects of training in strategic questioning on children's problem-solving performance. *Journal of Educational Psychology, 83 ,* 307–317.

King, A. (1992a). Comparison of self-questioning, summarizing, and notetaking-review as strategies for learning from lectures. *American Educational Research Journal, 29,* 303–323.

King, A. (1992b). Facilitating elaborative learning through guided student-generated questioning. *Educational Psychologist, 27,* 111–126.

King, A. (1993). *ASK Your Partner to Think.*[KC] Unpublished manuscript and materials, California State University San Marcos.

King, A. (1994a). *ASK Your Partner to Think—TEL WHY.*[KC] Unpublished manuscript and materials, California State University San Marcos.

King, A. (1994b). Guiding knowledge construction in the classroom: Effects of teaching children how to question and how to explain. *American Educational Research Journal, 31,* 338–368.

King, A. (1994c). Autonomy and question asking: The role of personal control in guided student-generated questioning. *Learning and Individual Differences, 6*(2), 163–185.

King, A. (1997). ASK Your Partner to Think—TEL WHY:[KC] A Model of transactive peer tutoring for scaffolding higher-level complex learning. *Educational Psychologist, 32,* 221–235.

King, A. (1998a). Teaching effective discourse patterns for small group learning. In R. Stevens (Ed.), *Teaching in American Schools* (pp. 7–17). Upper Saddle River, NJ: Prentice-Hall.

King, A. (1998b). Transactive peer tutoring: Distributing cognition and metacognition. *Educational Psychology Review, 10,* 57–74.

King, A., Burton, S., Galloway, L., & Verdusco, E. (1996). *Effects of metacognitive questioning during sequenced inquiry peer tutoring on fourth graders' higher-level learning.* Unpublished manuscript, California State University San Marcos.

King, A., & Rosenshine, B. (1993). Effects of guided cooperative questioning on children's knowledge construction. *Journal of Experimental Education, 61,* 127–148.

King, A., Staffieri, A., & Adelgais, A. (1998). Structuring tutorial interaction for mutual peer tutoring: Effects on knowledge construction and responsibility for learning. *Journal of Educational Psychology, 90,* 134–152.

Kohlberg, L. (1963). The development of children's orientations toward a moral order: Sequence in the development of moral thought. *Vita Humana, 6,* 11–33.

Kohlberg, L., & Lickona, T. (1987). Moral discussion and the class meeting. In E. DeVries & L. Kohlberg (Eds.), *Constructivist early education: Overview and comparison with other programs* (pp. 143–180). Washington, DC: NAEYC.

Konold, C. (1989). Informal conceptions of probability. *Cognition and Instruction, 6,* 59–98.

Koschmann, T. D., Myers, A. C., Feltovich, P. J., & Barrows, H. S. (1994). Using technology to assist in realizing effective learning and instruction: A principled approach to the use of computers in collaborative learning. *Journal of the Learning Sciences, 3,* 227–264.

Kruger, A. (1992). The effect of peer and adult-child transactive discussion on moral reasoning. *Merrill-Palmer Quarterly, 38,* 191–211.

Kruger, A., & Tomasello, M. (1986). Transactive discussions with peer and adults. *Developmental Psychology, 22,* 681–685.

Kuhn, D. (1972). Mechanisms of change in the development of cognitive structures. *Child Development, 43,* 833–844.

Kuhn, D. (1991). *The skills of argument.* New York: Cambridge University Press.

Kuhn, D. (1992). Thinking as argument. *Harvard Educational Review, 62,* 155–178.

Kuhn, D. (1993). Science as argument: Implications for teaching and learning scientific thinking. *Science Education, 77,* 319–337.

Lambiotte, J. G., Dansereau, D. F., O'Donnell, A. M., Young, M. D., Skaggs, L. P., Hall, R. H., & Rocklin, T. R. (1987). Manipulating cooperative scripts for teaching and learning. *Journal of Educational Psychology, 79,* 424–430.

Lambiotte, J. G., Dansereau, D. F., O'Donnell, A. M., Young, M. D., Skaggs, L. P., Hall, R. H., & Rocklin, T. R. (1988). Effects of script manipulations on initial learning and transfer. *Cognition and Instruction, 5,* 103–121.

Larkin, J. H., & Chabay, R. W. (Eds.). (1992). *Computer-insisted instruction and intelligent tutoring systems.* Hillsdale, NJ: Lawrence Erlbaum Associates.

Larson, C. O., Dansereau, D. F., O'Donnell, A. M., Hythecker, V. I., Lambiotte, J. G., & Rocklin, T. R. (1985). Effects of a metacognitive and elaborative activity on cooperative learning and transfer. *Contemporary Educational Psychology, 10,* 342–348.

Laughlin, P. R., & Ellis, A. L. (1986). Demonstrability and social combination processes on mathematical intellective tasks. *Journal of Experimental Social Psychology, 22,* 177–189.

Lave, J. (1988). *Cognition in practice.* New York: Cambridge University Press.

Laws, P. (1991). Workshop physics: Learning introductory physics by doing it. *Change (July/August),* 20–27.

Laws, P. (1997). A new order for mechanics. In J. M. Wilson (Ed.), *Conference on the introductory physics course* (pp. 125–136). New York: Wiley.

Lebeau, R. B. (1998). Cognitive tools in a clinical encounter in medicine: Supporting empathy and expertise in distributed systems. *Educational Psychology Review, 10,* 3–24.

Leinhardt, G. (1988). Situated knowledge and expertise in teaching. In J. Calderhead (Ed.), *Teachers' professional learning* (pp. 146–168). London: Falmer.

Leinhardt, G. (1990). Capturing craft knowledge in teaching. *Educational Researcher, 19*(2), 18–25.

Lemke, J. L. (1990). *Talking science: Language, learning, and values.* Norwood, NJ: Ablex.

Leont'ev, A. N. (1932). Studies in the cultural development of the child, 3: The development of vocabulary attention in the child. *Journal of Genetic Psychology, 37,* 52–81.

Leont'ev, A. N. (1978). The problem of activity in psychology. In J. V. Wertsch (Ed.), *The concept of activity in Soviet psychology* (pp. 37–71). White Plains, NY: Sharpe.

Leont'ev, A. N. (1981). *Problems of the development of mind.* Moscow: Progress Press.

Lepper, M. R., Aspinwall, L. G., Mumme, D. L., & Chabay, R. W. (1990). Self-perception and social-perception processes in tutoring: Subtle social control strategies of expert tutors. In J. M. Olson & M. P. Zanna (Eds.), *Self-inference processes: The Ontario symposium* (pp. 217–237). Hillsdale, NJ: Lawrence Erlbaum Associates.

Lerner, G. H. (1991). On the syntax of sentences-in-progress. *Language in Society, 21,* 441–458.

Lesgold, A., Lajoie, S., Buzno, M., & Eggan, G. (1992). SHERLOCK: A coached practice environment for an electronics troubleshooting job. In J. H. Larkin & R. W. Chabay (Eds.), *Computer-assisted instruction and intelligent tutoring systems* (pp. 201–238). Hillsdale, NJ: Lawrence Erlbaum Associates.

Levin, I., & Druyan, S. (1993). When sociocognitive transaction among peers fails: The case of misconceptions in science. *Child Development, 64,* 1571–1591.

Light, P. (1983). Social interaction and cognitive development: A review of post-Piagetian research. In S. Meadows (Ed.), *Developing thinking: Approaches to children's cognitive development* (pp. 67–88). London: Meuthen.

Light P. (1986). Context, conservation and conversation. In M. Richards & P. Light (Eds.), *Children of social worlds: Development in social context* (pp. 170–190). Cambridge, MA: Harvard University Press.

Lockheed, M. E., Harris, A., & Memceff, W. P. (1983). Sex and social influence: Does sex influence as a status characteristic in mixed-sex groups of children? *Journal of Educational Psychology, 75,* 877–886.

Lortie, D. (1975). *Schoolteacher: A sociological study.* Chicago: University of Chicago Press.

Lourenço, O., & Machado, A. (1996). In defense of Piaget's theory: A reply to 10 common criticisms. *Psychological Review, 103,* 143–164.

Luria, A. R. (1928). The problem of the cultural development of the child. *Journal of Genetic Psychology, 35,* 506.

Mackie, D. (1983). The effect of social interaction on conservation of spatial relations. *Journal of Cross-Cultural Psychology, 14,* 131–151.

Marx, R., & Walsh, J. (1988). Learning from academic tasks. *Elementary School Journal, 88,* 207–219.

Mason, E. (1971). *Collaborative learning.* New York: Agathon.

Matthews, M. R. (1994). *Science teaching: The role of history and philosophy of science.* New York: Routledge.

Matusov, E. (1996). Intersubjectivity without agreement. *Mind, Culture, and Activity, 3,* 25–45.

Mayer, R. E. (1984). Aids to prose comprehension. *Educational Psychologist, 19,* 30–42.

McArthur, D., Stasz, C., & Zmuidzinas, M. (1990). Tutoring techniques in algebra. *Cognition and Instruction, 7,* 197–244.

McAuliffe, T., & Dembo, M. (1994). Status rules of behavior in scenarios of peer learning. *Journal of Educational Psychology, 86,* 163–172 .

McCarthy, S. J., & McMahon, S. (1992). From convention to invention: Three approaches to peer interaction during writing. In R. Hertz-Lazarowitz & N. Miller (Eds.), *Interaction in cooperative groups: The theoretical anatomy of group learning* (pp. 17–35). New York: Cambridge University Press.

McCaslin, M., & Good, T. (1996). The informal curriculum. In D. Berliner & R. Calfee (Eds.), *Handbook of educational psychology* (pp. 622–670). New York: Macmillan.

McDermott, L. C. (1997). How research can guide us in improving the introductory course. In J. M. Wilson (Ed.), *Conference on the introductory physics course* (pp. 33–45). New York: Wiley.

McLaughlin, J. (1991). Reconciling care and control: Authority in classroom relationships. *Journal of Teacher Education, 40*(3), 182–195.

Meeker, B. F. (1981). Expectation states and interpersonal behavior. In M. Rosenberg & R. H. Turner (Eds.), *Social psychology: Sociological perspectives* (pp. 290–319). New York: Basic Books.

Mehan, H. (1979). *Learning lessons: Social organization in the classroom.* Cambridge, MA: Harvard University Press.

Meloth, M. S. (1991). Enhancing literacy through cooperative learning. In E. Hiebert (Ed.), *Literacy for a diverse society: Perspectives, practices, and policies* (pp. 172–183). New York: Teachers College Press.

Meloth, M. S., & Barbe, J. (1992, April). *The relationship between instruction and cooperative peer-group discussions about reading comprehension strategies.* Paper presented at the Annual Meeting of the American Educational Research Association, San Francisco.

Meloth, M. S., & Deering, P. D. (1990, April). *Cooperative reading tasks, student awareness, and group discussions.* Paper presented at the Annual Meeting of the American Educational Research Association, Boston.

Meloth, M. S., & Deering, P. D. (1992). The effects of two cooperative conditions on peer-group discussions, reading comprehension, and metacognition. *Contemporary Educational Psychology, 17,* 175–193.

Meloth, M. S., & Deering, P. D. (1994). Task talk and task awareness under different cooperative learning conditions. *American Educational Research Journal, 31,* 138–165.

Meloth, M. S., Deering, P. D., & Sanders, A. B. (1993, April). *Teacher influences on cognitive processes during cooperative learning.* Paper presented at the Annual Meeting of the American Educational Research Association, Atlanta.

Meloth, M. S., & Sanders, A. (1991, December). *Teachers' beliefs about learning through cooperation.* Paper presented at the Annual Meeting of the National Reading Conference, Palm Springs, CA.

Merrill, D. C., Reiser, B. J., Ranney, M., & Trafton, J. G. (1992). Effective tutoring techniques: A comparison of human tutors and intelligent tutoring systems. *Journal of the Learning Sciences, 2,* 277–305.

Mevarech, Z. R. (1994). The effectiveness of individualized versus cooperative computer-based integrated learning systems. *International Journal of Educational Research, 21,* 39–52.

Miller, S., & Brownell, C. (1975). Peers, persuasion and Piaget: Dyadic interaction between conservers and non-conservers. *Child Development, 46,* 992–997.

Miller, N., & Harrington, H. J. (1990). A situational identity perspective on cultural diversity and teamwork in the classroom. In S. Sharan (Ed.), *Cooperative learning: Theory and research* (pp. 39–76). New York: Praeger.

Miller, N., & Harrington, H. J. (1993). Social categorization and intergroup acceptance: Principles for the development an design of cooperative learning teams. In R. Hertz-Lasarowitz & N. Miller (Eds.), *Interaction in cooperative groups: The theoretical anatomy of group learning* (pp. 203–227). New York: Cambridge University Press.

Mink, J. (1992, March). *Communities and collaboration: An alternative research assignment for literature courses.* Paper presented at the Annual Meeting of the Conference on College Composition and Communication, Cincinnati, OH.

Mohan, M. (1972). *Peer tutoring as a technique for teaching the unmotivated.* Fredonia: State University of New York, Teacher Education Research Center. (ERIC Document Reproduction Service No. ED 061 154)

Moore, J. L., & Rocklin, T. R. (1998). The distribution of distributed cognition: Multiple interpretations and uses. *Educational Psychology Review, 10,* 97–113.

Morine-Dershimer, G. (1993). Tracing conceptual change in preservice teachers. *Teaching and Teacher Education, 9,* 15–26.

Morton, C. (1996). The modern land of Laputa. *Phi Delta Kappan, 77,* 416–419.

Moshman, D., & Geil, M. (1998). Collaborative reasoning: Evidence for collective rationality. *Thinking & Reasoning, 4,* 231–248.

Mugny, G., & Doise, W. (1978). Socio-cognitive conflict and the structure of individual and collective performances. *European Journal of Social Psychology, 8,* 181–192.

Mulryan, C. (1992). Student passivity during cooperative small groups in mathematics. *Journal of Educational Research, 85,* 261–273.

Murray, F. B. (1972). Acquisition of conservation through social interaction. *Developmental Psychology, 6,* 1–6.

Murray, F. B. (1983a). Equilibration as cognitive conflict. *Developmental Review, 3,* 54–61.

Murray, F. B. (1983b). Learning and development through social interaction and conflict: A challenge to social learning theory. In L. S. Liben (Ed.), *Piaget and the foundations of knowledge* (pp. 231–247). Hillsdale, NJ: Lawrence Erlbaum Associates.

Murray, F. B., Ames, G., & Botvin, G. (1977). Acquisition of conservation through dissonance. *Journal of Educational Psychology, 69,* 519–527.

Naisbett, J., & Aburdene, P. (1990). *Megatrends 2000: Ten new directions for the 1990's.* New York: Morrow and Co.

National Commission on Excellence in Education. (1983). *A nation at risk: The imperative for educational reform.* Washington, DC: U.S. Government Printing Office.

National Council of Teachers of Mathematics. (1989). *Professional standards for teaching mathematics.* Reston, VA: NCTM.

Nelson, J., & Aboud, F. E. (1985). The resolution of social conflict between friends. *Child Development, 56,* 1009–1017.

Nelson-Le Gall, S. (1981). Help-seeking: An understudied problem-solving skill in children. *Developmental Review, 1,* 224–246.

Nelson-Le Gall, S. (1985). Help-seeking behavior in learning. In E. V. Gordon (Ed.), *Review of Research in Education, Vol. 12* (pp. 55–90). Washington, DC: American Educational Research Association.

Nelson-Le Gall, S. (1992). Children's instrumental help-seeking: Its role in social acquisition and construction of knowledge. In R. Hertz-Lazarowitz & N. Miller (Eds.), *Interaction in cooperative groups: The theoretical anatomy of group learning* (pp. 49–70). New York: Cambridge University Press.

Nelson-Le Gall, S., Gumerman, R. A., & Scott-Jones, D. (1983). Instrumental help-seeking and everyday problem-solving: A developmental perspective. *New directions in helping, Vol. 2* (pp. 265–283). New York: Academic Press.

Newman, D., Griffin, P., & Cole, M. (1989). *The construction zone: Working for cognitive change in schools.* Cambridge, UK: Cambridge University Press.

Nicolopolou, A. (1993). Play, cognitive development, and the social world: Piaget, Vygotsky, and beyond. *Human Development, 36,* 1–23.

Nisbett, R. E., Fong, G. T., Lehman, D. R., & Cheng, P. W. (1987). Teaching reasoning. *Science, 198,* 625–631.

Noddings, N. (1984). *Caring—A feminine approach to ethics and moral education.* Berkeley: University of California Press.

Noddings, N. (1985). Small groups as a setting for research on mathematical problem solving. In E. A. Silver (Ed.), *Teaching and learning mathematical problem solving* (pp. 345–360). Hillsdale, NJ: Lawrence Erlbaum Associates.

Noddings, N. (1989). Theoretical and practical concerns about small groups in mathematics. *Elementary School Journal, 89,* 607–623.

Noddings, N. (1995). *Philosophy of education.* Boulder, CO: Westview.

Ochs, E. (1990). Indexicality and socialization. In J. W. Stigler, R. A. Shweder, & G. Gerdt (Eds.), *Cultural psychology: Essays on comparative human development* (pp. 287–308). New York: Cambridge University Press.

O'Connor, M. C. (1998). Managing the intermental: Classroom group discussion and the social context of learning. In D. I. Slobin, J. Gerhardt, A. Kyratzis, & J. Guo (Eds.), *Social interaction, social context, and language: Essays in honor of Susan Ervin-Tripp* (pp. 495–512). Hillsdale, NJ: Lawrence Erlbaum Associates.

O'Connor, M. C., & Michaels, S. (1993). Aligning academic task and participation status through revoicing: Analysis of a classroom discourse strategy. *Anthropology and Education Quarterly, 24,* 318–335.

O'Donnell, A. M. (1986). Cooperative procedural learning: The effects of prompting and planning activities. *Dissertation Abstracts International, 47*(08), 3561B. (University Microfilms No. AAI86-26100)

O'Donnell, A. M. (1996). The effects of explicit incentives on scripted and unscripted cooperation. *Journal of Educational Psychology, 88*, 74–86.

O'Donnell, A. M., & Dansereau, D. F. (1992). Scripted cooperation in student dyads: A method for analyzing and enhancing academic learning and performance. In N. Miller & R. Hertz-Lazarowitz (Eds.), *Interaction in cooperative groups: The theoretical anatomy of group learning* (pp. 121–140). New York: Cambridge University Press.

O'Donnell, A. M., Dansereau, D. F., Hall, R. H., & Rocklin, T. R. (1987). Cognitive, social/affective, and metacognitive outcomes in scripted cooperative learning. *Journal of Educational Psychology, 79*, 431–437.

O'Donnell, A, M., Dansereau, D. F., Hall, R. H., Skaggs, L. P, Hythecker, V. I., Peel, J. L., & Rewey, K. L. (1990). Learning concrete procedures: Effects of processing strategies and cooperative learning. *Journal of Educational Psychology, 82*, 171–177.

O'Donnell, A, M., Dansereau, D. F., Hythecker, V. I., Hall, R. H., Skaggs, L. P., Lambiotte, J. G., & Young, M. D. (1988). Cooperative procedural learning: The effects of prompting and pre- vs. distributed planning activities. *Journal of Educational Psychology, 80*, 167–171.

O'Donnell, A. M., Dansereau, D. F., Rocklin, T. R., Hythecker, V. I., Hall, R. H., Young, M. D., & Lambiotte, J. G., (1988). Promoting functional literacy through cooperative learning. *Journal of Reading Behavior, 20*, 339–356.

O'Donnell, A. M., Dansereau, D. F., Rocklin, T. R., Lambiotte, J. G., Larson, C. O., & Young, M. D. (1985). Effects of elaboration frequency on cooperative learning. *Journal of Educational Psychology, 77*, 572–580.

O'Donnell, A. M., DuRussel, L. A., & Derry, S. J. (1997). *Cognitive processes in interdisciplinary groups: Problems and possibilities.* Madison, WI: National Institute for Science Education Research Report.

O'Donnell, A. M., & O'Kelly, J. (1994). Learning from peers: Beyond the rhetoric of positive results. *Educational Psychology Review, 6*, 321–349.

Ohlsson, S. (1986). Some principles of intelligent tutoring. *Instructional Science, 14*, 293–326.

Osbom, A. (1953). *Applied imagination.* New York: Scribner's.

Pajares, F. (1992). Teachers' beliefs and educational research; Cleaning up a messy construct. *Review or Educational Research, 62*, 307–332.

Pajares, F. (1993). Preservice teacher beliefs: A focus for teacher education. *Action in Teacher Education, 15*(2), 45–54.

Palincsar, A. (1992, April). *Reciprocal teaching: A retrospective and prospective view.* Paper presented at the Annual Meeting of the American Educational Research Association, San Francisco.

Palincsar, A. S. (1986). The role of dialogue in scaffolded instruction. *Educational Psychologist, 21*, 71–98.

Palincsar, A. S. (1998a). Keeping the metaphor of scaffolding fresh. To appear in *Learning Disability Quarterly.*

Palincsar, A. S. (1998b). Social constructivist perspectives on teaching and learning. *Annual Review of Psychology, 49*, 345–375.

Palincsar, A. S., Anderson, C. W., & David, Y. (1993). Pursuing scientific literacy in the middle grades through collaborative problem solving. *Elementary School Journal, 93*, 643–658.

Palincsar, A. S., Anderson, C. W., & Ford, D. J. (1998). *Collaborative problem solving: The learning experiences of sixth graders exploring the particulate theory of matter.* Manuscript in preparation.

Palincsar, A. S., & Brown, A. L. (1984). Reciprocal teaching of comprehension fostering and monitoring activities. *Cognition and Instruction, 1*, 117175.

Palincsar, A. S., & Brown, A. L. (1989). Classroom dialogues to promote self-regulated comprehension. In J. Brophy (Ed.), *Advances in research on teaching* (pp. 35–72). Greenwich: JAI.

Palincsar, A. S., Brown, A. L., & Campione, J. C. (1993). First grade dialogues for knowledge acquisition and use. In E. Forman, N. Minick, & A. Stone (Eds.), *Contexts for Learning: Sociocultural dynamics in children's development* (pp. 43–57). New York: Oxford University Press.

Palincsar, A., Stevens, D., & Gavelek, J. (1989). Collaborating with teachers in the interest of student collaboration. *International Journal of Educational Research, 13*, 41–54.

Papert, S. (1980). *Mindstorms: Children, computers and powerful ideas.* New York: Basic Books.

Pea, R. D. (1985). Beyond amplification: Using the computer to reorganize mental functioning. *Educational Psychologist, 20*, 167–182.

Pea, R. D. (1993). Practices of distributed intelligence and designs for education. In G. Salomon (Ed.), *Distributed cognitions: Psychological and educational considerations* (pp. 47–87). New York: Cambridge University Press.

Perret-Clermont, A. (1980). *Social interaction and cognitive development in children.* New York: Academic Press.

Perret-Clermont, A. N., Perret, J. F., & Bell, N. (1993). The social construction of meaning and cognitive activity in elementary school children. In L. B. Resnick, J. M. Levine, & S. D. Teasley (Eds.), *Perspectives on socially shared cognition* (pp. 41–62). Washington, DC: American Psychological Association.

Perret-Clermont, A. N., & Schubauer-Leoni, M. L. (1981). Conflict and cooperation as opportunities for learning. In P. Robinson (Ed.), *Communication in development* (pp. 203–233). London: Academic Press.

Person, N. K. (1994). *An analysis of the examples that tutors generate during naturalistic tutoring.* Unpublished doctoral dissertation, University of Memphis.

Person, N. K, Graesser, A. C., Magliano, J. P., & Kreuz, R. J. (1994). Inferring what the student knows in one-to-one tutoring: The role of student questions and answers. *Learning and Individual Differences, 6*, 205–229.

Person, N. K., Kreuz, R. J., Zwaan, R., & Graesser, A. C. (1995). Pragmatics and pedagogy: Conversational rules and politeness strategies may inhibit effective tutoring. *Cognition and Instruction, 13*, 161–188.

Peterson, C. C., & Peterson, J. L. (1990). Sociocognitive conflict and spatial perspective-taking in deaf children. *Journal of Applied Developmental Psychology, 11*, 267–281.

Peterson, P. L., Janicki, T. C., & Swing, S. R. (1981). Ability × treatment interaction effects on children's learning in large-group and small-group approaches. *American Educational Research Journal, 18*, 453–473.

Peterson, P. L., Wilkinson, L. C., Spinelli, F., & Swing, S. R. (1984). Merging the process-product and the sociolinguistic paradigms: Research on small-group process. In P. L. Peterson, L. C. Wilkinson, & M. Hallinan (Eds.), *The social context of instruction* (pp. 126–152). Orlando, FL: Academic Press.

Phelps, E., & Damon, W. (1989). Problem solving with equals: Peer collaboration as a context for learning mathematics and spatial concepts. *Journal of Educational Psychology, 81*, 639–646.

Phillips, D. C. (1995). The good, the bad and the ugly: The many faces of constructivism. *Educational Researcher, 24*(7), 5–12.

Phillips, D. C. (1997). How, why, what, when, and where: Perspectives on constructivism in psychology and education. *Issues in Education: Contributions from Educational Psychology, 3*, 151–194.

Phillips, S. (1972). Participant structures and communicative competence: Warm Springs children in community and classroom. In C. B. Cazden, V. P. John, & D. Hymes (Eds.), *Functions of language in the classroom* (pp. 370–394). New York: Teachers College Press.

Piaget, J. (1932a). *The language and thought of the child* (2nd. ed.). London: Routledge & Kegan Paul.

Piaget, J. (1932b). *The moral judgment of the child.* London: Routledge & Kegan Paul.

Piaget, J. (1952). *The origins of intelligence.* New York: International University Press.

Piaget, J. (1954). *The construction of reality in the child.* New York: Basic Books.

Piaget, J. (1962). *Play, dreams,and imitation in childhood.* New York: Norton.

Piaget, J. (1966). *The psychology of intelligence.* Totowa, NJ: Littlefield, Adams, & Co.

Piaget, J. (1970a). *Genetic epistemology* (E. Duckworth, Trans.). New York: Columbia University Press.

Piaget, J. (1970b). Piaget's theory. In P. H. Mussen (Ed.), *Carmichael's manual of child psychology* (pp. 703–732). New York: Wiley.

Piaget, J. (1971). *Biology and knowledge. An essay on the relations between organic regulations and cognitive processes*. Chicago: University of Chicago Press.

Piaget, J. (1976). *The grasp of consciousness: Action and concept in the young child*. Cambridge, MA: Harvard University Press.

Piaget, J. (1978a). *Behavior and evolution*. New York: Random House.

Piaget, J. (1978b). *Success and understanding*. Cambridge, MA: Harvard University Press.

Piaget, J. (1980). *Adaptation and intelligence: Organic selection and phenocopy*. Chicago: University of Chicago Press.

Piaget, J. (1981). *Intelligence and affectivity: Their relationship during child development*. Palo Alto, CA: Annual Reviews Inc.

Piaget, J. (1985). *The equilibrium of cognitive structures: The central problem of intellectual development* (T. Brown & K. L. Thampy, Trans.). Chicago: University of Chicago Press.

Piaget, J. & Inhelder, B. (1969). *The psychology of the child*. New York: Basic Books.

Piaget, J., & Inhelder, B. (1973). *Memory and intelligence*. New York: Basic Books.

Prawat, R. (1992). Teachers' beliefs about teaching and learning: A constructivist perspective. *American Journal of Education, 100*, 354–395.

Pressley, M. (1990). *Cognitive strategy instruction that really improves children's academic performance*. Cambridge, MA: Brookline Books.

Pressley, M., El-Dinary, P. B., & Brown, R. (1992). Skilled and not-so-skilled reading: Good information processing and not-so-good information processing. In M. Pressley, K. R. Harris, & J. R. Guthrie (Eds.), *Promoting academic competence and literacy in school* (pp. 91–127). San Diego, CA: Academic Press.

Pressley, M., McDaniel, M. A., Turnure, J. E., Wood, E., & Ahmad, M. (1987). Generation and precision of elaboration: Effects on intentional and incidental learning. *Journal of Experimental Psychology: Learning, Memory, and Cognition, 13*, 291–300.

Putnam, R. T. (1987). Structuring and adjusting content for students: A live and simulated tutoring of addition. *American Educational Research Journal, 24*, 13–48.

Putnam, R. T., & Borko, H. (1997). Teacher learning: Implications of new views of cognition. In B. J. Biddle, T. L. Good, & I. F. Goodson (Eds.), *The international handbook of teachers and teaching* (Vol. 2, pp. 1223–1296). Dordrecht, The Netherlands: Kluwer.

Radziszewska, B., & Rogoff, B. (1988). Influence of adult and peer collaborators on children's planning skills. *Developmental Psychology, 24*, 840–848.

Radziszewska, B., & Rogoff, B. (1991). Children's guided participation in planning imaginary errands with skilled adult or peer partners. *Developmental Psychology, 27*, 381–389.

Reder, L. M. (1980). The role of elaboration in the comprehension and retention of prose: A critical review. *Review of Educational Research, 50*, 5–53.

Redish, E. F. (1997). What can a physics teacher do with a computer? In J. M. Wilson (Ed.) *Conference on the introductory physics course* (pp. 47–60). New York: Wiley.

Reeve, J. (1996). *Motivation: Nurturing our inner resources*. Needham Heights, MA: Allyn and Bacon.

Reif, F., & Allen, S. (1992). Cognition for interpreting scientific concepts. *Cognition and Instruction, 9*, 1–44.

Reiser, B. J., Connelly, J. W., Ranney, M., & Ritter, C. (1992). *The role of explanatory feedback in skill acquisition*. Unpublished manuscript, Princeton University, Princeton, NJ.

Resnick, L. B. (1989). Introduction. In L. B. Resnick (Ed.), *Knowing, learning, and instruction: Essays in honor of Robert Glaser* (pp. 1–24). Hillsdale, NJ: Lawrence Erlbaum Associates.

Resnick, L. B., Levine, J. M., & Teasley, S. D. (Eds.). (1991). *Perspectives on socially shared cognition*. Washington, DC: American Psychological Association.

Resnick, L. B., Salmon, M., Zeitz, C. M., Wathen, S. H., & Holowchak, M. (1993). Reasoning and conversation. *Cognition and Instruction, 11*, 347–364.

Rewey, K., Dansereau, D. F., Skaggs, L. P., Hall, R. H., & Pitre, U. (1990). Effects of scripted cooperation and knowledge maps on the processing of technical information. *Journal of Educational Psychology, 81,* 604–609.

Rich, Y. (1990). Ideological impediments to instructional innovation: The case of cooperative learning. *Teaching and Teacher Education, 6,* 81–91.

Richardson, V. (1994). Teacher inquiry as professional staff development. In S. Hollingsworth & H. Sockett (Eds.), *Teacher research and educational reform: Ninety-third Yearbook of the National Society for the Study of Education* (pp. 186–203). Chicago: University of Chicago Press.

Robinson, B., & Schaible, R. M. (1995). Collaborative teaching: Reaping the benefits. *College Teaching, 43*(2), 57–59.

Roehler, L. R., & Duffy, G. G. (1991). Teachers' instructional actions. In R. Barr, M. L. Kamill, P. Mosenthal, & P. D. Pearson (Eds.), *Handbook of reading research. Vol. 2* (pp. 861–884). Mahwah, NJ: Lawrence Erlbaum Associates.

Rogoff, B. (1990). *Apprenticeship in thinking: Cognitive development in social context.* Oxford, UK: Oxford University Press.

Rogoff, B. (1991). Guidance and participation in spatial planning. In L. Resnick, J. Levine, & S. Teasley (Eds.), *Perspectives on socially shared cognition* (pp. 349–383). Washington, DC: American Psychological Association.

Rogoff, B. (1998). Cognition as a collaborative process. In W. Damon (Ed.), *Handbook of Child Psychology: Vol. 2* (pp. 679–744). New York: Wiley.

Rogoff, B., & Gardner, W. (1984). Adult guidance of cognitive development. In B. Rogoff & J. Lave (Eds.), *Everyday cognition: Its development in social context* (pp. 95–116). Cambridge, MA: Harvard University Press.

Rogoff, B., Matusov, E., & White, C. (1996). Models of teaching and learning: Participation in a community of learners. In D. Olson & N. Terrance (Eds.), *Handbook of education and human development: New models of learning, teaching, and schooling* (pp. 388–414). London: Basil Blackwell.

Rokeach, M. (1968). *Beliefs, attitudes, and values: A theory of organization and change.* San Francisco: Jossey-Bass.

Rommetveit, R. (1974). *On message structure.* London: Wiley.

Rommetveit, R. (1975). On the architecture of intersubjectivity. In R. Rommetveit & R. M. Blakar (Eds.), *Studies of language, thought and verbal communication* (pp. 93–107). London: Academic Press.

Roschelle, J. (1992). Learning by collaborating: Converging conceptual change. *Journal of the Learning Sciences, 2,* 235–276.

Rosenshine, B., & Meister, C. (1994). Reciprocal teaching: A review of the research. *Review of Educational Research, 64,* 479–530.

Rosenshine, B., Meister, C., & Chapman, S. (1996). Teaching students to generate questions: A review of the intervention studies. *Review of Educational Research, 66,* 181–221.

Rosenthal, T. L., & Zimmerman, B. J. (1972). Modeling by exemplification and instruction in training conservation. *Developmental Psychology, 6,* 392–401.

Rosenthal, T. L., & Zimmerman, B. J. (1978). *Social learning and cognition.* New York: Academic Press.

Ross, D. D., Johnson, M., & Smith, E. (1991, April). *Developing a professional teacher at the University of Florida.* Paper presented at the Annual Meeting of the American Educational Research Association, Chicago.

Ross, J. A., & Raphael, D. (1990). Communication and problem solving achievement in cooperative learning groups. *Journal of Curriculum Studies, 22,* 149–164.

Rottman, T., & Cross, D. R. (1990, April). *Scripted cooperative reading: Using student-student interaction to enhance comprehension.* Paper presented at the Annual Meeting of the American Educational Research Association, San Francisco.

Rowe, M. B. (1986). Wait time: Slowing down may be a way to speeding up! *Journal of Teacher Education, 37,* 43–50.

Russell, J. (1982). Cognitive conflict, transmission and justification: Conservation attainment through dyadic interaction. *Journal of Genetic Psychology, 142,* 283–297.

Ryan, R. M., & Grolnick, W. (1984). *Origins and pawns in the classroom: A self-report and projective assessment of children's perceptions.* Unpublished manuscript, University of Rochester, New York.

Salomon, G. (1993). No distribution without individual's cognition: A dynamic interactional view. In G. Salomon (Ed.), *Distributed cognitions: Psychological and educational considerations* (pp. 111–138). New York: Cambridge University Press.

Salomon, G., & Almog, T. (1994). *Project SELA: Background, goals, and implementation.* Haifa: University of Haifa, School of Education. (in Hebrew)

Salomon, G., & Almog, T. (1996, September). *SELA: Knowledge networking through shared problem solving.* Paper presented at the Growing Mind Conference, Geneva, Switzerland.

Salomon, G., & Globerson, T. (1989). When teams do not function they way they ought to. *International Journal of Educational Research, 13,* 89–99.

Sanders, A. B., & Meloth, M. S. (1997). Cooperative learning, staff development, and change. In D. M. Byrd & D. J. McIntyre (Eds.), *Teacher education yearbook: Research on the education of our nation's teachers* (Vol. 5, pp. 92–113). Thousand Oaks, CA: Corwin Press.

Sarason, S. B. (1996). *Revisiting "the culture of the school and the problem of change."* New York: Teachers College Press.

Saxe, G. B., Gearhart, M., Note, M., & Paduano, P. (1993). Peer interaction and the development of mathematical understanding. In H. Daniels (Ed.), *Charting the agenda: Educational activity after Vygotsky* (pp. 107–144). London: Routledge.

Scardamalia, M., & Bereiter, C. (1991). Higher levels of agency for children in knowledge building: A challenge for the design of new knowledge media. *Journal of the Learning Sciences, 1,* 37–68.

Scardamalia, M., Bereiter, C., & Lamon, M. (1994). The CSILE project: Trying to bring the classroom into World 3. In K. McGilly (Ed.), *Classroom lessons: Integrating cognitive theory and classroom practice* (pp. 201–228). Cambridge, MA: MIT Press.

Schank, R. C., & Jona, M. Y. (1991). Empowering the student: New perspectives on the design of teaching systems. *Journal of the Learning Sciences, 1,* 7–35.

Schmuck, R., & Schmuck, P. (1992). *Group processes in the classroom (6th ed.).* Dubuque, IA: Brown.

Schon, D. A. (1983). *The reflective practitioner.* New York: Basic Books.

Schon, D. A. (1987). *Educating the reflective practitioner.* San Francisco: Jossey Bass.

Schonman, S. (1995). *Theatre of the classroom.* Tel Aviv: Charikover Publishers. (in Hebrew)

Schwab, J. J. (1978). Education and the structure of the disciplines. In I. Westbury & N. J. Wikof (Eds.), *Science, curriculum, and liberal arts: Selected essays* (pp. 229–272). Chicago: University of Chicago Press.

Scott, L. U., & Heller, P. (1991). Team work works. *The Science Teacher,* January, p. 26.

Selman, R. (1980). *The growth of interpersonal understanding.* New York: Academic Press.

Sharan, S., & Hertz-Lazarowitz, R. (1980). A group investigation method of cooperative learning in the classroom. In S. Sharan, P. Hare, C. Webb, & R. Hertz-Lazarowitz (Eds.), *Cooperation in education* (pp. 14–46). Provo, UT: BYU Press.

Sharan, S., & Sharan, Y. (1992). *Expanding cooperative learning through group investigation.* New York: Teachers College, Columbia University.

Shavelson, R. J., Webb, N. M., Stasz, C., & McArthur, D. (1988). In R. Charles & E. Silver (Eds.), *Teaching and assessing mathematical problem-solving: A research agenda* (pp. 203–231) Hillsdale, NJ: Lawrence Erlbaum Associates.

Shuell, T. J. (1996). Teaching and learning in a classroom context. In D. C. Berliner & R. C. Calfee (Eds.), *Handbook of educational psychology* (pp. 726–764). New York: Simon & Schuster Macmillan.

Shulman, L. (1990). Reconnecting foundations to the substance of teacher education. *Teacher College Record, 91,* 300–310.

Shulman, L. (1995, August). *Psycholigizing the subject matter: Old problems, new agendas.* Paper presented at the Annual Meeting of the American Psychological Association, New York.

Shulman, L., & Sparks, D. (1992). Merging content knowledge and pedagogy: An interview with Lee Shulman. *Journal of Staff Development, 13,* 14–16.

Silverman, I., & Geiringer, E. (1973). Dyadic interaction and conservation induction: A test of Piaget's equilibrium model. *Child Development, 44,* 815–820.

Silverman, W., & Stone, J. (1972). Modeling cognitive functioning through participation in a problem solving group. *Journal of Educational Psychology, 63,* 603–608.

Sinclair, J. M., & Coulthart, R. M. (1975). *Toward an analysis of discourse.* New York: Oxford University Press.

Slavin, R. E. (1983). When does cooperative learning increase student achievement? *Psychological Bulletin, 94,* 429–444.

Slavin, R. E. (1986). *Using student team learning* (3rd ed.). Baltimore, MD: The Johns Hopkins University Press.

Slavin, R. E. (1987). Developmental and motivational perspectives on cooperative learning: A reconciliation. *Child Development, 58,* 1161–1167.

Slavin, R. E. (1992). When and why does cooperative learning increase achievement? Theoretical and empirical perspectives. In N. Miller & R. Hertz-Lazarowitz (Eds.), *Interaction in cooperative groups: The theoretical anatomy of group learning* (pp. 145–173). New York: Cambridge University Press.

Slavin, R. E. (1989–1990). Here to stay—or gone tomorrow? *Educational Leadership, 47,* 1.

Slavin, R. E. (1995). *Cooperative learning* (2nd ed.). Boston: Allyn & Bacon.

Slavin, R. E., Leavey, M., & Madden, N. A. (1984). Combining cooperative learning and individualized instruction: Effects on student mathematics achievement, attitudes, and behaviors. *Elementary School Journal, 84,* 409–422.

Slavin, R. E., Madden, N. A., & Leavey, M. (1984). Effects of team assisted individualization on mathematics achievement of academically-handicapped students and nonhandicapped students. *Journal of Educational Psychology, 76,* 813–819.

Sleeman, D. H., & Brown, J. S. (Eds.). (1982). *Intelligent tutoring systems.* New York: Academic Press.

Sparks, D., & Loucks-Horsley, S. (1990). Models of staff development. In W. R. Houston (Ed.), *Handbook of research on teacher education* (pp. 234–250). New York: Macmillan.

Spires, H. A., Donley, J., & Penrose, A. M. (1990, April). *Prior knowledge activation: Inducing text engagement in reading to learn.* Paper presented at the Annual Meeting of the American Educational Research Association, Boston.

Spurlin, J. E., Dansereau, D. F., Larson, C. O., & Brooks, L. W. (1984). Cooperative learning strategies in processing descriptive text: Effects of role and activity level of the learner. *Cognition and Instruction, 1,* 451–463.

Stein, B. S., Way, K. R., Benningfield, S. E., & Hedgecough, C. A. (1986). Constraints on spontaneous transfer in problem-solving tasks. *Memory & Cognition, 14,* 432–441.

Stern, K. (1996). Scripted cooperation and explicit incentives: Impact on cognitive and affective outcomes. *Dissertation Abstracts International, 57*(11), 4650A. (University Microfilms No. ADG97-11484)

Stevens, A., Collins, A., & Goldin, S. E. (1982). Misconceptions in students' understanding. In D. Sleeman & J. S. Brown (Eds.), *Intelligent tutoring systems* (pp. 13–24). New York: Academic Press.

Stevens, R., Madden, N., Slavin, R., & Farnish, A. (1987). Cooperative integrated reading and composition: Two field experiments. *Reading Research Quarterly, 22,* 433–454.

Stipek, D. (1988). *Motivation to learn: From theory to practice.* Englewood Cliffs, NJ: Prentice-Hall.

Stodolsky, S. (1984). Frameworks for studying instructional processes in peer work-groups. In P. Peterson & L. C. Wilkinson (Eds.), *The social context of instruction: Group organization and group processes* (pp. 107–124). Orlando, FL: Academic Press.

Strauss, S. (1993). Teachers' pedagogical content knowledge about children's minds and learning: Implications for teacher education. *Educational Psychologist, 28,* 279–290.

Strauss, S. (1996). Confessions of a born-again constructivist. *Educational Psychologist, 31,* 15–22.

Sweller, J. (1989). Cognitive technology: Some procedures for facilitating learning and problem solving in mathematics and science. *Journal of Educational Psychology, 81,* 457–466.

Swing, S., & Peterson, P. (1982). The relationship of student ability and small group interaction to student achievement. *American Educational Research Journal, 19,* 259–274.

Sykes, G., & Bird, T. (1992). Teacher education and the case idea. *Review of Research in Education, 9,* 457–521.

Taylor, J., & Cox, B. D. (1997). Microgenetic analysis of group-based solutions of complex two-step mathematical word problems by fourth graders. *Journal of the Learning Sciences, 6,* 183–226.

Teasley, S. (1995). The role of talk in children's peer collaborations. *Developmental Psychology, 31,* 207–220.

Tharp, R. G., & Gallimore, R. (1988). *Rousing minds to life: Teaching, learning, and schooling in a social context.* New York: Cambridge University Press.

The Holmes Group. (1996). *Tomorow's schools of education.* East Lansing, MI: Author.

Thelen, H. A. (1981). *The classroom society: The construction of social experience.* London: Croom-Helm Halsted.

Thorndike, E. L. (1911). *Animal intelligence: Experimental studies.* New York: Macmillan.

Thornton, R., & Sokoloff, D. R. (1990). Learning motion concepts using real-time microcomputer-based laboratory tools. *American Journal of Physics, 58,* 858–867.

Tobias, S. (1990). *They're not dumb, they're different: Stalking the second tier.* Tucson, AZ: Research Corporation

Tobias, S. (1992a). *Revitalizing undergraduate science: Why some things work and most don't.* Tucson, AZ: Research Corporation.

Tobias, S. (1992b). Science education reform: What's wrong with the process? *Change, May/June,* 13–19.

Toffler, A. (1981). *The third wave.* New York: Bantam.

Toffler, A. (1990). *Power shift: Knowledge, wealth, and violence at the edge of the twenty-first centrury.* New York: Bantam.

Trevarthen, R. (1980). Instincts for human understanding and cultural cooperation: Their development in infancy. In M. von Cranach, K. Foppa, W. Lepenies, & D. Ploog (Eds.), *Human ethology: Claims and limits of a new discipline* (pp. 530–594). Cambridge, UK: Cambridge University Press.

Tudge, J. R. H. (1989). When collaboration leads to regression: Some negative consequences of socio-cognitive conflict. *European Journal of Social Psychology, 19,* 123–138.

Tudge, J. R. H. (1990a, April). *Cooperative problem solving and the zone of proximal development.* Paper presented at the Annual Meeting of the American Educational Research Asociation, Boston.

Tudge, J. R. H. (1990b). Vygotsky: The zone of proximal development and peer collaboration: Implications for classroom practice. In L. Moll (Ed.), *Vygotsky and education: Instructional implications and applications of sociohistorical psychology.* New York: Columbia University Press.

Tudge, J. R. H. (1992). Processes and consequences of peer collaboration: A Vygotskian analysis. *Child Development, 63,* 1364–1379.

Tudge, J. R. H., Gray, J., & Hogan, D. (1996). Ecological perspectives in human development: A comparison of Gibson and Bronfenbrenner. In J. Tudge, M. Shanahan, & J. Valsiner (Eds.), *Comparisons in human development: Understanding time and context* (pp. 72–105). New York: Cambridge University Press.

Tudge, J. R. H., & Rogoff, B. (1989). Peer influences on cognitive development: Piagetian and Vygotskian perspectives. In M. Bornstein & J. S. Bruner (Eds.), *Interaction in human development* (pp. 17–40). Hillsdale, NJ: Lawrence Erlbaum Associates.

Tudge, J. R. H., Shanahan, M., & Valsiner, J. (1996). *Comparisons in human development: Understanding time and context.* New York: Cambridge University Press.

Tudge, J. R. H., & Winterhoff, P. A. (1993a). Can young children benefit from collaborative problem solving? Tracing the effects of partner competence and feedback. *Social Development, 2,* 242–259.

Tudge, J. R. H., & Winterhoff, P. (1993b). Vygotsky, Piaget, and Bandura: Perspectives on the relations between the social world and cognitive development. *Human Development, 36,* 61–81.

Tudge, J. R. H, Winterhoff, P. A., & Hogan, D. M. (1996). The cognitive consequences of collaboration and feedback. *Child Development, 67,* 2892–2909.

Tversky, A., & Kahneman, D. (1971). Belief in the law of small numbers. Psychological Bulletin, 76, 105110.

Valsiner, J. (1987). *Culture and the development of children's action.* New York: John Wiley.

Valsiner, J., & Litvinovic, G. (1996). Processes of generalization in parental reasoning. In S. Harkness & C. M. Super (Eds.), *Parents' cultural belief systems: Their origins, expressions, and consequences* (pp. 56–82). New York: Guildford.

van der Veer, R., & Valsiner, J. (1991). *A quest for synthesis: Life and work of Lev Vygotsky.* London: Routledge.

van der Veer, R., & Valsiner, J. (Eds.). (1994). *The Vygotsky reader,* Cambridge, MA: Basil Blackwell.

VanDusen, L., & Worthen, B. R. (1994). The impact of integrated learning system implementation for student outcomes: Implications for research and evaluation. *International Journal of Educational Research, 21,* 13–24.

VanLehn, K. (1990). *Mind bugs: The origins of procedural misconceptions.* Cambridge, MA: MIT Press.

VanLehn, K., Jones, R. M, & Chi, M. T. (1992). A model of the self-explanation effect. *Journal of the Learning Sciences, 2,* 1–59.

Vedder, P. (1985). *Cooperative learning. A study on processes and effects of cooperation between primary school children.* Westerhaven Groningen, The Netherlands: Rijkuniversiteit Groningen.

von Glasersfeld, E. (1989). Cognition, construction of knowledge, and teaching. *Synthese, 80,* 121–140.

Vygotsky, L. S. (1929). The problem of the cultural development of the child. *Journal of Genetic Psychology, 36,* 415–434.

Vygotsky, L. S. (1962). *Thought and language* (E. Hanfmann & G. Vakar, Trans. & Eds.). Cambridge, MA: The MIT Press.

Vygotsky, L. S. (1978). *Mind in society: The development of higher psychological processes.* In M. Cole, V. John-Steiner, S. Scribner, & E. Souberman (Eds.). Cambridge, MA: Harvard University Press.

Vygotsky, L. S. (1981a). The genesis of higher mental functioning. In J. V. Wertsch (Ed.), *The concept of activity in Soviet psychology* (pp. 144–188). Armonk, NY: Sharpe.

Vygotsky, L. (1981b). The instrumental method in psychology. In J. Wertsch (Ed.), *The concept of activity in soviet psychology.* Armonk, NY: Sharpe.

Vygotsky, L. S. (1987). Thinking and speech. In R. W. Rieber & A. S. Carton (Eds.), *The collected works of L. S. Vygotsky,* Vol. 1. (N. Minick, Trans.; pp. 39–385). New York: Plenum.

Vygotsky, L. S. (1994a). The problem of the cultural development of the child. In R. van der Veer & J. Valsiner (Eds.), *The Vygotsky reader* (pp. 57–72). Cambridge, MA: Basil Blackwell.

Vygotsky, L. S. (1994b). The problem of the environment. In R. van der Veer & J. Valsiner (Eds.), *The Vygotsky reader* (pp. 338–354). Cambridge, MA: Basil Blackwell.

Vygotsky, L. S. (1997). *The collected works of L. S. Vygotsky, Vol. 4: The history of the development of higher mental functions.* New York: Plenum Press.

Vygotsky, L. S., & Luria, A. R. (1993). *Studies on the history of behavior: Ape, primitive, and child* (V. I. Golod & J. E. Knox, Trans. & Eds.). Hillsdale, NJ: Lawrence Erlbaum Associates.

Vygotsky, L. S., & Luria, A. R. (1994). Tool and symbol in child development. In R. van der Veer & J. Valsiner (Eds.), *The Vygotsky reader* (pp. 99–174). Oxford: Blackwell.

Walker, C. H. (1987). Relative importance of domain knowledge and overall aptitude on acquisition of domain-related information. *Cognition and Instruction, 4,* 25–42.

Webb, N. M. (1984). Sex differences in interaction and achievement in cooperative small groups. *Journal of Educational Psychology, 76,* 33–44.

Webb, N. M. (1985). Student interaction and learning in small groups: A research summary. In R. Slavin, S. Sharan, S. Kagan, R. Hertz-Lazarowitz, N. Webb, & R. Schmuck (Eds.), *Learning to cooperative, cooperating to learn* (pp. 147–172). New York: Plenum.

Webb, N. M. (1989). Peer interaction and learning in small groups. *International Journal of Educational Research, 13*, 21–40.

Webb, N. M. (1991) Task related verbal interactions and mathematics learning in small groups. *Journal for Research in Mathematic Education, 22*, 366–389.

Webb, N. M. (1992). Testing a theoretical model of student interaction and learning in small groups. In R. Hertz-Lazarowitz & N. Miller (Eds.), *Interaction in cooperative groups: The theoretical anatomy of group learning* (pp. 102–119). New York: Cambridge University Press.

Webb, N. M., & Cullian, L. K. (1983). Group interaction and achievement in small groups: Stability over time. *American Educational Research Journal, 20*, 411–423.

Webb, N., Ender, P., & Lewis, S. (1986). Problem solving strategies and group processes in small group learning computer programming. *American Educational Research Journal, 23*, 243–251.

Webb, N. M., & Farivar, S. (1994). Promoting helping behavior in cooperative small groups in middle school mathematics. *American Educational Research Journal, 31*, 369–395.

Webb, N. M., & Kenderski, C. M. (1984). Student interaction and learning in small group and whole class settings. In P. L. Peterson, L. C. Wilkinson, & M. Hallinan (Eds.), *The social context of instruction: Group organization and group processes* (pp. 153–170). New York: Academic Press.

Webb, N. M., & Palinscar, A. S. (1996). Group processes in the classroom. In D. Berliner & R. Calfee (Eds.), *Handbook of educational psychology* (pp. 841–873). New York: Macmillan.

Webb, N.M., & Palincsar, A.S. (1996). Group processes in the classroom. In D. Berliner & R. Calfee (Eds.), *Handbook of educational psychology* (pp. 841–873). New York: Macmillan.

Webb, N. M., Troper, J. D., & Fall, R. (1995). Constructive activity and learning in collaborative small groups. *Journal of Educational Psychology, 87*, 406–423.

Weinstein, C. S. (1989). Teacher education students' perceptions of teaching. *Journal of Teacher Education, 40*(2), 53–60.

Weinstein, C. S. (1996). *Secondary classroom management: Lessons from research and practice.* New York: McGraw-Hill.

Weinstein, C. S., & Mignano, A. J., Jr. (1997). *Elementary classroom management: Lessons from research and practice* (2nd ed.). New York: McGraw-Hill.

Weinstein, C. S., Woolfolk, A., Dittmeier, L., & Shanker, U. (1994). Protector or prison guard: Using metaphors and media to explore student teachers' thinking about classroom management. *Action in Teacher Education, 16*(1), 41–54

Wertsch, J. (1979). From social interaction to higher psychological processes: A clarification and application of Vygotsky's theory. *Human Development, 22*, 1–22.

Wertsch, J. (1985). *Vygotsky and the social formation of mind.* Cambridge: MA: Harvard University Press.

Wertsch, J. (1991). *Voices of the mind: A sociocultural approach to mediated action.* Cambridge, MA: Harvard University Press.

Wertsch, J., & Bivens, J. (1992). The social origins of individual mental functioning: Alternatives and perspectives. *Quarterly Newsletter of the Laboratory of Comparative Human Cognition, 14*, 35–44.

Wertsch, J. V., & Hickmann, M. (1987). A microgenetic analysis of problem-solving in social interaction. In M. Hickmann (Ed.), *Social and functional approaches to language and thought* (pp. 241–266). Orlando, FL: Academic Press.

Wertsch, J. V., & Tulviste, P. (1992). L. S. Vygotsky and contemporary developmental psychology. *Developmental Psychology, 28*, 548–557.

Whiting, B. B., & Edwards C. P. (1988). *Children of different worlds: The formation of social behavior.* Cambridge, MA: Harvard University Press.

Wilkinson, L. C. (1985). Communication in all-student mathematics groups. *Theory into Practice, 24*, 8–13.

Wilkinson, L. C., & Calculator, S. (1982a). Effective speakers: Students' use of language to request and obtain information and action in the classroom. In L. C. Wilkinson (Ed.), *Communicating in the classroom* (pp. 85–99). New York: Academic Press.

Wilkinson, L. C., & Calculator, S. (1982b). Requests and responses in peer-directed reading groups. *American Educational Research Journal, 19,* 107–120.

Wilkinson, L. C., & Spinelli, F. (1983). Using requests effectively in peer-directed instructional groups. *American Educational Research Journal, 20,* 479–502.

Williams, M. (1996). Learner-control and instructional technologies. In D. H. Jonassen (Ed.), *Handbook of research for educational communications and technology* (pp. 957–983). New York: Macmillan.

Winn, W. (1990). Some implications of cognitive theory for instructional design. *Instructional Science, 19,* 53–69.

Wittrock, M. C. (1978). The cognitive movement in instruction. *Educational Psychologist, 13,* 15–29.

Wittrock, M. C. (1990). Generative processes of comprehension. *Educational Psychologist, 24,* 345–376.

Wood, D., Bruner, J. S., & Ross, G. (1976). The role of tutoring in problem solving. *Journal of Child Psychology Psychiatry, 17,* 89–100.

Wood, D., & Middleton, D. (1975).The study of assisted problem-solving. *British Journal of Psychology, 66,* 181–91

Wood, T., & Yackel, E. (1990). The development of collaborative dialogue within small group interactions. In L. P. Steffe & T. Wood (Eds.), *Transforming early childhood mathematics education: An international perspective* (pp. 244–252). Hillsdale, NJ: Erlbaum.

Woolfolk Hoy, A. E. (1998). *Educational psychology.* (7th ed.). Boston: Allyn & Bacon.

Worthen, B. R., VanDusen, L., & Sailor, P. J. (1994). A comparative study of the impact of integrated learning systems on students' time-on-task. *International Journal of Educational Research, 21,* 25–37.

Yackel, E., Cobb, P., & Wood, T. (1991). Small-group interactions as a source of learning opportunities in second-grade mathematics. *Journal for Research in Mathematics Education, 22,* 390–408.

Yackel, E., Cobb, P., Wood, T., Wheatley, G., & Merkel, G. (1990). The importance of social interaction in children's construction of mathematical knowledge. In T. J. Cooney & C. R. Hirsch (Eds.), *Teaching and learning mathematics in the 1990s* (pp. 12–21). Reston, VA: National Council of Teachers of Mathematics.

Yager, S., Johnson, D. W., & Johnson, R. T. (1985). Oral discussion, group-to-individual transfer, and achievement in cooperative learning groups. *Journal of Educational Psychology, 77,* 60–66.

Youniss, J. (1981). *Parents and peers in social development.* Chicago: University of Chicago Press.

Youniss, J., & Damon, W. (1992). Social construction and Piaget's theory. In H. Beilin & P. Pufall (Eds.), *Piaget's theory: Prospects and possibilities* (pp. 267–286). Hillsdale: Lawrence Erlbaum Associates.

Zeichner, K., & Gore, J. (1990). Teacher socialization. In W. R. Houston (Ed.), *Handbook of research on teacher education* (pp. 329–348). New York: Macmillan

Zelditch, M., Jr. (1985). Three questions about status. In J. B. Berger & M. Zelditch, Jr. (Eds.), *Status, rewards, and influence* (pp. 73–107). San Francisco: Jossey-Bass.

Zimmerman, B. J. (1974). Modification of young children's grouping strategies: The effects of modelling, verbalization, incentives, and age. *Child Development, 45,* 1032–1041.

Zimmerman, B. J., Bandura, A., & Martinez-Pons, M. (1992). Self-motivation for academic attainment: The role of self-efficacy beliefs and personal goal setting. *American Educational Research Journal, 29,* 663–676.

Zimmerman, B. J., & Lanaro, P. (1974). Acquiring and retaining conservation through modeling and reversibility cues. *Merrill Palmer Quarterly, 20,* 145–161.

Zuber, R. L. (1992). Cooperative learning by fifth-grade students: The effects of scripted and unscripted techniques. *Dissertation Abstracts International, 53*(08), 2684A. (University Microfilms No. AAI92–31396)

Author Index

A

Abelson, R. P., 209, 210
Aboud, F. E., 64
Aburden, P., 286
Adams, D. D., 230
Adelgais, A., 91
Aeillo, N., 77
Ahmad, M., 90
Allen, S., 227
Almog, T., 285, 288, 302, 309, 311
Ames, C., 237
Ames, G., 29, 30, 46
Anderson, C. A., 163
Anderson, C. W., 160, 161, 163, 164, 165, 231, 272, 273
Anderson, J. R., 69, 73, 74, 216, 225
Anderson, L. M., 250, 253, 268, 269, 270, 272, 274, 275, 277, 314, 315
Anderson, S., 215
Andrews, S. V., 222, 224, 226, 227
Arechevala-Vargas, R., 262
Argyris, C., 307
Arons, A. B., 220
Asoka, H., 216
Aspinwall, L. G., 69
Assaf, S., 291
Au, K. H., 173
Azmitia, M., 40, 47, 56, 64

B

Bandura, A., 73, 223
Barbe, J., 238, 241, 245, 246, 254, 269
Bargh, J. A., 89, 106, 119, 145
Barrell, J., 169
Barrows, H. S., 217
Bassock, M., 121, 127, 162
Battistich, V., 282
Bayer, A. S., 250
Beare, H., 287
Bearison, D. J., 18, 31, 32, 46, 47, 89, 98, 117, 265

Beilin, H., 3
Bell, N., 27
Benningfield, S. E., 223
Benware, C. A., 119, 145
Berardi-Coletta, B., 223
Bereiter, C., 73, 88, 121, 152, 219, 233, 301, 314
Berg, K. F., 190
Berger, J. B., 147, 185, 195
Berkheimer, G., 163
Berkowitz, M., 22
Berliner, D. C., 271, 305
Berman, B. P., 216
Berndt, T., 64
Berry, D. C., 223, 224
Biehler, R. F., 271
Bird, T., 269
Bivens, J., 153
Blakeslee, T., 163
Blatt, M., 22
Bloom, B. S., 69, 113
Blumenfeld, P., 270, 272, 274, 275, 276
Blunk, M. L., 165
Bobier, D., 195, 196
Borko, H., 268, 269, 273, 274
Bornstein, M. H., 41
Bossert, S., 237, 250
Botvin, G., 28, 29
Bovet, M., 3
Bowers, C.A., 69
Bransford, J. D., 74
Britton, B. K., 89
Broadbent, D. E., 223, 224
Bronfenbrenner, U., 40
Brooks, L. W., 180
Brookhart, S. M., 268
Brophy, J. E., 236, 262, 275, 279
Brown, A. L., 73, 86, 89, 90, 117, 118, 152, 155, 156, 158, 215, 218, 235, 237, 241, 244, 245, 250, 252, 254, 292, 301
Brown, J. S., 74, 76, 217, 218, 230, 314, 315
Brown, P., 75, 242

345

Subject Index

List of Contributors

Tamar Almog, Assistant Professor, School of Education, University of Haifa, Haifa 31999, Israel. E-mail: almogt@construct.haifa.ac.il

Marie A. Cooper, I. H. M., Assistant Professor, Immaculata College, Immaculata, PA 19345. E-mail: mcooper2@immaculata.edu

Paul D. Deering, Assistant Professor, Department of Teacher Education and Curriculum Studies, University of Hawaii, 1776 University Ave., Honolulu, HI 96822. E-mail: deering@hawaii.edu

Sharon J. Derry, Professor, Department of Educational Psychology, 1025 W. Johnson Street, University of Wisconsin a Madison, Madison, WI 53706. E-mail: sderry@macc.wisc.edu

Richard De Lisi, Professor, Department of Educational Psychology, 10 Seminary Place, Rutgers University, New Brunswick, NJ 08901-1183. E-mail: delisi@rci.rutgers.edu

Sydney Farivar, Associate Professor, Department of Elementary Education, School of Education, California State University, Northridge, CA 91130-8265.

Susan L. Golbeck, Associate Professor, Department of Educational Psychology, 10 Seminary Place, Rutgers University, New Brunswick, NJ 08901-1183. E-mail: golbeck@rci.rutgers.edu

Art G. Graesser, Professor, Department of Psychology, University of Memphis, Memphis, TN 38152. E-Mail: agraesser@memphis.edu

Leslie Rupert Herrenkohl, Assistant Professor, Department of Educational Psychology, University of Washington, Educational Psychology, 312 Miller Hall, P.O. Box 353600, Seattle, WA 98195-3600. E-mail: leslieh@u.washington.edu

Rachel Hertz-Larazowitz, Professor, School of Education, University of Haifa, Haifa 31999, Israel. E-Mail: rachelhl@construct.haifa.ac.ll

Diane M. Hogan, Research Officer, The Children's Research Centre, Áras an Phiarsaigh, Trinity College, Dublin 2, Ireland. E-mail: dmhogan@tcd.ie

Alison King, Professor, California State University San Marcos, San Marcos, CA 92096. E-mail: aking@mailhost1.csusm.edu

Michael S. Meloth, Associate Professor, Department of Educational Psychology, School of Education, University of Colorado, Boulder, CO 80309. E-mail: meloth@spot.colorado.edu

Megan Tschannen-Moran, School of Educational Policy and Leadership, College of Education - Ramseyer Hall, 29 West Woodruff Ave., The Ohio State University, Columbus, OH 43210. E-mail: megantm@aol.com

Angela M. O'Donnell, Associate Professor, Department of Educational Psychology, Rutgers University, 10 Seminary Place, New Brunswick, NJ 08901-1183. E-mail: angelao@rci.rutgers.edu

Annemarie Sullivan Palincsar, Professor, University of Michigan, 1360 SEB, 610 E. University, Ann Arbor, MI 48109. E-mail: annemari@umich.edu

Natalie K. Person, Assistant Professor, Department of Psychology, Rhodes College, 2000 North Parkway, Memphis, TN 38112. E-mail: person@rhodes.edu

Jonathan R. H. Tudge, Associate Professor, Department of Human Development and Family Studies, University of North Carolina, HDFS, Greensboro, NC 27411-5001. E-mail: tudgej@hamlet.uncg.edu

Noreen M. Webb, Professor, Graduate School of Education, University of California, Los Angeles, CA 90024. E-mail: webb@ucla.edu

Anita Woolfolk Hoy, Professor, School of Educational Policy and Leadership, College of Education - Ramseyer hall, 29 West Woodruff Ave., The Ohio State University, Columbus, OH 43210. E-mail: awoolfolk@aol.com